Blacks in the Adirondacks

Blacks IN THE Adirondacks

Sally E. Svenson

With an Afterword by

Alice Paden Green

Syracuse University Press

Syracuse, New York 13244-5290

First Edition 2017
17 18 19 20 21 22 6 5 4 3 2 1

∞ The paper used in this publication meets the minimum requirements of the American National Standard for Information Sciences—Permanence of Paper for Printed Library Materials, ANSI Z39.48-1992.

For a listing of books published and distributed by Syracuse University Press, visit www.SyracuseUniversityPress.syr.edu.

ISBN: 978-0-8156-3555-0 (hardcover) 978-0-8156-1093-9 (paperback)
978-0-8156-5421-6 (e-book)

Library of Congress Cataloging-in-Publication Data

Names: Svenson, Sally E., author

Title: Blacks in the Adirondacks : a history / Sally E. Svenson.

Description: First edition. | Syracuse : Syracuse University Press, 2017. | Includes bibliographical references and index.

Identifiers: LCCN 2017036168 (print) | LCCN 2017038208 (ebook) | ISBN 9780815654216 (e-book) | ISBN 9780815635550 (hardcover : alk. paper) | ISBN 9780815610939 (pbk. : alk. paper)

Subjects: LCSH: African Americans—New York (State)—Adirondack Mountains—History. | African Americans—New York (State)—Adirondack Mountains—Biography. | Adirondack Mountains (N.Y.)—History, Local.

Classification: LCC E185.93.N56 (ebook) | LCC E185.93.N56 S84 2017 (print) | DDC 305.896/0730747—dc23

LC record available at https://lccn.loc.gov/2017036168

Manufactured in the United States of America

To the next generations:
Alicia, Tait, Matt, Lindsay, and now, Mason and Porter.

Contents

Illustrations

Preface

SOME TEN YEARS AGO I was scrolling through microfilmed copies of the *Lake George Mirror*, a newspaper that began publication in the late nineteenth century to document life in the summer resort communities strung out along the western shore of Lake George. I was interested in an altogether different aspect of Adirondack history at the time, but items referencing hotel wait staffs composed entirely of African Americans caught my eye, as did articles about the fundraising visits of singing student groups from traditionally black southern schools. For no particular reason, I began to collect these bits of newsprint and file them away. Other finds linking blacks in a surprising way to regional life followed. As my file expanded it became clear that there was an untold story here, and also, that black transients were an important part it. Thus *Blacks in the Adirondacks* is about blacks who settled in the region, as well as about individuals and groups who spent brief periods there—among them those resort waiters and singing students. Other part-timers covered include railroad workers, tuberculosis patients, summer domestic employees, minstrel and vaudeville players, tourists, even barnstorming baseball and basketball players. In many cases, these visitors were the only African Americans with whom local whites had contact.

The black history of the Adirondack interior has been explored only tangentially—most often in stories relating to abolitionist John Brown and philanthropist Gerrit Smith. But tantalizing other references to a black presence surface from time to time. Who, for instance, was Mr. Emory, the "colored gentleman" who resided in the Deerhead hamlet of Lewis, Essex County, between 1854 and 1856 and left for "parts unknown" after the tavern he operated was destroyed by fire?[1] Who was the "master-workman" and "most able layer of stone wall in the country" who once lived in Liberia, worked near Sabbath Day Point on Lake George in 1860, and led twice-daily religious exercises for his white employees?[2] What explained the 1880 presence at Moody's isolated Tupper Lake hunting lodge of one "colored woman" among the handful of females at a "ball" planned by lodge guides?[3] And who was Jack Lake, a black lumberjack remembered for the song he sang as he worked in the woods near Newcomb in the early twentieth century?[4] Their stories are unlikely to be discovered, but others are known, at least in part. This book is an attempt to pull them together before they, too, are lost.

As a Boston newspaper recorded of a small Hamilton County town in 1869: "Fancy a village whose inmates had passed through the anti-slavery agitation, the war of the rebellion, and the suffrage campaigns, and known of the great apple of discord, the negro, only by hearsay. A family brought a colored nurse to Long Lake, and the people from miles around came to the hotel to see her, looking for the first time in their lives on a black face."[5] Other Adirondack residents were as cut off from the national conversation on race relations as the curious denizens of Long Lake.

Blacks left behind almost no record of their Adirondack lives. Thus, this history is woefully unfinished in its failure to portray what author Zora Neale Hurston called "a sense of black people as complete, complex, *undiminished* human beings."[6] Most of the material presented in this book was culled from regional and national newspapers, from public records, and from the written memories of white residents. Thus, it sometimes exudes a condescending, caricatured, white perspective. Accounts of events as reported in African American journals provide the occasional black point of view.

Current practice is followed in the book in regard to language, and the terms "black" and "African American" are used interchangeably when referring to people of African descent. The word "colored," an out-of-date term used by blacks among themselves as both adjective and noun through the first half of the twentieth century, appears only in quotation marks, as does the word "Negro," with and without a capital "N." This term was denigrated by Isabel Wilkerson, author of the masterful study of black migration, *The Warmth of Other Suns*, who wrote of it: "On the whole, I found that people who had most felt the sting of the word and the violence that undergirded it were less likely to use the word in casual speech than people who had never had to step off a sidewalk because of the color of their skin."[7] The occasional reproduction of black dialect reflects stereotyped representations of African American speech in texts of an earlier period.

My profoundest thanks go to Alice Paden Green, who was kind enough to contribute an autobiographical afterword to this text. The story of her experience growing up black in the Adirondacks ventures into subtle territory that I, as a white author, could not have begun to plumb. Thanks to her, too, for her contributions in highlighting the recent history of blacks in the region that so effectively complement my own emphasis on the century between 1850 and 1950, and for her synopsis of ongoing efforts to encourage diversity in the Adirondacks.

It is difficult to know where to begin in acknowledging institutions and other individuals who helped with this project. The Schomburg Center for Research in Black Culture, an arm of the New York Public Library, was always a first source in locating relevant general material. The New York Society Library holds many germane books. Among institutional resources in and near the Adirondacks were the New York State Archives and the Adirondack Museum, particularly its knowledgeable librarian, Jerold Pepper, and the assistant curator in charge of photographs, Angela Snye. Michele Tucker, curator of the Adirondack Room at the Saranac Lake Free Library, not only knows her subject matter well but has done some useful work on the genealogy of early blacks who settled near Saranac Lake. The index-card employment records of Witherbee, Sherman and Company held at the Adirondack History Center Museum/Essex County Historical Society in Elizabethtown were invaluable; I owe special thanks to volunteer Carol Haber for the many hours she spent hosting me at the society as I worked through the collection. Special collections librarian Debra Kimok and associate Michael Burgess were more than helpful at the Feinberg Library, SUNY Plattsburgh, as was Brendan Mills, site manager at the John Brown Farm State Historic Site. Don Papson, founding president of the North Country Underground Railroad Historical Association, was generous in sharing relevant material he uncovered during many years of research.

My warm thanks to county, town, and village historians, so many of whom were able to point me toward or knew details about stories that I would never have found on my own. Nancy Deitch of Mayfield, Fulton County, deserves special mention for introducing me to the slave records held in Mayfield town files. Other local historians, past and present, who contributed include Ron Bruno, Willsboro; Ted Caldwell, Bolton; Linda A. Casserly, Canton; Jan Couture, Saranac; Gail Cramer, Northampton; Janet Cross, Elizabethtown; Jean W. Dickerson, Lewis; William Dolback, Ticonderoga; Priscilla L. Edwards, Edinburg; Kelly A. Farquhar, Montgomery County; Janet Hall, Keene; Samantha Hall-Saladino, Fulton County; Sharron L. Hewston, Black Brook; Mary Hotaling, Harrietstown; Joan Hunsdow, Crown Point; John W. Krueger, Plattsburgh; Betty LaMoria, Moriah; Pete Light, Dannemora; Margaret Mannix, Lake George; Peg Masters, Webb; Ann McCann, Warren County; Richard Nilsen, Caroga; Sandi Parisi, Warrensburg; Anastasia Pratt, Clinton County; Bev Reid, North Elba/Lake Placid; Mary Ellen Salls, Brighton; Abbie Verner, Long Lake archivist; and Betty White, Westport.

Gratitude, too, to everyone else who offered help along the way. Ted Comstock often passed along relevant morsels of information. Other collaborators included descendants of African American park residents, academics, historical society personnel and volunteers, strangers, and friends—among them Joan Aldous, Jaclyn Anderson, Russell Baker, Margaret Bartley, Louis Baum, Heather Beattie, Mary Behr, Wayne Blanchard, Sheila Borden, Michael R. Bridgen, Roland M. Brown, Erica Burke, Amy Catania, Frank Carey, Jessica L. Clemons, Tom Colarco, Joseph Collea, Ed and Sue Curtis, James Dawson, Wayne Dewey, Betsy Dirnberger, Stephen Elliott, Bea Evans, Sarah Farrar, Susan Forrest, Jim Frenette, Gary Glebus, Charles Gosselink,

Elise Guyette, Alison Haas, Judy Haggett, Lisa H. Hall, Michael Hill, Janet G. Hudson, Basil Johnson, Sr., Barbara Kelly, David Krutz, Paul Larner, Jan Letteron, Kate Lewis, Elizabeth Lowe, Lee Manchester, J. Peter Martin, Fred Mayo, Vonda McCrae, Caleb McDaniel, Pat McDonough, James McMaster, Larry Miller, John Moravek, Ann Nickloy, Bambi Pedu, Karen Peters, Frank Pine, Marjorie Ochs Powers, Dawn Richardson, Debby Robinson, Mary Roden, Michelle SanAntonio, Susan Smeby, Marsha Smith, Kelly Stanyon, Michael Sullivan, Neil Surprenant, Jane M. Verostek, William S. Walker, Alice Ridenour Wareham, John Warren, Aurora Wheeler, Betty White, Dorsey M. Whitehead, Harvey A. Whitfield, Carolyn Wilkins, and Vanessa Wilson. My sincere apologies to others whom I have inadvertently failed to mention.

Finally, thanks to Syracuse University Press, which thought this project worth taking on, with special recognition going to acquisitions editor Alison Maura Shay and assistant editor Kelly L. Balenske, who made the collaboration easy. I owe a lot to my daughter, Alicia Svenson, who humanely volunteered for the task of organizing images for the completed project.

My thesis has been that the story of blacks in the Adirondacks is likely to have paralleled that of other rural districts and small towns across the northern United States. I hope that the book, despite its limitations, represents an early step in recovering a group history that enriches the more familiar historical account of Adirondack life, and that also encourages similar regional investigations elsewhere.

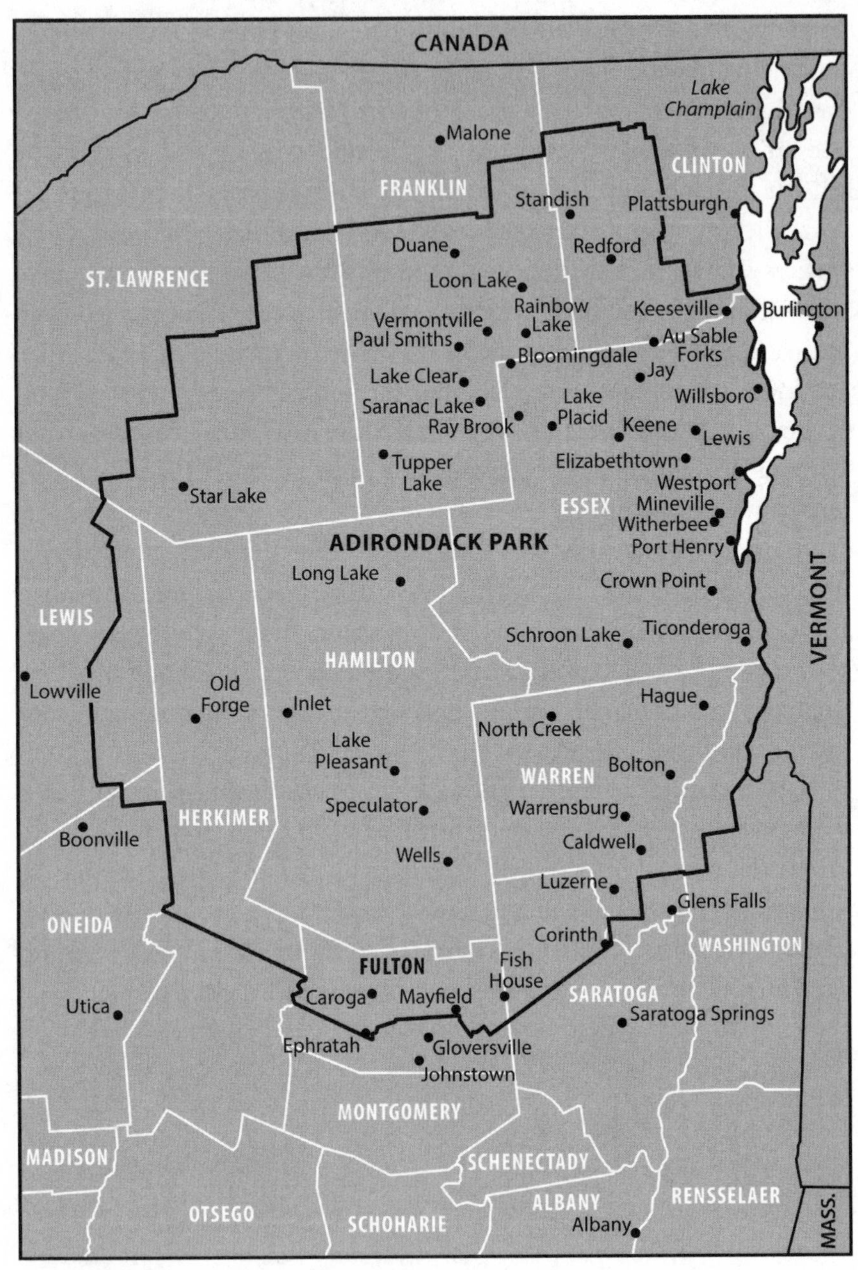

Map of the Adirondack Park. Syracuse University Cartographic Laboratory.

Blacks in the Adirondacks

Introduction

AS AUTHOR RUSSELL BANKS wrote in 2000 of Lake Placid, an Essex County village in northeastern New York State that twice served as the setting for the Winter Olympics:

> The population is sparse and, except for tourists and skiers, poor. Almost everyone, including the tourists and skiers, is white-skinned. On the surface of things, the place seems to be about as far from the history of race in America as one could get.
>
> But, there is no place in America that does not participate in that history, no place that is innocent of the five-hundred-year war between the races that began when Columbus dropped anchor in the warm Caribbean Sea.[1]

Banks's reference to "almost everyone" in Lake Placid as white acknowledged the minimal presence of African Americans as residents and visitors in the community. And, indeed, blacks have been living and working in the Adirondack region since it became a population center. In 1850 they were part of an ethnic mix that included indigenous Abenaki and Mohawk Indians, old-stock Yankees from Vermont and southern New York, and French Canadians from the north. Immigrants from Europe began arriving around midcentury, the first of them Irish fleeing the potato famine that killed more than a million of their countrymen in five years.

The chapters that follow concentrate for practical reasons on the largely rural region contained within the Adirondack Park, a six-million-acre administrative creation with boundaries roughly paralleling those of the Adirondack Mountain range that gives the park its name. A few communities outside the park will need to be mentioned, however, as nearby and distant population centers with larger concentrations of residents of African descent exerted their influence on the flow of migrants into and out of the region.

The Adirondacks' lightly peopled nucleus was set aside as a forest reserve by New York State in 1885 in an effort to guard it against over-logging, a prospect that it was feared might threaten the state's water supply and lead to climatic changes. A blue line, drawn on a state map when the reserve was incorporated in 1892 as the Adirondack Park, enclosed a much larger swath of territory that it was hoped the state might one day own or over which it might exert some control. The often used phrase "within the blue line" refers to the modern park, a patchwork of publicly and privately owned land that constitutes the largest state park in the country and represents a unique, innovative experience in shared land use. Its physical borders have little to do with political divisions. Only two counties, Essex and Hamilton, are wholly within the park, along with large and small segments of nine others: Clinton, Franklin, Fulton, Herkimer, Lewis, Oneida, St. Lawrence, Warren, and Washington.

Exact numbers referencing the historical Adirondack population of African heritage are hard to come by, but 1850 census figures for the two counties wholly within the park give some idea of early levels of black concentration. Essex County reported 50 African Americans in its overall population of 31,148 that year; Hamilton County, 2 in a population of 2,188. These figures contrast dramatically with those for New York County (Manhattan), then the largest county in the state, which in 1850 sustained 13,815 African Americans in a population of 515,547.

The earliest censuses detailing New York State's population, including one taken in 1698 when it was still a British colony, classified by race, with blacks usually specified as *slaves*. A New York census in 1774 estimated the state as home to 161,098 white and 21,149 black residents.[2] "Whites" were set apart from "all other free persons" as well as from "slaves" in the first federal census, compiled in

1790. This and later censuses were not overly accurate, as communities were widely scattered and not all census enumerators thought it necessary to count those whom they considered "marginal" residents of their districts. At the same time, many New York citizens of African descent chose, until the close of the Civil War, not to make their presence known.

Division by race was continued in later federal censuses, enumerated at ten-year intervals. The language used between the Civil War and World War II was subject to experimentation, much of it politically driven as southern politicians sought evidence to legitimize policies of racial exclusion,[3] and the US Census Office (later Bureau) toyed with a number of words to classify people of African heritage. "Black," as used in early censuses, was replaced in 1920 by "negro." Other labels represented efforts to measure shades of pigmentation. "Mulatto" (referring to persons of mixed white and black ancestry, particularly those with one white and one black parent) appeared in the federal census in 1850 and acknowledged the country's increasing racial mix. The category was thought to comprise some 25 percent of northern blacks at the time.[4] "Quadroon" ("one-quarter black blood") and "octoroon" ("one-eighth or any trace of black blood") were used only in the 1890 federal census—a census that was largely destroyed, in part by fire, in part by administrative order as politically suspect. All indicators of black-white racial mix were dropped from the census in 1900. "Mulatto" reappeared again in 1910 and 1920 and then vanished for good. The designation "negro" as used in the 1930 and 1940 censuses covered all persons of mixed "white and negro blood," making it easy for state legislators in the South to implement "one-drop" laws passed in the 1920s without having to rely on imprecise definitions.[5] New York State censuses enumerated in mid-decade between 1825 and 1875, in 1892, and between 1905 and 1925 roughly paralleled federal censuses in their wording.[6]

Color as documented in census data was in the eye of the beholder until 1970. Thus, many individuals in the Adirondacks with some African background will be seen in this account to have been labeled as "white" and "mulatto" as well as "black" and "negro" in the course of their lifetimes by census enumerators. The use of nomenclature based on color had ongoing political repercussions. As a director of the US Census Bureau in the late 1990s noted: "It would of course be an exaggeration to attribute the racialization of American politics to the census. But the availability of a racial taxonomy—counting and sorting by race—was handmaiden to the politics of race that continue to the present."[7]

The early histories of many individuals mentioned in the following chapters are unknown. Ray Stannard Baker, writing in 1908 about race in the North, speculated that a substantial percentage of the scattered assemblage of northern black settlers arrived there as fugitives from slavery or "during the period of philanthropic enthusiasm which followed it." As a group, he noted, "they have come to fit naturally into the life of the communities where they live, and no one thinks especially about their color. I have found no places anywhere which seemed so favorable to Negroes as smaller towns and cities in the North where the colored population is not increasing."[8]

No matter how it was measured, the relative darkness of one's skin played a significant role in determining place in the world. Light-skinned blacks generally dominated the elite tier in what developed as a rigid African American class structure, and obviously mixed-race individuals achieved higher social status in the white community than those of darker complexion while still sharing the legal disabilities of blacks. Light-complexioned blacks were also likely to realize greater economic success—a distinction that persisted into the late twentieth century, when it was estimated that dark-skinned African Americans earned only seventy cents for every dollar earned by those of lighter coloring.[9]

Interracial marriages, particularly those between black men and white women, occurred in the Adirondacks with some frequency. As was true in general of developing parts of the country where men outnumbered women in early censuses,[10] African American men were more likely than women to journey to and settle alone in the harsh region. Despite an intricate web of personal and kinship connections that brought isolated blacks together and enabled them to maintain racial and cultural cohesion, black wives could be hard to find. The apparent outward acceptance of mixed marriages does not mean that white (or black) residents were altogether comfortable with the phenomenon. New York is one of only nine states that never adopted laws against biracial unions, but failed efforts to bar them in 1900 and 1913 are reminders that the thought crossed legislators' minds.

A number of Adirondack residents of African heritage "crossed over" into whiteness when they could do so in order to make their lives, particularly their working lives, easier. Most such realignments took place in the nineteenth and early twentieth centuries, when, according to philosopher William James, "to be an assimilated American and to be an unassimilated Negro were both real and, more importantly, equally or nearly equally appealing choices."[11] It was not until the later twentieth century that racial consciousness and identification became charged issues and forgoing one's black history came to be seen by some as tantamount to "denial of one's genuine self."[12] Change was likely to follow a period of ambiguity, when, "neither denying nor actively claiming a black racial identity," an individual "simply lived in the spaces between absolutes." This was reported to be most pronounced in small, mostly white towns in which personal contacts rather than arbitrary definitions of race defined relationships between citizens.[13]

"Crossing over" differed subtly from "passing," a process that generally referred to light-skinned blacks who intentionally escaped the handicaps associated with race by slipping quietly into the white world—often shedding their black backgrounds and families in doing so. "Passing" as defined here would have been difficult to achieve in the small communities of the Adirondacks, but the Franklin County resort hotel Paul Smith's played an incidental role in one of the top ten news stories of 1925: the sensational *Rhinelander v. Rhinelander* marriage-annulment trial in Westchester County in which a young white man of aristocratic lineage, under family threat, accused his "octoroon" wife, a domestic worker with English-immigrant parents, of deceiving him about her racial background before marriage.[14] The trial grappled with concepts of self-identity as well as the meaning of race and the ambiguities of racial classification. Paul Smith's figured in the trial only as the postal address from which the defendant, Alice Jones Rhinelander, sent a number of letters to her future husband, Leonard "Kip" Rhinelander, that were introduced in court as "evidence" of Alice's aggressive, often sexually explicit, pursuit of her wealthy marital quarry. The letters offer no insight into race relations in the Adirondacks, where the twenty-two-year-old Alice spent the summer of 1922 as an employee of the William Alderson family and was accepted as white.[15] Leonard Rhinelander lost his suit against his wife, to the surprise of many, and later divorced Alice in Nevada. Another bill banning interracial marriage introduced in the New York State legislature directly after the 1925 trial was debated but did not pass.

The story told in this book is not linear. In its entirety it reflects trajectories of consistency and change in relationships between the black and white races in a single remote area of northern New York State during the one hundred years between 1850 and 1950. These relationships were not predetermined, although a majority of white residents were likely to have absorbed to some degree—from "perceived knowledge," from newspapers, from wherever—notions of racial difference. As we will see, few blacks in the Adirondacks were able to escape the casual racism that occasionally flared but stayed, for the most part, below the surface—"unwritten, mercurial, opaque and eminently deniable."[16] Nevertheless, they persevered, developing sufficient knowledge of the dominant white culture to read its ways and to adapt to its conventions. Their experiences are likely to have paralleled those of other blacks who found themselves in rural areas and small towns across the northern United States, but with some unusual exceptions.

1

Slavery

Backdrop to the Adirondack Story

A FRENCH AGENT for Paris-based land speculators operating in Castorland, a huge forested tract just west of the Adirondack Park in what is now Lewis County, offered a succinct statement vis-à-vis slavery in 1796. "It is," he observed, "nearly impossible to keep slaves in this region, where everyone encourages them to become free, and where the woods and the people are favorable to their escaping."[1] Despite his pronouncement that slaves were scarce, there were estimated to be about four hundred of them scattered about in the general Adirondack region, sometimes referred to as the North Country, in the late eighteenth century.[2] A few could be found in and near Plattsburgh, Clinton County, located in an area close to northeastern park borders but not included in the Adirondack Park because of its population density. Others were concentrated to the south and southeast of what became park borders in present-day Fulton, Washington, and Saratoga counties. In many cases, their owners were Dutch, who introduced slavery into the United States in 1624 and carried their culture north from New York City through the Hudson River Valley and beyond.

Sir William Johnson was perhaps the region's foremost slave owner. A Fulton County resident who arrived from Ireland in 1738 to oversee an uncle's landholding in the valley of the Mohawk River, Johnson stayed on to become a wealthy businessman, an influential public figure, and the proprietor of a large estate. His Johnson Hall, completed in 1763, was built a few miles south of the park boundary in what became Johnstown, and references to Johnson's slaves appeared from the early 1740s on in bills of sale, instructions to agents, personal correspondence, and orders for clothing and supplies. More than sixty slaves worked his farmlands and produced flour and wheat in his gristmill, as well as boards, staves, and masts in his sawmill—products that were profitably exported to the New York City market and the West Indies. A harsh overseer involved in supervising the construction of Johnson Hall was caught "flogging slaves" in 1760, and at least one order was placed in Johnson's name for the purchase of handcuffs for slaves. Among several references to escaped slaves was a 1761 New York City newspaper advertisement reading, "Run-away, about 2 weeks since from Sir William Johnson of Fort Johnson, a Negro Man named Joe, 5 feet 7 inches high of a yellow Cast, speaks good English, and is a very active fellow." Johnson's slaves lived in cabins across the Cayadutta Creek from Johnson Hall and were described as dressing very much like the Indians, "but wore coats made from blankets on the place."[3]

Slavery became an expensive economic system to maintain in New York. A high birth rate and a sharp increase in white immigration from other colonies after 1750 made it cheaper to engage workers on an as-needed basis,[4] and a steady decline in the ratio of slaves to free blacks in the Adirondack region marked the years leading up to the Revolutionary War. The language of liberty during this confusing period led many of those held in bondage to escape, while the war itself weakened the slave-owning system as American and British military forces competed for the allegiance and services of black residents. In 1777 the Continental Congress opened the ranks of the revolutionary army to slaves with the promise of freedom after service, and as of 1779 the British granted freedom to any slave belonging to patriots who fled to British lines and embraced British war policy. Slaves abandoned on forfeited New York estates by fleeing British loyalists were treated as contraband of war and subject to confiscation and sale. Those not sold before May 1786 were given their freedom.[5]

New York passed legislation in 1788 banning the slave trade within the state, but slavery itself continued to be legal. Furthermore, the state was obligated to implement laws relating to slavery elsewhere. The most contentious of these was the federal Fugitive Slave Act of 1793, which allowed slave hunters to capture escapees in any state or territory simply on the oral confirmation to a state or federal judge that the seized person was a runaway. Heavy fines were levied on those who concealed fugitives. The law was inconsistently enforced and aggravated ill feeling between North and South. A number of northern states reacted by passing personal liberty laws that impeded slave recapture—laws that were often successfully challenged in court.[6]

The New York legislature approved an Act for the Gradual Abolition of Slavery in 1799. Based on Pennsylvania legislation from 1780, the law provided for the eventual manumission (freeing) of slaves in the state, but did so in a manner intended to balance the property rights of slaveholders with the interests of abolitionists. Freedom was assured to the offspring of female slaves born on and subsequent to July 4, 1799, but only after they had spent long periods in indentured servitude to their mothers' legal owners: twenty-five years for women and twenty-eight for men. Slaves born before the 1799 date were to remain in bondage for the remainder of their lives.

The proportion of free blacks to slaves in the Adirondack region rose rapidly after the law took effect. A 1799 tax list for Plattsburgh recorded thirty-five slaves belonging to nine owners. By 1814 there were no slaves in Plattsburgh, but fifty-eight free blacks; only two slaves could be found in all of Clinton County.[7] (According to one Plattsburgh resident, his mother's slave "was given her freedom before her time was out, because she was so much excited about being a free woman that we thought it better to hire our work done than to try to get the work out of her."[8]) In 1817 New York's legislature abolished slavery altogether as of July 4, 1827. Fifteen other of the thirty-one United States did so by late 1850.

Mayfield, a Fulton County town largely inside Adirondack Park borders, holds well-preserved records from the late eighteenth and early nineteenth centuries relating to slaves and slaveholders. Settled around 1760 under the patronage of William Johnson, the town was home to at least eight slave owners during the decades bookending

1800. Francis Van Buren, a farmer of Dutch ancestry from Columbia County, owned seven slaves in 1790. His farmer brother Harmon, who followed Francis to Mayfield in 1792, was documented in 1790 as owning six slaves while a resident of Kinderhook, Columbia County. Ownership on the Van Buren scale was atypical, as most of the region's slaveholders owned only one or two slaves. Their insularity kept them from establishing families and living independent social and religious lives.

Slaveholders were required after passage of the state's Gradual Abolition Act to register the newborn children of female slaves with town clerks. Those who did not do so were subject to fines, and Mayfield's slaveholders were a law-abiding lot. Town records contain entries with wording along the following lines: "I Roswell Churchill of the Town of Mayfield do hereby certify that Mary a Slave belonging to me was on the 20th day of June 1814 delivered of a Female Child name Jude. Dated the 8th day of October 1814."[9]

A number of documents detail the slave-owning history of Harmon Van Buren. One from June 1802 addressed itself to a point inserted in the Gradual Abolition Act to gain the cooperation of slave owners: "I do hereby Notify you that my Negro woman has a male Child named Jacob over nine Months old and under one year old which Child the Town of Mayfield will consider as a pawpear [*sic*]."[10] Van Buren's declaration responded to a provision of the law that allowed owners to abandon the offspring of slave mothers at the age of one. This officially made them paupers and the financial responsibility of towns' Overseers of the Poor (predecessors to departments of social services) until they were old enough to be bound out to employers. Such children were then allowed to remain as boarders in the homes of their mothers' owners, who received generous monthly payments from the state for their maintenance. The thinly veiled program to compensate slaveholders for loss of services was amended in late 1802 by the state legislature to reduce the costs of monthly maintenance, and was abolished altogether in 1804.[11]

In 1811 Mayfield's Overseers of the Poor advised the town clerk, "We do Certify that it appears to us that Dean, a female slave Belonging to Harmon Van Buren of the Town of Mayfield is under fifty years of age and is of sufficient ability to provide for herself—and we do hereby require and command the Town Clerk of the town of Mayfield forthwith to make an entry of record of the same." Such certification, attesting to enslaved adults' capacity to support themselves, was a legal prerequisite to their manumission under the Gradual Abolition Act, and could take place once women reached the age of eighteen and men the age of twenty-one.[12] Given the timing of Van Buren's filing, it is possible that he was considering manumission as a way of cutting expenses during a period of national economic depression. While he may have been no more than practical in this instance, Van Buren never abandoned his belief in the right to hold African Americans in bondage. Within the body of his will, dated 1807, his slaves born before 1799 were dispassionately and somewhat erratically disposed of: "I Will and bequeath unto my son, Francis, my negro boy, Cap, to him, his heirs and assigns forever. And also I give to my said wife, Elizabeth, my negro wench Pana, during the life of my said wife. . . . I also give and bequeath to my son, Francis, one feather bed. I also give and bequeath to my daughter, Mariah Easton, my negro girl, Bet, and my negro boy, Leer, to her and her heirs and assigns forever." Van Buren died in 1819.[13]

References to slave baptisms and admissions to church membership appeared occasionally in Mayfield records. New York had taken an interest in the saving of enslaved Africans' souls as early as 1706, when the state's colonial legislature, fearful that the "children of the devil" might invoke evil against whites, passed an Act to Encourage the Baptizing of Negro, Indian, and Mulatto Slaves.[14] Those belonging to Mayfield farmer Abraham Wells occupied a high box pew near his family's pew in the community's Dutch Reformed Church and were well known to the church pastor—who was reported on one occasion to have interrupted his preaching to address a slave by name and request that she awaken her dozing husband.[15] Five slaves and "Biana, a free black woman," were admitted in 1816 to membership in Mayfield's Central Presbyterian Church, which baptized slaves at half price; seats were set aside "for the blacks" in the town's new

Presbyterian church, built in 1827. Such segregated seating was noted in 1840 by Kentucky-born abolitionist James G. Birney to be standard operating procedure in Methodist, Baptist, Presbyterian, and Episcopal churches, where it "applies to all colored persons, whether *members* or not." The "negro pew," he added, "is almost as rigidly kept up in the *free* States as in the slave."[16]

Only one individual is understood to have worked slaves in the Adirondack interior. Philip Rhinelander Jr. (1788–1830), a wealthy landowner and land speculator from downstate New York, settled on family-owned lands in Lake Pleasant, Hamilton County, in 1815 with the intention of developing them for profit. Building and lavishly furnishing a mansion as well as dedicating a large acreage to crops and a stock farm, he briefly became a leader of the community: twice elected as town supervisor and serving as a county representative to New York State's 1821 constitutional convention. "Seized with paralysis" in 1823, Rhinelander shortly thereafter departed the region for New York City, "never to return." Little is known about his slaveholding history, except that he reportedly arrived in Lake Pleasant with "numbers of slaves and servants," and built "outhouses for the negro servants, with a private cemetery where they might bury their dead" behind his home.[17]

Solomon Northup, born in 1808 in Minerva, Essex County, became, ironically, famous as a slave despite free-born Adirondack roots. His father, Mintus Northup, had been enslaved in Rensselaer County and manumitted upon his owner's death in the first years of the nineteenth century. The elder Northup farmed for several years in Minerva before relocating to Washington County, where his son Solomon became a farmer, Champlain Canal laborer, and raftsman before taking up urban life with his wife and children in Saratoga Springs, Saratoga County. There, he chanced in 1841 to meet two white men who, expressing knowledge of his known skill as a violinist, invited him to join a traveling circus they were promoting in Washington, DC. Northup journeyed south with his new friends to the nation's capital, where he was drugged and sold into slavery shortly after his arrival. *Twelve Years a Slave*, Northup's compelling account of his experience as a bondsman in the South before regaining his freedom in 1853, was a bestseller upon its publication later that year.[18] The book was made into a feature film in 2013. Details about Northup's subsequent life and death after his return to upstate New York remain sketchy.

White residents of the Adirondacks, like their compatriots elsewhere in the northern United States, held conflicting views when it came to the institution of slavery. The *Plattsburgh Republican*, a Clinton County newspaper that commenced publication in 1813 and usually reflected local majority sentiment, denounced abolitionism steadily throughout the 1830s and 1840s. It frequently expressed anti-black sentiment: implicitly endorsing segregated schools, disparaging a Whig as a "pretended Negro-loving personage," and declaring of a plan for educating black girls that it "smells badly."[19] Plattsburgh residents expressed themselves on both sides of the abolition issue in connection with two 1837 events: an April abolitionist convention and the founding meeting in July of the Clinton Anti-Slavery Society. Some 114 anti-abolition citizens signed a petition before the April gathering demanding that it be held elsewhere than the Clinton County Courthouse scheduled as the group's meeting place. Convention attendees were met by a name-calling, egg-throwing mob that forced them to repair to the Old Stone Methodist Church in nearby Beekmantown. Hecklers interfered with the July meeting of the Anti-Slavery Society at the town's First Presbyterian Church by tarring the church doorway beforehand; a retired judge spoke out in favor of "perpetual" slavery.[20] As an abolitionist wrote disparagingly of nearby Keeseville in 1856, the town's "moral atmosphere, in relation to slavery, is not very unlike that of South Carolina."[21]

During the same period, a number of Adirondack residents were acting on fervent anti-slavery sentiments and risking legal consequences by participating in a collaborative system of loosely organized local networks in what came to be known as the Underground Railroad. Initiated around 1830 to assist escaping slaves heading to Canada, where their freedom was assured, the clandestine undertaking represented an unusual instance of antebellum interracial teamwork in its pattern of cooperation between lower-class urban blacks, who took on responsibility for most of the daily operations involving the movement of escapees, and more affluent white supporters.[22] One popular escape route, thought to have facilitated the flight north of thousands of fugitive slaves in the thirty years before the Civil War, led from New York City through the cities of Albany and Troy, some sixty miles south of the Adirondack Park and separated from one another by the Hudson River.[23] From there, itineraries leading to Canada generally skirted the Adirondacks, with the favored route moving freedom seekers west through the Mohawk Valley via the Erie Canal and, from 1836, the Utica and Schenectady Railroad (part of the New York Central system after 1853) to cities such as Syracuse and Rochester on their way north. Lake Champlain, with its busy steamboat traffic, provided another escape route, although the French-speaking city of Montreal at the end of the journey was not known as a first choice of destination for blacks fleeing the United States.[24] Some fugitives traveled through the forested heart of the Adirondacks. A few no doubt stayed on.

Despite the divergence of Adirondack views on the subject of slaveholding (and perhaps, in part, because of the region's limited direct experience with the slave system), the region was generally more favorable to the rights of African Americans than some areas of New York. When an 1846 state referendum raised the issue of full voting rights for black men, only ten of the state's fifty-nine counties returned pluralities in favor of the measure. Three Adirondack counties provided the highest pro-suffrage votes: Clinton County with 72.8 percent in favor, Essex County with 71.1 percent, and Washington County with 59.9 percent. Two others, Franklin and Warren, were also among the top ten in supporting undiluted voting rights for black men.[25]

With the 1827 abolishment of slavery in New York, Americans of African heritage and their descendants once concentrated in northeastern slaveholding centers of the state dispersed. Plattsburgh, with its fifty-eight free blacks in 1814, was by 1850 home to only one black citizen. The routes former slaves followed to resettlement are impossible to trace, but a few individuals and families from Plattsburgh and nearby no doubt tried their luck in making a living in the region's villages and towns—a phenomenon documented in mid-nineteenth-century census records. Duane, Franklin County, for example, fifty miles from Plattsburgh and referred to in 1918 "as distinctively a rural town as can be found in the State,"[26] recorded twelve blacks (two families headed by male laborers) in its 1850 population of 222. There were no African Americans in Duane by 1860.

Despite its rapid loss of black population after state emancipation, Plattsburgh would continue to remain important in regional history as the site of the occasional race-based incident at Plattsburgh Barracks, a federal military installation. Other population centers outside the Adirondack Park were also intertwined with Adirondack history in launching early black settlers, many of them former slaves, into the region, and later evolving as destinations for African Americans who, after months or years of living in the Adirondack interior, relocated in search of more urban, black-centered lives and a wider range of job opportunities. The African American pasts of what can be called these "push-pull" towns and cities are relevant to the examination of our more circumscribed geographic area of interest.

Blacks accounted in 1771 for 9 percent of the population of Albany County,[27] a sprawling political district and the most populous county in New York before it was subdivided one year later. The cities of Albany and Troy (a municipality detached from Albany County in 1791) were within the old slave-owning "Dutch belt" and continued to sustain sizable black communities after 1827. A black church, the Hamilton-Israel African Methodist Episcopal (AME) Church, an offshoot of conventional Methodism, was organized in Albany in 1828 and a black Masonic lodge inaugurated in 1869. The Albany Female Lundy Society, established "by a few earnest and benevolent colored ladies for mutual benefit and the development of social, intellectual and religious principles," celebrated its fiftieth anniversary in 1883. A number of black Albany residents achieved professional success in the nineteenth century: among them a prosperous hotel owner; the city's foremost baker; a leading writer and orator (William H. Johnson, author of New York State's 1867 Civil Rights Bill); a doctor; and a lawyer. Albany was described in 1886 as free from "the race prejudice that exists in some cities."[28]

The early Dutch presence in Saratoga County and the county's unlikely reputation as a haven for free blacks explained its substantial African American population in 1800 (565 free and 107 enslaved). Many African American newcomers joined those long resident in Saratoga Springs after state emancipation. In 1840, blacks totaled nearly 6 percent of the population of the city, by then celebrated as the leading resort in America.[29] They filled jobs as hotel waiters and domestic servants to the tens of thousands of visitors who came, at first, to drink the healing mineralized water that gave the resort its name and, later, to see and be seen. A public gambling house opened in 1842 and became an immediate attraction; horse racing was added in 1863—the same year in which an AME Zion church was organized. Blacks were represented in small numbers among tourists and were key participants in the early days of Saratoga racing—as trainers, stable hands, grooms, hostlers, and rubbers. A New York City journalist reported in 1865 that half the jockeys at the track were black—evidence, he noted, of a "Democratic spirit" that did "not extend to the spectator's galleries, for an addendum to the Programme says: 'Colored persons not admitted to the stand.'"[30] Irish began replacing black jockeys in the late nineteenth century. Gambling was eventually banned, but the city continued to be a popular recreational outlet through the first third of the twentieth century, providing a diminished number of job opportunities for blacks in a competitive market as service workers and proprietors of small bars and restaurants.[31]

Slavery appears never to have thrived in Utica, Oneida County, thirty miles southwest of the park and strategically located along the well-traveled corridor to the West via the Mohawk Valley and Erie Canal. It nevertheless maintained a small population of early black residents, employed in the nineteenth century primarily as servants or in jobs generated by the city's transit-corridor location as provisioners to the canal trade, canalboat cooks, hotel waiters, and in stagecoach and livery stables. "A few children, mostly colored," were gathered together for Sunday school instruction (which provided some education of a secular nature) as early as 1815. Utica's population of roughly 25,000 included 184 blacks living at its economic margins when incorporated as a city in 1832. By 1840 the city had both a school for black children and an "African Church." Post Avenue, a center of black community life, was written off by a local newspaper in 1889 as "an African oasis . . . unsavory in every way, a plague spot in the very heart of the city."[32] The avenue was reported mockingly in 1912 to have long provided an outlet for Adirondack lumbermen, who reached it

> either by accident or design, and found the saloons and dance halls places of gaiety, where drinking was mingled with ragtime songs and buck dances by black boys and girls. Then there were dusky sirens who plied their wiles on half intoxicated men. Sometimes the final chapter of these adventures was written in Police Court the next morning; sometimes the woodsman awoke heartily ashamed of his conduct and footed it back north, or borrowed enough money to buy a railroad ticket, rather than make complaint that he had been "rolled" and face the publicity of a scene in court. This feature of shame always favored the thief on the avenue, for white men who had the nerve to confess that they had been consorting with negroes were scarce.[33]

Neither of the twinned cities of Johnstown and Gloversville, Fulton County, located just south of park borders and nicknamed the Glove Cities for their combined importance as a leather-glove manufacturing center, had substantial black populations. Yet both municipalities offered otherwise unavailable social opportunities and religious institutions to African Americans in nearby rural sections. Johnstown's AME Zion Church was founded in 1864, Gloversville's in 1896. The two communities came together in the mid-1890s at joint picnics in Sacandaga Park, an Adirondack pleasure ground on the Sacandaga River in nearby Northville financed and promoted by the short-line railway that shuttled tourists to the park from Gloversville. An 1893 "emancipation picnic," including emancipation "exercises" and a reading of the emancipation proclamation, was deemed "an unbounded success."[34] Three black men were mentioned by name in a history of Gloversville published in 1899 that incorporated a detailed list of well-known families and individuals: Cuffe Niver, former slave of Abram Niver, "a very honest and industrious Negro, and also a fiddler"; "Black Jack," former slave of Daniel Meeker, "a short, thick-set and jolly Negro, who died many years ago"; and James Thompson, Gloversville's "popular colored barber" in the 1860s.[35]

Burlington, Vermont, easily accessible across Lake Champlain, was, like the other cities just enumerated, both a source of black immigrants and a destination for those looking for a larger African American community. Burlington counted 62 black residents among its 1850 population of 7,585. This number rose and held steady at 115 through three federal censuses: 1880 (overall population 11,365), 1890 (population 14,590), and 1900 (population 18,640). The city developed one organization associated with African Americans during these years: a "colored" lodge of a temperance organization, the Independent Order of Good Templars, that persisted from the late 1870s through the mid-1880s.[36] A researcher who studied Burlington's black population between 1880 and 1900 found it "astonishing" that only 18 of the 115 black individuals present in the community in 1880 were among those enumerated twenty years later. Transient populations, he noted, tended to include the most casually employed and financially insecure in an aggregation, and he speculated that Burlington's black out-migration, some of it to the Adirondacks, was driven by a lack of social and economic opportunities.[37]

The transience found in Burlington was later to characterize African American population centers on the other side of Lake Champlain. As blacks with short- and long-term ties to the region moved on, they would be replaced by African Americans from further afield, often from the South.

2

Gerrit Smith

Essex and Franklin County Colonists

ANY EXAMINATION of post-1850 black history in the Adirondacks has to begin with Gerrit Smith (1797–1874), a wealthy white philanthropist, social reformer, and politician from Peterboro, New York, who gave away thousands of acres of rural upstate land to poor New Yorkers in the mid-nineteenth century. Peter Smith, Gerrit's father, had become rich through fur trading and land speculation. Much of his real estate passed to his son, an enthusiastic land speculator in his own right, and by 1845 the younger Smith owned three quarters of a million acres of real estate in New York, making him one of the state's largest landholders. A fervent abolitionist, he committed in 1846 to donating some 120,000 acres, most of it in 40- to 50-acre plots in Essex and Franklin counties, to three thousand African Americans.[1] Thanks to his largesse, a number of black individuals and families, many of them with no background in husbandry, ventured to and settled—some briefly and a few for the long haul—in the Adirondacks. Land ownership would, by Smith's reckoning, be an important step in securing grantees' eventual qualification to vote, a right diminished for them with ratification of the state's second (1821) constitution, which raised black men's property qualification for voting from $100 to $250 while abolishing it altogether for white men. This legislation achieved virtually complete disenfranchisement of African American citizens: Only 298, or .007 percent, of the 39,999 blacks living in the state were declared eligible to vote in 1826.[2] Unconditional black male suffrage would not be achieved until passage of the Fifteenth Amendment in 1870.

Mid-nineteenth-century black leaders looking to the "elevation of the race" romanticized agriculture as "a means of sustenance and real happiness" as well as an escape from the more iniquitous forms of prejudice encountered in urban life. As Austin Steward, a onetime Virginia slave who became a successful grocer in Rochester, New York, noted in his 1857 autobiography: "Our people mostly flock to cities . . . when, if they would but retire to the country and purchase a piece of land, cultivate and improve it, they would be far richer and happier than they can be in the crowded city. It is a mistaken idea that there is more prejudice against color in the country. True, it exists everywhere, but I regard it less potent in the country, where a farmer can live less dependent on his oppressors."[3] Farming was also regarded as a means of attaining political influence. As black activist Mary Ann Shadd wrote in a letter to abolitionist Frederick Douglass's newspaper, *North Star*, in 1849, "The estimation in which we would be held by those in power, would be quite different, were we producers, and not merely, as now, consumers."[4]

Smith's Adirondack land giveaway accorded with the philosophy of black self-realization through agriculture. Lots were granted to applicants from a wide swathe of New York State, among them men from New York City, from Hudson River counties, and from central New York. At least two parcels were gifted to black farmers living within what later became park boundaries—Lafayette Mason of Elizabethtown, Essex County, and William Mott of Edinburg, Saratoga County—parcels that they, like most recipients of Smith's bounty, never bothered to claim.[5]

The proximity of many Smith land parcels to one another encouraged the development of colonies of settlers able to support one another's endeavors. The most fully documented colony to date was located in the lightly populated township of North Elba, Essex County (encompassing the later village of Lake Placid). Thirteen black families, most of them Smith grantees, appeared in town records between 1850 and 1870, although few of them lived there for the full twenty-year period, and others may have arrived and departed between census enumerations.[6] The first to settle in the colony, briefly dubbed Timbucto after the ancient West African "golden place" that evolved in western mythology into one known for its inaccessibility,[7] is thought to have been thirty-year-old James H. Henderson. A Virginia-born shoemaker, Henderson arrived from Troy in the summer of 1848 with his wife, mother, and five young children. "I have been here eight months," he wrote in January 1849, "and I like the land and the country well."[8] Henderson died tragically in the winter of 1852, becoming lost while walking home from a neighbor's during a snowstorm and freezing to death. His family subsequently left the region.[9]

The one Smith grantee to make his permanent home in North Elba was Lyman Erastus Epps, employed on a Hudson River steamboat out of Troy before his arrival around 1849 in the settlement with his wife and the first two of their eight children. Born in 1813 in Colchester, Connecticut, where he attended the local School for Colored Children and "fitted himself for a teacher," Epps farmed and became a well-known guide in the High Peaks region of the central Adirondacks. He taught music to local residents, organized and taught at North Elba's first Sabbath school, was an 1875 charter member of its first church, and was one of the founders and an early trustee of the Lake Placid Public Library. At Epps's 1897 death he was eulogized for his use of "such choice language" and because he "was so well informed, and more than this because of his gentle dignity and benevolence."[10] His wife and four of his children were still in North Elba in 1900. His son Lyman Jr. spent the rest of his life in the town.

The rural community of struggling blacks in the Adirondack hinterland attracted an unusual white man to North Elba: John Brown (1800–1859), the controversial, fiery abolitionist whose violent antislavery confrontations escalated existing sectional tensions leading to the commencement of the Civil War. Brown, who "always pushed his religious convictions and philanthropic impulses to their legitimate consequence,"[11] first visited North Elba's black community in 1848. As the peripatetic farmer, surveyor, and wool merchant wrote to Gerrit Smith: "I am something of a pioneer; I grew up among the woods and wild Indians of Ohio, and am used to the climate and the way of life that your colony find so trying. I will take one of your farms myself, clear it up and plant it, and show my colored neighbors how such work should be done; will give them work as I have occasion, look after them in all needful ways and be a kind of father to them."[12] As settler James Henderson wrote in a January 1849 letter to black Troy minister Henry Garnet, "I have seen Mr. J. B. of Springfield, Mass., and he says that he will move here in the Spring, and will give us a start if we will try and help ourselves."[13]

Brown took up farming in North Elba in 1849, at first renting a farm to which he moved some of his "family and flocks and herds"—including "a number of very choice and beautiful Devons [cattle]" that he exhibited at the Essex County fair that year.[14] Brown was, however, a political activist "in no mood to undertake the quiet life of counselor and guide to a few black farmers,"[15] and he spent little extended time in North Elba. He relocated his family to Ohio in 1851, leaving behind his eldest daughter, Ruth, who had married the previous year into the abolitionist Thompson family of North Elba.[16] Brown's son-in-law Henry Thompson built a simple house on the 244-acre holding that Brown purchased from Smith before his departure. Returning briefly in 1855, Brown settled his wife and younger children into their new home before himself heading west to join five grown sons living in Kansas and involved in a regional conflict between pro- and anti-slavery forces. Brown sporadically visited his family, noting of North Elba that it was a place where "every thing you see reminds one of Omnipotence."[17] He chose to be buried there after he was captured, tried for treason, and hanged following his disastrously unsuccessful 1859 raid on Harpers Ferry, West Virginia. Half the people assembled at the lightly attended North Elba farmhouse funeral service six days after his execution were said to be blacks living in the area. Newspapers reported the presence as mourners of Lyman Epps (a confidante but not a follower of Brown) and his "silver-voiced . . . family [who] sang sweet music" at the service, choosing what was said to be Brown's favorite hymn, "Blow Ye the Trumpets, Blow."[18] The remnants of the

Brown family who were still in North Elba relocated to California not long after Brown's death.

Among black landowners in the North Elba colony was one who had little in common with its hardscrabble farmers. This was William Appo, whose family counted among Philadelphia's colored aristocracy—in particular, the so-called West Indian strand of the city's black elite that settled and established businesses in the city in the late eighteenth and early nineteenth centuries.[19] His father, St. John Appo, was listed in an 1804 Philadelphia directory as the proprietor of a confectionery store; he later added catering to his business offerings. William, born around 1808, was schooled in Haiti, where he married in 1828 and served as an officer in the Haitian army. He took up music as a profession upon returning to the United States and became what one contemporary black historian referred to as "the most learned musician of his race." An accomplished conductor, composer, singer, and multi-instrumentalist (piano, violin, and brasses), he performed regularly with musical ensembles organized by his brother-in-law Francis (Frank) Johnson, a pioneering black musician in Philadelphia. Appo visited London in 1837 as a member of Johnson's five-man ensemble and played with his Cotillion Band during summer seasons at the Congress Hotel in Saratoga Springs for several years prior to 1840. He eventually settled in New York City as a teacher of music and French.[20]

William Appo was not a beneficiary of Gerrit Smith's land giveaway, but like many members of Philadelphia's black elite, he closely identified with the abolitionist cause.[21] Familiar with upstate New York from his Saratoga days and brief residences in Troy and Utica (where in 1846 he advertised that he tuned pianos and arranged music for military bands "and for any kind of instrument or voice"),[22] he expressed his active support for Smith's settlement scheme in 1848 by purchasing from him a 148.6-acre North Elba plot that he at first used as a summer retreat. In 1860 he was listed in the federal census as a North Elba farmer and music teacher; he continued to teach music in New York City's "colored" schools through at least 1870.[23] He retired to North Elba in the late 1870s, having as a widower married Lyman Epps's daughter Albertine, who was some forty years younger than himself and with whom he had a daughter. Appo died there in 1880 and is buried in the Epps family plot in the town cemetery. His wife and daughter sold the last of their Adirondack landholdings in 1906.[24]

Despite the enthusiasm with which black leaders promoted Smith's initiative, the North Elba colony proved a failure, with most incomers drifting away within months or years of settling on their land grants. One reason for the colony's collapse may have been fear of vulnerability after the 1850 passage of Congress's second Fugitive Slave Act, a strengthened version of the 1793 legislation authorizing the capture and return of escaped slaves to their masters. Part of a compromise plan to effect the sectional reconciliation on which many white citizens felt the preservation of the Union depended, the act's draconian provisions included the loss of rights previously granted under federal and state laws and created havoc in upstate New York communities among free as well as fugitive blacks. Indeed, one-third of the six hundred blacks living in and around Syracuse, and nearly the entire congregation of Rochester's Abyssinian Baptist Church (including its minister), left the country shortly after the act's passage for the safety of Canada.[25]

Other likely explanations for the colony's failure were based in practical considerations. It is clear that little real thought had been given to the undertaking. The settlers were provided with no capital with which to commence operations or to maintain their families until farms became self-sustaining. Some of the neat, square lots designated on maps were found to be located on terrain unsuitable for husbandry. (Smith expressed the hope that these would be "more or less valuable for lumber"—in many cases, wishful thinking on his part.) Some parcels had not been surveyed and were difficult to locate on the ground, making it easy for swindlers to cheat grantees out of the best allotments; some came with delinquent taxes owed. The "rigorous clime" of northern New York State, and even would-be settlers' "disabling infirmities and vices" were among other reasons suggested for the venture's breakdown.[26]

Not all white residents of the region had welcomed the idea of black settlers in North Elba. As Essex County historian Winslow Watson wrote in 1852, not long after formation of the colony: "A reluctance, innate to the New England sentiment, to mingle with a colored population . . . has been another potent influence that has tended to arrest the course of [white] emigration to this territory." Noting that at one period "it seemed probable that the colored freeholders would obtain the political preponderance in the town" (two black settlers having been elected as North Elba's inspectors of elections in 1851), Watson raised the specter of "an African supervisor occupying a seat in the county legislature." The "people of this region," he added, "are deeply and vehemently opposed to being made the theatre of these so-called social and political experiments."[27] Seventeen years later Watson was still railing against the now failed North Elba colony, denouncing Smith's act of generosity as having "exercised a depressing and sinister influence upon the prosperity and reputation of the county."[28] Such sentiments, as well as contemporary allegations that some white citizens overcharged for or even refused to sell supplies to the settlers,[29] could have been among motivations for colonists' decisions to desert North Elba in search of more auspicious receptions elsewhere.

North Elba's black colony was a noble experiment. But it was not the only Gerrit Smith settlement in the proximate wilderness. A number of grantees established themselves in the adjacent towns of St. Armand, Essex County, and Franklin, Franklin County, some twenty-five to forty miles to the northwest of North Elba. Thirty African Americans—six families and three single males—were recorded in the 1850 census as living in the town of Franklin, representing 4.14 percent of its population of 724. Eight of Franklin's black male residents owned real estate, of which the average value was between thirty-eight and fifty dollars.

The most organized and centralized, albeit ephemeral, of Franklin's black settlements was located in what is today the hamlet of Loon Lake. Known as Blacksville, the colony was made up of African Americans from Williamsburg, Kings County (Brooklyn), under the de facto leadership of Willis Augustus Hodges, a black abolitionist and the cofounder of a short-lived abolitionist newspaper, *Ram's Horn*. Born free in Virginia in 1815, Hodges was one of those influential blacks who advocated agriculture as a good "life for a proscribed caste to pursue, because it tends to break down all proscriptions" and was well adapted to their "pecuniary circumstances."[30] The thirty-three-year-old pioneer enlisted five families and four single men to settle on Smith lands, where, in May 1848, he declaimed, "under our own vine and fig trees in the Promised Land, God speed the plough!"[31] John Brown, a friend and supporter, sent six barrels of pork and flour to the Blacksville settlers in October of that year with instructions to Hodges "to divide with the different families as to make all as happy and comfortable as possible." But it is apparent from correspondence between Brown and Hodges that the colony endured hard times from the outset. In January 1849 Brown wrote to Hodges that he understood his "colored friends" were getting through the winter "middling well." By early May he was urging Hodges, "Do not get discouraged."[32] Nevertheless, settlers began drifting away. Hodges did not appear in the 1850 Franklin County census and was known to be living again in Brooklyn by 1853. The colony disappeared completely by 1855.[33] The land became the site of the Loon Lake House, a popular resort hotel that opened in 1878.

Vermontville, another Franklin hamlet, absorbed at least two Smith grantees. The background of one of them, John Thomas, is well known. Born a plantation slave in Queen Anne County, Maryland, around 1810, he married in 1833 and fathered two children who died in infancy before his wife was sold away to Georgia. Thomas escaped Maryland in 1840 and traveled on foot to Philadelphia, where friends hid him before sending him northward on the Underground Railroad to Troy, New York. There he married again and started a new family.[34] Thomas took up the Smith grant given to him in 1846 and relocated to a forty-acre parcel in Franklin but, "owing to the inconvenience of Church and School privileges," sold it not long afterward and returned to Troy.[35] He later purchased fifty acres of land in Vermontville and settled permanently in the Adirondack interior. It was rumored after passage of the Fugitive Slave Act that his former Maryland master had heard of his whereabouts and sent agents to Franklin County to retrieve him, "but upon being warned there that Thomas was armed and would never be taken alive, and that the local whites would stand by him," his pursuers "abandoned their purpose, and turned back."[36] Thomas expanded his original farm holding, one that, according to a perhaps embellished letter he sent to Gerrit Smith in 1872, "by labor and economy has been enlarged into a hansome farm of two hundred acres; with all necessary Stock and farming implements. I generally have surplus of two or three hundred dollars worth of farm produce to sell, every year. . . . I have breasted the storm of prejudice and opposition, until I begin to be regarded as an 'American Citizen.'"[37] Thomas died in 1894.

Settler Stephen Warren Morehouse moved to Vermontville from Waterford, Saratoga County, and settled with his family on a forty-acre Smith grant by 1850. He seems not to have farmed for long, as he and his wife, both forty-nine years old, were listed as living in the adjoining Franklin County town of Brighton in the 1860 census. They were then the only blacks on the seven-member service staff of Apollos Smith, an innkeeper who a year earlier had opened what later became Paul Smith's Hotel. The couple's one son, another Stephen Warren (known as Warren), relocated to Boston, where he found employment as a waiter. He returned to Vermontville after serving in the Civil War.

One other possible Smith grantee, William A. Smith, was living in Vermontville in 1850 but departed by 1855. James Brady, born in 1824 in Frenchtown, Maryland, appeared in 1860 census records as a Vermontville farmer possessing real estate valued at $300 and a personal estate of $150 (although no land deed was ever recorded in his name). He had no known connection to Gerrit Smith but may have been acquainted with other colonists. Brady's seventeen-year-old son, James, born, like his father, in Maryland, lived on a neighboring farm as a servant.

A number of early Franklin residents (among them Samuel Brady and Stephen Warren Morehouse Jr.) had post office addresses in the adjoining hamlet of Bloomingdale in St. Armand, Essex County. By 1855 there was a Smith grantee living in Bloomingdale itself: Avery Hazzard, a son of Revolutionary War veteran Levi Hazzard.[38]

Avery had migrated to St. Armand from Union Village, Washington County,[39] and was then the head of a household of seven. Three Hazzard sons—Charles Henry (twenty-seven), George (twenty-two), and Leonard (twenty)—farmed with their father in Bloomingdale in 1855. Another son, Alexander (twenty-five), was not enumerated with them that year, but by 1860 he and Charles Henry were the only Hazzard sons living on the family farm. The descendants and extended families of both men would have a longtime presence in the region.

Avery Hazzard had been granted a forty-acre lot, but he increased his acreage. By 1855 his farm comprised 130 acres, some of which may have been leased. In December 1864, a 160-acre St. Armand farm was conveyed to nine heirs of the recently deceased Hazzard by Ira Marks, an Elizabethtown businessman and real estate speculator, for the sum of $300.[40]

Avery Hazzard's son Charles Henry served as a soldier during the Civil War and, like many other soldiers, found a bride where he was stationed. He married widow Julia Newton Smith of Beaufort, South Carolina, and brought her, as well as her two daughters, home after the war to Bloomingdale, where he purchased his own farm in 1870. Julia's daughter Clara married Abial Anthony of Burlington, Vermont, son of Burlington steamboat cook and Underground Railroad agent Tony Anthony, in the late 1860s.[41] The couple may have met during one of several summers in which Anthony worked as a barber at nearby Paul Smith's Hotel, where he was reported to have shaved the faces of future president Grover Cleveland and impresario P. T. Barnum.[42]

The Charles Henry Hazzards had no offspring of their own. They were close, however, to the children of Julia's daughter Genevia, who stayed in the region after marrying Jate Johnson in 1877. Johnson, from West Virginia, appeared in the 1875 census as both a black farm laborer in St. Armand and a hotel hostler (employed to look after horses) in nearby Malone, Franklin County.[43] When Genevia died in 1887, her husband relocated to the New York City area. The couple's three children—Charles (born 1878), Mabel (1880), and Laura (1882)—stayed behind. Charles and Mabel were recorded as living in the home of Charles Henry and Julia Hazzard in 1892. Their sister, Laura, may have been raised by her aunt and uncle Clara and Abial Anthony. She is listed as a member of their Burlington household in the 1900 census.

Alexander Hazzard, Charles Henry's brother, and his wife, Elizabeth, parented ten children. Their son George, born in Bloomingdale in 1869, married Warren and Charlotte Morehouse's daughter, Elizabeth, or Libby, and by 1905 had relocated his family to Saranac Lake. Further binding the Hazzard and Morehouse families was the marriage of Alexander and Libby's daughter Anna M., known as Mary, to John Morehouse in 1902. By 1910 the Morehouses were also residing in Saranac Lake.

Alexander Hazzard died at the age of sixty-nine in 1898. By 1905 there were only three of his descendants still resident in Bloomingdale. Ada (or Adelaide), born around 1871, was the wife of black farmer William Langley from Williston, Vermont. The Langleys' two-year-old son and Ada's sister Lizzie, age twenty, lived with them; Lizzie was listed in census records as a servant. The Langleys farmed briefly in the area and then disappeared from local records. Jate and Genevia Johnson's three children were also in Bloomingdale in 1905. Mabel, age twenty-five, was married to farmer William M. Greene and working at what would be her lifelong occupation as a cook. Living with the Greenes were Mabel's brother, Charles, a twenty-six-year-old liveryman, and her sister, Laura, twenty-three. The three Johnson siblings were to remain close.

The center of black life in the region henceforth shifted to Saranac Lake, where third, fourth, and fifth generations of Smith land grant families from Franklin and St. Armand would become part of the town's black community in the first half of the twentieth century. Their stories will be taken up again in chapter 11.

3

Soldiers of the Civil War

THE CIVIL WAR (1861–65) was initiated by the Confederacy to protect the institution of slavery. The federal government's goal was to preserve the Union, not to proscribe the practice, and public opinion at the outset of hostilities would not have supported abolition. As the war lengthened and escalated, ending slavery became a political possibility, and on January 1, 1863, President Abraham Lincoln issued the Emancipation Proclamation, freeing all slaves in areas still in rebellion. The announcement was not universally applauded in the North Country. As James Estes, a twenty-year-old farmer's son from Keene serving with the 118th New York Infantry (the "Adirondack Regiment") wrote to his mother from Maryland about the pending announcement in October 1862: "I think it is good but some are out against it with all their might."[1]

The federal government was not initially enthusiastic about recruiting blacks into the military. Lincoln's position evolved during the course of the conflict as manpower needs became pressing. At the outset, he was concerned that enrolling black soldiers would alarm slaveholders in the crucial border states of Delaware, Maryland, Kentucky, and Missouri, whose loyalty kept them in the Union as long as their right to own slaves was not threatened. In the summer of 1862 he approved the principle of recruiting free blacks and the slaves of "loyal owners" who gave their consent, as well as the concept of "compensated emancipation." The Emancipation Proclamation authorized the entry of blacks into military service,[2] and in May 1863 the government, sensitive to racial prejudice, established the Bureau of Colored

Troops—creating a segregated military that would serve as the country's model for some eighty years.

State governors were responsible for raising regiments, and abolitionist John A. Andrew of Massachusetts was the first northern governor to embrace the recruitment of black soldiers. The Fifty-Fourth Massachusetts Volunteer Infantry, a black regiment, began organizing in mid-February 1863, less than two months after the Emancipation Proclamation was issued. It was a controversial undertaking. Despite Governor Andrew's trust in African Americans' capacity for leadership, it was settled that commissioned officers in the unit were to be white, a precedent that would be followed in the staffing of black regiments across the country. The Fifty-Fourth saw extensive service and gained recognition in July 1863 for gallantly fronting an assault on Fort Wagner near Charleston, South Carolina, an incident memorialized in the 1989 Academy Award–winning film *Glory.*

Massachusetts's population of black men was insufficient to fill the ranks of the Fifty-Fourth from within the state's borders, so a committee of prominent white abolitionists, later known as the Black Committee, was formed to superintend the raising of recruits outside the state. The committee subscribed nearly $100,000 for the unit (Gerrit Smith sent in his check for $500), and a call for enlistees was published in one hundred journals "from east to west." An agent closely identified with abolitionist John Brown was headquartered in Buffalo to establish a line of recruiting offices from Boston to St. Louis, and on a March 1863 trip through Rochester he enrolled twenty-two-year-old Lewis H. Douglass, a son of Frederick Douglass—the renowned black spokesman of the abolition struggle during the Civil War years.[3]

Two African Americans from the Adirondacks joined the Fifty-Fourth Massachusetts. One of them, Stephen Warren Morehouse, appeared in the last chapter as the son of Gerrit Smith grantee Stephen Morehouse of Vermontville, Franklin, Franklin County. Enrolling as a twenty-year-old waiter from Boston in September 1863, Morehouse was mentioned twice by name in the history of the Fifty-Fourth compiled after the war by Luis Emilio, the captain of Morehouse's Company E. According to one entry, private Morehouse was "scouting in the woods" when he discovered and alerted his major to the presence of "Rebs" hiding in a barn. He was cited again as a "sharpshooter" who exposed himself in creeping out of hiding during a lull in the February 1864 Battle of Olustee (Florida) when "the men began to chafe, and exhibit a desire for aggressive action."[4]

Amos King, the second Adirondack resident to serve in the Fifty-Fourth Massachusetts, came from Caroga, Fulton County, and was enrolled in the unit in April 1863 by two recruiters active in the Mohawk Valley. At forty-three years of age, he was one of the oldest enlistees in the regiment and is likely to have been among a group cited in a mid-April newspaper report from Albany: "A squad of forty-five colored men recruited in Little Falls [Herkimer County] and elsewhere . . . left this city to-day for the camp of the 54th Massachusetts (colored) Regiment at Readville near Boston. The men are mostly canallers, and will make brave and hardy soldiers. Previous to their departure, they were each furnished with a copy of the New Testament by the Albany Young Men's Christian Association which slight token of regard was fully appreciated and thankfully received."[5] King was a member of Company G and served in all of the Fifty-Fourth's major battles. As his superior officer wrote in the margin of his discharge papers, "At Olustee he conducted himself with great bravery."[6]

What circumstances, one wonders, had led to the clustering in the early 1850s of King's family and those of two other black farmers in Caroga—a town with an 1865 population of roughly 625. All adults and children born before 1852 into these families claimed Dutchess County as their place of birth.[7] The first of them to settle appears to have been Philip Leonard, who bought property in the town in 1851.[8] An 1856 Caroga map identified him and the two other black householders—Peter Millett, like Leonard, a farmer, and King, a farm laborer—by name.[9] They were then living on adjacent or near-adjacent plots in what became North Bush, thought to have been the town's first settlement. Four members of these families in addition to Amos King participated as soldiers in the Civil War. Three of them did not return.

New York's governor, Horatio Seymour, held racist views and did what he could to impede the mobilizing of African American units in New York.[10] Consequently, recruitment for the state's first black regiment did not begin until December 1863, nearly a year after the issuance of the Emancipation Proclamation. But several blacks who called the Adirondacks home had already enrolled or were about to be enrolled in predominantly white units of the Union army, an army in which the color line had not yet been firmly drawn.

The earliest African American to join the war effort from the Adirondacks is likely to have been twenty-one-year-old William Appo, namesake son of the musician, who enlisted in September 1861 from North Elba. He was assigned to the Thirtieth Regiment New York Infantry, organized at Troy. A private in Company I, Appo may have been light-skinned enough to pass for white in the unit (although he was listed as "colored" in military documents), as his siblings adopted both black and white identities. His sister Helen Appo Cook, whose "complexion was that of a Spaniard," married into a prominent and wealthy black family in the District of Columbia. Once described as "the mother of organizations among colored women in the country," she was the long-term president of the Colored Women's League of Washington, DC, and a professor of romance languages at Howard University. William's brother, St. John Appo, "became white," according to family papers. He was for many years the publisher of the *Army and Navy Register* in Washington, "where his scholarly attainments and courtly manner made him a familiar figure in national affairs." He was also a trophy-winning amateur golfer.[11] Young William Appo was promoted to corporal in February 1862 and died in August of that year during the Second Battle of Bull Run.

Franklin County farmer James Brady, described as "mulatoe" in the town of Franklin's Civil War records, enlisted in July 1862 from St. Armand, Essex County. He served as a private in Company C of the 118th New York Regiment, made up mostly of recruits from Clinton, Essex, and Warren counties. Brady was mustered out with the unit on June 22, 1865, and relocated to Malone, Franklin County, leaving behind in Vermontville a wife, Louisa, who acted as housekeeper for

John Thomas, Gerrit Smith land grantee, after the 1875 death of his wife, Mary.[12]

Adolphus and Henry James were sons of Joseph James, born around 1812 in Jay, Essex County, to Peter and Dolly James. Joseph James first appeared in the federal census of 1850 as a resident of Westport, Essex County—the town in which he had spent the previous eight years. His wife, Adeline Ober of Crown Point, was white, and the couple's ten children were enumerated in census documents for more than fifty years as "black," "mulatto," and "white."[13] Adolphus and Henry, identified in Essex County war records as "colored," enlisted in New York units from Westport in August and September 1862. Adolphus, eighteen years old at the time of enlistment, served as a private in Company F with the 118th Regiment for nearly three years and was mustered out with the company in June 1865. Henry James, also eighteen at enlistment, became a private in the Seventy-Seventh New York Infantry Regiment. Known as the Saratoga Regiment, its Company A, of which he was a member, was recruited primarily at Westport. Henry lost a forearm at Fredericksburg, Virginia, in May 1863 and was discharged in Washington "for wounds" the following year.[14] By June 1865 he was living with his parents and farming in Westport. A third James son, Harvey (also "colored," according to war records), tried unsuccessfully to enlist in the army at Westport in 1862. Born, like his mother, in Vermont, he applied again from Burlington in December 1863 and was assigned to Company G of the First Vermont Cavalry. He died at Brandy Station, Virginia, in March 1864 of disease—the wartime killer of four times as many soldiers as died in battle, and three times more black than white soldiers.[15] James is buried at Culpeper National Cemetery in Virginia.

Lafayette Mason, born in 1827 in Ellenburg, Clinton County, was another member of the 118th Infantry Regiment with African American roots. Married to Essex County–born Mary Wheeler of Willsboro, with whom he had eleven children, Mason was a small farmer and collier in the Elizabethtown hamlet of New Russia and was later described by his longtime employer as a "good steady industrious man."[16] He enlisted in the military on December 21, 1863, from Elizabethtown, and was mustered into the 118th's Company G one week later. His enrollment record noted his physical features as "eyes black; hair black; complexion dark." His race was not recorded on his enlistment muster, but he was consistently listed as "mulatto" in New York census records.

Mason was one of fifty-one members of his regiment to be captured on October 27, 1864, at the Second Battle of Fair Oaks, Virginia,[17] a Union attack on Richmond with disastrous results that, according to one participant, "came near wiping out of existence the 118th Regiment, but not quite."[18] The captured men were sent to North Carolina's Salisbury Prison on November 4,[19] a notorious Confederate holding pen known for overcrowding and suffering. Four days later the prison attained its highest capacity during the war (8,740 prisoners in quarters intended to hold 2,500).[20] "Coatless, hatless, and shoeless" detainees were said to live in open stockades, in tents, or burrows they dug themselves inside an open stockade, sometimes in below-freezing weather and without food or fuel.[21] Salisbury's death rate was higher than that of any war prison, North or South, during the months in which it held soldiers from the 118th,[22] and Mason spent two months in hospital after being evacuated from Salisbury to Richmond in late February 1865—just weeks before the last major Confederate army surrendered at Appomattox.[23]

One wonders what sort of treatment Appo, Brady, the James brothers, and Mason received from officers and other soldiers in their regiments. They were undoubtedly light-skinned, and it is possible that, because they enlisted with neighbors and came from a region in which there was little outward racial conflict, they were welcomed into their units as individuals. But this was not necessarily the case. As the company commander of a white Ohio regiment wrote to the War Department in 1864 asking for the transfer of four "mulattoes ('one of them very dark')" to a black unit: "The presence of these men cause great dissatisfaction among the white soldiers and occasion myself a great deal of trouble to keep order and quiet in the company and is I think an injustice both to myself and the men to have them where they now are." A black soldier in a white Ohio unit expressed unhappiness as well. "I am a colored man," he wrote, "and my position as private in a white Regiment is very unpleasant. My feelings are constantly outraged by the conduct of those who have no respect for my race."[24]

Because New York's Governor Seymour divorced himself from the process of recruiting blacks into the military, three black units were raised privately in the state by New York City's Union League Club: "five hundred of the wealthiest and most influential gentlemen of the city, who have no purpose to serve, but the support of the Government."[25] Designated the Twentieth, Twenty-Sixth, and Thirty-First infantry regiments United States Colored Troops (USCT), they were recognized as federal rather than state units in keeping with the Union army's effort to assuage latent hostility to the use of black soldiers.[26] Approximately 175 regiments of USCT, representing 10 percent of all Union forces, were raised during the war. New York State's three black regiments enrolled 4,125 servicemen, or about 2 percent of the total black enlistment.[27]

The Union League Club's committee in charge of recruiting its first black regiment, the Twentieth Infantry Regiment USCT, held its initial organizational meeting in November 1863 and began recruitment in mid-December. This was only five months after New York City had been the scene of bitter draft riots in which a mob demonstration of working-class, mostly Irish, protestors against new draft laws turned into a violent four-day race riot that resulted in the killing of at least 119 African Americans. The enlistment experience of Samuel Brady, twenty-year-old son of James, the Franklin County farmer enrolled since July 1862 in New York's 118th Infantry Regiment, suggests early confusion in connection with recruitment for the USCT. Samuel enlisted in the army from Plattsburgh, Clinton County, on December 15, 1863, and was immediately assigned to his father's regiment. The following day, however, he was "unassigned" from the 118th,[28] and reallocated to the newly formed Twentieth USCT. The reason for this is unlikely to be discovered, but may have signaled a closer attention to color engendered by the anticipated segregation of New York State's army units.

The Twentieth trained at Riker's Island in New York Harbor, marched down Manhattan's Broadway on March 5, 1864 (although it had been difficult to find a white band willing to accompany the unit), and embarked by sea for New Orleans.[29] Like most black regiments, it would participate in no major campaigns but spent most of its time in garrison and nonmilitary fatigue duties in Louisiana: cleaning, cooking, repairing roads, and digging trenches. As one member of the regiment wrote bitterly to President Lincoln in August 1864, "Instead of the musket It is the spad and the Whelbarrow and the Axe cuting in one of the most horable swamps in Louisiana stinking and misery."[30] A single enlisted man in the unit died of wounds received in battle; 263 died of disease.[31] Among them were Samuel Brady and three young men from Caroga: Joseph King (son of Amos King and sixteen years old at the time of his death) and Charles and George Leonard (twenty and twenty-two years old, respectively). Brady and George Leonard are buried under marked tombstones in the Chalmette National Cemetery in New Orleans; King and Charles Leonard (who joined the regiment as a corporal and was promoted to sergeant) are said to lie among the seven thousand unmarked graves in the burial ground.

Recruitment into the Twentieth Regiment USCT moved quickly, and only two weeks after enrollment commenced the Union League Club applied for authorization to raise a second black unit. Permission was granted in January 1864. The Twenty-Sixth Regiment USCT was briefly deployed to Annapolis, Maryland, before serving in and around Beaufort, South Carolina. Several members of the regiment came from towns within and partially within the future Adirondack Park at the time of their enrollment:

- William Carasaw: Farmer. Born in Watervliet, Albany County, and resident in North Elba, Essex County. Private, Company A.[32] His gravestone in Vergennes, Vermont, records his outgoing rank as sergeant.
- Daniel Fitch: Laborer. Born in Vermont and resident in Garoga, a hamlet of Ephratah, Fulton County. Private, Company A.[33]

- Josiah Hasbrook Jr.: Farmer. Born in Fishkill, Dutchess County, and resident in North Elba, Essex County. Private, Company B.[34]
- Charles Henry Hazzard: Farmer. Born in Washington County and resident in the hamlet of Bloomingdale, St. Armand, Essex County. Private, Company G.[35]
- Leonard Kettle: Laborer. Born in Schoharie County and resident in Vail Mills, a hamlet of Mayfield, Fulton County. Private, Company F.[36]
- Thomas Millett: Laborer. Born in Dutchess County and resident in Caroga, Fulton County. Entered as private; promoted to second sergeant, Company A.[37]

Daniel Fitch was the only one of these soldiers to become a war casualty. Losing his hand "by accidental discharge of musket," he was taken to hospital in Beaufort and died there of infection in November 1864.[38] He is buried in Beaufort National Cemetery.

Perhaps the most unusual Civil War record for a black combatant with an Adirondack connection was that compiled by Silas Frazier, born in Sullivan County in 1821 and first appearing as an Adirondack resident in 1854 with his purchase of a thirty-acre plot in Gerrit Smith's North Elba colony.[39] Frazier and his wife, Jane Oakley, were listed in the 1855 North Elba census as "mulatto"; in every other state and federal census from 1850 (when the newly married Fraziers lived in Newburgh, Orange County) through 1870 they were enumerated as "black." By 1860 the couple relocated to Westport, where Frazier was recorded as "black" in Essex County records of men eligible for the draft in 1863.

Thirty-six men from Westport (1860 population 1,981) served in cavalry units during the war. Fourteen of these soldiers were members of the Second New York Veterans Volunteer Cavalry,[40] including Frazier, who joined its Company A on December 15, 1863. He went to the front and tented with other members of the unit from Westport, and was later recalled by one of them as "a splendid soldier." Frazier was injured in the late spring of 1864 near Morganza, Louisiana, the site of a Union army encampment, when going to the aid of a tentmate from home, Allen Talbot, whose horse failed to clear a ditch during a raid and fell on its rider. Getting off his own mount to assist his comrade, Frazier was kicked in the groin by the rear legs of Talbot's horse, after which doctors pronounced him unfit to ride again. "There being a call for men to go into the Navy," Frazier, who according to his wife "had been to sea considerable" before his marriage, volunteered and was transferred to the US Navy on July 1, 1864. He was assigned the job of cabin cook (officer's cook) on the *Augusta Dinsmore*,[41] a screw steamer operating out of New Orleans that carried information and materiel to warships of the West Gulf Blockading Squadron.[42]

The Union navy was racially integrated at this time, and African Americans, a majority of them former slaves, represented some 20 percent of its enlisted wartime force—nearly double the proportion of black soldiers in the army. On supply steamers such as the *Augusta Dinsmore* this number might rise to between 63 and 100 percent. The cultural bias of the northern white officers under whom they served meant that most African Americans were assigned to duties as laborers and personal servants. Frazier would have had some advantage over the recently freed slaves as both a free black man and a speaker with an accent familiar to his superiors. He was one of the approximately 8 percent of black sailors rated as cooks and stewards during the war, earned premium pay, and was technically a petty officer, albeit one with no authority over other enlisted men.[43] Discharged from the navy in August 1865, Frazier returned to Westport, where he purchased a twenty-acre farm on the outskirts of the village. He appears, as did many other Civil War soldiers, to have suffered from untreated (and in those days untreatable) war injuries, for he complained of constant pain in his abdomen, "grew weaker, and gradually wore out," dying at the age of fifty-four in April 1874.[44]

Like Frazier, most black men who participated in the Civil War from the Adirondacks resumed their old lives when it was over, at least for a while. Henry James returned to Essex, Essex County, after being wounded. His brother Adolphus located nearby in the town of Willsboro. Both men married white women and lived white lives thereafter, although Henry was identified as "black" in the 1892 state census.

Alternately classified as a laborer and a farmer in census records, he was buried in the Old Burt Cemetery in Essex upon his death in 1919. Adolphus took up the occupation of "grocery man" by 1892; Dolphus James of "Africa" appeared as an 1880s entry in Willsboro's Riverside Hotel guest book, where his name was inscribed a number of times.[45] He died in 1898 and lies in the Gilliland Cemetery in Willsboro.

Lafayette Mason briefly returned to his New Russia home, although he was, according to the Mason family's physician, "a skeleton of his former self" after his incarceration in Salisbury Prison.[46] He, his wife, and seven of their children departed the Adirondacks in 1866 and moved westward, following in the footsteps of other farming families who abandoned their farms when soil lost fertility. The Masons landed first in Vernon Springs, Howard County, Iowa (where all family members were designated in the 1870 census as "mulatto") and Mason and his second son, twenty-one-year-old Lewis, worked as farm laborers. The family moved at least once more before settling in 1877 or 1878 in Minnehaha County, Dakota Territory, where Mason died in 1879.[47] Of Mason's older children who stayed in the East, the eldest, George, remained for a time in Elizabethtown and was recorded there as a twenty-seven-year-old laborer in the 1875 census. Daughter Thirza Storms raised a family in Vermont and then followed her children to Boston, where she became a noted evangelist.[48] Several Mason children settled in Minneapolis.

Caroga's Amos King was able to purchase a farm of his own in October 1865 with his accumulated soldier's wages and the bounty he earned in joining the Fifty-Fourth Massachusetts Regiment.[49] He died in 1908 at the age of eighty-nine. The US Department of Veterans Affairs provided a government headstone for King in Caroga's old North Bush cemetery in 1996 at the request of the Fulton County historian. Its installation was celebrated with a memorial service to honor the long-forgotten Civil War soldier.[50]

Warren Morehouse returned to farm in Vermontville, Franklin County, after serving with the Fifty-Fourth Massachusetts, and in 1866 married one of Smith grantee John Thomas's two daughters,

Charlotte. The couple had four children before Morehouse's 1882 death at the age of forty-five.

Charles Henry Hazzard also resumed his Adirondack life, returning to Bloomingdale, Essex County, and bringing with him a bride from Beaufort, South Carolina, as discussed in chapter 2. He died in 1899 at the age of seventy-three and is buried in Bloomingdale's Brookside Cemetery. Descendants of his stepdaughter Genevia Smith Johnson still live in the area.

William Carasaw made a brief reappearance in North Elba after the war. By 1880 he was a sixty-year-old hostler in Vergennes, Vermont, where he died in 1886. His former neighbor and comrade in arms, Josiah Hasbrook Jr., also spent a few postwar years in North Elba, although his parents and siblings had left the town by 1860. In 1868 he married Jane Ann Hazzard, sister of veteran Charles Henry Hazzard. The couple farmed in North Elba until 1871, when they relocated to a farm in Westport, Essex County. They moved twice more, to Worcester, Vermont, where Hasbrook was elected commander of the local chapter of the Grand Army of the Republic, and then to Amherst, Massachusetts, where he died in 1915 at the age of seventy-five. His obituary mentioned that he had received his early schooling from Sarah and Annie Brown, daughters of abolitionist John Brown.[51]

Leonard Kettle (also known as Jack Kittle) returned to Mayfield, Fulton County, where censuses through 1890 recorded his occupation as farmer, and the local newspaper occasionally referenced his lively personality. Thomas Millett went back to upstate New York as well. His father, pioneer settler Peter Millett, remained in his Caroga home until moving in with a daughter in Gloversville several years before his 1892 death. Thomas, however, relocated not long after the war to Fonda, the county seat of Montgomery County, where he was a longtime employee of the Snell House, later the Hotel Roy. He died in 1927 at eighty-four years of age and was reported in his obituary to have been a member of Fonda's Van Derveer Post of the Grand Army of the Republic.[52]

1. William Carasaw, Civil War veteran, Twenty-Sixth Regiment, USCT. Courtesy of New York State Military Museum.

The Grand Army of the Republic (GAR) to which Millett and Hasbrook belonged was an anomaly in the late nineteenth and early twentieth centuries as a largely integrated organization in an era when American society was steadily becoming divided along the color line. A fraternal, charitable, and political association founded in 1866 by

2. Josiah Hasbrook Jr., Civil War veteran, Twenty-Sixth Regiment, USCT. Courtesy of Jones Library, Inc., Amherst, MA.

and for Union veterans, it went through a period of eclipse in the 1870s and reemerged in the 1880s as perhaps the most powerful political lobby of the age.[53] In large urban agglomerations, African Americans generally maintained separate posts, but in less densely populated areas of the North, such as the Adirondacks, black members were integrated into mostly white posts. Their acceptance as equals by their white comrades was based on their shared wartime experiences, a fellow feeling that did not extend beyond the organization, as racism shaped the political response of white veterans and the GAR to civil rights and other issues affecting blacks. The organization died in 1956 with the death of its last member; its last black representative died in in 1951.[54]

4

Wartime and Early Postwar Migration

THE BLACK POPULATION of the Adirondacks remained static or diminished slightly in the years before the Civil War. But, as national hostilities escalated and populations shifted, a few uprooted southern blacks found their way to the region as a result of interactions with its residents during the war and early postwar decades.

Four young African Americans from Virginia arrived, presumably together, sometime before 1865 in Fish House, a hamlet of Northampton Township in Fulton County. Dr. Langdon Marvin, a local resident who served briefly in the South as a surgeon with a New York regiment in 1862, is believed to have arranged for their transportation north.[1] The motivation for providing homes in the North to displaced blacks from southern states during the war was generally altruistic, but it was not unheard of for northerners who found themselves in the war zone to secure inexpensive retainers where they were stationed.[2] Marvin's four imports—Ash, a fourteen-year-old male; Re, a sixteen-year-old male; S. Jackson, a fifteen-year-old male; and L. Jackson, a twenty-year-old female—were immediately parceled out, one per family, as servants to various members of the Marvin clan. Unlike many who saw to it that southern blacks they were responsible for bringing north received some level of education, the Marvins made no apparent effort to school their charges. Ash, the youngest of the four upon arrival, was still unable to read or write fifteen years later.

Three of the four Fish House transplants left the community before 1870. But Ash remained. He spent the rest of his life with the Marvins, much of it working at the dairy farm that served as a summer home for the family of Lucy, a Marvin daughter who married Brooklyn merchant Frank Sinclaire in 1855.[3] Ash gradually achieved his own identity. Recorded in 1870 census records as Ash Marvin, he became Ashton Hodge by 1880. His occupation rose in stature from servant to laborer to farmer. By the 1920s Hodge was manager of the Sinclaire farm and its registered herd of Jersey cows that provided fine butter on a weekly basis to a Brooklyn clientele.[4] Remaining single, he became a respected citizen of Northampton as evidenced by the deference paid him by local newspapers. A column in a Gloversville journal devoted to the social news of Broadalbin, a Fulton County town some sixteen miles south of Fish House, occasionally noted his presence as a visitor to the town; in 1918 he was recorded as a subscriber to a Third Liberty Loan issued to help meet expenses related to the First World War. When Hodge died in 1925, his largely attended funeral was held from the Sinclaire home, now owned by a new generation of Marvin descendants.[5] He was buried in the Marvin family plot in the Northampton cemetery under a tombstone patronizingly, but no doubt lovingly, worded "faithful retainer in the family for 62 years."

Slaves began freeing themselves and streaming into Union army camps not long after the first shots of the war were exchanged at Charleston's Fort Sumter in April 1861. Officially, the Fugitive Slave Act required that runaways be returned to their masters. But, building on an initiative of Union general Benjamin Butler, it was determined early on that slaves in seceded states should be considered as Confederate assets that would be used by the enemy to promote its war efforts. Thus Congress passed, and President Lincoln signed into law in August 1861, a Confiscation Act that defined slaves as property to be "seized, confiscated, and condemned" as contraband of war.[6] This calculated half measure did not challenge the status of enslaved people as property, but it encouraged an increasing number of slaves to seek protection behind Union lines. Their willingness to work and fight against the Confederacy gradually led the Union army to accept runaways as a practical necessity. Indeed, many slaves found themselves behind Union lines without even leaving their plantations when Union armies seized Confederate territory.[7]

A number of "contrabands" were brought by local residents or found their own way to the Adirondacks after the war, where they were generally welcomed. A few stayed on. A memoirist who compiled a 1902 history of Westport, Essex County, recalled "a black boy" named William Mallory, brought home by the town's Dr. Platt Sawyer, whom Mallory had attended during the war "as a kind of body-servant." She evoked the interest excited by the boy's arrival among the town's children, few of whom had seen a black person, writing of him that he "was very quiet and well mannered, and often admonished us children in points of etiquette." Mallory remained with the family for several years (although his name never appeared in census records) before returning to his home state of Virginia.[8]

The hamlet of Vermontville in Franklin, Franklin County, is believed to have absorbed two former slaves as a result of Civil War contacts. One of them, Walter Scott of North Carolina, purportedly traveled north at the age of nineteen with Alfred N. Skiff, a lieutenant with the Sixtieth Regiment, New York Infantry. Nicknamed "Ums" for his southern way of referring to himself (as in "Ums did the chores"), he had no formal education but "was nobody's fool." Scott married Caroline, the second daughter of Gerrit Smith grantee John Thomas. He bought a fifty-acre Vermontville farm from Skiff in 1874 on which he and his wife raised two children; two others died in childhood.[9] The farm did not prosper. In 1890 Scott mortgaged his property to another member of the extended Skiff family, receiving $114.50 in the transaction. Interest was never paid, nor was any of the principal repaid, and yet another Skiff sued to recover the debt in 1916. Scott's home of forty-three years was auctioned off on February 3, 1917, "at the front door of the Court House in the Village of Malone," the county seat. It went for $221.50 ($3.15 above the amount owed) and the Scotts disappeared from Franklin County records.[10] Anecdotal evidence also attributes the post–Civil War presence in Vermontville of a black woman, Bettie Burns, to her arrival with a Civil War soldier—in this case, Luther Bryant, a lieutenant in the 118th Infantry Regiment.[11] Burns did not reside long in the community.

Surrey (Joe) Herring was born into slavery in 1844 and raised as a house slave on a Wilmington, North Carolina, plantation. Rented out by his master to a Wilmington hotel at the start of the war, he freed himself and joined the Union cause as a contraband. Attaching himself to the army, he became unofficial orderly to William H. Shaw, a farmer from Mayfield, Fulton County, and the captain of Company E of New York's 115th Infantry Regiment, recruited almost exclusively from Fulton County. After the war, Captain Shaw brought Herring to Mayfield, where he spent three years at Shaw's farm before relocating to Gloversville. There he married, fathered four children, worked as a hotel porter and, later, office janitor, and became a trustee of the local African Methodist Episcopal Church. Informally but never officially acknowledged as a Civil War veteran, Herring was honored on his 1933 death by Gloversville's Ansel Denison Post of the Grand Army of the Republic.[12]

Like Herring, the majority of southern blacks employed in the service of white Union regiments had no legal standing as soldiers. One group, however, did: men recorded as "colored cook" or "colored under-cook" on regimental muster rolls, which they did on the rosters of nearly 13 percent of New York State's infantry regiments at the close of the war. These men were, almost without exception, recruited locally when regiments were quartered in the South.[13] Unlike Herring, they and their widows were entitled to soldiers' benefits, including pensions, after the war.

At least three of the seven black men recruited in the South to cook for the Ninety-Sixth New York Infantry relocated after the war to the proximate region from which most members of the regiment originated: Clinton, Essex, Washington, and Warren counties. William Satchel and Thomas Elliott joined the unit at Fort Gray, North Carolina, and Joshua Aldridge at Coinjock when the Ninety-Sixth was stationed near Plymouth in the eastern part of that state in January 1864. Satchel and Elliott were assigned to Company K, Aldridge to Company I. All three were mustered out with their companies at City Point, Virginia, in February 1866. Aldridge became a laborer in Vergennes, Vermont, by 1870 and died there in 1907. Satchel and Elliott landed in the Adirondacks.

Satchel, from "Little" Washington, North Carolina, had been a slave before his enlistment. It is likely that Elliott and Aldridge shared his background. As Satchel explained in an 1890 Civil War pension application, he was unable to provide a formal birth document with his application owing to the circumstance:

> That I was born in Beaufort County, in the State of North Carolina, on the 2d day of January, A.D. 1837, of slave parents, who were then the property of Solomon Satchel; that I remained a slave for Solomon Satchel until I was twenty-four years of age; that I then escaped to the Northern Army, but was not enlisted regularly until 1864; that since the War, I have lived in the North and have not returned to the place of my birth, and that I am unable to furnish any of the evidence of my birth except this, my own statement, for the reason that I do not know anyone else who would know of my birth.[14]

Satchel travelled north with his company to its discharge point at Hart's Island, New York, and then settled in Burlington, Vermont. By 1872 he was living in Elizabethtown, Essex County, where he was joined in 1878 by Sophronia Davis, daughter of Burlington barber William Davis, whom he married in Burlington that year and with whom he had three sons. He followed his father-in-law's profession as a barber, an occupation known for producing "the most successful African American businessmen in the nineteenth century."[15] Working at first out of a basement room in Elizabethtown's Market Building, he later took over a tiny building next to the town's Methodist Church.[16] As an embedded 1889 advertisement in the town newspaper read: "If you want a clean shave or your hair cut in the latest style, call on Wm. Satchell [*sic*]."[17] Running on Elizabethtown's single (Republican) ticket, Satchel was elected in 1886 as the town's Sealer of Weights and Measures,[18] a minor position that entailed the testing of instruments used by the town's merchants for weighing and measuring.

Satchel subsequently spent a brief period in Keene Valley before relocating his family to St. Albans, Vermont, in 1890.[19] He was unable to repeat the success he had realized as an Elizabethtown barber. Recorded in the 1910 census as a gardener, he was thereafter listed as a laborer in St. Albans directories until his death at the age of eighty-one in 1918.

Thomas Elliott, the second of the southern black cooks to have signed on with the Ninety-Sixth and relocate to the Adirondacks, appeared in 1870 census records as a farm laborer in the North Elba, Essex County, colony of Gerrit Smith grantees. By 1875 he was a "bloomer" in Jay; in 1880 he was recorded in the Elizabethtown census as a bloomer and in the North Hudson census as an "iron maker in forge." Elliott was documented in the 1870, 1875, and 1880 censuses as a single man before disappearing from Adirondack accounts.

On the premise that lawful governments did not exist in the South after the war, anti-slavery or "Radical" Republicans in Congress united in March 1867 to pass—over President Johnson's veto—what became known as the Reconstruction Act, by which the ten former Confederate states were temporarily reorganized into five military districts until new governments could be created. Among the responsibilities of military commanders was the appointment of politically acceptable government officials to replace local office holders.[20] One such appointee was twenty-nine-year-old George Chahoon, who became the mayor of Richmond, Virginia—the former capital of the Confederacy—in May 1868. Born in Sherburne, New York, but raised in Virginia, Chahoon sat out the war as a Treasury Department clerk in the District of Columbia. Recently married to Mary Rogers, a daughter of James Rogers of the J and J Rogers Iron Company in Au Sable Forks (on the border of Essex and Clinton counties), he stirred controversy in Richmond by purging its government of former Confederates and creating a special black police force. The local white community attempted to oust Chahoon when military government ended in 1870 by designating a new mayor before formal elections were held, but Chahoon refused to step down, citing dubious job appointments by the new mayoral assignee. He won the popular vote in the legitimate election but was defeated in a second round of voting held after a critical ballot box from the earlier count was found to have been stolen. Republican (and integrationist) rule in Richmond ended with his departure from office, and Chahoon was arrested by local officials, tried, and convicted on forgery charges ("Ku-Kluxism in high life" and "scienced political rascality," as the episode was referred to by a Plattsburgh newspaper in 1871).[21] Chahoon was pardoned by the state governor after serving six months of a two-year prison sentence on the condition that he leave the state. He did so, relocating to his wife's hometown of Au Sable Forks and taking on leadership roles in the Rogers enterprise and as a representative in the state senate.[22] Travelling with or following Chahoon from Richmond was a black man, James (or John) Mosby.

By 1880, thirty-year-old Mosby was a coachman living in the household of Henry D. Graves, husband of Mary Rogers Chahoon's sister and, like George Chahoon, engaged at the upper level of the Rogers family businesses. Mosby appeared in several local photographs during the following decade: in his coachman's top hat on the driver's seat of a carriage in front of the Graves family residence; in a fireman's uniform holding the reins of a pair of horses drawing the hose wheel maintained by Graves Hose Company No. 1 of the Au Sable Forks volunteer fire department. Henry Graves "retired" from the Rogers Company in 1890 after it was discovered that he had embezzled funds from the firm to build an ostentatious home.[23] He did not thereafter employ a live-in coachman. An intriguing portrait photograph of Mosby in the Au Sable Forks historian's collection suggests that the onetime coachman returned to Richmond after his ten- or fifteen-year tenure in the Adirondacks.[24]

George Jackson followed a somewhat later trajectory to the North Country. Born in Maryland around 1855, he was employed by 1880 in Washington, DC, as a servant at the exclusive Arlington Hotel, located one block from the White House and popular with great capitalists of the day as well as members of Congress. Jackson's wife, Martha Curtis, was the granddaughter of Virginia slaveholder Charles Curtis, who manumitted his mixed-race offspring in 1828.[25] She married Jackson in 1875 and bore him three children in Washington between 1876 and 1882; another child would be born in upstate New York.

Union general John Hammond, member of a prominent Crown Point family, was responsible for Jackson's move to the Adirondacks. The organizer of Company H of the Fifth New York Cavalry during the early days of the Civil War, he later became president of the Crown Point Iron Company and served as a United States Representative from 1879 to 1883. Hammond presumably met Jackson at the Arlington Hotel while boarding there during a congressional session, for Jackson relocated his family to Crown Point in the mid-1880s and became Hammond's coachman. He worked for Hammond's wife for ten years after her husband's 1889 death and then resettled his family in the adjoining village of Port Henry.[26] There he entered the employ of George D. Sherman, a principal stockholder in Witherbee, Sherman and Company, the Port Henry mining operation of which his father had been a founder.

The fertile flatlands of the Champlain Valley, home of Crown Point and Port Henry, were known as a center for horse breeding. During the industry's heyday between 1870 and 1895 the region was famous for its production of "trotters," horses trained to race at a trot while pulling two-wheeled carts or "sulkies." The sport was popular at Saratoga Springs to the south and also had a huge local following; nine tracks were located during those decades in the Essex County town of Ticonderoga.[27] Sherman was a horse aficionado and owned large stock farms both in Port Henry and in Messina Springs, outside of Syracuse. Jackson worked for Sherman at both locations until Sherman's death in 1921. His occupation between 1905 and 1920 was listed in census records as coachman, "horsler" (stableman), and horse trainer. Sherman left $4,200 (more than $56,000 in 2016 dollars) to Jackson in his will, and $1,200 to Jackson's eldest son, Walter, another employee.[28]

The Jacksons and their three surviving children were identified in census records over the years as "negro," "black," "mulatto," and "white." Their daughter and two sons stayed on in Port Henry, marrying white spouses and adopting white identities. Walter worked as a laborer, a "caretaker, house and garden," and a "rock watch man" with a "steam railroad." His brother, Edward, became a bookkeeper and eventually the manager of a Port Henry hotel.[29]

Lloyd Brown, another African American skilled with horses, relocated to the Adirondacks at about the same time Jackson settled in Crown Point. Born in 1840 in Howard County, Virginia, he was possibly sold as a slave to Louisiana, where he served during the Civil War as a private, later sergeant, with the Seventy-Sixth United States Colored Infantry: a successor to the Corps d'Afrique formed by black volunteers from the region prior to the establishment of the United States Colored Troops. Directly after the war he relocated to Newburgh, Orange County. According to his Civil War pension records, Brown spent "most of the time since 1874" in Schroon Lake, Essex County,[30] where he appeared in the 1880 census as a widower and one of four live-in servants in the household of New Yorker Bayard Clarke Jr., part owner of Isola Bella, an elegant summer home built by his father on a private island in the middle of Schroon Lake. Brown was again in Schroon Lake in 1892, where he was listed in the state census as a fifty-two-year-old "trainer." Enumerated with him were his second wife, Annie Schencks, whom he married in Newburgh in 1881, and three children between the ages of eight and eleven. Brown died in 1911 and is buried with his wife in Schroon Lake's Protestant Cemetery. His wife, Annie, became a Schroon Lake personage in her own right, running a boardinghouse for a black clientele on Main Street in the home she purchased in 1904.

Brown's connection with horses manifested itself in a surprising manner in the following generation. His son, George, raised in Schroon Lake, was employed by the City of New York for some twenty-five years before retiring in 1935 to his widowed mother's Schroon Lake home.[31] Not long thereafter he began rehabilitating an abandoned racetrack just north of the village once belonging to William Pickhardt, a New York City–based multimillionaire and onetime owner of Schroon Lake's Wilbrook Stud Farm—breeder of many fast trotters in the 1870s and 1880s.[32] Renamed Maypine Lawns under his enthusiastic leadership, the track restoration project was "a dream come true" for Brown, known as the "progressive president of the Summer Sports Club." He cleared the underbrush from the old track and drove a sulky behind his own horse, Just Dillon, at the venue's first Sunday harness race in 1936.[33] Brown was remembered by late Schroon Lake resident Marjorie Ochs Powers as a "very tall and good-looking" man and a regular among the men who gathered around the winter stove at her father's general feed and produce store. He once drove her around the restored track when she was a young girl.[34] Brown died in Schroon Lake in 1950.

Reconstruction greatly improved the lives of African Americans in compelling former Confederate states to ratify the Fourteenth Amendment in 1868, which gave blacks full rights of citizenship, and forcing them to adopt new constitutions embodying the principle of male suffrage without regard to race. The still Republican-controlled Congress was able to pass a civil rights bill in 1875 that insured access, regardless of race, to public accommodations and facilities. But the situation changed as postwar military governments gave way to local rule, a process completed by 1877. Southern whites, left again to their own devices, were deeply resentful of African Americans' brief era of influence and authority. They dismantled the postwar freedoms granted to former slaves and moved once more toward segregationist extremes—enacting poll taxes and requiring literacy tests for voters that they knew blacks could not pass. Many Reconstruction statutes were declared unconstitutional in the 1880s, among them the 1875 Civil Rights Act. By the early 1890s, Jim Crow laws, named after a nineteenth-century minstrel figure and shorthand for legislation designed to isolate and humiliate black people, were in place throughout the South. The North, where so many had rejoiced at the anti-slavery triumph of 1865, experienced a parallel backlash. Idealism faded as Civil War memories dimmed and, tired of the "Negro cause," a growing number of residents moved in step with their southern neighbors to express antipathy to black advancement. Race-based proscriptions began to find their way, albeit to a far lesser degree than in the South, into northern custom.[35]

The final nail in the coffin of racial progress was the US Supreme Court's notorious 1896 *Plessy v. Ferguson* decision determining that "separate" facilities for blacks and whites were constitutional as long as they were "equal." The case arose from an orchestrated event in which a mixed-race man, Homer Plessy, refused to move from a "whites only" railway car in Louisiana, thereby breaking a state law. In a seven-to-one decision, the court ruled that the law did not violate Plessy's constitutional rights. The judgement caused little stir at the time (the *New York Times* mentioning it only briefly in an inside article on railway news).[36] But the "separate but equal" doctrine was never "equal" in practice, and racial interdictions intensified as the principle was quickly extended to other areas of southern public life, from restrooms to overnight accommodations to public schools. As before, northern sentiment made a corresponding move toward racial exclusion. The period from roughly 1890 to 1940, sometimes referred to as "the Nadir of race relations," was one of profound despair throughout the country for the black race as its members discovered the national vision of "freedom and justice for all" to be far from what they had anticipated after the Civil War.[37]

Despite diminished opportunities, the North continued to offer a better life to African Americans than the South, and the trickle of black migrants became a steady stream. Some 194,000 left southern coastal and border states between 1900 and 1910, a prelude to the greater migration that would commence with World War I.[38] Most transplants landed in northeastern cities, but a few—thanks to family and personal connections or specific employment opportunities—relocated to the Adirondacks.

5

Making a Living

THE PREVIOUS CHAPTERS have introduced several occupations by which black residents supported themselves in the Adirondack interior during the nineteenth century. This chapter takes up the matter of livelihoods in greater detail. At the same time, it points up the subtle but persistent manifestations of racial bias in the economic sphere that penetrated the isolated Adirondacks as African Americans were, almost without exception, confined to the modest occupational niches to which they were assigned elsewhere in the North.

During the second half of the nineteenth century, the influx of European immigrants escaping intractable problems at home had the effect of diminishing the already-limited economic opportunities for blacks in upstate New York. Willing to compete with African Americans for low-paying jobs (and often doing what they could to denigrate the black competition), the newcomers systematically displaced blacks from occupations in which they had once held sway.[1] Among the hardest hit job categories were barbering and coach-driving, with the percentage of black barbers in the Hudson River city of Poughkeepsie, for example, dropping from 27 percent to 13 percent between 1850 and 1880, and of black coachmen and drivers from 43 to 18 percent. Other callings in which black participation decreased included dressmaking, catering, tailoring, whitewashing, and laundering.[2] Black waiters, in vogue in elegant settings and ascendant in high-end Adirondack resorts in the early decades of the second half of the nineteenth century, were to suffer the same fate. Their distinctive history will be taken up in chapter 7.

Three enterprises dominated the year-round Adirondack economy in midcentury: agriculture, mining, and lumbering. None of these were conventional means by which blacks earned their livings in the North, as African Americans were concentrated in cities: home to seven-eighths of the northern black population before World War I.[3] According to census records, only twenty-four black farmers were documented as living in New York State in 1850,[4] but, as we have seen, Gerrit Smith's gift of land to black men led to the settlement of a number of black agriculturalists in the Adirondacks.

There had been at least one black farmer resident in the region in the late eighteenth century, Prince Taylor, whose undertaking future president James Madison documented in the rough journal he kept during a tour made with Thomas Jefferson through northern New York and Vermont in 1791. Describing the pair's June visit to Lake George, where they stopped for a night in Ticonderoga, Essex County, Madison wrote, "On the East Side [of Lake George] not a House is seen except one at the North end owned & inhabited by a free Negro. He possesses a good farm of about 250 Acres which he cultivates with 6 white hirelings for which he is said to have paid about 2½ Dollrs. per Acre and by his industry & good management turns to good account. He is intelligent; reads writes & understands accounts, and is dexterous in his affairs. . . . He has no wife, and is said to be disinclined to marriage: nor any woman on his farm."[5]

The sight of a black man overseeing white employees no doubt surprised Virginian slaveholders Madison and Jefferson. Taylor was a colorful character, mentioned in several accounts of early life in Ticonderoga. Born in 1755 in Lunenburg, Massachusetts, he served in the Revolutionary War, winning his freedom in doing so if he had been enslaved before entering military service. The circumstances of his arrival in Ticonderoga are unknown, but he abandoned farming by 1811 and opened an inn on the shore of Lake George, receiving a tavern license from Essex County the following year (the first such license in Ticonderoga). A skilled tailor, cooper, surveyor, and, reputedly, tap dancer, he was remembered in 1858 "as a man of wit, of good parts, and withal of sincere piety, and few were the weddings, or parties or festivals in town in which his art as cook, waiter, and chief director of the eatables, was not brought into contribution." Taylor died in 1828 at the age of seventy-three.[6]

Madison recorded no details of his farming operation, but Taylor, like most Adirondack farmers, had a great deal to overcome in coping with the region's hilly geography and harsh climate. The most conducive topography and weather for agriculture were found at the outer edges of the region: toward the St. Lawrence River in the northwest, Lake Champlain in the east (not far from Taylor's farm), and the Mohawk River in the south. Farms there also had better access to markets than did those of the interior, access that became increasingly important with the move from subsistence to competitive production for outside markets.[7]

Mixed planting was the prevalent agricultural pattern in the Adirondacks in the mid-nineteenth century. Tending a farm was often combined with other pursuits, among them logging, charcoal making, hemlock barking for tannery use, wage work in hotels, guiding, and taking in boarders.[8] New York closely tracked farming practice in mid-decade censuses, tallying the production of individual farmers. Statistics from the 1865 and 1875 censuses for four black farmers highlight variations on the kind of patchwork agriculture practiced by most smallholders in the region until around 1900. These were not peculiarly "black" approaches to farming but were attuned to the realities of Adirondack conditions.

Lyman Epps, the settler who remained for life in North Elba after taking up a Gerrit Smith land grant in 1849, farmed 123 acres estimated to be worth $700 in 1875. He, his wife, and four mostly grown children lived in a house of wood valued at $100. Stock was valued that year at $650 and included six milch (milking) cows, three heifer calves, three horses, three colts, and two pigs—preferred as meat and a staple of the farm diet.[9] Epps's small dairy operation, which produced 700 pounds of butter in 1874, required broad and fertile fields.[10] Thus some 50 of Epps's acres were given over to animal feed: 20 to pasture for grazing, 20 to meadow for hay (an important local crop as it commanded high prices),[11] and 10 to oats. Buckwheat was cultivated on 3 acres, and potatoes for starch and direct consumption on 2 acres. Epps also produced 400 pounds of maple sugar on his 60 acres of wood and timberland. This would have entailed tapping roughly 100 sugar maples, found in high density in Adirondack hardwood forests.[12]

John Thomas, the Vermontville, Franklin County, settler who in 1872 wrote to Gerrit Smith thanking him for his generosity in giving free land to blacks, was sixty-five years old at the time of the 1875 census and reported lesser agricultural activity than that detailed in his letter to Smith three years earlier. His "hansome farm" of 200 acres had shrunk to 60 acres and was estimated to be worth $700; his log cabin was valued at $50. Twenty-five acres were planted in oats in 1874, yielding 300 bushels; 2 in wheat; 5 in pasture; and 12 in meadow. Gross sales came to $150. Thomas possessed one horse and 9 apple trees.

All 7 acres of Peter Millett's farm in Caroga, Fulton County, were in pasture. The 1865 census valued his holding at $284 with improvements, and recorded the presence of one calf in 1864 and one ox in 1865. A pig slaughtered in 1864 produced 250 pounds of pork, and poultry worth $10 laid eggs valued at $5.50. Three apple trees produced 10 barrels of apples. It is likely that Millett supplemented his farm income as a farm laborer elsewhere.

Benjamin Van Buren gave his name to Van Buren Bay on the northwestern shore of Lake George. A "mulatto" born around 1800 in Rensselaer County, he began farming in Hague, Warren County, around 1847 on 161 acres of land that he either rented or simply occupied. (The family did not legally own the property until 1875, when it was bought by Van Buren's daughter.)[13] Only 6 acres were improved in 1865, on which Van Buren planted a little corn, a little rye, and a few potatoes. Four acres were given over to meadow, and 25 apple trees produced 100 bushels of apples, suggesting that apples were a market crop rather than grown simply for home consumption. Van Buren's other specialty was sheep. His 19 mature animals produced 78 pounds of wool in 1864. This farm product had risen in regional popularity in the two decades prior to the 1840s, declined as a result of local and western competition, and resurged temporarily in response to Civil

War demand for woolen uniforms and blankets; the number of sheep and amount of wool produced in the Adirondacks essentially doubled between 1855 and 1865. Sheep farming resumed its steady decline throughout New York after the war.[14] Van Buren died in 1877 and his farm was sold out of the family in 1885. Sons Hiland and Martin stayed on in Hague as farmers and farm laborers through at least 1915 before the family disappeared from local records.[15]

The Adirondack trend at the turn of the twentieth century was away from agriculture, the region accounting for a quarter of the acreage taken out of production in all of New York between 1885 and 1925.[16] Remote from markets and overendowed with hilly terrain unsuited to mechanization, farmland reverted to forest as farmers and their descendants migrated to more urbanized population centers or westward in search of more fertile land. Black farmers were part of the movement, and few were to be found in the Adirondack region by the early years of the twentieth century.

Despite their disappearance as landed farmers, African Americans were identified by race as potential Adirondack agricultural laborers in a curious manner in 1917. Shortly after the United States entered World War I the New York State Food Supply Commission appointed an Essex County representative to survey local agricultural resources with the goal of increasing food production and conservation. The agent exposed the pervasiveness of racial bias in inserting the following notice in local newspapers:

> **Labor May Be Found**
>
> Persons desiring labor should write their wants to Food Supply Representative, Essex, N. Y., stating
>
> 1. When labor is needed.
> 2. Maximum price they will pay.
> 3. If transportation will be paid.
> 4. If colored experienced help can be used.
> 5. If colored experienced college boys can be used.
> 6. If untrained help can be used.[17]

3. Benjamin Van Buren. Tintype, circa 1870. Courtesy of Hague Historical Society.

It was not, however, until the 1950s that seasonal black farm laborers were systematically introduced in small numbers into the region. There were by 1951 an estimated 25,000 blacks, a majority of them from Florida, among the 110,000 seasonal employees engaged in harvesting and processing New York's fruit and vegetable crops.[18] Arriving during the Sunshine State's slack summer agricultural season, they fanned out across New York, but not into the Adirondacks, where apples grown in a narrow band bordering Lake Champlain were the only crop that required intensive hand-harvesting. Local sources and nearby Canada supplied the manpower necessary for the annual two- or two-and-a-half-week apple harvest for many years, but in 1955 the New York State Department of Labor announced that "one county, Essex, used a southern [i.e., mostly black] migrant crew this year to pick an apple crop for the first time and reported a satisfactory experience." Twenty-five workers made up this workforce.[19] Twenty-one southern migrant apple-pickers were tallied in 1956 in Clinton County, and twenty-five in 1957. As the state Department of Labor's annual report noted in 1958: "A nucleus of Southern migrants has been growing here slowly; look for greater expansion from this source, if available."[20] There was some increase in ensuing years, but migrant farming would remain a small-scale operation in the Adirondacks.

More than two hundred iron mines and forges operated in the Adirondacks during the 1800s, propelling a regional industry that produced nearly one-quarter of the iron ore in the United States before peaking at the end of the century.[21] African Americans had long been employed throughout the country in the heavy work demanded in the forges that processed iron, and two black men achieved regional status thanks to their specialized skills in this aspect of iron production. Joseph James, father of the three Civil War soldiers whose military service was documented in the previous chapter, was a "bloomer" by 1850 at an iron forge in Wadhams, a bustling industrial hamlet of Westport. His job—maintaining a charcoal-burning fire in which he fashioned lumps of semimolten, malleable iron into "blooms"—was critical at the early stage of the iron-making process. Bloomers were at least semiskilled workers and near the top of the pay scale in the forge hierarchy. James died in 1887. He and his wife are buried in Riverside Cemetery in Wadhams.

When a bloom reached the proper consistency, the bloomer handed it over to a "hammerman," who beat it repeatedly to expel impurities and shaped it into marketable iron bars. Thomas Thompson was a hammerman in the early 1870s for the J and J Rogers Iron Company in Au Sable Forks. Born a slave in North Carolina, he reportedly escaped into a Union army regiment, enlisting as a cook and later following the regiment north, although no war records corroborate this story. Thompson became a respected citizen of the nearby town of Jay and was profiled by H. P. Smith in his 1885 *History of Essex County* as a man who "has by industry and frugal habits acquired some property and a good education. He is a member and class leader of the First M[ethodist] E[piscopal] Church of Jay."[22]

Martin Tankard, like James and Thompson, made his living in connection with concentrated fire. According to a deposition filed in Plattsburgh in 1821, Tankard was a freeborn "Black or Mulatto Person" about twenty-two years old whose family the witness had known in Vermont.[23] Ten years later, Tankard was "melt master" at the new Redford Crown Glass Works in the Saranac, Clinton County, hamlet of Redford—a position he held until the works closed in 1851. The company made window glass by a process of blowing a red-hot mix of sand and other ingredients into a large, hollow globe that was later flattened and cut to size. The melting furnace was the backbone of the operation, and it was Tankard's responsibility to maintain its high heat during a "melt" and to determine when the molten glass was ready for working. A witness to the Redford operation referred indirectly to Tankard twenty-five years after the closure of the glassworks in describing an early stage of the manufacturing process, in which "a mighty magician," the glassblower, "approaches the heated furnace with a long hollow rod. . . . A dark man is also hovering about with whom the magician consults and presently he dips the end of the rod into a huge pot of what appears to be liquid fire." The furnaces burned day and night, and a melt could last up to sixteen hours. As a later reporter noted, "there were no Sabbaths in glass making."[24]

Tankard's labor appears to have been adequately recompensed. In 1838 he bought the first of several lots of Redford land he would own from Matthew Lane, a partner in the glassworks from 1836 and its sole proprietor after a three-year plant closure that began in 1843. (Like all of Lane's deeds at this time, Tankard's contained a clause forbidding the sale of "ardent spirits" on premises.)[25] When the Redford works closed for good, Tankard relocated to the Berkshire Glass Company in Lanesborough, Massachusetts, where he was recorded as a "glass factory laborer" in the 1860 census. He returned the following year to Redford, leaving behind his son Henry, who had followed his father into the Lanesborough glassworks, and Henry's family. Tankard and his wife, Elizabeth, spent the rest of their lives in Redford, where he supported them both with a little farming, a little lumbering, and occasional gravedigging. The couple is buried in the town's Protestant Cemetery. So, too, are five of their children who died between 1835 and 1851.

Both Tankards left behind wills—proof of their engagement in the Redford community and its rituals as well as of their material success. The documents are intriguing in their provision of details for the disposition of possessions of small property-holders. Elizabeth left all of her "wearing apparel of every kind so ever made or unmade and my rings" to a granddaughter. George Tankard bequeathed his "real and personal estate of every name and kind so-ever," to his only daughter, Maria Williams, with the exception of a town lot and over forty-five acres of farmland that he divided unequally among four sons. Son John received more than twenty-one acres of land as well as Tankard's "gray horse Known as the Sharlow Colt and lumber wagon and one pare [*sic*] of one horse lumber sleds." Henry, the son who had transferred with him to Massachusetts, received twenty acres, "on condition he comes and lives on it."[26] Son George, a laborer, appears to have settled for a time on the two acres he received from his father. His white wife, "heard to say that she would fix him the first chance she got," shot him in the back in their Redford home in 1896 but did not kill him.[27]

Forest-related industries employed few black workers. Very rarely, an African American resident of the Adirondacks was denominated a lumberman in census documents, but few black faces were captured in the hundreds of photographs of some of the several thousand men whose occupations took them into the region's forests.

By far the greatest number of African Americans resident in the Adirondacks were employed in domestic service. Black men tended campfires and the food needs of early white sportsmen. They worked as cooks on household, hotel, and, later, children's camp staffs; as coachmen (subsequently chauffeurs); and occasionally as butlers and

4. Cedar River/Upper Hudson loggers, early twentieth century. Courtesy of Indian Lake Museum, Wayne Blanchard, Town Historian.

valets—often to part-time residents who spent only the summer season in the Adirondacks. Black women were almost exclusively employed in private homes as housekeepers, cooks, maids, and nursemaids. Such service workers might be part of otherwise white (usually Irish) staffs, and resided in the households in which they worked. Often they were the only black people in the villages or towns in which they lived.

Grace Noyes, a domestic worker in Warrensburg, Warren County, left behind two diaries documenting her life in the Adirondacks. Born in Connecticut in 1825, she first appeared in Warrensburg records in 1840 as one of six people presenting themselves for membership in the town's Presbyterian church. By 1850 she was living in the home of Pelatiah Richards, a white resident with income from a variety of enterprises including farming and insurance. When he died in 1870, Richards left a bequest to Noyes that provided her with a small independent income for the rest of her life: the quarterly interest on a United States bond valued at one thousand dollars (later exchanged for an interest-bearing mortgage in the same amount).[28] Noyes, who never married, was by then a cook in the Main Street home of Richards's widowed daughter, Minerva King, and the four youngest of her six children. She spent the rest of her life with Mrs. King, who

5. Grace Noyes. Photograph by Frank M. Taft, Glens Falls, circa 1880. Courtesy of Richards Library, Warrensburg.

occasionally took in student boarders attending a local teachers' training institute and oversaw a thirty-six-acre farm.

Noyes's journals cover the years 1878 and 1879. Entries are succinct, their length dictated by the format of the palm-sized pocket diaries she used—each with space for two days' entries per page and originally created to meet the record-keeping needs of businessmen. Surprisingly, perhaps, she never mentioned race in her journals, suggesting either that racism held little sway in Warrensburg at that period, or that she found the subject irrelevant in her personal life. She recorded day-to-day events in a household dominated by women: Mrs. King and her (generally) three female servants. She reported on weather conditions, the doings of the King family and family friends, church attendance, sicknesses, deaths, funerals, and "sociables." She focused in particular on her own chores and the chores of others, among them an Irish coworker, Biddie, with whom she often clashed, and the white hired man, Jim. She had little regard for punctuation. As entries from her 1878 diary read:

> *January 24*: We just heard of the death of Mrs. Farlin thawing Jim sawing wood
>
> *March 25*: Biddie Washing & about as mean as Cain Jim sawing wood
>
> *May 7*: Real plesent & warm Jim drawing out manure I baking and went out to ride in PM with Mrs King & had a lovely ride

Now and again, Noyes alluded to national, even international, events:

> *February 7*: Pope of Rome died today
>
> *April 12*: Tweed died today at noon Boss I mean[29]

Like many domestic retainers, Noyes identified with and was dependent on the family she served. The pronouns "we" and "us" appeared frequently in her writing. Her bond with the Kings was expressed in a will executed shortly before her 1881 death in which she left to "my friend, Mrs. Minerva King . . . all of my wearing apparel, bed, bedding & household furniture books pictures both usefull and ornamental." After a bequest of fifty dollars to a sister living in Connecticut, the residue of her small estate was divided among her "friends," the four youngest King sons, "share and share alike."[30]

A few African Americans who filled service roles, often on a seasonal basis, made lasting impressions on their employers, coworkers, or others who recalled them years after the chronicled events took place. Chef Tim Collins was remembered as accompanying members in the early 1900s from Springfield, Massachusetts, to the Grasse River Outing Club, located just beyond the western edge of the Adirondack Park and reached by wagon from the train station at Childwold, St. Lawrence County. Collins "lived in a one-room log cabin located about 20 feet from the kitchen. He slept with a meat axe handy in case of an attack by a bear, which he always expected to encounter but never did." He claimed to be a great swimmer and once challenged himself to swim in the frigid water of the river. He "took one dive, swam to the other side and summoned a boat for his return trip. He had had enough."[31]

More than one member of the extended family of Calvin Durand, a prosperous Chicago grocery owner who established a private camp in 1907 at the northern, water-access-only end of Hamilton County's Long Lake, wrote about the family's black help. "Henry" appeared in a 1909 diary "as cook and man of general work and especially for such tasks as the boys chose to omit." Eli Williams, born in 1892 in Virginia and a Baltimore resident, became a regular in the extended camp household by 1913. He "cooked, split wood, milked the cow [rented in the town of Long Lake and brought up the lake by scow every summer], and helped with many other chores." "A very modest, quiet and unassuming man," he was remembered by family members as playing the fiddle in his lighted tent behind the camp "at night and Sunday afternoon on his time off—rather squawky way up in the woods" and an "eerie" and "weird lonely sound." Eli's sons, Foster and Smith Williams, born around 1917 and 1918, joined Durand Camp's summer staff when they were of an age to do so, carrying the Williams family tradition into the 1930s.[32]

Valets ranked high in the social pantheon of domestic workers. Perry Thomas took pride in his profession and his Adirondack connections, reporting to *New York Age* in 1921 that he, "valet to Judge Freeman," and his wife had "returned home after spending a delightful summer at Hague-on-Lake-George."[33] Arthur Brooks joined President Calvin Coolidge and his wife at White Pine Camp on Osgood Pond near Paul Smith's Hotel in Franklin County, where the presidential couple enjoyed an eleven-week summer vacation in 1926. Brooks had worked as the White House valet under Coolidge as well as his three presidential predecessors: Taft, Wilson, and Harding. Known for his intelligence, beautiful manners, and discretion, as well as his "nose for the newsy" and ability to tell a good story, Brooks was referred to by Coolidge as "one of the finest men in Washington."[34] Forced

6. Henry "gentling" a cow en route to Calvin Durand family's Long Lake camp, circa 1910. Courtesy of Calvin Durand Family Archives.

to retire in 1925 as the result of a heart condition, he was invited to the Adirondacks "not to work, but to obtain a rest and the beneficial effects of life in the mountain country." A heart attack forced him to return to Washington two weeks after his arrival, where he died in early September. The executive offices of the "Summer White House" were closed on the afternoon of his funeral out of respect for Brooks's memory.[35]

Chauffeurs had, perhaps, more free time and more money than other members of domestic staffs. "The Boys of Lake Placid" who hosted an August 1931 dance at the Pine Ridge Pavilion in Ray Brook, on the highway between Saranac Lake and Lake Placid, are likely to have held this job title.[36] Another black chauffeur-sponsored entertainment, the "Chauffeurs' First Special Dance" at the Ray Brook Inn in August 1938 featured African American bandleader Clem Banks, who fronted a number of Westchester County bands in the 1930s. The Westchester County town of Scarsdale had a Chauffeurs Club; one or more of its members was perhaps working in the Adirondacks, knew Banks, and hired him for the occasion.[37]

Time magazine published a tribute to longtime Adirondack boys' camp cook James Hankins in 1950. Hankins joined the kitchen staff of New York's Peekskill Military Academy as a teenager in 1900. When the school's headmaster, Dr. Charles Robinson, founded Camp Pok-O-Moonshine in Willsboro, Essex County, five years later, he went to work in its kitchen as well. Eventually becoming head chef at the academy, Hankins returned to Pok-O-Moonshine every summer for forty-five years, estimating in 1950 that he had turned out about nine million meals and "handed out plenty of man-to-man advice" in the course of his long career. "The impact of James was substantial," noted Stephen Elliott, a grandson of the camp founder-owner and a onetime camper. "We had Vespers every Sunday night, conducted by various staff members. James often took one of the services late in the season—he was quite religious, knew his Bible and lots of hymns, and gave good short sermons." His inventiveness with ice-cream flavors led to a reference in the Pok-O-Moonshine camp song, written in 1921, to "James's Ice Cream" that is still part of today's camp song at coeducational Camp Pok-O-MacCready, successor to the earlier camp.[38]

Hankins's partner for thirty-seven years in the Pok-O-Moonshine kitchen was another member of the Peekskill Military Academy kitchen staff: Robert Childress. "Uncle Rob," remembered Elliott, met him by arrangement on the train to Willsboro one summer "dressed in worn work clothes and carrying two overflowing shopping bags." Second-in-command of the camp kitchen and operator of the camp's ice cream churn, he "chopped down trees that no one else wanted to tackle, or moved things no one else could move. With one bad eye and a hip that gave him trouble, he wasn't the quickest person around camp—just the strongest and most competent."[39] Hankins and Childress, Elliott later observed, "I'm sure, changed the attitude towards 'Negroes' that most of the campers had in those days."[40]

James Coswell and Clarence Moore, chef and assistant chef at the Eagle Bay Hotel on Fourth Lake in Webb, Herkimer County, were credited with saving nearly two hundred lives on the summer night in 1945 when flames destroyed the hotel in little more than an hour. Racing through the smoke-filled building to awaken guests, they sustained the only injuries received in the fire. Moore was given a surprising thank-you gift for his brave exploit nearly sixty years later, when a New Jersey man, reading a news story about a housing-related misfortune that had befallen Moore, recognized the name of the man whose quick thinking had saved the lives of his wife and mother—guests at the hotel at the time—and sent a $7,000 check to a lawyer representing Moore to pay for repairs to his Florida home.[41]

A local woman who lived near Upper St. Regis Lake and served one summer in a nearby household as a kitchen maid retained affectionate memories of the only African American she is likely to have known, writing of her: "One of the sweetest, most considerate ladies I ever worked with was a black woman. She came one summer to care for the Toomey children, great niece and nephew of the Slades. . . . She was 'black as coal' with a heart as big as all outdoors. Actually this widow had educated all of her children in Boston and was beloved as a seamstress in that city."[42] The Toomeys' nanny was not the only black employee to experience warm contacts with local employers and/or coworkers, warmth that sometimes extended into the larger communities. There was honest affection, for example, expressed in the *Essex County Republican*'s 1930 farewell to Mrs. Romayne Spriggs, who had spent several summers in the area as a maid to Mrs. George Ladd and was heading "south to work among her own colored people as a teacher. She leaves many friends here who wish her success."[43]

No self-identifying black professionals (doctors, lawyers, educators), government employees, or storekeepers (although perhaps one or two store clerks) called the region home during the nineteenth or first half of the twentieth century. But one man and several women carved out occupational niches as proprietors of boardinghouses catering to African Americans. Three other individuals shaped roles for themselves as businessmen and a writer, which placed them firmly on a par with the region's otherwise white middle class. They and their careers will be discussed in chapters 10, 13, 18, and 19.

6

Railroad Building

AN INFLUX OF BLACK WORKERS into the Adirondacks took place during 1891–92 with the laying of track for the Adirondack and St. Lawrence Railroad, also known as the Mohawk and Malone. This line would run through the heart of the region, connecting Herkimer on the New York Central line with Malone, close to the Canadian border, and eventually with Montreal. A project of Dr. William Seward Webb, a son-in-law of William H. Vanderbilt, the railroad was a controversial undertaking. It elicited admiration for the speed with which it was built and for opening up the central and western Adirondacks, but at the same time provoked ire for its desecration of the Adirondack wilderness. The railroad bed, which covered 165.12 miles between Herkimer and Malone Junction, took eighteen months to build.

Webb was in a hurry, and he drove his numerous contractors. Crews made up of several thousand men started work in spring 1891 from both ends of the route toward the center. Labor, regionally and more widely sourced, included Canadians and St. Regis Indians as well as recent immigrants imported from New York City—many of them Italian. Several superintendents of companies with grading contracts for the line hailed from Tennessee, and they chose to bring in the kind of laborer they were most used to overseeing: African Americans from the South. An early shipment of two rail cars carrying thirty-two sturdy Tennessee mules and black teamsters to drive them attracted considerable attention when it arrived in northern Franklin County in June 1891.[1]

A seventy-mile stretch of road south and southwest of Tupper Lake, Franklin County, proved unexpectedly difficult to work. What could be accomplished elsewhere with modern machinery often had to be done here by hand, and it was necessary to cart in many supplies, including hay for horses, from Boonville and Lowville (Oneida and Lewis County stops on the Rome, Watertown and Ogdensburg Railroad) and carry them overland on men's backs to isolated camps miles away. The Enterprise Construction Company, which had the grading contract for this section, went bankrupt before its work was half finished, as did its subcontractors. Webb, according to a laudatory book about the railroad commissioned by his wife after her husband's death, paid them "enough to keep them going, whether they were entitled to it or not," and wiped out their debts to him when the job was completed.[2] Not surprisingly, these contractors worked their laborers with particular zeal.

To counter the insatiable demand for cheap manpower as overworked, transient crewmembers departed, agents for Enterprise and its subcontractors recruited additional black laborers from Alabama, North Carolina, and Tennessee. As one southern contractor expressed it, when asked by a Syracuse reporter to explain his preference for bringing in black laborers: "Well, you see you can't drive a white man like you can a negro."[3] Would-be southern black employees were offered golden inducements to sign on: pay of between $1.25 and $1.50 a day, comfortable lodgings, and a reasonable weekly board charge. They were not apprised, however, that their prepaid transportation to upstate New York would have to be reimbursed, that if they chose to leave the job their pay might be held back for more than a month, or that the actual board rate would be more than double that quoted and would eat up half their weekly pay. They were told that the job site was further south than it was (one draftee was informed that it was only twelve miles from New York City), and that its climate was little colder than that to which they were accustomed.[4] They came totally unprepared for the weather and conditions they encountered.

The New York State census of 1892, enumerated on February 16, provides a glimpse into project organization in its record of residents

7. "Two Phases of a Crime Which Disgraces the Very Name of Freedom." *Utica Globe*, April 2, 1892. Courtesy of Adirondack Museum.

at a railroad encampment adjoining the work site—one located along the western border of the town of Long Lake, Hamilton County. Some 350 people were documented in the camp, among them senior (white) personnel including four railroad contractors, two civil engineers, three bookkeepers, one timekeeper, two clerks, and one park superintendent and his assistant. Sixty-three African Americans were part of the Long Lake crew, as were large immigrant clusters from Ireland (fifty-seven workers), Canada (fifty-four), and Germany (twenty-one).[5] Three black men held skilled or semiskilled jobs at the site—as one of three blacksmiths and two of ten cooks. The others were laborers, as were the majority of camp residents. A thirty-three-year-old black women was recorded as a laundress, as was her fourteen-year-old daughter; three children with the same last name between the ages of three and seven were enumerated with them.[6]

Housing in the Long Lake camp is likely to have been inadequate for February conditions. Workers at other camps described winter living in tents surrounding large bonfires or in rough, unchinked log shanties with leaky tarpaper roofs and no bunks on which to sleep. Frostbite was a widespread problem. Typical meals at one camp were "one piece of filthy bread smeared with vile molasses" for breakfast and supper, and "a small piece of partially boiled and very fat salt pork" for midday dinner.[7]

News of labor abuse surfaced in early October 1891, when the *New York Times* reported that a contractor from Tennessee had shot and killed one of his black workers (also from Tennessee and at work since July) in a fit of pique near Woodgate, Oneida County, just outside park borders.[8] Nineteen Italians who had been at work on the southern section of the road walked off the job and into Lowville early in December, complaining of cruelty and intolerable working conditions, substandard accommodations, insufficient food, inadequate clothing, and no pay. What began as a trickle of deserters became a steady stream, and it was reported in mid-December that "much uneasiness prevails along Dr. Webb's railway."[9]

Newspapers across the country covered the unfolding story. Black deserters provided stark accounts of their travails to journalists after leaving the work camps and, generally penniless, working their way home through villages and towns across the state to Buffalo and on to Cleveland before heading south. Contractors spoke out bitterly against the adverse reporting, blaming northerners' unwarranted sympathy "toward the darkies" on their lack of experience with "Southern usages." They attributed sensational stories to muckrakers and blackmailers, and dismissed what they considered inflated accounts given by black interviewees, who "can easily impose on Northerners, and they know it, and practice the deception for all its worth."[10] Journal coverage in white-owned southern newspapers about incidents relating to black workers on the job tended to highlight what they considered northern hypocrisy when it came to race. According to the *Keowee Courier* of Walhalla, South Carolina:

"Deceived, fleeced, and persecuted, they are worse off than the Jews in Russia, notwithstanding the fact that they are surrounded by millions of people who profess to make the welfare of the negro race one of their most cherished objects."[11]

One black man heading home to Knoxville, Tennessee, in early March 1892 through Lyons, Wayne County (some fifty miles east of Rochester), recounted that he and the one hundred other workers with whom he had traveled north to work on the Enterprise section of the road had never been paid. He had not, he related, been allowed to leave his camp because he was in debt to the "commissary" or company store for warm clothing (a frequent complaint), but had finally escaped through waist-deep snow in the middle of the night. Another deserter passing through Lyons reported that he and seventy-one others from Birmingham, Alabama, labored on the railroad for thirty-eight days and received little or no pay. "The weather was so cold," he continued, "that four of our number froze to death, and we were not allowed to bury them, but they were thrown out of the picket line to be devoured by the animals. . . . There were bosses arranged all along the line of work, one to each 25 men, all armed with Winchester rifles. If one of us was sick we had to work just the same, and several that tried to escape were shot and their dead bodies were hung up to show us that escape was dangerous."[12] Men were buried where they died, if they were buried at all. One black laborer was reportedly placed under a railroad crossing in the hamlet of Big Moose in the town of Webb, Herkimer County. Another was laid to rest nearby under a bank in a coffin made of railroad ties under a crude wooden cross still visible in the 1930s.[13]

The mid-March arrival in Boonville of a trainload of black recruits from Tennessee captured public attention when a howling blizzard detained the workers in town for nearly a week. Stoves were installed in the empty house where they were lodged to provide some degree of warmth (although there was no soap or water), and the Women's Christian Temperance Union and other organizations conducted used-clothing drives to provide them with a basic level of appropriate attire. The visitors reportedly showed their appreciation with a Saturday evening entertainment before a packed crowd in the local opera house that featured "songs, dances, and plantation humor. Folks passed the hat and collected twenty dollars for their entertainers."[14]

A sympathetic local journalist, after reminding readers of the layers of clothing they donned in anticipation of winter travel, described the scene as the Tennesseans were hauled off by sleigh to campsites in the woods. "These poor fellows, used to a warm climate, but not to cold, with thin clothing and half-worn wrappings, started in a temperature nearly down to zero, with a sharp cold wind, in such a rig as this: Flooring over two runners, no back, no sides, no seats, not even straw on some of them. On this in a group, steadying each other, stood the black men. One sleigh was loaded with baled hay and on top of it rode a lot of men, legs and feet dangling in the cold, with such covering as rubber boots."[15]

When one group of black laborers saw the conditions in the camp to which they were taken, thirty or forty of them rebelled and the next day walked back to Boonville during a storm. They were arrested on a complaint from contractors "determined to make them work out what had been paid in transportation, board and clothing. The negroes claimed misrepresentation, overcharge and camps unfit to shelter them." Eventually the contractors' complaint was withdrawn and the men released, "the contractors agreeing to remit the charge for transportation against such as did return." About half accepted the offer.[16] Those who did not became the charges of poormasters in successive villages and towns who, after addressing their immediate needs, gave them tickets to the next rail stop on their route and eagerly saw them away before they triggered additional local expense. Lewis County reportedly admitted 164 men, black and white, from the railroad job to its poorhouse in March who stayed there from a day to a week. The poormaster's book at Remsen, Oneida County, listed "Africans" on its roster, and residents of Holland Patent, also in Oneida County, pooled their money to ease the journey of an African American with frozen feet who showed up in the village.[17]

Other charitable collections were taken up as blacks fled south, and the recipients did their best to give value for the money they received. The mayor of Erie, Pennsylvania, gave a group returning on foot to Tennessee permission to tour residential streets in the company of a local black pastor outside the business district, where they made music and the pastor, Rev. Pride, told their story. It was, reported the African American *Cleveland Gazette*, "the most pitiable sight ever seen in Erie. Old, gray-haired men, young men, middle-aged men, and boys, sad-faced, tired, disheartened. People went to the windows and doors and money and sympathy were freely given. Passes over the road to Cincinnati, food and God-speed, were given them and they went on their way."[18]

Contractors continued to reckon the costs of their fleeing work force. The flight of ninety-three men and five women (hired to work in camp kitchens) from Columbia, Tennessee, who turned back from Utica before reporting to work in late March 1892 meant a loss, it was calculated, of more than $1,500 in transportation expenses.[19]

Recurring tales of mistreatment in camps associated with the Enterprise Construction Company led concerned citizens to call for an investigation by the New York State Board of Mediation and Arbitration. The board's three commissioners, appointed by the governor, were mandated to attempt settlement of grievances and disputes between employers and employees, and on March 28 Commissioner Florence F. Donovan took testimony from fleeing workers in Boonville and Lowville in preparation for making an investigatory tour of camps along the line. According to one of the black witnesses called, the Enterprise representative in charge of the project, a man from Knoxville by the name of Kenefick, had a reputation in the South for not paying his employees, and "very few men in eastern Tennessee would go to work for Kenefick if they knew it."[20] Kenefick, for his part, maintained that jobsite problems could be laid at the feet of the "15 to 20 per cent of every 100 men hired who were tramps and thieves" of the worst character and "not afraid to commit any deed."[21] He claimed to be entirely ignorant of New York State labor laws and took no responsibility for what agents had promised the one to two thousand men under contract to Enterprise, or for the extortionate prices charged for commissary goods, which he asserted were set independently by the commissary clerk. Kenefick admitted to insisting that hirees be held on the job against their wishes until they could "work out" their transportation debts, and allowed that men were sent on horseback to capture runaways.[22] One white worker testified that a mounted boss had "put a rope around a negro's body and chased him back to camp." There was, a resident engineer explained philosophically, always trouble between contractors and employees on public works jobs. He had known many greater misunderstandings.[23]

Commissioner Donovan and an entourage, including journalists, left for a two-day fact-finding tour on March 29. They traveled in the wake of Dr. Webb, who had felt it necessary to respond to criticism by visiting camps himself a few days earlier. Webb and his colleagues pronounced themselves "more than ever satisfied" with conditions as they found them. The laborers were described as "well and hearty, and were frequently heard laughing and singing at their work, and among them some of the southern workers were ready to dance for a dime."[24] One journalist noted quietly that Webb's optimistic findings might, despite the supposed "surprise" nature of his visit, have come about because "telegraph and telephone lines extended even into the woods, and a man cannot travel in a special car, even on special business, without some one sending heralds of his coming."[25]

Donovan's visit was similarly broadcast before he entered the wilderness. He and his party were warmly welcomed by railroad spokesmen who impressed them with new, tightly chinked log shacks in which brisk wood fires burned, and provided them with a dinner so good that "it excited wonder that it could be prepared so many miles from civilization." Only the occasional disconcerting incident marred the party's comfortable passage through the camps, as when "a negro attempted to commit suicide in a cabin and within thirty feet of the investigating party. He did not succeed in his undertaking, as his skull was too thick and would not let the 23-calibre bullet go into his brain." One white laborer, a brother of a contractor on the job, testified that, "except for clubbing," men were well treated.[26] Donovan's entourage spent the second night of its trip in a hunting lodge at Little Rapids, Hamilton County, owned by Dr. Webb.[27]

The Board of Mediation and Arbitration's report concluded that, while there was evidence that contractors' agents might have provided false data about climate, cost of living, and transportation charges, no blame for worker complaints accrued to the contractors themselves, and camp and work conditions were generally good.[28] It was discovered a few months later that Commissioner Donovan had accepted a $500 bribe from a job contractor in exchange for his favorable report—a fee that Donovan did not dispute but claimed had been paid in compensation for providing the contractor with laborers. Donovan was not reappointed to the board when his term expired in early 1893.[29]

As winter turned to spring, fewer accounts of cruelty came from the camps housing the men building the Adirondack Railroad. This was not because the contractors and subcontractors had changed their ways, but because workers were better able to endure job conditions as the weather grew warmer. Nevertheless, both black and white laborers continued to desert. A few African American site workers stayed on in northern New York when the job was finished. As one laborer replied in answer to a journalist's question when he passed through Cleveland on his way south: "The north? I like it better than Tennessee. The white folks are better to us up here. I might get work and stay, but I am too sick." He was given a rail ticket to Galion, Ohio. Two women secured jobs as waitresses in Syracuse and several men were said to be looking for work in the city in late March.[30]

Crews from the northern and southern ends of the railroad project came together near Big Moose in the western Adirondacks in mid-October 1892. Less than two weeks later, trains were running on the line. William Seward Webb was lauded for his "wonderful vision, magnetism, and leadership" in building the Adirondack and St. Lawrence Railroad. But, as an 1892 commentator concluded after writing about the exploitation of manpower during the course of the project:

"We are told that the men who build railroads are public benefactors, and the foregoing is in the nature of an application of ice water in toning down feverish adulation of such philanthropists."[31] In the spring of 1893, Webb leased his railroad to the New York Central and Hudson River Railroad, which changed its southern terminus from Herkimer to Utica and operated it as its Adirondack Division. By 1913 the railroad had been absorbed into the New York Central.

7

The Summer Resort Industry

THE FORT WILLIAM HENRY and Sagamore hotels on Lake George, and the Hotel Champlain on the Champlain lakeshore just north of the park, were centerpieces of the Adirondacks' early summer tourism industry. Situated in romantic landscapes surrounded by lushly ornamental grounds, catering to clients' every social and recreational need while providing modern amenities, and easily accessible by rail (or rail and stagecoach) from New York and other major eastern cities, they attracted thousands of guests during their heyday. All three hotels employed large numbers of black workers in the second half of the nineteenth and early years of the twentieth century.

African American men served as hotel waiters, bellboys (or bellhops), hostlers, mail clerks, kitchen help, gas fitters, and metal polishers. A few women could be found working as chambermaids and in hotel kitchens and laundries. "To a large number of our people the Summer time is the harvest time," noted an African American journalist in 1883. "When others spend they reap; when others madly pursue an echo over the mountain side, they calmly pursue the mighty dollar."[1] The aggregate $7,500 monthly income of three hundred such resort workers in the North, it was estimated, went "directly into the pockets of Negroes" throughout the country, with most of it going to the South, "land of ignorance and darkness."[2]

Exclusively black wait staffs served in the dining rooms of all three hotels. They constituted the elite tier of black employment in terms of status and earnings, and were markers of prestige for the hotels' white clientele in obliging them as servers/servants. The Fort William

Henry Hotel, built in 1854–55 in Caldwell (now the town of Lake George) at the southern end of Lake George and catering to nine hundred guests at its peak, employed black waiters from its earliest days.[3] It was of the Fort William Henry's staff that a correspondent for a New Jersey newspaper wrote in reporting on the Lake George summer season of 1865:

> At one of the hotels the servants' department is filled with colored men, neatly uniformed with white jackets, and every one skilled in his business. One of the best vocal and instrumental serenades ever heard was got up by them one mellow moonlight night, in front of the hotel. During an afternoon stroll to a wood adjoining the lake, four colored men were seen writing, three reading and one sketching the scenery. In answer to an inquiry one of them replied, that out of forty or fifty waiters employed in the hotel, every one could read, and, with one exception, all could write! Can you find the same number of white servants in any hotel in Saratoga or New York equally intelligent and educated?[4]

A year later the *Christian Recorder*, journal of the African Methodist Episcopal Church, detailed the general background of black summer workers at Lake George and other popular resorts (Saratoga and Niagara, New York; Newport, Rhode Island; and Cape May and Long Branch, New Jersey). "The class of men who go are mostly young men, many of them are highly intelligent, some of them have trades, and not a few of them are members of Church. Prejudice, keeping them out of other business, forces them to engage in this kind of employment to so great an extent."[5]

Hotel waiters were selected with care by headwaiters, who were themselves black when dining rooms were manned by African Americans. Celebrated for their "suavity of manner, pleasing address, and . . . qualities of leadership,"[6] headwaiters were responsible for greeting and seating guests, ensuring efficient food service, maintaining standards, and overseeing the outside activities of employees. The best headwaiters returned to the same hotels year after year and held positions of power within management. Each had a well-established hiring network, and black headwaiters in the eastern Adirondacks relied primarily on staff members of southern winter resorts and on students from privately supported Southern schools—liberally dubbed colleges, institutes, and universities—that offered various degrees of education to African Americans. Two schools, the Hampton Normal and Agricultural Institute in Hampton, Virginia (founded 1868), and Howard University in Washington, DC (1866), were the educational institutions most represented in the Adirondacks before and just after 1900, presumably because of their geographic proximity to the Northeast. The schools embodied competing philosophies when it came to education.

Northern missionaries, financially supported by northern philanthropists, led the black education initiative in the South after the Civil War. They planted institutions in a region where there was intense resentment to educating rural blacks; where, as late as 1910, there were no public schools that offered them as much as an eighth-grade education; and where few black teachers had more education than their students.[7] Many benefactors and the school heads they supported accepted segregation as an operating principle, and training was geared to practical education that would enable students to take their place within that system while encouraging them to "avoid social questions; leave politics alone; . . . learn that it is a mistake to be educated out of your environment."[8] As reformers, they guided the development of "industrial" schools, patterned along the lines of Hampton Institute, that sought to prepare students to increase their labor value to white society by pursuing character-building education that equipped them for self-supporting opportunities in the agricultural, mechanical, and household industries. Some schools in the Hampton tradition also offered "normal departments" to prepare teachers for public school classrooms.[9]

Washington's Howard University, along with Fisk University in Nashville, Tennessee, and Atlanta University in Georgia, offered another model of education in advocating advanced curricula that included both classical and professional programs. Booker T. Washington, whom some labeled an accommodationist, was the black voice of the industrial, or Hampton, ideal for many years. W. E. B. Du Bois pushed for racial equality, a distinct black identity, and the alternative educational model: "Negro colleges as a source of educated Negroes who could guide their own destiny."[10]

Because so many waiters at Lake George and Champlain hotels were college students (or college graduates unable to procure jobs commensurate with their educational attainment),[11] they tended to be a sophisticated lot. Their contributions to African American newspapers between the 1880s and the first years of the twentieth century reflected the exuberant optimism of the first generations of blacks born after the Civil War, when it seemed possible that the race would be successfully integrated into American society. According to their accounts, they led a convivial life and were given a fair amount of free time and access to hotel facilities. They "stick closer than brothers," effused a correspondent for the African American *Washington Bee* on the Fort William Henry wait staff in 1887, and "amuse themselves with singing or roaming around, viewing the grand scenery, and once in a while some of them partake rather freely of the juice of the forbidden fruit."[12] Sporting activities were popular: tennis, croquet, "rowing, fishing, gunning, bathing, base ball, and rambling in the forest; all are merry."[13] The Fort William Henry's season that year opened with a staff boat race on Lake George offering a fifty dollar purse for the winners that was watched by "hundreds of spectators, thronging the piers fronting the Hotels." By late August it was reported that "all the men are getting along nicely, and though the season is not as good as it might be and there is but one colored young lady at the Hotel, nevertheless the men are well satisfied with the proprietor, the head and second waiter, and will doubtless remain until the first of September." The staff gifted both the head and second waiter with "very handsome and costly" watch chains as tokens of their appreciation.[14]

The huge Hotel Champlain opened in 1890 and was "one of the most important resort hotel complexes ever to be constructed in the Adirondack Region."[15] Owned in part by the Delaware and Hudson Railroad (as was the Fort William Henry Hotel at a later date),

8. Hotel Champlain Dining Room. Photograph by S. R. Stoddard, circa 1891. Courtesy of Adirondack Museum.

it accommodated four hundred guests. The Champlain maintained a large black staff, its manager, it was reported in 1897, formally opening the summer season by "reviewing the army" of its three hundred African American servants.[16]

The headwaiter at the Champlain from its 1890 opening day through 1903 was Frank P. Thompson, "possibly the most prominent head-waiter in the country." Born in 1855 in Virginia, Thompson grew up in Pennsylvania, entered hotel service at the age of sixteen, and rose to the position of headwaiter seven years later. He spent winters as headwaiter at industrialist Henry Flagler's Ponce de Leon Hotel in St. Augustine, Florida, and accompanied its manager, Osborn Dunlap Seavey, north when Seavey was tapped as the Hotel Champlain's first manager.[17]

The hotel deferred to Thompson, whose relationship with Seavey bolstered his commanding staff position. The Champlain sponsored occasional "tournaments" for the benefit of its black employees:

9. Frank Thompson, headwaiter, Hotel Champlain. From *Commanders of the Dining Room: Biographic Sketches and Portraits of Successful Head Waiters*, by E. A. Maccannon. Courtesy of Jean Blackwell Hutson Research and Reference Division, Schomburg Center for Research in Black Culture, New York Public Library.

one- or two-day affairs at which money prizes were given to winners in a series of events, from real athletic challenges such as high jumping, hurdles, distance running, and bicycling to frivolous races of the sack, potato, and three-legged variety. (Thompson's thirteen-year-old son, Frank Jr., won a bicycle race in 1896 after receiving a substantial handicap.)[18] Thompson's flare for promotion and his compelling interest in baseball, discussed in chapter 9, brought a good deal of

10. F. H. Griffin, headwaiter, Sagamore Hotel. From *Commanders of the Dining Room: Biographic Sketches and Portraits of Successful Head Waiters*, by E. A. Maccannon. Courtesy of Jean Blackwell Hutson Research and Reference Division, Schomburg Center for Research in Black Culture, New York Public Library.

local attention to the Hotel Champlain waiters during his reign. It is surmised that 1903 was Thompson's last summer at the hotel. "A very sick man" when he returned in the spring of 1904 from St. Augustine, he died in late 1905 of longstanding "stomach trouble" at the age of fifty. His position was filled the summer after his death by his former "second" at the Ponce de Leon.[19] The hotel succumbed to fire in the spring of 1910 but was closed for only one season. A smaller but no less elaborate structure opened the following summer.

The Sagamore Hotel in Bolton, financed by a quartet of wealthy investors who summered nearby, opened in 1883, burned to the ground in 1893, was rebuilt with a capacity for four hundred guests, and reopened with some fanfare in 1894. The hotel's initial wait staff had been white, but in its second incarnation it employed blacks in the dining room. "That the change is for the best is already decided," reported a writer for the *Lake George Mirror* early that summer, "for a more attractive or obliging lot of colored boys I never met." There was no longer any "hurly burly in the dining room," he later added. "The colored boys flit by silently and reappear in a twinkling with trays loaded with delicacies."[20]

F. H. Griffin from Savannah, Georgia, was the popular head-waiter at the Sagamore for at least eleven years.[21] Under his leadership, according to a correspondent writing for an African American newspaper in September 1904, "waiters have had a very successful and pleasant season, for which we all are very grateful to him." Staff diversions that year included the Magnolia Literary Society, an organization with antecedents in black history and devoted to intellectual development and racial uplift (for which Griffin served as "critic"), and a tennis tournament with prizes: a silver loving cup for the winner and a tennis racket for the second-place finisher.[22]

Black staff members, with the exception of a few who arrived with spouses, generally lived in hotel-owned dormitories. This meant that they could be easily mustered when wanted, and also that wages might be minimized in emphasizing the perquisites of room and board. Waiters benefited in social terms from the enforced closeness, but dormitory living magnified the transitory and segregated nature of their experience.[23] A three-story residence built by the Sagamore in 1913 for its "colored help" contained one hundred sleeping rooms, baths with toilets and running water on each floor, and a large assembly hall equipped with an organ for use as a general meeting room and Sunday religious services.[24] The building served for only one summer in its original guise, as the second Sagamore burned to the ground in early 1914 and the dormitory was repurposed as a kitchen and dining facility for residents of privately owned cottages on hotel property.[25]

Rules for Dining Room Waiters at the Sagamore Hotel
Lake George, 1913

1. Every waiter must clean his teeth and finger nails before each meal.
2. Every waiter must frequent the bath tub after ball games and other athletic sports.
3. Every waiter must be in his room at 11 o'clock at night.
4. No card playing for money is permissible at any time.
5. All waiters must be courteous, obliging and attentive.

By Thomas A. Madison, Headwaiter

Source: *Lake George Mirror*, July 5, 1913
Note: Thomas Madison, the headwaiter at the Sagamore Hotel in the summer of 1913, was born in Augusta, Georgia, in 1875 and made his home in Albany for forty years. It was, he pronounced, "the fault of the headwaiter that colored waiters are not more in demand throughout the country." Madison held twice-a-week "mock service" sessions during June to instruct Sagamore waiters in the proper use of various dishes, and gave weekly lessons throughout the season in "the art of carrying the tray, etc."

Not rebuilt until 1921–22, the Sagamore did not employ black waiters in its new dining room.

The names of black men who spent summers working in Adirondack resorts were likely to be common ones, and little is known about most of those employed. One exception was William John Anderson, born in Shoreham, Vermont, and a graduate of Mount Hermon School in Northfield, Massachusetts. A staff member of the Hotel Champlain in the late 1890s, he went on to become a leading apple grower in Shoreham, president of the Vermont Horticultural Society, and a member of the Vermont State Legislature.[26] Another exception was Samuel Jesse Battle, born in 1883 in New Bern, North Carolina, to a former slave and the daughter of slaves. Having had some training as a servant in a private New Bern home where, as he later recalled, he "learned the proper way of laying a linen cloth and placing silver" as well as "how people of real culture and refinement behave, converse and live," he headed north and worked briefly at the Sagamore around 1900. After subsequent stints as a waiter at Yale University, a houseman in a private New York City home, and a redcap porter at Grand Central Station, he became in 1911 the first African American appointed to the New York City police force.[27]

Mary Johnson, a thirty-two-year-old black woman from Washington, DC, kept a diary during the summer of 1917 when she worked as a servant for a family living in or near the village of Caldwell. A midsummer entry mourned her lack of freedom as a domestic worker:

> *July 17*: We went to the Falls today. A tiresome trip with no rest for me. Is this my life?

But later entries suggest a mode of quiet, domesticated social life available to blacks working in village homes and hotels during the summer:

> *August 6*: Went to a demonstration at the old School House. Mr. Wormley walked up with me.
>
> *August 11*: Mr. Wormley, Mr. Lindsey, and Miss Stella came and played cards this evening we had lots of fun.
>
> *August 16*: Went to the dance tonight in the village had a nice time.
>
> *September 11*: Three of the boys from Fort William Henry came out had quite a party over to Stella's.
>
> *September 17*: Chicken and another man came out to Stella and we had a fine game of whist.[28]

The Fort William Henry, the Sagamore, and the Champlain employed the greatest number of African Americans, but black contingents filled staff positions at other high-end regional hotels as well. Paramount among these was the short-lived Prospect House, an ambitious venture in the interior wilderness of Blue Mountain Lake, Hamilton County. Opening in 1882 with a maximum capacity of five hundred guests, the Prospect House offered year-round accommodations in its early years. It was never a financial success, and after changing its name to the Hotel Utowana in 1900, closed its doors in 1903. The hotel's first owner, Frederick C. Durant, lived in Philadelphia, as did the hotel's only two black staff members known by name:

11. Taylor House staff, Schroon Lake, 1898. Courtesy of Schroon–North Hudson Historical Society.

Alec Erskine, the hotel's wine steward for several years and said to have been a former slave and the butler at Durant's home during the winter; and Martin Cowdrey, the house steward in 1882, who became a well-known Philadelphia caterer and a member of the city's "ultra aristocratic" black elite.[29]

Smaller hotels employed black staff members in various capacities. The Wayside Inn in Luzerne (later Lake Luzerne), which housed around two hundred guests at its peak, welcomed thirteen "colored help" in June 1906 from the District of Columbia.[30] Fifteen black employees at a hotel in Keene founded a social organization, St. Hubert's Whist and Social Club, in the summer of 1929; thirteen members were listed on the club roster in 1930 from as far afield as Portsmouth, Virginia; St, Louis, Missouri; and Charleston, South Carolina.[31]

Racial incidents at Adirondack hotels, if not rare, were rarely reported. The *Lake George Mirror* noted the 1907 beating of a "gentlemanly young negro" bellboy in the noisy barroom of the Fort William Henry by "two young men with an evident desire for trouble." The attack caused the bellboy to lose his front teeth and triggered a skirmish between the perpetrators and black staff members that was quickly broken up. "Not a single feature of the episode," recorded the

Mirror, "can be construed to the discredit of either management or attachés."[32]

Race relations deteriorated in the North during the last decade of the nineteenth century, as Civil War idealism faded and white northerners absorbed some of the South's outspoken post-Reconstruction hostility to the black race. The new attitude undermined the previous strength of waitering as an occupation for African Americans, as did the availability of European immigrants who increasingly won out in competition for low-paying jobs. In an effort to counteract their growing marginality, the livelihood's black leaders established the Head and Second Waiters' National Benefit Association in 1899, one of several quasi-unions for black waiters. Among its goals was the training of waiters to a high degree of proficiency—particularly in their ability to handle the new European "a la carte" style of dining then supplanting the old resort tradition of American-style set meals. Frank Thompson of the Hotel Champlain was elected association president in 1902.[33]

Hardly immune to racist pressures, Adirondack resort hotels moved away from employing blacks in their dining rooms in the early twentieth century. The exact timing of the shift to white waiters is unclear. The *Washington Bee* reported in early September 1915 that a number of black waiters from Saratoga Springs had moved north after the closing of its seasonal hotels to Lake George and Lake Champlain "where the September business is great."[34] At the Fort William Henry, a local newspaper article detailing the 1920 drowning death of the hotel's "negro assistant headwaiter" suggests that the hotel still maintained a black dining room staff at that time.[35] But the overall number of African American resort employees in the region plummeted by 1925. The Sagamore did continue to utilize African Americans in other capacities than waiter in its new guise. Thomas Wesley Benn, a college graduate who taught briefly in Virginia's public schools, was, according to his 1946 obituary, the chief bellman at the hotel for thirty years.[36])

One smaller Lake George resort facility, the Rogers Rock Hotel, maintained an unusual relationship with black student personnel well into the twentieth century. A seasonal fifty-room operation in Hague at the northern end of Lake George, the hotel opened in 1875 and was bought in 1903 by New York publisher David Williams as a hobby enterprise. Williams knew the work ethic of young men from Virginia's Hampton Institute through contact with them at other hotels on the lake, and shortly after taking over ownership of Rogers Rock began to engage Hampton students as bellboys. The tradition continued—despite Williams's 1927 death—through 1941, the summer before the hotel (part of a private club and cottage community from 1925) was torn down.[37]

Williams, noted Rogers Rock memoirist Geoffrey Wilson, "happily expected the African Americans he imported from Hampton to play roles almost as subservient as those in any plantation big house." His businessman's viewpoint was, however, offset by the personal interest he took in his young hirees and his expectation that they accomplish great things after their graduation from Hampton. Many of his recruits rose to the challenge. Among the first seven blacks on the Rogers Rock staff, it was reported in 1922, were "one physician, one dentist, one carpenter and contractor, two agriculturists, one businessman, and one lawyer. All married but one." As a 1907 employee who became an Indianapolis attorney wrote in 1921, "one of the most important factors in my life has been the Rogers Rock Community, headed by Mr. David Williams, and composed of people like members of his family and associates."[38] A onetime black employee who became ill around 1918 was reported to have been cared for in hospital and then by a private nurse until his death "through the kindness of a friend" made at the hotel.[39]

Robert E. Williams, an early black staff member, returned to Rogers Rock every summer for more than thirty years. As he described himself in a 1907 *Lake George Mirror* article devoted to the "exceptionally fine lot of fellows" who made up that summer's Rogers Rock cadre, "I was born in Oconee County and in the State of South Carolina. After attending the country public schools I graduated from the Seneca High School and taught a country school for one term. The next school I entered was Hampton Institute. After finishing a work year, I completed the tailor's trade, which covers a period of three years. I have one more year in which to complete the academic course. My aim is to be an ideal business man."[40]

No one involved with the hotel knew how Robert Williams passed his winters, but he eventually presided at the front desk of Rogers Rock and became, in essence, its assistant manager. His title, however, remained that of bell captain, and he always dressed in the same Spartan white uniform he had worn as a young bellboy. "It never seemed to cross anyone's mind," wrote memoirist Wilson, "that as he grew older and his role gained more importance, he might have preferred to wear a business suit." Williams's "very presence helped foster the pleasant social equilibrium that usually prevailed." Among his other duties, he directed the Rogers Rock Quartet, a hotel institution that performed for guests (a midseason telegram was purportedly once sent to Hampton requesting a replacement "dishwasher who could sing bass").[41] The quartet occasionally took its music beyond the hotel to wider audiences, among them a 1923 carnival sponsored in Ticonderoga by the Knights of Columbus.[42]

The character of the black staff at Rogers Rock changed over the years. Students hired from Hampton and a few other traditionally black colleges—convinced "that if they continued to 'know their place' they were doomed"—developed a race consciousness by the 1930s and were no longer willing to adopt the obsequious manners of their predecessors. They became difficult for old-timers like Williams (whom some of them might have called an Uncle Tom) to supervise.[43] The 1941 closing of the Rogers Rock marked the definitive end of the long era in which black staff members figured prominently in the regional resort industry.

Adirondack hotels, as has been suggested, did no more than follow in the footsteps of the industry in abandoning their African American staffs and replacing them with white European immigrants. A 1950s study documented the loss of status by blacks in the New York City hotel industry and their displacement by white workers in the preceding half-century. According to this report, there were then only 223 blacks among 3,428 employees in thirty of the city's hotels, representing 6.5 percent of the total workforce. (Of these, only five individuals served among 1,064 waiters and waitresses in dining rooms of twelve hotels of "the better type.") Bellmen were predominantly white, and most hotels in the study barred African Americans from employment in their bars and front service departments.[44]

Blacks were seldom seen around Lake George outside of the summer season and were rarely recorded in resident censuses (generally taken in June) in the Lake George communities of Caldwell and Bolton, where the Fort William Henry and Sagamore hotels were located.[45] Mrs. Bertie Champion was a member of one of the two African American households documented in the Caldwell census of 1915.[46] The only regional black woman known by name to have made a career in the resort industry, she was born in 1877 in Jacksonville, Florida, and had by 1910 made her way to New York City, where she and two other black women were laundresses working in their "own laundry" for their "own account." Champion, "of Lake George, New York," was reported in 1928 to be supervising the maintenance of the living quarters for the several hundred blacks who made up the winter staff of the Poinciana Hotel in Palm Beach, Florida, a job she had held "for years."[47] It is likely that she occupied a similar position at a Lake George hotel during the summer months. Champion relocated to Saratoga Springs in the late 1920s and died there in 1949.[48]

By 1940 there were no year-round black residents in either Caldwell (population 1,487) or Bolton (1,310). But the black population of the city of Glens Falls, immediately to the south of Caldwell, had expanded from a 1910 population of 22 black among 15,243 inhabitants to 78 among 18,836 (0.4 percent). Eleven of these residents reported working that year at hotel jobs as porters, bellmen, and elevator operators (but not as waiters); nine were musicians. Any of these individuals might have first ventured to the region as Lake George summer employees and chosen to stay on, living nearby in a more urban agglomeration with a small but established black population.

8

Resort Entertainment

Employees and Students

AS THE 1865 NEWSPAPER quoted in the last chapter suggested in its report of Fort William Henry Hotel waiters serenading hotel guests on a "mellow moonlight night," Adirondack resorts discovered early on that black personnel had musical talents that could be exploited to entertain patrons. Employees enjoyed performing before an audience, hotel proprietors allowed them to make money at it, and playful minstrel and vaudeville shows as well as serious drama produced by black staff members became surprisingly regular features of resort life.

A "dramatic entertainment" featuring Shakespearean and other recitations presented in the parlor at the Fort William Henry by student waiters from Howard University in 1887 "received great credit and was financially encouraged" by the hotel's clientele.[1] One guest, a correspondent for the *Louisville (KY) Courier Journal*, singled out student waiter Charles S. Morris from Louisville for his acting skill in this performance. Noting the young man's "decided dramatic talent" and his "yearnings . . . for the stage," he queried, "Where is the philanthropist who will help the man to attain the goal toward which he is reaching?"[2] In fact, Morris did quite well without the intervention of white philanthropy. He trained for the law and briefly practiced in Washington, DC, before becoming a protégé of and private secretary to black statesman Frederick Douglass, with whom he traveled the nation. He married Douglass's granddaughter Annie Sprague, and after her 1893 death became a well-known Baptist minister and missionary to Africa. Adam Clayton Powell Sr., pastor of New York City's Abyssinian Church, once headed by Morris, preached the sermon at Morris's 1931 New York memorial service.[3]

Dramatic recitations were one thing, but minstrelsy was the entertainment vehicle most enjoyed by black members of Lake George hotel staffs. Indeed, the minstrel club was "chief of all" the several associations enthusiastically organized by waiters at the Sagamore in 1903.[4]

The art of minstrelsy had roots in African folk as well as English and Irish culture. It was introduced and broadly disseminated from the 1840s on by white performers who blackened their faces with burnt cork and travelled from town to town, providing popular entertainment for lower- and middle-class white Americans. The array of stereotypically degraded black characters delineated in minstrel routines enabled white actors to loosen up and play with nonsensical themes, slang, bad grammar, and mispronunciation.[5] African Americans (sometimes in blackface) took up minstrelsy themselves in the late 1850s. Their programs incorporated religious music and offered a more intense focus on plantation themes than those of white minstrels to create what they viewed as a liberating, authentically black art form.[6] They lampooned their own people in pursuit of laughs while using and demonstrating the value of black culture, but in stooping to meet the expectations of their audiences they were often considered "among the chief purveyors of negative racial stereotypes."[7]

Both the Fort William Henry and Sagamore hotels were known at the turn of the twentieth century for their annual minstrel shows. These were produced by black staff members and given wide publicity and editorial support by the local newspaper catering to resort clientele, the *Lake George Mirror.* The Sagamore's sophisticated 1899 show (see program) followed the three-part structure of such performances: opening with dancing and singing, followed by an "olio" or variety show that might include a comic speech, ethnic dances, and instrumental performances, and closing with a slapstick plantation skit or parody of a popular play. Tambo and Bones, as presented in the Sagamore program, were stock minstrel figures named after the instruments they played—tambourines and curved animal bones clicked together like castanets. The characters were part of a trio and spoke in loud, exaggerated black dialect while quarreling with an interlocutor or straight man and one another in rapid-fire patter. Buck dancing was a precursor to tap dancing; the singing quartet was a wholly black contribution to minstrelsy.[8]

Contemporary popular music was a fundamental feature of Lake George shows, and its Adirondack performance indicative of how quickly it penetrated black culture. The singer of "That's the Way to Spell Chicken," a racially stereotyped "coon song" hit of 1902, was obliged to encore the song at the Sagamore's 1903 show. Another number in the Sagamore production that year, "On Broadway in Dahomey," had debuted in New York City less than six months earlier in "In Dahomey," the first full-length musical written and played by blacks to be performed at a major Broadway theater.[9]

Fort William Henry waiters, occasionally assisted by black staff members from Delaware and Hudson steamboats (under the same ownership as the hotel) that plied Lake George waters, financed their own musical presentations and split house receipts among themselves—as presumably, did Sagamore waiters.[10] Between four and five hundred guests from nearby hotels and cottages attended the concert and minstrel performance at the Fort William Henry in 1898 upon purchasing tickets priced at fifty cents for adults and twenty-five cents for children.[11] The hotel troupe hired several "colored Stars of the first magnitude from Saratoga" and elsewhere to perform as singers and female partners in the "cakewalks" included in their annual shows of 1898 and 1899.[12] This dance phenomenon had come into vogue in the mid-1880s as an exhibition dance and was by then a mainstay of the black minstrel show. Also known as the walkabout or the strut, it was said to have its roots in the plantation life of southern slaves as a parody of the pretentious, courtly quadrilles once danced by their masters. Stylized and rigorously physical, the high-stepping cakewalk was performed competitively by mixed couples wearing fancy dress in processionals or in the round. The "cake" awarded at the close of the performance purportedly had its origin, again, in slave life, when one had been given to the most creative of contending

Sagamore Waiters' Program of Musical Entertainment
August 22, 1899, at 9 o'clock
In the Music Hall of the Hotel

William Rollins, interlocutor; F. W. Addison, J. H. Gibbs, bones; S. H. Frazier, F. F. Pierce, tambos; M. J. Moore, F. W. Addison, E. R. Gray, C. J. Smith, J. R. Burroughs, vocal choir.

PART FIRST.

1. Grand Chorus: "De Captain of De Coon Town Guards." De Captain, F. W. Addison.
2. Grand Opening Overture by Prof. Zita's Orchestra.
3. Song: "All I Want Is My Black Baby Back." Mr. Pierce.
4. Solo and Chorus: "My Creole Sue." Mr. Moore.
5. Song: "I Guess I'll Have to Telegraph My Baby." Mr. Frazier. And the arrival of Mr. Cooper in his latest hit, "I'm Livin Easy."
6. Song: "I Ain't Seen No Messenger Boy." Mr. Addison.
7. Solo and Chorus: "She Was Happy 'Till She Met You." Mr. Smith.
8. Song: "Hello, Ma Baby." Mr. Gibbs.

QUARTETTE

Messrs. Moore, Addison, Gray and Burroughs

PART SECOND.

1. Clarionet Solo: "Angels Serenade." Mr. Burroughs.
2. Smith, Addison and Gray in their funny sayings and doings.
3. J. H. Gibbs in his Buck Dancing Specialties.
4. A Few Minutes with Frazier and Pierce.
5. Guitar Selection. Mr. Cooper.
6. "Contest for a Melon." Messrs. Moore, Frazier, Addison and Cooper.
7. Quartette: Messrs. Moore, Addison, Gray and Burroughs.
8. Grand Finale and Cake Walk.

P.S.: The melon in the above contest will be awarded to the singer getting the loudest applause.

F. W. ADDISON
General Manager and Musical Director
S. H. FRAZIER
Stage Manager

Source: *Lake George Mirror*, August 19, 1899

pairs who cakewalked for the entertainment of plantation owners at harvest time.[13]

Hotel employees from Lake George sometimes took their performances to wider audiences. Among staff groups to travel afield was a "West Indian Quartette" of Fort William Henry waiters, who not only sang on the hotel's grand piazza in 1900 but also at least contemplated giving concerts at other local venues around Caldwell. A group of Fort William Henry and nearby Lake House bellboys from "the sunny South and cotton fields" staged a concert, cakewalk, and pie- and watermelon-eating contest at the Music Hall in Warrensburg some six miles from Lake George Village in 1901.[14]

Hotel staff members were not the only African Americans making music at Adirondack resorts during the late nineteenth century. The region became a regular summer destination of singers from southern black industrial-style schools endeavoring to raise money for and interest in their institutions. George Foster Peabody (1852–1938), a prosperous New York investment banker who bought a summer (later, year-round) home in Bolton on Lake George in 1891, gave them early encouragement and support. He had long taken an interest in the education of blacks in the South and served over the years on the boards of trustees of a number of schools promoting industrial education.[15] As he pronounced in 1925, "The South is entitled to have the most generous aid from the wealth of the North and West, to help educate the negro to an understanding of agriculture and the coincident production of wealth."[16]

A delegation from Hampton Institute visited Lake George at least as early as 1893. The school had a musical fundraising tradition that had begun when General Samuel Armstrong, the son of a white missionary and Hampton's first principal, observed the 1871–72 success of a touring ensemble of students—the Jubilee Singers from Fisk University in Nashville, Tennessee—at attracting financial support in the North. Armstrong determined that Hampton should follow Fisk's lead, and a choral group left Hampton for northern states in February 1873, returning ten months later with $10,000 in new funds for the institute. Many Hampton campus buildings would henceforth

Performance Schedule and Donations Received

Adirondack Campaign, Hampton Institute, 1901

August 4	
Caldwell [Lake George], Fort William Henry Hotel	65.84
Caldwell [Lake George], Presbyterian Church	15.75
August 5	
Lake George, Hundred Island House	45.91
Lake George, Lake View House	5.00
Lake George, Marion House	30.40
Lake George, Sagamore Hotel	116.44
Lake George, Silver Bay Hotel	303.00
August 9	
Elizabethtown, Hotel Windsor	15.04
August 11	
Keene Valley, Congregational Church	45.12
St. Hubert's, St. Hubert's Inn	127.43
August 13	
Cascadeville [Keene Valley], Cascade Lake House	13.77
Lake Placid, Grand View House	22.64
August 14	
Lake George, Bolton House	6.11
Lake Placid, Whiteface Inn	236.92
August 20	
Saranac Lake, Algonquin Hotel	28.25
Saranac Inn, Saranac Inn	52.28
August 21	
Long Lake, Sagamore Hotel	26.68
Long Lake, Grove House	22.73
Blue Mountain Lake, Blue Mountain Lake House	28.68
August 22	
Brighton, Paul Smith's Hotel	139.92
August 23	
Childwold, Childwold Park House	46.92
August 25	
Westport, Westport Inn	88.69
TOTAL DONATIONS RECEIVED	$1,483.52

(continued from p.103)

Source: Reconstructed from *Hampton Normal and Agricultural Institute, Treasurer's Statement for the Year Ending June 30, 1902*, Hampton, VA: Hampton Institute, 1902, 17–48.
Note: The Bolton House entry is obviously misplaced.

be "sung-up" with money collected by students and recent graduates on similar tours,[17] and the school's roaming singers drew appreciative Lake George audiences. Presentations included more than song. Speeches by current and past students, distinguished residents, and committed friends were part of the programs; school principals were sometimes on hand. Hampton's campaigns penetrated deeply into the Adirondack woods. A three-week visit to other resort venues in 1901 covered some six hundred miles of rough terrain and raised over $1,400.[18] (See schedule.)

More than a decade before this tour took place, a black student, without a musical entourage, had given a presentation on education as a representative of his race in the Adirondacks. John Langalibalele Dube arrived in the United States in 1887, having travelled from his home in Natal (now a province of South Africa) with former African missionary William Cullen Wilcox, who became the minister of the Congregational Church in Keene Valley, Essex County. Dube was in the country to study at Oberlin Preparatory School and later Oberlin College, of which Wilcox was an alumnus, and Wilcox invited him to spend the summers of 1887 and 1888 with him in Keene Valley. During his second summer's residence, Wilcox asked the seventeen-year-old Zulu boy to address an afternoon church meeting "crowded with curious city people" on the subject of "Self Help for My People," where he spoke "like a veteran of the platform" in delivering his first public address. Dube went on to spend a number of years in the United States, often lecturing, before settling in Natal in 1899 and founding a school based on the American industrial model. He was chosen unanimously in 1912 to become the first president of the organization that later became the African National Congress.[19]

At the heart of Hampton and other visiting black schools' choral programs was the "spiritual," a synthesis of African and American music with roots in plantation life. Its unusual intonations, variable tones in pitch, and apparent irregularities in rhythm were unfamiliar to white Americans. Surprisingly, however, the spiritual had penetrated the Adirondacks as early as 1874. Two years after the New York publication of a songbook entitled *Jubilee Songs: As Sung by the Jubilee Singers of Fisk University,* a double quartet of white choir singers from the local Congregational church performed a program of spirituals at an evening social in Lewis, Essex County. The songs, reported an attendee at the event, "were wild, weird pieces, yet many of them were very sweet."[20] As arranged for the songbook and sung by black singers at regional summer resorts, noted black author and anthropologist Zora Neale Hurston, the style of presentation would have "conformed more to Conservatory rules of music" than to spirituals sung, "let us say, in the Macedonia Baptist Church."[21]

Quartets—known for their dignity, elegance, and repertoire—were more economical to send on the road than large choirs and were the most frequent school representatives to appear in the Adirondacks. Among schools other than Hampton to perform in the region between 1900 and 1930 were Shaw University, Raleigh, North Carolina; Tuskegee Institute, Tuskegee, Alabama; and Wilberforce University, Wilberforce, Ohio.[22] Five representatives of the Snow Hill Institute in Alabama followed a less-traveled route in the summer of 1901—appearing at the Forge House in Old Forge and the Arrowhead Hotel in Inlet on the Fulton Chain of Lakes in the western Adirondacks.[23]

Hampton and Tuskegee's campaign tours were well-organized and well-financed, but travel could be difficult for smaller schools that trod in their footsteps. The assistant principal of the Fort Valley High and Industrial School in Fort Valley, Georgia, and his party were reported by a mocking South Carolina journalist to have been denied accommodations by three Saranac Lake hotels during a 1901 summer tour after giving a concert in the village. Served a too costly meal of hash and tea on the ground in the backyard of one of the hotels, according to the reporter, the group "finally secured the privilege of sleeping in a hay loft. This was pretty rough treatment to receive in the land of great moral ideas and the brotherhood of man. We do not know that they would have fared any better at Southern hotels nor would they have applied at them, but they had a right to expect different and better treatment at the hands of these loud-mouthed friends in the Adirondacks."[24] Five years later, Fort Valley's assistant principal was back in the Adirondacks—again sleeping in haylofts and "without enough money at day's end even to buy a 'wholesome meal.'" He reported surprising fundraising success in the area encompassing Franklin County's St. Regis and Saranac lakes, where he rowed a small boat between resort hotels and raised $1,500 for current expenses and for the school's blacksmithing department.[25]

As a Hampton campaign member recounted in the first years of the twentieth century, seven schools had already visited one hotel on its summer route through the North before Hampton's arrival. This proliferation of campaigns dampened donor enthusiasm, and as early as 1907 George Peabody was advising Hampton from Lake George to give "the people hereabouts a rest."[26] His plea, however, did little to staunch the school's pursuit of Adirondack support. Its 1914 tour took students on a one-hundred-day circuit from Virginia by schooner to Bar Harbor, Maine, and then overland through the White Mountains, the Adirondacks, and the Berkshire Hills. Hampton's first "motor campaign," launched in 1920, included stops in Lake George, Schroon Lake, Paul Smiths, Saranac Lake, and Lake Placid. A student automobile mechanic was present on the excursion to guarantee that the two vehicles carrying the party were never held up for long by automobile breakdowns.[27]

As philanthropists developed new interests, and the summer population of Lake George and other northeastern resorts changed in character, southern black schools gradually abandoned the tradition of fundraising in the region's large hotels. But a few school choral groups were taken on by commercial sponsors, among them the Redpath Chautauqua lecture bureau—known for providing "culture" to some ten thousand small towns and cities across the United States in the 1920s. One southern black boarding school made its first visit to the Adirondacks under Redpath's auspices in 1925, when the founder of the Piney Woods Country Life School near Braxton, Mississippi, transported a female quartet of "Cotton Blossom Singers" to the region in a green and white "house on wheels" built on the chassis of a Ford Model T. Its self-contained living arrangements were intended to minimize racial incidents and cut down on costs. At the close of the group's 1925 entertainment at the Methodist Church in St. Regis Falls, Franklin County, the congregation was invited to inspect the house-car's interior with its Pullman-style bunk beds, and to view a display of rugs and baskets made by students.[28]

The Cotton Blossom Singers who performed in the Adirondacks constituted only one of up to thirteen male, female, and mixed trios, quartets, and quintets that Piney Woods sent out on the country's roads—singing spirituals and secular "plantation" songs and reading dialect poems by black poet Paul Lawrence Dunbar.[29] The group performed in Adirondack venues a long way from resort centers habituated to the appearance of such groups: among them Broadalbin, Fulton County (where their annual visits in the late 1920s and 1930s were "eagerly anticipated by all music lovers"), and the tiny summer communities of Otter Lake in Forestport, Oneida County, and Star Lake in Clifton, St. Lawrence County.[30] Their and similar tours came to an end with the Great Depression.

9

Baseball, and a Little Basketball

BASEBALL WAS DUBBED THE NATIONAL GAME as early as 1867, and professional teams began playing against one another in the 1870s. The sport was central to community life in the Adirondacks as it was elsewhere. Every town wanted to field a team, but few were large enough to support one. Cities, on the other hand, such as Schenectady, some forty miles south of the park, might have dozens of them in the early twentieth century: neighborhood teams, factory teams, occupational teams, service club teams.[1] Most were amateur clubs, but a number were semiprofessional (meaning that members were compensated on a per game basis), and a very few were professional—made up of full-time, paid players. African Americans were included on the rosters of a number of top teams throughout the country (principally in the North) until 1887, when baseball's unwritten color line was firmly drawn with the refusal of a Chicago-based all-white team to play against an integrated team from Newark, New Jersey. Organized baseball recognized the League of Colored Baseball Clubs as a legitimate minor league that same year. The sport's color line would not be knowingly crossed again for six decades.[2]

The first black American thought to have played baseball in the Adirondacks was John Carsaw, who earned a reputation "as a good catcher, a strong thrower to bases and a heavy hitter" in Port Henry, Essex County, in the early 1880s. Carsaw was particularly remembered for wearing the first chest protector seen in the region: a "white contraption" that "contrasted strongly with the color of the man who wore it."[3]

Black baseball players arrived in the Adirondacks in numbers with Frank Thompson, the Hotel Champlain's headwaiter from 1890 to 1903. Thompson had seen moneymaking possibilities in the sport, and he is known in baseball circles as a founder of the Cuban Giants, the first African American team to achieve national renown. Initially based in Newark, New Jersey, the team's first roster included players who worked under Thompson as waiters at a summer hotel on New York's Long Island where he was headwaiter in 1885.[4] In the winter, Cuban Giants followed Thompson to St. Augustine, Florida, when he took on the role of headwaiter at Henry Flagler's Hotel Ponce de Leon. A local newspaper reported in January 1889 that "a pick nine" of "colored" staff members from the hotel would play a baseball game against a "colored" team from the Hotel Alcazar—another Flagler hotel. The two teams, it was said, possessed some of the best black talent in the country and were composed mostly of Cuban Giants.[5]

Thompson immediately organized a team of waiters and other black staff members upon his arrival at the Hotel Champlain. At first designated the Ponce de Leons,[6] the hotel's "colored nine" was in short order renamed the Hotel Champlains. It played against local teams based on both sides of Lake Champlain, against teams fielded by other Adirondack hotels (many of which packed their summer staffs with local and college baseball players), and against the Cuban Giants, who, thanks to the Thompson association, played the region during eight consecutive summers from 1890 through 1897. It was said that several Cuban Giants doubled as employees at the Hotel Champlain.[7]

Thompson's skill as a publicist led to the scheduling of well-advertised special trains to carry spectators to game venues, and the local press reported enthusiastically on the black teams' "lively," "closely contested and exciting" performances.[8] Coverage reflected contemporary attitudes to race, but appreciation of the players' skills and the teams' consciously constructed image of middle-class respectability meant that it was rarely offensive. "No people can play ball with greater vim than the colored gentlemen from Hotel Champlain," announced one regional newspaper in 1898.[9] Another commented

12. Cuban X-Giants, 1895. Courtesy of National Baseball Hall of Fame Library, Cooperstown, NY.

that the team's opponents "will have foemen worthy of their steel as ballplayers or as men who know how to conduct themselves with dignity on all occasions."[10] The Cuban X-Giants, a team made up in part of defectors from the Giants, began playing the region in 1896 and was lauded in the Plattsburgh press as "the strongest team of colored players in the country."[11]

Both the Cuban Giants and the X-Giants played dual roles as entertainers and sportsmen, incorporating vaudevillian buffoonery into their playing to release racial tension and keep their white audiences interested.[12] Shadowball, a fast-paced pantomime of live baseball played without a ball, was a comic favorite. The Cuban Giants' playing style was on display in 1897, when a Plattsburgh newspaper reported under the headline "They Are Real Giants" that team members "generated much amusement by their ridiculous remarks and antics, but played ball all the same, and not one of them was caught napping on the bases."[13]

One of Thompson's summer hires was a young African American who came close to becoming a major league baseball player. William Clarence Matthews was an Alabama-born member of the Hotel Champlain staff and baseball team for two summers in the early 1900s.[14] Having prepared at Tuskegee Institute for Phillips Academy in Andover, Massachusetts, he was then a member of the class of 1905 at Harvard, where he completed more than the required academic coursework while working year-round to support himself. He also played college baseball: as a crackerjack shortstop and the Harvard team's leading hitter during his final three years at the university. Directly after graduation, Matthews became the only black player in a professional baseball league when he joined the Burlington team of the independent Northern League of Vermont, against which he had played as a Champlain employee. It was rumored that summer that the Boston Nationals (later the Braves) were interested in hiring him—some forty years before Jackie Robinson made history by signing with the Brooklyn Dodgers—but open hostility to the scheme scotched the young man's chance of playing professional ball. Matthews went directly on to law school, was admitted to the bar in 1907, and was serving as an Assistant US Attorney General in San Francisco at his early death in 1926.[15]

Black staff members at the Sagamore and Fort William Henry hotels followed the lead of the Hotel Champlain in organizing baseball teams of their own. There were at one point in the mid-1890s three Sagamore teams under longtime headwaiter F. H. Griffin's management—the Bostons, the Washingtons, and the New Yorks—playing against one another on the hotel's baseball field and attracting enthusiastic audiences.[16] A team of waiters from the Fort William Henry occasionally played against a "picked nine" made up of recruits from the village of Caldwell on a baseball diamond across from the post office.[17] In the absence of Frank Thompson's promotional skills, however, both the Sagamore and the Fort William Henry teams played strictly local games, and it was not long before homegrown support transferred to all-white squads made up of vacationing guests and town residents. But black teams continued to resurface, at least at the Sagamore. A team of players from Warrensburg "applied a coat of whitewash" to the hotel squad in 1912 in defeating a team "made up entirely of colored men," among whom were "some excellent players." Sagamore's black bellboys issued a challenge to "any and all teams on the lake" during the summer of 1913.[18]

Local Adirondack promoters sponsored amateur town teams that competed against one another in loosely organized, often short-lived, leagues. Fans wanted to see other opponents than the two or three clubs that managers were able to rustle up nearby, and in the 1920s some teams began contracting to play exhibition games against black "barnstorming" or traveling teams to attract larger audiences and increase gate receipts. Popular between the two world wars, these nomadic teams had no home field, but headquartered wherever their manager felt he could make a few dollars: playing a "home game" on Sundays and traveling to neighboring venues (which could be anywhere within a 150-mile radius) for exhibition games during the rest of the week. The teams played for a set fee or for a percentage of admission revenue. A small audience turnout meant low reimbursement, while a rainy day could mean no compensation at all.[19] Barnstorming black teams now and again fielded players gifted enough to compete in the major leagues had they been allowed to do so, and represented the highest level of play seen in many localities.

"Port Henry is certainly going strong on colored teams this season," it was announced in late July 1923. "Next Sunday they have a game scheduled with the Havana Colored Giants, this being the third negro aggregation to play in Port Henry this summer. This team trimmed the Saranac Lake outfit last Sunday by a score of 10 to 2 and they will evidently give the fast Port Henryites a stiff battle."[20]

The black team that visited the region most frequently during the 1920s and 1930s was managed and partly owned by African American George "Chappie" Johnson. Born in Ohio in 1870, Johnson became a professional baseball player in 1896. He played for the next two decades with black teams in the Midwest and the East, acquiring a reputation as an "exciting, colorful, unique character who was probably the outstanding Negro catcher during the pre–World War I years." In 1913 and 1914 Johnson was on the roster of the Mohawk Colored Giants, a professional team of African Americans based in Schenectady. He managed the team in 1914.[21]

As Johnson aged and his skills eroded, he played less and managed more. He first appeared in the Adirondacks with a barnstorming team in 1922 known as Chappie Johnson's Philadelphia All-Coloured Stars.[22] Two years later his recently organized Stars or All-Stars, a team that would play extensively in eastern and central New York during the next decade, contracted with Ticonderoga's local team to play an exhibition game for a guaranteed fee of $175. The game broke all attendance records at Ticonderoga's Weed Field with 830 paid admissions and pulled the Ticonderoga club out of an impending financial hole.[23] In 1925 the Ticonderoga team invited "our old favorite rivals" to compete again in what the local newspaper would call "the fastest, most exciting and closest played game" of the season. The Stars confronted the Ticonderoga team at least twice more that summer, winning every game (designedly, by small margins) and proving the biggest drawing card among visiting challengers.[24]

Johnson was a popular figure, and his players were considered "good boys": known for showing up on time, never causing trouble, and always giving an audience its money's worth.[25] The team earned respect with its skillful play, one Adirondack newspaper reporting in 1924 that it was "rated by many experts the best semi-professional club in New York State."[26] In the tradition of the old Cuban Giants, the Stars and other black barnstormers engaged in vaudevillian horseplay on the ball field, at least during pregame practice sessions and between innings. Shadowball, the onetime mainstay of the Cuban Giants and X-Giants, was a drawing card for the Stars, and their singing between innings was "especially commented on" in 1925.[27] Such hijinks were considered by many blacks to be demeaning to the race, but players recognized that what they offered was in part show business, and Johnson's team produced a good show. A few black road clubs took clowning too far. Particularly offensive to an Adirondack audience was a team called the Zulu Cannibal Giants, whose members wore grass skirts, sported straggling hair and war paint, and played under assumed African names. They showed up in the region twice in the mid-1930s, where their "weird" antics drew strong reactions. "Please cancel all further 'circus games,' such as the Zulu Cannibals, or whatever that baseball atrocity masquerading as a team called themselves," admonished Ticonderoga's newspaper in 1936.[28]

Johnson's players liked and respected their manager, who, according to one of them, knew "every place where a black man could get something to eat or a bed to sleep in, just as he knew the real redneck towns to pass by, just as he remembered every level crossing, river, honest garage man, and maybe every last damn blade of grass, in North America."[29] His reputation meant that he was able to attract high-class talent to the Stars. On the team's early roster was colorful personality William "Buck" Ewing, an exciting young catcher from Ohio nicknamed the "colored Babe Ruth." Ewing eventually settled in Schenectady, played with the Mohawk Colored Giants, and became a local legend.[30] Years later, Ticonderoga fans still recalled the 1926 game when "Big Buck Ewing, giant colored catcher for Chappie Johnson's All Stars, slapped that super-home run 'way out past that tree back of center field, and the echoes from spectators' gasps could still be heard . . . on the following Sunday."[31]

The Stars were based at various times in Schenectady, Amsterdam, Saratoga, Glens Falls, Ogdensburg, Oneonta, and Montreal, and they generally moved about the countryside in a fleet of three gaily decorated Oldsmobile touring cars. The players themselves were peripatetic. Johnson's club, like other black teams, was subject to frequent raids by other teams. Contracts meant little, there were no reserve clauses that tied players to one team, and money talked. Players made the best deals for themselves that they could. Jimmy Shields, for example, a black college student from Richmond, Virginia, was a summer porter at a Lake George hotel and already committed to pitching some games for Johnson's Stars and Schenectady's Mohawk Colored Giants when he signed on with the local Warrensburg team to prop up its shaky season in the summer of 1926.[32] An interracial baseball team was a rare phenomenon in the Adirondacks, and Warrensburg promoted its "colored ace," taken on "at a considerable added expense," in pleading for greater audience turnout than its usual three to five hundred spectators. "Unless the games are better supported," threatened Warrensburg's management at the beginning of August, "the team will be taken out of town on Sundays, as there is a big demand for the club in other places with the brand of baseball they are offering." Shields missed a game on August 8 in fulfilling a commitment to Johnson in Saratoga Springs, and Warrensburg lost its game.[33] There was no subsequent newspaper reportage of the team; it may not have survived. Shields pitched for the Mohawk Colored Giants in 1927 before disappearing from upstate New York's baseball history.[34]

Johnson's Stars played the region every season but one between 1924 and 1935. Johnson himself still participated in the occasional game into his fifties—often as an outfielder. In 1927, the year he did not field a team in the Adirondacks, he concentrated his energies on managing a black team in the Semi-Pro League of Montreal, where he was referred to as "the most picturesque baseball figure in the city."[35] Most of Johnson's former team members stayed behind in New York, playing with a team owned and agented by Hank Bozzi, white owner of the Mohawk Colored Giants, and managed by Johnson's former star catcher Buck Ewing.[36] Ewing's Colored Stars briefly "represented" Ticonderoga during the season, playing three early games in its Weed Park against out-of-town teams: the D and H Generals (sponsored by the Delaware and Hudson Railroad); the Rochester Cuban Giants; and the Howe Scale Company of Rutland, Vermont. "The manner in which the fans cheered the colored boys and razzed the D and H Generals was indicative of the fact that in baseball all thoughts and opinions of race, color and creed are thrown to the four winds," according to one journalist.[37] A 1929 exhibition game in Lake Placid between Johnson's All-Stars, still based in Montreal, and the (black) All-Cubans of Havana was a pricey undertaking, noted the local paper: "the guarantee exceeding anything ever before given for baseball here."[38]

The Great Depression took its toll on Chappie Johnson's Stars, as it did on all touring black baseball clubs. The Stars played the region in 1933, making a "clean sweep" of a two-day series against a

"Tupper-Sunmount" team on the grounds of the Veterans Administration Hospital in Tupper Lake, but by 1935 the team was struggling financially.[39] It participated in two leagues that season: the Northern League (Chateaugay, Lyon Mountain, Malone, Plattsburgh, Saranac Lake, and Tupper Lake) and the Eastern Ontario League. Nevertheless, it was unable to make ends meet.[40] In Ogdensburg, where the team based itself in the early part of the summer, "they didn't have a nickel," according to their local promoter. He "was hitting people up for five dollars and ten dollars to keep them eating. . . . They had it rough."[41] Ogdensburg fans held a benefit to meet the team's outstanding debts in midsummer—raising three hundred dollars to pay its hotel, restaurant, gas station, and sporting goods store bills—but the team played badly, missed dates, and abandoned Ogdensburg in August.[42] Johnson never again brought his team back to northeastern New York. He continued to manage the Stars, however, through 1939, playing them mostly in Canada and in midwestern states just south of the Canadian border. In 1940, at the age of sixty-three, he accepted a position as sports trainer at Clemson University in South Carolina, twenty-three years before the school welcomed its first black student. He remained at Clemson until his 1949 death and was, according to Clemson's baseball coach, "well-liked and a most efficient workman, despite his advanced age."[43]

Although Chappie Johnson's Stars were the crowd-pleasing favorite, other black clubs made regular forays into the Adirondacks before, during, and after the team's reign. The most frequent of them was Schenectady's Mohawk Colored Giants. Port Henry's team, editorialized a local journalist in 1937, "has as much chance to defeat the Giants as we have of cuffing Joe Louis on the jaw and getting away with it."[44] Among other black teams to play the area were the Red Socks (1921), Manhattan Colored Giants (1922), Brooklyn Royal Giants (1923), Boston Black Sox (1926), Cuban Red Sox (1927), Ithaca Red Caps (1932), Brooklyn Colored Giants (1932), Newark Colored Giants (1947), and Chicago Bombers (1948).

The number of black players recruited to organized baseball's minor leagues gradually increased after Jackie Robinson joined the major league's Brooklyn Dodgers in 1947, and the talent that had made black touring teams exciting to watch in out-of-the-way venues like the Adirondacks was no longer available. It was an improving world for black baseball players, but residents of small towns in the Adirondacks lost the opportunity to see some of the best athletes in the country at work on their own playing fields.

Baseball had a long history as a developing American sport. Basketball "sprang full-blown" in the winter of 1891–92 from the inventive brain of James Naismith, a physical education instructor at the International YMCA Training School (now Springfield College) in Massachusetts. Naismith created the game as a fast-paced alternative to the indoor calisthenics, gymnastics, and children's games endured by restless college men during long New England winters. The first professional teams began playing the sport in 1896.[45]

Like baseball, basketball was a segregated sport, although a handful of blacks played for white professional teams before World War II. There were only two nationally known black teams in the game's first fifty years, the earliest of them being the New York Renaissance: named after the Renaissance Casino in Harlem where black players, forbidden the use of whites' gymnasiums, practiced in the high-ceilinged casino ballroom. By the late 1920s, the "Rens" were barnstorming widely in the East and Midwest, playing about 130 games between November and mid-April every year, most of them against semiprofessional teams in small towns and cities. The team won the first professional basketball championship in 1939, when the quintet beat out the white Oshkosh All-Stars at the World Professional Basketball Tournament in Chicago. At the close of the team's final season, 1948–49, when racial bars in professional sports were falling, it boasted a 2,318 to 381 won-lost record over twenty-six years.[46]

The Renaissance played a few games in the Adirondacks, basing itself in a major city nearby—Albany, Troy, or perhaps Schenectady—to avoid racial incidents in hotels and restaurants in smaller communities on the road. (What the team called "eating out of a grocery store bag" was automatic on their tours, with players making their own sandwiches from store-bought ingredients.[47]) For several years the team played a near-annual game against a semiprofessional team sponsored by the International Paper Company and based in Corinth, Saratoga County, partly inside the Adirondack Park. As reported by a regional newspaper of the two teams' first encounter in February 1927, the Rens' "most wonderful exhibition of team work, speed, and everything else that goes to make a high class" quintet made it "apparent from the very opening of play that the Corinth outfit had not a chance"; the visiting team "held the locals bewildered the greater part of the 40 minutes of play."[48] Despite the lopsided competition, fans traveled long distances to enjoy the contests through 1934. The Rens played once in 1927–28 in Warren County against North Creek's American Legion squad, but a scheduled 1931 game against the National Home Stores club of Plattsburgh was cancelled due to "King Winter" and an accumulation of treacherous snow.[49]

The black basketball landscape changed in the East with the ascendance of the Harlem Globetrotters. This team had its genesis in Chicago in the mid-1930s and never ventured further east than western Pennsylvania before winning the World Tournament in 1940. At first a "straight" basketball team, it developed crowd-pleasing tricks—spinning the ball on a fingertip, fancy dribbling, comedy routines—to combat boredom during the one-sided games it played as a barnstorming team.[50] The Globetrotters made two known forays into the Adirondack region, playing in Plattsburgh and Lake Placid in November 1952 and Lake Placid in 1955. Other black basketball teams that made at least one Adirondack appearance included the Philadelphia Colored Giants (Corinth) in 1930; the Harlem Aces (Lake Placid, Port Henry, Tupper Lake) in 1947, 1948, and 1950; and the Harlem Roadkings (Edinburgh in Saratoga County, Port Henry, Tupper Lake) in the early 1950s.

The Adirondacks produced two African American basketball players of its own. Born in the South but raised in the mining community of Moriah, Essex County (see chapter 15), both Norman Gates and Murray "Pops" Bullock were baseball stars at the town's Port Henry High School, graduating in 1946 and 1949, respectively. Thanks in large part to their skills, Port Henry fielded the Adirondack Park's first and only semiprofessional basketball team for five years beginning in late 1949. Initially dubbed the Port Henry Orioles, the integrated squad changed its name to the Port Henry Hawks and joined the short-lived (one season only) New York Semi-Pro Basketball League in November 1953.[51] The Hawks won twenty-seven of their twenty-eight league games and the league title that season.[52] Gates and Bullock both served in the military before returning to school for college degrees and becoming teachers.

The 1950 draft by the Boston Celtics of Chuck Cooper, the first black player to join a National Basketball Association team, changed basketball. Again, national sport was enriched by the breakdown of the color line, but signaled the end of an exciting era for Adirondack sports enthusiasts.

10

Saranac Lake and Tuberculosis

SARANAC LAKE IS, and has been for more than one hundred years, the largest center of year-round population in the Adirondack Park. It came to prominence as the hub of a bustling industry in the treatment of tuberculosis (popularly known as consumption) that began with the founding in 1884 of the Adirondack Cottage Sanitarium, a private, subsidized facility for working men and women in the early stages of the disease. The sanitarium was established by Dr. Edward Livingston Trudeau, himself a tuberculosis sufferer who traveled north from New York City in 1873 to die in the Adirondacks, where he had enjoyed hunting and fishing vacations. Following a regime of rest, good food, and hours spent outside in the mountain air, he regained much of his strength.[1]

Trudeau was not the only early seeker of relief from poor health in the region. Henry Ossawa Tanner, born in 1858 to a minister of the African Methodist Episcopal Church and his wife, a former slave, was one of the first blacks to achieve international fame as an artist. In 1878 the twenty-year-old Tanner made the first of three journeys from Philadelphia to the modest Rainbow Inn on Rainbow Lake in Brighton, Franklin County, some eleven miles northwest of Saranac Lake, in search of a cure for what he called "a severe illness, from which I did not completely recover for many years."[2] The inn was launched in 1860 by James Wardner, an early Brighton pioneer who had come to the area for his own health. It accommodated fifty guests and was popular with hunting and fishing parties.[3]

"Not a little benefitted from this trip," according to Tanner, he returned to Philadelphia in 1879, where he studied at the Pennsylvania Academy of Fine Arts as the school's only black student and a mentee of artist and teacher Thomas Eakins. He made two more pilgrimages to Brighton, one in 1882 and another in 1886, later recalling "those lovely friends at Rainbow Lake—how I have wished I might be able to repay them for some of their kindnesses." Tanner relocated to France in 1891, where the 1897 purchase of one of his paintings by the French government cemented his reputation. He was elected to the French Légion d'Honneur in 1923, and in 1927 he became the first black artist honored with full membership in New York's National Academy of Art and Design.[4]

Dr. Trudeau took up winter residence in Saranac Lake in 1876 and opened a small medical practice. Doctors elsewhere began sending their consumptive patients to the village, where Trudeau and a growing medical team (among them other doctors with tuberculosis) oversaw treatment at what became the first successful treatment center for the disease in the country. The Adirondack Cottage Sanitarium, renamed the Trudeau Sanatorium after Trudeau's death in 1915, provided a temporary home for some three to four hundred consumptive patients a year on a broad campus dotted with stylish living and service buildings, many of them gifts from wealthy donors.[5]

The village grew rapidly as its reputation as a "health resort" spread, nearly sextupling its population in twenty years: from 768 in 1890 to 4,983 in 1910. Hotels, privately run boardinghouses (many of which functioned as small sanatoria, or cure cottages), and single-family homes accommodated tuberculosis patients. Charitable organizations followed Trudeau's lead in opening sanatoria nearby to take advantage of the region's supposedly curative climate and Saranac Lake's specialized medical practice. The village continued to expand: by 1918 it was home to roughly 5,000 full-time inhabitants and a floating population of 1,200 to 1,500 health seekers and their relatives who spent months or even years in the town.[6] A 1917 town map documented over 520 buildings—almost half of its structures—as providing lodgings for tuberculosis sufferers.[7]

Black patients were not welcome at the Trudeau Sanatorium. Nor were black physicians. Indeed, white medical practitioners had shown themselves slow to accept black health professionals into established institutions. New York City's Bellevue Hospital, for example, founded in 1736 and the oldest public hospital in the country, did not open its doors to black interns and residents until faced with a wartime shortage of white medical staff in 1918; a black physician was not appointed to the house staff of a New York municipal hospital until 1929.[8] The situation was no different upstate. The University of Rochester's medical school refused as late as 1939 to provide a comprehensive degree program to black medical students on the pretext that it could not offer them clinical training in the sensitive areas of obstetrics and gynecology. "When the attitude of society changes sufficiently to permit further medical training for Negroes in medicine and nursing," it announced testily, "we shall provide the training." Needless to say, no black doctors or nurses were then on staff at the university hospital.[9]

Tuberculosis was a ruthless killer of African Americans—responsible for the death of 445.8 per 100,000 blacks across the country in 1910 as compared to 153 per 100,000 whites.[10] And despite their exclusion from Trudeau, a number of blacks with the disease chose to travel to Saranac Lake for medical treatment. Many or most doctors in the village were willing to treat them, and they presumably had access to the free dispensary maintained by the Trudeau Sanatorium that provided daily medical advice to those living in the community. They were accepted as patients at Saranac Lake's privately supported Reception Hospital, opened in 1905 and originally serving as a facility for those seriously ill with tuberculosis, and at the General Hospital, a twelve-bed facility established in 1913 for surgical and non-tuberculosis-related cases that offered "aid to sick or disabled persons of every creed, nationality and color."[11]

Black Americans' trust in Saranac Lake, a health center overseen wholly by white doctors and far from most black residential concentrations, had roots in a phenomenon observed in New York City in 1905. The city's Department of Health, which had a less stormy relationship with race than that found in its hospitals,[12] offered a special clinic that year for black tuberculosis patients staffed by black doctors. "It was thought that such patients would attend the clinic more readily were they treated by physicians of their own race," it was reported. But, in fact, the clinic was poorly patronized and closed after less than seven months following the discovery that blacks were "not only willing, but often eager" to attend mixed classes run by white practitioners.[13] A study of interracial social behavior in the late 1930s corroborated the earlier finding in noting the inclination of African Americans with critical illnesses to prefer white above black doctors because of their greater prestige and their possession of more sophisticated equipment.[14]

Dr. Lawrason Brown, the resident physician at Trudeau from 1901 to 1912, organized the Saranac Lake Society for the Control of Tuberculosis in 1907. The society acted as a clearinghouse for the steady influx of tuberculosis patients who arrived unannounced in Saranac Lake, many of them destitute or in the advanced stages of the disease. Most were met at the train station, taken to a hotel where they were examined and, if not bound for a particular address, given the names of several approved boardinghouses or cure cottages with vacancies that met their perceived requirements.[15] Ethnic and racial compatibility were deemed fundamental considerations in patient placement.

Boarding cottages were generally rented from individuals or agencies serving the local industry. They changed hands frequently and were run, not by longtime Saranac Lake residents, but by proprietors who arrived in the village as a result of their own or a family member's poor health or what they saw as a business opportunity.[16] Amenities varied but included basic nursing care, meals, and access to the open-air "cure porches" that were an essential feature of the Saranac Lake regimen and on which patients passed hours a day lying still and quietly breathing. Individual cottages specialized in specific populations: Jews, Greeks, Spanish-speakers. A very few catered to African Americans.

Disinfection records for Saranac Lake noted the death of a black tuberculosis patient in June 1912. Identified by race rather than by name, the deceased had resided in a boarding cottage at 94 Lake

Flower Avenue, a main street into town on the lakeside edge of a neighborhood in which a number of black residents then lived.[17] Also chronicled that year was the May departure of "Mr. Harris," a patient from "Poyas Cottage" at 41 Pine Street, for Baltimore.[18] This entry made no mention of race, but Warren and Carmen Poyas were enumerated as "black" in the 1915 state census. It is unknown what brought the couple, whose occupations were recorded in that year's state census as chauffeur and dressmaker, to the village, but they appear to have maintained a small boardinghouse catering to a black clientele for a brief period. The Poyases relocated to Plainfield, New Jersey, later in the decade, where they were active in black organizations.

James H. Garner, for ten years the South Carolina state agent of the "largest colored insurance company in the world," died in Saranac Lake in 1915.[19] But it was not until around 1917 that another boardinghouse appealing explicitly to black tenants opened. Its African American proprietor, Sylvia Alston, was from South Carolina and had arrived in Saranac Lake by 1915, when she and her husband were cook and butler in the household of J. Peyton Clark, a civil engineer with a consumptive wife. Not long thereafter, Mrs. Alston left the Clarks' employ and opened a cottage at 26 Lake Flower Avenue from which several black patients registered with the society during the next two years. The thirty-five-year-old Alston was recorded in the 1920 census as the keeper of a boardinghouse without boarders. Her name thereafter disappeared from Saranac Lake records.

Hunter C. Haynes, originally from Alabama, settled in as a patient next door to Alston's boardinghouse at 28 Lake Flower Avenue in April 1917. He had begun his career as a barber and was the inventor of the Haynes Razor Strop, the patent for which he profitably sold. During a subsequent career as a motion picture producer and director, he achieved some celebrity with his motion picture *Uncle Remus's First Visit to New York*, popular with a black audience upon its 1914 release.[20] Haynes died in Saranac Lake in January 1918.

John and Viola Ramsey opened a boarding facility for African Americans at 24 Lake Flower Avenue in 1923. John Ramsey, born in 1886 and the son of a former slave, had relocated to Saranac Lake in

1908 after spending several winters as an elevator attendant in New York City and summers as a waiter at the Hotel Champlain. He moved to Saranac Lake on the recommendation of an elevator passenger whose brother-in-law George L. Starks owned the town's Adirondack Hardware Store. Ramsey became the store's janitor (and later Starks's chauffeur) and bought the Lake Flower building lot in 1921.[21] He personally built the house that his wife, Viola (whom he married in New York City in 1922),[22] would operate as a boardinghouse accommodating four or five lodgers. This, like other boardinghouses run by black proprietors, was not a "cure cottage" in the formal sense, as it welcomed healthy as well as consumptive lodgers. However, since neither of the two black boarders living with the Ramseys at the time of the 1930 census—an English-born hotel clerk and an eighteen-year-old girl from Georgia—was working, it can be assumed that both were tuberculosis victims.

John Ramsey's sister Mattie Reid followed her brother to Saranac Lake, where she bought a home in 1927 at 155 Pine Street and operated it as a boarding cottage. Ten years older than her brother and the eldest sister among nine children, Mattie had moved her siblings from Georgia and raised them in New York City after their mother's early death. She was in her mid-forties when she arrived in Saranac Lake. Her husband, Claud Reid, whom she had married in New Mexico,[23] was a career soldier before his discharge there from the army in 1919 with disabilities, among them heart disease. He spent much of his subsequent life as a patient in veterans hospitals but often joined his wife in Saranac Lake during the summer.

One of Mattie Reid's early tuberculosis patients was Lucius Eugene "Bud" Aiken, a thirty-year-old trombonist and cornet player with Perry Bradford's Jazz Phools in New York City (a band with which Louis Armstrong also played). Aiken's musician friends raised the money to send him to Saranac Lake, but he arrived in town in 1927 with a "far advanced" case of the disease and died less than a week after settling in.[24] The generosity shown to Aiken by his professional associates was not exceptional in the black musical community. Bandleader, drummer, and first "King of Swing" William Henry

"Chick" Webb saved the life of guitarist John Trueheart, a longtime friend, by paying his salary and expenses while he cured in Saranac Lake during 1937 and 1938. Webb died of tuberculosis himself in 1939 at the age of thirty-four.[25]

Boarders at Viola Ramsey's cottage came through word-of-mouth referrals. Mattie Reid, whose facility was somewhat larger, advertised in African American newspapers. A 1931 classified announcement in the *Norfolk (VA) Journal and Guide* read:

> Sanitorium for sick and convalescent patents [*sic*] in the Adirondack Mountains. Specially fitted for tuberculosis patients—for particulars, write—Mrs. Mattie B. Reid, Superintendent.[26]

"Private" was included in the occupational listing of two of the three nonworking residents among seven boarders at Reid's cottage in the 1930 census: a waitress in a "private" home (thirty, from Nova Scotia); and a "private chauffeur" (twenty, from Virginia). It is possible that their employers covered their Saranac Lake expenses.

Two other black entrepreneurs marketed mixed boarding facilities to an African American clientele in the 1920s and 1930s. Peter Green arrived in Saranac Lake as a domestic servant; his occupation was listed as cook in a private home in the 1925 state census. Green managed a rented cottage at 147 Pine Street while pursuing his primary occupation. Like Mattie Reid, he promoted his venture beyond Saranac Lake. An October 1928 advertisement in the African American newspaper *New York Amsterdam News* announced:

> **Green's Sanitarium**
>
> Adirondack Pine View Cottage
>
> A place for broken-down and convalescent patients, also railroad porters. Clean, airy rooms, absolutely free from city noises, also one apartment for tubercular patients. Reasonable rates.
>
> Pete Green, Superintendent[27]

By 1940 Green, listed in that year's census as a general worker for a private family, was managing another boarding establishment, this one at 24 Olive Street. Two of the five black men lodging with him were employed: one as a domestic servant and one as a dishwasher in a private sanatorium. All of his tenants, like Green himself, had been living at the same address for the previous five years.

Yet another advertisement for a Saranac Lake boarding cottage appeared in the *New York Amsterdam News* in September 1931:

> **Hopkins Cottage**
>
> Now open for business; overlooking Lake Flower. Vacation, rest and health resort. We take in Tubercular cases.[28]

This boardinghouse was operated by Isidore and Margaret Clark, a Bermuda-born tailor and his wife who had been boarders at Mattie Reid's at the time of the 1930 census. It was customary to give names to boarding cottages, and the Clarks christened their enterprise Hopkins Cottage in honor of its previous owner: Margaret Hopkins, a practical nurse who had maintained a well-regarded, albeit expensive, facility for white patients elsewhere in Saranac Lake until her 1932 departure for New York City.[29] Hopkins Cottage did not appear in any local records as housing boarders, and may not have succeeded as a business venture. The Clarks were still living on Lake Flower Avenue in 1940, when Clark was a tailor in a dry cleaning shop.

Few blacks could afford to cure in private, single-family cottages, the luxurious Saranac Lake housing option for those who rented, bought, or built their own residences to provide a homelike atmosphere for tubercular family members. The wife of perhaps the only African American to opt for such housing left behind a record of the experience.

William Alphaeus Hunton was a son of Stanton Hunton, a one-time Virginia slave who purchased his freedom and migrated to Chatham, Ontario, where he was among a small group of abolitionists who worked with John Brown in 1858 to prepare for the following year's raid on Harper's Ferry. Born in 1863, William Hunton made a career with the Young Men's Christian Association, becoming the secretary of its newly created Colored Men's Department in 1890,

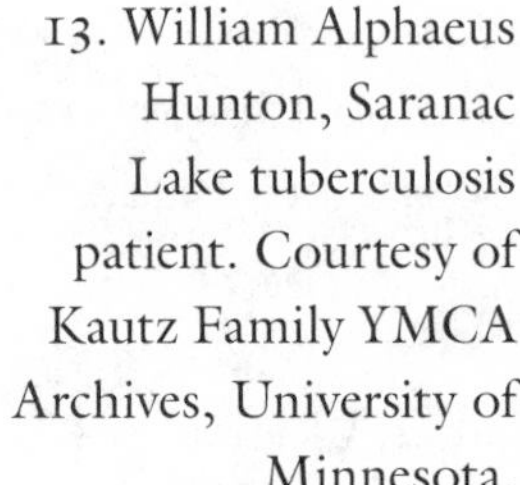

13. William Alphaeus Hunton, Saranac Lake tuberculosis patient. Courtesy of Kautz Family YMCA Archives, University of Minnesota.

and later the organization's international secretary. Gravely ill with tuberculosis, Hunton arrived in Saranac Lake with his wife and ten-year-old son in June 1914.[30] Their housing at 30 Franklin Avenue was arranged ahead of time, and W. F. Roberts, the proprietor of a number of local cure cottages,[31] met his tenants at the train station. A physician and trained nurse were waiting for the family at their cottage, and Hunton was put to bed on a sleeping porch with a panoramic mountain view. The family remained in Saranac Lake for seventeen months. Their son, Alphaeus Jr., went to school in the village,[32] a circumstance so common that by the 1920s it was estimated that the town accommodated some three to four hundred children of transients in its schools each year.[33] Hunton's health improved, and during his second Saranac Lake summer he was well enough to "thoroughly boss" his wife and son as they planted and maintained a garden that provided vegetables for their own and friends' consumption and won blue ribbons at the Essex County Fair. By November 1915 Hunton was considered well enough to leave for New York, where he suffered a relapse not many months later. Too ill to return to Saranac Lake, he died in November 1916.[34]

Hunton's wife later wrote that her husband had found living in Saranac Lake a "profound experience," thanks in part to his immersion in "the daily miracle of that visible world of beauty that stretched before us." "Every one there," she added, "whom he had touched and known had been exceptionally kind—ministers, physicians, and civic leaders had all called and invited him to participate in their affairs."[35] As there were no black ministers, physicians, or civic leaders in town, it is safe to assume that, thanks to his background and his network of connections, the Huntons lived largely in a white world during their Saranac Lake sojourn.

An energetic minister of the AME Zion Church arrived in Saranac Lake in the fall of 1923, taking up residence at Mattie Reid's boardinghouse. What brought the Reverend W. B. Carr to Saranac Lake is not clear. The African American newspaper *New York Age* suggested before his arrival that he was "en route to the Adirondack Mountains in the interest of the education work of the race." By the following spring Carr was recorded as having conducted AME Zion services at the church "mission" at his Pine Street address during the winter while occasionally preaching in Syracuse.[36]

Reverend Carr had followed a peripatetic career. Educated at traditionally black Guadalupe College in Seguin, Texas, he landed in Watertown, New York, in 1916 and held later ministries in Amsterdam and Gloversville.[37] In March 1924, he announced from Saranac Lake the need for a tuberculosis sanatorium "for afflicted members of his race" and publicized a campaign to purchase a specific facility for this purpose: Fletcher's Farm, ten miles northeast of Saranac Lake in the Franklin, Franklin County, hamlet of Vermontville. The 225-acre property commanded "a beautiful outlook" and was touted as "long famous as a tuberculosis resort." It accommodated some sixty patients; came equipped with a main building, an annex, and several outbuildings; and could be bought, according to Carr, for $30,000.[38] The minister's ambitious plans for raising the funds to secure the property included a drive directed by "leading members of the race" in every New York county and "a monster benefit boxing show" in New York City featuring Harry White, a young black boxer from Niagara Falls.[39] Despite Carr's ability to garner newspaper attention, his plan did not materialize, and he disappeared from local view after May 1924. Carr might have been a tuberculosis patient who either died or recovered his health and left Saranac Lake, or he might have simply transferred his enthusiasms to other themes and another part of the country.

Two substantial sanatoria, one funded by the Catholic Church and one by private donors, were built at the turn of the twentieth century to the north of Saranac Lake in the vicinity of Brighton, Franklin County. Gabriels, a nonsectarian facility run by the Catholic Sisters of Mercy, opened in 1897. It theoretically accepted all comers, but there were no blacks in residence during census counts. Stony Wold, founded in 1901, was established by wealthy women, most of them from New York City, to care for consumptive working girls unable to afford treatment. In 1939 it began admitting men. A 1949 photograph suggests that it took seriously its mission to accept applicants "regardless of race, creed, religion or ability to pay." Stony Wold accommodated 150 and eventually treated over 6,000 patients.[40]

State approval was given in 1901 for the construction of the New York State Hospital for Incipient Pulmonary Tuberculosis in Ray Brook, a North Elba hamlet some three miles east of Saranac Lake. Ray Brook, as the hospital was known, accepted only patients with inadequate resources to pay for their own care. Opened in 1904, it was the second state-operated sanatorium to go up in the country. Welfare agencies in New York towns, cities, and counties submitted cases to physicians who selected patients for referral. There was room for racial bias among doctors who made these medical decisions (only 222 of 940 applicants were recommended for admission from the 1906 pool);[41] a physician made the "obvious" point in 1911 that "patients should be chosen along lines calculated to return the greatest possible

14. Stony Wold Christmas, 1949. Courtesy of Adirondack Collection, Saranac Lake Free Library.

good to the community."[42] District governments paid most fees for Ray Brook residents. Albany, Buffalo, and New York City furnished the bulk of patients in the sanatorium's early years. By the close of 1911 the Ray Brook facility housed a resident monthly population of 234, which later grew to 300. Its patients stayed for an average of somewhat over seven months.[43]

Ray Brook was racially inclusive in neither its patient population nor its staff. It did not accommodate blacks in any capacity on the day that federal census data was first gathered there in 1910. Later census figures for the sanatorium indicate that it housed one black patient in 1920 (Bristow Fitts, a Pullman porter who spent some seven years curing in the Adirondacks), none in 1930, and three in 1940. While no census data is yet available for 1950 or beyond, photographic evidence suggests that Ray Brook's patient body became more diverse over the years.

There were reportedly 650 World War I veterans with tuberculosis or mustard gas poisoning of the lungs living in Saranac Lake by 1922, and some 45 cure cottages in town had contracts with the US Veterans Administration to provide for their care.[44] The federal government constructed a 500-bed hospital that year for veterans with lung damage in Tupper Lake, twenty miles southwest of Saranac Lake. Sunmount Veterans Hospital eventually treated more than 35,000 former soldiers. Like Ray Brook, the hospital was not at first racially mixed. No black patients were in residence at the time of the 1930 census. By 1940, however, the facility housed 33 African Americans, representing nearly 8 percent of the 416 patients in the hospital population. The facility's 91-member resident staff included no blacks.

Most black veterans at Sunmount in 1940 were in their mid-forties. More than half recently hailed from New York City boroughs, but many of them had been born in southern states along the Atlantic coast: six from South Carolina, five from Virginia, four from North Carolina, and one from Georgia. Four patients had been employed as railroad porters in their active lives, and ten as porters in other industries. Four were listed as clerks (two of them with the post office), three as laborers, and two as automobile mechanics. Those with unusual careers included one club manager and one comedian.

The ninety-patient National Vaudeville Artists Association sanatorium, built by the association in 1928–29 in Saranac Lake to provide free tuberculosis treatment to members of its union, was the last large institutional facility to go up in the region. Ownership was transferred in 1935 to the Will Rogers Memorial Commission and the facility renamed in honor of the recently deceased actor and humorist; eligibility was extended to anyone involved in the "amusement" business. In 1949, when the hospital was beset by financial difficulties, the motion picture industry stepped in, and operations were taken over by Variety Clubs International, an organization of showmen, theatre operators, and film exhibitors. Fundraising succeeded in part by passing the hat during annual "Will Rogers audience collections" at movie theaters.[45]

No black patients were recorded at Will Rogers in the censuses of 1930 and 1940, but the facility did accept African Americans. The earliest known to have received medical attention there was Marshall "Garbage" Rogers, "one of the best known comedians on the vaudeville stage," who died of tuberculosis at the sanatorium in 1934.[46] Others included Louis Williams, musician and member of the popular tap-dancing team "Pops and Louis," who transferred in from a ward at Harlem Hospital with the assistance of the Negro Actors Guild in 1952 and subsequently reported receiving "good food, fresh air and sunshine, and plenty of rest"; and Bill Bailey, tap-dancing brother of Pearl Bailey and the first known performer of the "Moonwalk" later made famous by Michael Jackson.[47] Will Rogers began accepting patients suffering from all chest diseases in 1957, and the following year actress Evelyn Ellis, who in 1927 created the role of Bess in the Broadway play "Porgy" that became the basis for George Gershwin's "Porgy and Bess," died at Will Rogers of a heart ailment.[48]

Black tuberculosis patients in the Adirondacks were the subjects of at least two literary endeavors. A romantic little story entitled "The Mascot of Troop 1" coupled tuberculosis and racial harmony in Saranac Lake in 1917. This piece first appeared in *Boy's Life*, the journal of the Boy Scouts of America, an organization that officially did not discriminate on the basis of race. Its author was Stephen Chalmers, a onetime New York City journalist who had by now spent ten years curing in Saranac Lake. The story's protagonists were two Grand Central Station newsboys: black "Smokey" and white "Jimmy." When Smokey developed tuberculosis, Jimmy, "who read the papers he sold," arranged for his free train transport to Saranac Lake, where Smokey found a job delivering newspapers and Jimmy joined him when he too contracted the disease. The boys became progressively unwell but were providentially discovered in the loft above a paint shop in which they lived by members of the local scout troop. The scouts arranged for the famous Dr. Trudeau to visit them (climbing a ladder to their loft to do so). He secured their admittance to hospital, where they were cured. The boys joined the troop and wore its uniform, although the story pandered to racial prejudice in suggesting that Smokey became the troop's mascot rather than a full-fledged scout.[49]

Edgar T. Rouzeau, a black journalist who wrote the occasional short story for African American newspapers, came up with another Adirondack tuberculosis tale in 1939. His central character, a Red Cap porter at New York's West Side Station, had been stricken with tuberculosis and gone north on medical advice (to Lake Placid, according to the narrative), where he gradually recovered. His wife met the expenses of his cure by working, the protagonist believed, as a cook. He later discovered that she had, in fact, prostituted herself with another man during his absence, one she told she could never love but submitted to only "because her children were starving." The porter's moral dilemma—whether or not a wife was "ever justified in dishonoring her marital vows"—was resolved with his happy decision to forgive, and, what's more, to forget.[50]

The 1910 census for Saranac Lake recorded fifty-six African Americans among 4,963 residents, a number representing little more than 1 percent of the town's population. The percentage figure meant, however, that Saranac Lake was then home to the largest percentage agglomeration of African Americans within the Adirondack Park. Only Gloversville, Fulton County, among close-in neighboring population centers claimed more black residents in 1910: 194 in a substantially larger population of 20,642. Relative figures for other towns close to the park included Malone, Franklin County, four black among 6,467 residents; Plattsburgh, Clinton County, nine among 11,138; and Glens Falls, Warren County, twenty-two among 15,243.[51]

As noted in this chapter, a number of Saranac Lake's African American residents were tuberculosis patients and those who cared for them. But who were the others? What had brought them to the village? And how did they get along with the dominant white community and with one another?

11

Community Life in Saranac Lake

ITS ECONOMY may have been driven by tuberculosis and its treatment, but Saranac Lake was not a gloomy place—exuding "the natural high spirits of a boom town" and a "determination to preserve good cheer at all costs."[1] There was little stigma attached to the disease: one local doctor estimated in 1909 that as many as one in every six people walking the town's streets was a "lunger."[2] Residents and ambulatory patients mixed in the movie theaters and at sporting and cultural events. Residents made an effort to remain quiet during patients' compulsory afternoon rest period,[3] but Saranac Lake was in most ways similar to other northern communities of its size.

The proliferation of sanatorium facilities and related housing created an early demand for unskilled labor, and among the first African Americans to arrive in the village were descendants of settlers on Gerrit Smith's mid-nineteenth century Vermontville and Bloomingdale land grants. George Hazzard, grandson of Avery and son of Alexander Hazzard, and his wife, Libby, granddaughter of the first Stephen Warren Morehouse, appeared in town records in 1905 with three children; George was listed in 1915 census records as a building laborer, his wife as a washerwoman. Libby's brother John Morehouse and his wife (George's sister Mary) were in Saranac Lake with two children by 1910, when John was a "teamster, general trucking,"[4] and Mary a laundress, at home. Charles Johnson, step-grandson of Charles Henry Hazzard, farmed in Bloomingdale for a number of years before relocating to Saranac Lake as a teamster by 1920.

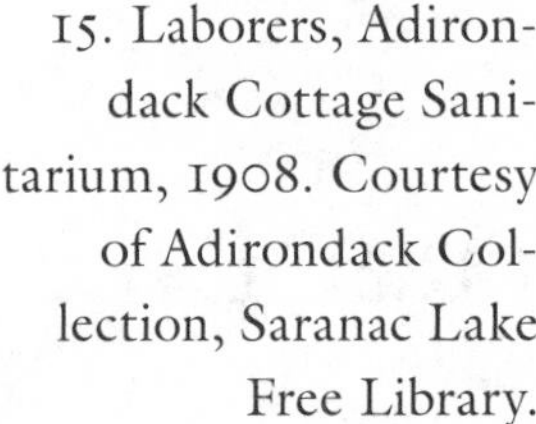

15. Laborers, Adirondack Cottage Sanitarium, 1908. Courtesy of Adirondack Collection, Saranac Lake Free Library.

The presence of family in the growing village attracted relatives in a typical pattern of community building. George and Mary Hazzard's sister Lizzie married teamster Charles Hazzard (a resident of New York City and perhaps a cousin) in 1907 at the Methodist church in Saranac Lake.[5] The couple remained in town through at least 1920, when Charles was listed in the census as a "mason, day work."

George Hazzard spent the rest of his life as a day laborer in Saranac Lake, dying at the age of seventy-nine in 1948. A local journalist occasionally reported in the 1940s on this elderly Saranac Lake "character," tendering him a small tribute upon his 1948 death: "We are going to miss the ready smile of George Hazzard around these parts. He, with all the discomfort that he must have experienced in recent years, was always cheerful, and always had a comeback to somebody's kidding remarks. I probably remember him as well as anyone in my 31 years here, and I always liked him."[6] The three children of George and Libby had long since relocated to the New York City area and to Washington, DC, by the time of their father's death.[7] When Libby Hazzard died in 1954 the Hazzard name disappeared from the Saranac Lake region after more than one hundred years. John and Mary

Morehouse and Charles Johnson also stayed on. The Morehouses' son Marshall, born in 1904, married Elizabeth Gorrow, a woman of Mohawk Indian ancestry, in the late 1930s, fathered nine children, and worked for thirty-five years at D. Cohen and Sons, a hardware store just outside of Saranac Lake. When his wife died of cancer in 1956, most of the couple's living children relocated to Baltimore, where an older sister had preceded them. But two Morehouse sons, Oscar and Victor, remained in Saranac Lake as fifth-generation descendants of Smith's land grant families. They still lived in the region in 2007.[8]

Other early incomers arrived in this moderately urbanized center from not far away. The Al Gordinier, "teamster, work team," living in Saranac Lake in 1910 with his wife and children was certainly the Albert Gordonier who had appeared in 1880 census records as a bachelor teamster domiciled in Wells, Hamilton County. John Emery was a farmer with a wife and seven children in Willsboro, Essex County, before relocating to Saranac Lake in 1910, where he was a "laborer, livery stable." The Emerys settled next door to their eldest daughter, Elizabeth, married to Ernest Williams, a laborer and woodsman born in 1888 in Redford, Clinton County, who had resided in Saranac Lake from childhood. When Williams died in 1955, he was buried, like many deceased Saranac Lake residents, black and white, from the Fortune Funeral Home, a longtime local institution. His obituary in the *Saranac Lake Adirondack Enterprise* made no reference to race: standard practice for the newspaper by early midcentury. Williams's three children all returned from homes in Buffalo for their father's funeral.[9]

As the occupations mentioned above suggest, African Americans in Saranac Lake did not climb far on the economic ladder. Black men were employed as "day," "odd jobs," and "common" laborers. Those who worked in the early decades of the twentieth century as teamsters or in livery stables were later supplanted by truck drivers, car washers, and car mechanics. Women, who for financial reasons seldom retired from the work force upon marriage, were likely to work as by-the-day or by-the-hour domestic servants, laundresses in their own homes, and "ironers" in commercial laundries.[10] Job instability meant that, as had been the case in Burlington, Vermont, the black population was highly mobile. Only four of the nine male family heads present in the community in 1910, for example, were still there in 1920. The village would not again claim as many black residents in the first half of the twentieth century as the fifty-six enumerated in the 1910 census.

Most early African American residents in Saranac Lake clustered on the southwestern edge of town—near where early cottages catering to black tuberculosis patients would be established on Lake Flower Avenue. Thirty-three blacks, for example, including seven heads of family, were crowded in 1910 into the neighborhood in three houses on one-block-long Center Street. By 1920 a pocket of black concentration (fifteen people in five families) could be found in an apartment house at 55½ Broadway in the heart of Saranac Lake's commercial district. Seven black residents—three couples and one daughter-in-law—were still living there in 1930. Down an alley behind the Colonial Theater, the building offered living quarters above a poolroom that was expanded around 1918 to accommodate a bakery shop and its oven at ground-floor level. Other African American individuals and families lived in mixed neighborhoods throughout the village.

Black social reformer Frederick Douglass verbalized the northern relationship between the black and white races as early as 1855 in writing: "Here at the North, our white friends—not our friends but our fellow citizens—have a regard for us—like us very well in our places,—and they have selected our places for us, and they have marked out the boundary lines for us,—and while we remain in the narrow circumference they describe for us, we are 'good fellows,' and they pat us on the head and say we are good boys."[11] Members of the white majority in Saranac Lake assiduously maintained their social distance from black neighbors, and there was little contact outside of work-based relationships.

The degree of social separation was highlighted in the 1920s in connection with fundraising for the Day Nursery, a daycare program for working parents with what whites called a "liberal" racial policy. Theatrical talent agent William Morris, who cured in Saranac Lake in the early 1900s and eventually built a summer home there, founded the nursery in 1919 and hosted annual summer benefits on its behalf

16. Saranac Lake Day Nursery, 1921. Courtesy of Adirondack Collection, Saranac Lake Free Library.

during the 1920s. It is apparent that no invitations to this event were issued to black village residents in 1923, for that year the nursery's white supporters organized a special "dance for the dusky hued" so that "colored folk" might, through their purchase of tickets, "cooperate with the community in aiding the enterprise, which has helped them." The evening program featured a cake walk—that outdated dance phenomenon of the 1890s—and a prize cup for the couple judged by their white hosts to have executed it "in the most correct and graceful manner."[12] How self-conscious must have been the paying guests at this shades-of-the-plantation evening.

In the absence of an African American church of any denomination, black residents belonged to a variety of Saranac Lake's white Protestant congregations: affiliations that claimed less than 1 percent of blacks in American Protestantism in midcentury. The most common choice for black churchgoers in Saranac Lake and elsewhere was Methodism, the majority preference of white Protestants across the country as well. But Presbyterianism and Episcopalianism, considered by the socially aspirational to be higher on the class scale, claimed a few adherents, as did Catholicism, said to appeal to some African Americans looking for an "escape from Negro identification."

Longtime resident Peter Green was active in the Jehovah's Witnesses, an evangelical Christian faith popular with the working and lower classes that had a larger percentage of black members than any other white-dominated religion in the United States in the early 1960s.[13]

Newspaper cartoons denigrating "niggers" elicited no negative feedback in Saranac Lake in the 1920s and 1930s, nor did white residents feel at all uncomfortable masquerading in blackface as "cannibals" or "mammies" in parade floats at annual winter carnivals. There appears, however, to have been little overt white hostility toward the black minority. In fact, religion may have been a more divisive local issue than race.

The Ku Klux Klan, a secret vigilante organization that flourished in the South during the post–Civil War Reconstruction era, had as its initial mission the quashing by intimidation and violence of government policies intended to assure political and economic equality for blacks. In seeking to restore white supremacy, members disguised in white robes, conical hats, and masks targeted and terrorized blacks and their allies with surprise attacks that sometimes ended in random murder. The enforcement of federal laws passed to prosecute the Klan's crimes in 1870 and 1871 led to the organization's quiescence until the early 1920s, when its name, rituals, and costume were revived by a new national organization comprised mostly of white Protestants who came together to denounce blacks, immigrants, Catholics, Jews, organized labor, and communism. Both country dwellers and urbanites were among the solid citizens who made up Klan membership, and the group was primarily known for staging harmless parades, rallies, and marches. The burning of a fiery Latin cross—an intimidating, attention-getting symbol appropriated by the 1920s Klan as its own—climaxed clandestine meetings and was left behind on the properties of those it harassed.[14]

The Klan was, for the most part, indifferently received by northern New York communities and ignored or derided by local journalists.[15] Saranac Lake's *Adirondack Enterprise* reacted coolly to a January 1927 letter received from a purported spokesman for the nearby Bloomingdale–Peck's Corners branch of the organization. The writer's primary complaint, according to the *Enterprise*, was that the paper listed the services of the town's Catholic church first in its "church notes" column (which the journal did on the principle, noted the published response, that it was the largest congregation in the village). The Klan would "burn a cross," threatened the anonymous correspondent. "On a hill, we suppose," was the paper's rejoinder. "In this way . . . we could all watch the procedure which is going to make us all One Hundred Per Cent American, and which is going to Place America First."[16]

Jan and Cora Gordon, an English couple who wrote and illustrated some twenty-four unconventional travel books between the two world wars, attended a nighttime Ku Klux Klan meeting some eighteen miles from Lake Placid during a 1927 visit to the United States—a meeting rousingly expected to be attacked by the Klan's "deadly enemies," the Knights of Columbus, a fraternal benefit society actively dedicated to defending Catholicism. The setting as the Gordons described it was "not-unimpressive": a bowl-shaped field in "a lonely spot of the mountains" ringed by a circle of darkened cars, at the center of which stood a truck. This was "dressed as a platform" sporting "an affair of ruby electric bulbs" mounted above the truck's hood as a substitute for a fiery cross. The speaker of the evening, a woman shrouded in white satin, railed against Catholics and, in particular, against the potential presidential candidacy of Al Smith, New York State's Catholic governor. The rest of the evening was "a mere touting for new membership"; the Gordons were certain that one black man was among those who lined up after the event to pay the required fifteen-dollar membership fee.[17] The organization was largely defunct in New York State before 1930. Its demise was hastened by the US Supreme Court's upholding in 1928 of a state law enacted five years earlier requiring all associations but labor unions and benevolent societies to make public their membership lists—a ruling that damped the Klan enthusiasm of many supporters.

Despite the preponderance of working-class African Americans in Saranac Lake, its black community was not cohesive. The village was the only population center in the Adirondack Park to develop a distinctive, self-identifying middle class, comprised largely of domestic servants who worked full-time for wealthy residents and enjoyed titles of butler, cook, and maid. A few black tuberculosis patients identified with the group—if they were well enough or cared to do so. Their position was underscored by their access to sufficient means to have enabled them to make the trip to Saranac Lake to cure. A number of black residents or couples held dual affiliations: C. W. Lanier, for example, came to the village as a tuberculosis patient in the early 1910s; his wife supported them both as a full-time domestic servant and stayed on in town for several years after her husband's 1915 death. Shades of skin color and family background were, as in other northern black communities, irrelevant when it came to assigning status within the group.[18]

The black middle class has historically been defined as a group sharing "an active desire to be recognized as 'respectable'" and characterized by home ownership, church membership, and regular employment.[19] To compensate for exclusion from participation in the community's broader culture, African Americans occupying the self-determined middle-class niche in Saranac Lake, like their peers elsewhere, created an active social life of their own. This was, according to leading black sociologist E. Franklin Frazier, a typical pattern of escape from racial isolation for members of the black bourgeoisie, who tried hard to imitate white "society" in their standards of consumption and recreation and to differentiate themselves from poorer blacks in their segregated community. Their flight into what Frazier characterized as a "make-believe" world had, he noted, little basis in the American economic system and was difficult to pull off on "what could be squeezed from the meager earnings of Negro workers."[20]

The African American press abetted the quest for collective consequence by printing items of interest proposed by readers. Such reportage was a necessary staple of all community newspapers and recorded the comings, goings, and petty achievements of self-identified "society" in the journals' catchment areas: areas that were unusually wide in the case of African American papers. Social news from Saranac Lake appeared from time to time in journals headquartered in New

York City and as far afield as Baltimore, Washington, DC, and Norfolk, Virginia.

New York Age and the *New York Amsterdam News* provided intimate glimpses into the social life of Saranac Lake's middle-class blacks at two brief periods: *New York Age* from February 1914 through December 1915, and the *Amsterdam News* from July through September 1931. Columns submitted by members of the local black community and headlined "Saranac Lake" recorded tea, supper, and bridge parties; visits from out-of-town guests; vacation motor trips; and the health status of tuberculosis patients. Social clubs received frequent mention. Names of hosts and attendees at individual events were scrupulously noted, as were their addresses—particularly if they were fashionable ones, which generally meant those of affluent white employers in whose homes domestic servants lived. Now and again there was coverage of festive events:

- *New York Age*: February 19, 1914: "Mr. and Mrs. Warren Poyas will give a social tea and dance for a few of their friends on Thursday evening at their residence, 41 Pine Street."
- *New York Age*, July 30, 1914: "Mr. and Mrs. C. W. Lanier gave a tango dance and lawn party to their visiting friends on July 23. Ices and all the delicacies of the season were served on the lawn. The Saranac Orchestra furnished the music. . . . A flashlight picture [night photograph] of the guests was a feature of the entertainment."
- *New York Age*, July 15, 1915: "The Rockledge Social club [most likely comprised of the four black servants then working in the Rockledge neighborhood home of civil engineer J. Peyton Clark] gave an excursion Monday, July 5, up Saranac Lake to Underwater Mt. Camp and was served with dinner at Hotel Colba. . . . In the evening a full dress reception was given by the club at Mt. Baker Hall which was beautifully decorated for the occasion. The reception was well attended. Dancing lasted until 3 o'clock. Music by Willis Haywood's orchestra of nine pieces."

- *New York Amsterdam News*, July 22, 1931: "Mr. and Mrs. R. H. Watson entertained the Ladies Club and the None Such Good Fellows at a supper and barn dance the other evening. . . . Mrs. George Tyre entertained a few friends at bridge."

Two women with roots in the black settlements of nearby Vermontville and Bloomingdale joined the rarefied world of Saranac Lake's African American middle class. Both deserve special mention as strong women with solid work ethics who became domestic servants to wealthy white villagers and absorbed the social ambitions that accompanied their perceived status.

Queenie Minnifield was born in 1882 in Vermontville, Franklin County. Her father, stonemason Wallace Minnifield, was rumored to have been a onetime slave from either Virginia or South Carolina and worked in New York City before landing in upstate New York. His wife and Queenie's mother, Cornelia, was the daughter of Beekmantown, Clinton County, farm laborer William Tankard, perhaps related to Redford glass-factory "melt master" George Tankard.[21] The Minnifields purchased a one-acre Vermontville property in 1890, and four of their many children were in school in Vermontville at the time of the 1905 census—from Florence, age eight, through Hattie, age fourteen.

Queenie Minnifield was the only black and the only woman among three servants living in 1900 in the home of Dana Davis, a white "grocery merchant" and farmer in Lake Clear (a hamlet of Harrietstown, Franklin County, that also encompassed part of Saranac Lake). Her occupation was listed in the census that year as "grocery, saleslady"; the male servants were farm laborers. By 1905, Minnifield was married to Davis, some twenty-seven years her senior. The first of four property transactions awarding Lake Clear real estate to Queenie Davis took place the following year; other parcels were conferred in 1907 and 1910.[22] Real estate was a good investment, and the lots may have been gifted to Queenie by her husband. The couple had no children, and Queenie Davis worked for twenty-five years as a servant to C. M. Palmer, a well-to-do newspaper broker who arrived in Saranac

Lake from St. Louis in the early 1900s in pursuit of a cure for a tubercular son. She was later employed for eighteen summers at the Holcombe camp at Paul Smiths in Brighton, Franklin County. Davis was mentioned in the Saranac Lake social columns of African American newspapers as a participant in local black outings in 1914 and 1915. When her husband died in 1926, she stayed on. By the 1930s she had taken on a leadership role in the black community:

- *New York Amsterdam News*, September 9, 1931: "Mesdames Queenie Davis and Hanzil Smith gave a thirty-mile cruise and picnic on Lower Saranac Lake last Tuesday."
- *Baltimore Afro-American*, November 9, 1935: "Mrs. Queenie Davis of Lake Clar [*sic*], gave a party Saturday night."
- *Baltimore Afro-American*, February 22, 1936: "Mrs. Queenie Davis has returned after spending ten days in New York and Washington, D.C."

Davis remarried in Saranac Lake in October 1936, becoming the wife of Theodore Simmons,[23] a car washer ten years her junior from Baltimore, Maryland. Her husband's name did not appear again in Davis's known history or in Saranac Lake records. Queenie Simmons retired to her Lake Clear property and died in 1970 at the age of eighty-seven. She is buried in Saranac Lake's Pine Ridge Cemetery in an unmarked grave in the spacious plot purchased on the death of her first husband, Dana Davis, forty-four years earlier.[24]

The second local black woman to achieve middle-class status was Mabel Johnson Greene, step-granddaughter of Charles Henry Hazzard and daughter of 1860s South Carolina transplant Genevia Smith Johnson. Recorded in the 1905 state census as living with her husband, William, on a Bloomingdale farm, she was by 1910 a live-in domestic servant on Saranac Lake's prestigious Park Avenue, where she would remain for several years.

Greene and her sister, Laura Johnson Anderson, maintained black identities throughout their lives. Both spent their middle years in New York City, where they resided in Harlem and were employed in domestic service. Their brother, Charles, stayed on in Saranac Lake as a teamster and married a local white woman, Jesse Woodruff. He and the first three of his and Jesse's seven children were recorded as "mulatto" in the 1920 census; by 1930 the family was designated as "white" and had adopted a white identity. Its mixed-race heritage would have been well known in the village, but the Johnsons were accepted on their own terms. Despite their success in the white world, they remained close to Charles's sisters. Mabel Greene, whose only child, Gordon, died in 1928 at the age of twenty-two, spent many summers with a family that vacationed on the St. Regis lakes in Franklin County. She was active in the Johnsons' family life and was remembered as strict. Not only did she boss her brother around, but she also taught his children table matters—lessons that the children dreaded, but some of which were absorbed. Greene retired to Saranac Lake, where her sister, Laura Anderson, and cousin Grace Anthony, daughter of Burlington's Abial and Clara Anthony, later joined her. She died at the age of ninety-two in 1972. Anthony and Anderson predeceased her: Anthony at the age of eighty-seven in 1964 and Anderson at eighty-three in 1965.[25] The three women are buried in Brookside Cemetery in Bloomingdale among four generations of Johnsons in a harmonious olio of black and white. An obelisk bearing the name of Charles Henry Hazzard dominates the family plot and establishes Hazzard, son of Gerrit Smith grantee Avery Hazzard, as a family patriarch despite his having no blood relationship to either of his wife's daughters.

Alice Wareham, born in 1922 and a daughter of John Ridenour, longtime owner and publisher of the *Adirondack Enterprise*, had the opportunity to observe the close but complex bond between her parents and a black couple who worked for the family from 1924 to 1939. George Washington Tyre and his wife, Georgia, known as Zoe, lived in a large apartment on the third floor of the Ridenours' home with Zoe's son, Edward Plummer, born in 1910. The couple was actively involved in the village's black middle-class social life, and George Tyre sometimes provided local news under his own byline to far-flung African American newspapers in the mid-1930s.[26]

17. George and Zoe Tyre with Alice Ridenour, Saranac Lake, circa 1928. Courtesy of Alice Ridenour Wareham.

Tyre, from Pennsylvania, had lived in Saranac Lake before his employment with the Ridenours as a domestic servant for J. Peyton Clark; his name appeared as one of three black among 202 Essex County men who attained the draft age of twenty-one during the year ending June 5, 1918.[27] He relocated around 1919 to Mount Vernon, Westchester County, where he was employed as a restaurant chef.[28] Upon returning to Saranac Lake as a married man he worked as the Ridenours' cook, while Zoe served as their maid. Much of her time was devoted to caring for Alice and her younger sister, and the Ridenour girls met many of the Tyres' social set in the family kitchen and at the homes of the Tyres' friends—who called the girls "George and Zoe's little white children."[29]

In explaining her parents' relationship with the Tyres, Alice recalled an incident from her childhood:

> [The Tyres'] friends were mostly chauffeurs in Lake Placid who came up for the summer, as well as some friends who lived here. Once, since the seasonal people were about to leave, George and Zoe asked if they could entertain them. By all means, said my parents, and George and Zoe told them they expected to be through by ten, so mother and daddy went out to dinner and then returned.

> We had a Chevrolet, not an expensive car . . . and when they got home, there, across from our house, were all these Mercedes and other fancy cars—one with an ambassadorial crest on it. Mother and daddy thought that George and Zoe would be so humiliated by our Chevrolet that they drove around and drove around until everybody left.[30]

The Ridenours' regard for the Tyres' perceived status within their social community manifested itself as one aspect of the employer-employee tie. Another was Wareham's uncomfortable memory of her father's treatment of Zoe's son, Howard Plummer. When Plummer was a high school senior, she recalled, he crossed what her father (who according to his daughter had a "southern" upbringing) considered an unwritten line in "just talking with" a white female classmate. Ridenour threw the young man out of his house. Plummer spent the winter of 1931–32 as a boarder with John and Viola Ramsey at 24 Lake Flower Avenue.[31] He went on to Howard University, served in the armed forces during World War II, and became a postal worker in Washington, DC. Having achieved a perfect twenty-year record with the post office, he died in 1960.[32] The tenacity of personal connection was demonstrated by the attendance of the Ridenours, then living part-time in Washington, at Plummer's funeral. Plummer's mother and stepfather, recalled Wareham, "were so grateful that they came. I," she added, "would have been resentful."[33]

The Tyres returned to Westchester County after leaving the Ridenours' employ but spent summer vacations in Saranac Lake through at least the 1950s. Alice Wareham's sister and her husband attended the Tyres' fiftieth wedding anniversary celebration, where the party table was laid with a tablecloth once given to them by Mrs. Ridenour. Alice Wareham's gift of flowers stood at the table's center.[34]

Among later social leaders of Saranac Lake's black community were William and Sadie Hall. Sadie, born in Maryland, was by 1930 a live-in waitress in a Park Avenue home. Her husband, believed to have arrived in Saranac Lake as a tuberculosis patient, was not then listed as a town resident. Bill Hall had once been chef to the Catholic archbishop

EDWARD L. PLUMMER
"Eddie"
24 Lake Flower Avenue
Boys' Varsity Club (2, 3); First Vice-President (4); Fire Squad (4); Canaras *(4); Red and White (3); Operetta (2); Sailor Maids (4); Band (1); Boys' Glee Club (2, 3, 4); Football (2, 3, 4); Cross Country (1); Basketball (2, 3, 4); Track (1, 2, 3, 4); Interclass Athletics (1); Secretary-Treasurer Home Room (2).*
A right, smart boy, never sullen or shy.
UNDECIDED

18. Edward L. Plummer, senior class entry in *Canaras*, Saranac Lake High School yearbook, 1931. Courtesy of Adirondack Collection, Saranac Lake Free Library.

of Baltimore and was perhaps unique among Saranac Lake's African Americans of their generation in having had two years of college education. Both Halls were members of the Catholic Church. Bill Hall was butler, gardener, chef, and chauffeur for a local family in the later 1930s and 1940s. He was remembered by George Packard, son of a doctor who lived across the street from Hall's employers, as the man who tutored him in a number of important areas, among them how to play chess, as well as "some horticulture and also elementary etiquette, such as how boys should pull out the chairs for girls at a party. I was convinced that he knew a great deal more useful stuff than Dad."[35]

The Halls leased an apartment in the village until 1946, when they purchased a large home out of foreclosure on the edge of the fashionable Park Avenue neighborhood.[36] They ran a successful catering business, took in occasional boarders, and were long remembered as providing a social center and weekly meal for Saranac Lake's black domestic help when they were collectively off-duty on Thursday evenings. William Hall died in Saranac Lake at the age of ninety-three in 1965, Sadie at eighty in 1966.[37]

Saranac Lake's growth peaked around 1930, when its population stood at 8,020. The onset of the Depression damped the boom that had propelled the village's growth. At the same time, its primary economic driver, tuberculosis, was losing its power to kill as the manner of transmission became better understood and patients received appropriate care. The 1943 discovery of streptomycin, the first antibiotic drug effective against the disease, intensified the rate of decrease, and the tuberculosis death rate dropped annually (27.1 per 100,000 whites, and 88.0 for blacks in 1947).[38] Both Saranac Lake's overall and black populations drifted downward. By 1940 only forty African Americans were living in Saranac Lake. Trudeau Sanatorium closed in 1954; Stony Wold in 1955, the Veterans Hospital and Sanatorium Gabriels in 1965; Ray Brook in 1974; and Will Rogers in 1975. All five facilities were repurposed. As population stagnated, most of the black children of longtime Saranac Lake residents, like the offspring of white families there and in other isolated communities throughout northern New York, moved elsewhere, generally to urban centers, in search of a wider life and better job opportunities. Saranac Lake was left in many ways a diminished municipality. It would take a long time to rebuild.

12

Popular Culture

Professional Performers

LIVELY, OUT-OF-TOWN ENTERTAINMENT was available to guests at urbane Adirondack resorts during the late nineteenth and early twentieth centuries, but most dramatic and musical amusements enjoyed by resident citizens were locally produced. Managers of traveling shows from outside the region sought out sizable population centers served by rail transportation and equipped with performance venues, of which the Adirondacks had few to offer. Indeed, only four towns and villages within what became Adirondack Park borders were deemed to meet the criteria in 1889: Au Sable Forks (with 1,000 residents), Port Henry (2,500), Ticonderoga (4,000), and Keeseville (3,500)—although Keeseville's four-and-a-half-mile distance by stage from a rail connection made it a less-than-ideal tour destination. Large towns and cities nearby that offered both access and suitable performance spaces in 1889 included Glens Falls (population 15,000), Gloversville (10,500), Malone (9,000), and Plattsburgh (9,000).[1]

Waiters at Lake George summer resorts performed in the minstrel tradition primarily for fun, but another strain of black minstrel player—one that relied on performance to make a living—brought the African American version of minstrelsy to the region's towns and villages. The first such show to visit the Adirondacks in the art form's pre-1890 heyday may have been the Georgia Minstrels, a troupe of "genuine darkies" that originated in Indianapolis in 1865. The group toured widely for five years and played Plattsburgh in December 1866, drawing a large audience curious about newly emancipated slaves. As a local journal noted, "There is no burnt cork about this show, the performers complexions being fast colors."[2] The term "Georgia Minstrels" became synonymous with "Colored" or "Slave Minstrels" and distinguished these performers from white actors performing in blackface, who called themselves "Negro" or "Nigger Minstrels."[3] White impresario and former tavern owner Charles Callender purchased the rights to the Georgia Minstrels in 1872. His long-lived Original Georgia Minstrels, headquartered on the East Coast and known at the time as the best black minstrel group in the business, visited Malone in October 1875 and Gloversville in February 1878. The show's success led to the addition of "Callender" to the list of words denoting black minstrel companies.[4]

Performers began in the 1880s to experiment with new show formats that, while retaining comedians as well as song and dance routines from the minstrel tradition, added an assortment of other, unrelated acts: acrobats, jugglers, ventriloquists, magicians, plate spinners. Backers took what they called the vaudeville show—a refined, family-oriented version of the spicy variety show—on the road. As with minstrelsy, a number of these entertainments showcased only black performers, of which a wide range was available. Indeed, musicians and actors constituted the two largest census categories of professional employment among African Americans in 1900.[5] Several black troupes visited the Adirondacks—particularly in the years immediately before and after 1911 (considered the glory era of black vaudeville). Players performed in the auditoriums of "opera houses" that continued to spring up in Adirondack towns until World War I. Generally accommodated in the second stories of showy buildings housing stores or government offices at street level, the venues rarely presented opera but were named to avoid offending church people who railed at the evil connotations of the word "theater." The street parades of eccentrically dressed troupers accompanied by loud brass bands before shows were a carryover from traveling minstrelsy.

The Alabama Troubadours, a transitional touring group "composed of a fine looking lot of darkies" with roots in minstrelsy, "made a big hit" in 1902 and 1905 at Sacandaga Park, the Northville, Fulton County park and amusement venue.[6] The troupe, organized around 1897, reportedly focused on three skills in selecting its members: "good singing, great dancing, and the rendering of the cake walk."[7] By the early years of the new century it was under contract to the J. W. Gorman Amusement Company of Boston, an agency that specialized in providing summer attractions to amusement parks and booked the troupe into Sacandaga. Gorman's, which had some three hundred acts in its stable, also furnished entertainers to the open air casino at Lake George's Fort William Henry Hotel in 1902, including the Mitchells ("colored entertainers" whose "Coon Pastimes" were "exceedingly clever with jokes and fancy dancing"), as well as other "unobjectionable" acts: a dancing juggler, a daring exhibition of skillful wheeling, Professor Miet's trained dogs.[8]

The record of Jack W. Boone's short-lived "Southern Octoroons (Colored)," a company booked in 1906 for one May evening at the Elizabethtown Opera House, demonstrated the precarious life of vaudeville performers. Boone, the show's white promoter, was an English-born, teetotaling saloon and concert hall owner in Syracuse, home to many of the troupe's twenty-odd players. In 1905 the Octoroons played small towns just north of the Canadian border. Business was bad, salaries were due and overdue, and the stage manager ran off with what little income had been accumulated. Ten company members were detained in Oswego upon returning to New York by freighter from Deseronto, Canada, until Boone could journey north from Syracuse to pay what was still owed on their fares.[9]

The Octoroons made a circuit of St. Lawrence County towns and villages in spring 1906, among them Canton, Potsdam, and Norwood, where it presented "a very poor show" to a "big house" before heading east for its one-night stand in Elizabethtown.[10] There the troupe gave "one of the best negro shows we ever had the privilege of attending," according to a local reporter,[11] before returning to St. Lawrence County—where it again "went on the rocks, this time" at Madrid. "The manager had enough money to get the women out of town, but the men were stranded high and dry, and the properties,

19. Alabama Troubadours at Sacandaga Park, Northville, 1902. Courtesy of Adirondack Museum.

uniforms, etc., were attached. There was nothing left for the actors to do but hoof it, and three of them, who were dead broke, went on foot to Ogdensburg, where they applied for lodgings at the police station."[12]

A different kind of show played in Ticonderoga in November of that year. The Drury Colored Opera Company was the creation of Kentucky-born Theodore Drury (1867–circa 1943), a concert baritone and one of several black singers to study at the National Conservatory of Music in New York City in the 1890s.[13] Drury made a name for himself with his 1900 New York production of the first known serious opera to feature an exclusively black cast. But few blacks could afford to support classical music, and attendance went down when white audiences lost interest in the phenomenon. Drury was henceforth forced to water down his ambitions to meet white expectations of black musical entertainment. His traveling company, booked into Ticonderoga for one night, drew a sufficiently enthusiastic audience that it was called upon to repeat its performance the following evening. The show is likely to have been similar to one the troupe had presented several days earlier in Rutland, Vermont, which opened with truncated acts from Carmen and Aida followed by "specialties and a plantation scene." "The novelty of ragtime mixed with grand opera by colored singers proved a great drawing card," noted one Rutland journalist.[14] Drury later toured as a concert singer but continued to produce the occasional opera.[15]

Sissieretta Jones (circa 1868–1933) was, like Drury, a classically trained African American singer unable to command an audience with the financial wherewithal necessary to support her career. Nicknamed "the Black Patti" after acclaimed nineteenth-century Italian opera singer Adelina Patti, she toured as a concert singer for several years after 1888 before settling for financial stability in headlining a vaudevillian troupe known as the Black Patti Troubadours between 1896 and 1916. The company's 1910 schedule of grueling one-night stands in the eastern and central Adirondacks was typical for itinerant vaudevillians. It called for shows in Port Henry on August 18, Plattsburgh on August 19, Au Sable Forks on August 20, Lake Placid on August 22, and Saranac Lake on August 23, after which it headed west to perform in Ogdensburg on August 25.[16] The Troubadours toured in a well-appointed Pullman car, the preferred transportation for vaudeville ensembles that could afford the expense, and of special value to black troupers in reducing the hazards of making their way in an intolerant nation.

Ticonderoga, so accessible by railroad, was always a popular venue for traveling entertainers, and at least two black vaudeville companies passed through the town in 1913. As the local newspaper noted that year of J. C. Rockwell's Sunny South Company (which played the Adirondacks a number of times between 1905 and 1931): "Noise and action are about all there is to the show and for this sort of thing, it is about the best show on the road." Its 1917 performance in Au Sable Forks, in contrast, was reported to be "about as rotten . . . as could be wished for," although the company was recognized as having given "fair satisfaction" in the past.[17]

The Nashville Students (who were neither students nor from Nashville) played Ticonderoga in 1913 with a program featuring "twenty real colored artists" and incorporating "eight Creole girls" and five vaudeville acts. The company performed in Tupper Lake's opera house as well, where "the audience had nothing to say but praise of the entire entertainment."[18] W. S. (Bill) LeVard, a "colored comedian of rare ability" and longtime minstrel performer, took the troupe to Elizabethtown in 1914 and St. Regis Falls, Franklin County, in 1916.[19] J. W. Boone, onetime proprietor of the failed Southern Octoroons, took over LeVard's show in 1919 with plans to play it in northern New York, Pennsylvania, New Jersey, and Maine.[20]

Harvey's Greater Minstrels was perhaps the last black vaudeville troupe to entertain Adirondackers, doing so in 1921 and 1923. R. M. Harvey, the ensemble's Iowa-born white owner and first manager, had been a longtime circus advance man and general agent, spending several years with the Barnum and Bailey circus. He fulfilled his dream of reviving "old-time minstrelsy" in 1918 with a "two-car show" that crisscrossed the United States and into Canada until it disbanded around 1925.[21] Harvey's "Musical, Vaudeville, Girl, Minstrel Show Combined" was well financed and well equipped. Some of the company's performers were old-timers: Harry Fiddler, the featured 1923 comedian, had by then been performing for at least thirty years and was known as a first-class "Chinese imitator."[22] As usual, rail routes determined the company's schedule: in late 1923 it played Plattsburgh, Ticonderoga, Port Henry, Glens Falls, and Hoosick Falls (Rensselaer County) before moving on to Pittsfield, Massachusetts.[23] The show had been presented to New York City's demanding black audience less than a month before heading north, and according to a *Billboard* reviewer, "Harlem liked it." The comedians, he noted, provided "laughs enough to keep the sophisticated New York audience giggling when they were not laughing outright," and the crowd "liked the band well enough to follow the parade over the whole route. This, mind you, when the district is supposed to be blasé and 'hard-shelled.'"[24]

Flickering silent film shorts, introduced in the 1890s, appeared on vaudeville bills in the early years of the twentieth century. By the 1920s longer movies were displacing live performance. The introduction of talking pictures in 1926 dealt the heaviest blow to vaudeville, and the art form disappeared altogether with the advent of the Great Depression.

Performers of a more dignified brand of black musical entertainment were catering to refined Adirondack audiences at the same time as the lively minstrel players and, later, vaudevillians. These commercially motivated groups followed the concert format originally introduced by Fisk University, which gave up its grueling tours in 1878. Thus the Fisk Jubilee Singers, under the direction of a former singer with the group, became a private enterprise. They performed in Ticonderoga in 1890 (to a "standing room" audience at Weed's Opera House), and returned again in 1894, 1902, and 1903.[25] Imitators incorporating "Jubilee Singers" into their titles specialized in spirituals and so-called traditional black songs.[26]

The Canadian Jubilee Singers, a black company organized in 1878 in Hamilton, Ontario, combined orchestral with choral music. After touring Great Britain for five years in the 1880s, it returned to Canada and henceforth played there and in the United States.[27] The group made repeat visits between 1896 and 1910 to the northeastern Adirondacks: Chateaugay, Franklin County; Crown Point, Port Henry, Ticonderoga, and Westport, Essex County.[28] Its venues were more likely to be church halls than opera houses.

A men's group known as the Utica Jubilee Singers, founded in the late 1920s at the Utica Normal and Industrial Institute for the Training of Colored Young Men and Women in Utica, Mississippi, evolved like the Fisk Jubilee Singers into a professional enterprise. It performed in Ticonderoga in 1926 and elsewhere in the Adirondacks between 1933 and 1938 before breaking up in 1939.[29] The group's 1938 concert in the Minerva, Essex County, hamlet of Olmstedville featured traditional spirituals, Stephen Foster's "Old Black Joe," a Brahms lullaby, and two songs composed and with lyrics by white artists: "Shortnin' Bread" and "Sylvia" (a sentimental song popular in the early twentieth century).[30] This group represented the entertainment future. Between 1927 and 1929 it cut some eighteen sides for the RCA Victor record label while performing regularly over radio station WJZ in New York City. It would be heard for several years across the country on NBC's Blue Network.[31]

Touring minstrel players, vaudevillians, and jubilee singers introduced black culture into the Adirondacks and supplemented white residents' often foggy impressions of African Americans. Black musicians providing live music for listening and dancing, who first entered the region with groups brought in by the large resort hotels bordering Lake George, had a similar impact.

Waltzes, two-steps to a new military march beat introduced by John Philip Sousa, lancers (a stately relative of the square dance), and polkas were among the favorite dances at hotel entertainments in the late nineteenth century. Men and women in evening dress who patronized the occasional Saturday night ball participated in the formal, patterned group figures of a "german" or "cotillion." Orchestra leaders tended to be of Italian, German, or Russian extraction and hailed from New York City or nearby towns and cities—Glens Falls, Albany, Troy. In the 1890s hotels began to replace this dance music and the staid concerts provided as afternoon diversion with more modern fare. The cakewalk, the first popular dance with black roots to enter the mainstream culture, was supplanted by the second decade of the twentieth century by a wide selection of dances from which to choose: the Texas tommy, the turkey trot, the fox trot, the Charleston, the black bottom. Ragtime, the first music to accompany the sprightly new steps, also came from black culture, and black musicians with expertise in its rhythms found new job opportunities in the Adirondacks after 1900.[32]

The *Lake George Mirror* highlighted the conflicting appeals of traditional and modern music during the summer of 1915, when two orchestras were simultaneously under contract at the Fort William

Henry. In the hotel itself, a five-piece orchestra played evenings under the direction of white violinist Joseph Brodo (who would go on to become a member of the Philadelphia Symphony Orchestra in 1918 and direct the hotel's summer orchestra of Philadelphia Symphony musicians through at least 1923).[33] At the same time, a lively four-piece orchestra of black musicians under George L. Jones played every night in the sunken garden court at the waterfront pavilion/casino. As the *Mirror* phrased it, the two orchestras

> have the same effect on us as two good speakers on opposite sides at a debate. Each one is convincing in his own element. You hear Brodo play some more or less popular operatic selection . . . and you are swept off your feet to a conviction that "That is the stuff!" Then you wander down to the pergola and hear the Geo. L. Jones quartet in the African "wail" and rhythm of the "Memphis Blues" or in a vocal rendition of "Over the Hills to Mary" which they really do in a manner that might be styled "a caution." Instantly you cry: "A bas with the high-brow junk, me for this!" only to change your opinion again when you return to the hotel.[34]

"As for the daughters of the idle rich," the *Mirror* noted later that summer, they were Jones aficionados and "simply dote on that stuff." Indeed, the new dances to music introduced by Jones and other black musicians were a particular enthusiasm of the young, who enjoyed the informality, the spontaneous movements, and the more intimate physical connection they fostered between partners.[35]

The Jones Quartet was hired for the 1915 season at the Fort William Henry through the Clef Club, an association of black musicians founded in 1910 by James Reese Europe, who went on to lead the backing band for the celebrated ballroom dancers Vernon and Irene Castle. The club not only had its own 125-piece orchestra (substituting plucked-string instruments like mandolins and banjos for some or most classical stringed instruments) but also functioned as a fraternal organization and a union/hiring hall and booking agency for its members, many of whom were intuitive rather than professional musicians and could not read music. It gained respectability in white

20. Unidentified hotel band at Lake George, circa 1890. Photograph by J. A. Thatcher. Courtesy of Historical Society of the Town of Bolton.

society with concerts between 1912 and 1915 at Carnegie Hall featuring music of exclusively black composers.[36]

As the twentieth century gained headway, the Adirondack summer resort industry experienced profound changes. The concept of suburban living, which had begun infiltrating the region in the 1890s, moved more and more former hotel patrons from intense communal life into private cottages where they could enjoy informal holidays on their own terms. The rise of the automobile gave all vacationers flexibility in making travel plans, and once-exclusive centers were suddenly within striking distance of anyone who owned a car. Roadside cabins and tourist homes displaced the grand hotels that, no longer socially influential, ceased to provide constant entertainment. Musicians with urban backgrounds now found summer niches in more far-flung Adirondack venues with partying populations of sufficient size to sustain them. Regional bands and groups from afield might be called upon at any time of year by residents to provide dance music for society balls or, in humbler circles, those given by fraternal clubs or police departments.

A newspaper columnist for the *Ticonderoga Sentinel*, reminiscing in 1949 about local life as it used to be, recalled the November 1929 appearance of twenty-two-year-old Cab Calloway "with somebody's Cotton Pickers" at a "Victory Ball" hosted by the American Legion in Port Henry's high school auditorium. Calloway, a black entertainer who became famous for his singing, bouncing, and comedic skills, was the front man for the black band that played Port Henry that evening: Marion Hardy and his Alabamians (misconstrued in advertising for the event as "Hardy and His Albanians").[37] A great success in Chicago, Hardy's band had travelled to New York City a month earlier to play a gig at Harlem's upscale Savoy Ballroom. The band proved too unpolished for the Savoy's demanding white audience and was given two weeks' notice after its first-night performance. Its Port Henry appearance took place during the brief period it made music in eastern New York before returning to the Midwest. Calloway stayed on in New York City, hitting the big time a year or two later as a bandleader and performer. Subsequent Calloway sightings in the Adirondacks were generally limited to observing his passage through the region in a private Pullman car en route to or from Montreal.[38]

Demonstrations by the Castles and other exhibition ballroom dancers created a nationwide craze for public dancing after 1911. This, in turn, led to the installation of dance floors in new urban phenomena: the "cabaret," and later the "night club." The nationwide liquor ban in effect from 1920 to 1933 stimulated nightclub expansion, and North Country promoters and hotel proprietors tried to recreate the ambiance of urban venues in the Adirondacks with varying degrees of success. The emphasis on the word *club* meant that, as so-called private membership organizations, these endeavors were free from Prohibition restrictions.

The Fawn Club (later the Alpine Inn) opened as a summer-only hotel in Lake Placid in 1921 and advertised itself as operating on the same membership plan as the exclusive Lake Placid Club, one of the largest residential vacation associations in the United States and the town's prime economic driver during the early years of the twentieth century. From the beginning, the Fawn Club featured live jazz: the more rhythmically complex, less restrictive musical form that supplanted ragtime. In 1928, a nightclub called the Barn—built into an old barn behind the Fawn Club and decorated to resemble a street scene in old Spain—was added to the operation to appeal to Placid's "smart crowd."[39] Promoted as "one of the finest dancing and supper clubs in the Adirondacks or in New York State," the Barn sustained an orchestra and floorshow that not infrequently featured black musicians. Resident in 1932 was Marion Hardy and His Alabamians, now advertising itself self-importantly as "Cab Calloway's Original Orchestra."[40]

The Birches, a Ray Brook roadhouse on the highway between Lake Placid and Saranac Lake, opened as Prohibition ended in 1933 and offered live entertainment under various owners for more than three decades. Hudson Farrior, a black singer, pianist, trumpeter and orchestra leader born in Georgia, settled in Saranac Lake around 1950 with his singer wife, Effie Johnson. As "Jet Johnson" he played the Birches as well as Durgan's, a similar roadside establishment north of Saranac Lake, and other nearby venues for some twenty years. He died in Saranac Lake at the age of seventy-four in 1974 and is buried with his wife in Bloomingdale's Brookside Cemetery.[41] "Tea dances" at the Birches between three and six o'clock on Sunday afternoons featuring Johnson or another entertainer at the piano were popular with patients from the nearby Ray Book and Will Rogers sanatoria.[42]

Two young musicians and promoters from the Greene County town of Catskill, Harold Clapper and Steve Jones, took a stab at introducing nightlife into the southern Adirondacks in 1929. Clapper, a white saxophone player, and Jones, a black guitarist "known from Harlem to Horicon," opened the seasonal Red Mill Restaurant and Bathing Beach that year in Chestertown under the direction of Clapper and featuring music by "Jones and his Red-Mill-odians." A number of the band's musicians had played New York City, and their ties with Harlem, the center of progressive black music, were referenced in Red Mill advertising.[43]

Clapper and Jones's first enterprise failed. They tried again with the Rustic Inn Ballroom (with special arrangements for bridge parties, weddings, banquets, and club receptions), located three miles north of Warrensburg, and then with "Steve's Band Box" at the south end of Brant Lake. To make ends meet, Jones's group played one-night gigs at such regional venues as an Elks clambake or a benefit for the County Blind Committee. The pair's ventures were closed down more than once for violating Prohibition laws, and they retreated in late 1932 to the Catskills, where they both fronted local bands. Clapper was still performing in 1957.[44]

The near-universal embrace of radio and the phonograph as the century progressed meant that everyone now had access to jazz and other forms of black music. By 1950 there were few Adirondack venues with enough patrons to warrant live bands of any kind, and black performers became increasingly difficult to find. Black music would go on to become the underpinning of popular musical culture. Residents of the Adirondack region, without undue curiosity, observed the evolution from afar.

13

Lake Placid and the John Brown Memorial Association

A THOUSAND PEOPLE were on hand at John Brown's North Elba home and gravesite to celebrate the radical abolitionist's 122nd birthday on May 9, 1922. This was not the first time a large crowd had gathered there to pay homage to Brown, but it was the first such assemblage organized in response to a black initiative. As at other Brown observances, the physical focal point of the event was a tombstone that once marked the grave of Brown's grandfather, a Revolutionary War soldier who died in defending his country in 1776. Brown had relocated this prized family relic from Connecticut to North Elba in 1857 and had it inscribed on the reverse side with an epitaph for his son Frederick, recently killed in Kansas. At John Brown's request, three more names were added to the gravestone after his death: his own and those of his two sons who died at Harpers Ferry. The stone was installed near his own grave, next to a large boulder some twenty yards from his home.[1]

The 244-acre site where Brown once lived now belonged to the State of New York. It had been purchased in 1870 through the efforts of St. Louis–born Kate Parks, a journalist who toured the lecture circuit—an important source of contemporary information and entertainment. Parks believed with a growing number of others that Brown had been a heroic martyr and visionary. Despite advice to avoid mentioning him so soon after the close of the Civil War, the thirty-one-year-old Parks concluded her 1869 winter lecture tour, on the topic of camp life in the Adirondacks, with a eulogy to him wherever she spoke: from Boston to Chicago to Dubuque.[2] Learning that Brown's neglected farm was for sale, she badgered potential donors until a private consortium raised the $2,000 necessary to purchase the property. It was donated to the state for use as a public park in 1896; some 1,500 people attended the North Elba/Lake Placid ceremony celebrating transfer of ownership.[3] Another throng participated in an observance at Brown's farm in 1899 honoring ten men who had lost their lives fighting alongside Brown at Harpers Ferry. Their remains had been quietly disinterred that year from other gravesites to be reburied with much fanfare next to the resting place of their leader.[4]

Philadelphia African Americans Dr. J. Max Barber, a dentist, and Dr. T. Spotuas Burwell, a physician, were the instigators of the 1922 memorial event.[5] Barber was an ardent Brown enthusiast who believed that the abolitionist "really had more to do with the emancipation of the Negro than even Abraham Lincoln."[6] He reportedly came up with the idea of a pilgrimage to Brown's grave in response to an acquaintance's comment that "it seemed singularly ungrateful that the Negro had never shown any special honor to this great friend of the race." Barber brought the matter to the attention of the Philadelphia branch of the National Association for the Advancement of Colored People (NAACP), an organization founded in 1909 and a pioneer in countering evolving patterns of segregation.[7] The dentist had been the Philadelphia branch's first black president (from 1917 to 1921), and it unanimously voted to support his Lake Placid excursion. "Fancy our surprise," reported Barber, "to find when we reached Placid, that the public schools took a holiday for the occasion, the Chamber of Commerce sent a delegation to welcome us, and the distinguished people of the town came out to be at the memorial services. There were perhaps one hundred and fifty automobiles parked around the grave and a thousand people there to do honor to our hero. The school children walked the three and one half miles to be with us."[8]

Lake Placid's welcome delighted the two men. While their reception was no doubt sincere, village boosterism may have swelled the turnout to watch Barber and Burwell lay a wreath on Brown's grave.

For early May was a fallow season in a town reliant on tourism as an economic driver, and Barber had made it clear in organizing his visit that "this gathering was probably the forerunner of an annual pilgrimage of colored people from all parts of the Union." He emphasized that he and his associate were there "to secure facts and information which would enable them to intelligently plan for the first great pilgrimage next year."[9]

Local support for the proposed venture was encouraging, but the Philadelphia NAACP "did not see its way clear to sponsor" a pilgrimage the following year. Only Barber visited the John Brown homestead in 1923, arranging his vacation so that he could pass through Lake Placid and lay a second wreath on Brown's grave.[10] Despite the setback, Barber was undeterred. He organized and was elected president in March 1924 of the John Brown Memorial Association in Philadelphia, and two months later led a caravan of ten motorcars to Lake Placid, where May 8 and 9 were spent in the observance of Brown's birthday.[11] Barber announced before seventy-five visiting African Americans and many more local white residents that the association had three goals: "the promotion of a John Brown Cult, the promotion of an annual pilgrimage to the grave and the erection of a monument to John Brown." The monument, it was determined, should cost no less than $25,000.[12]

The 1924 outing, thereafter known as the John Brown Memorial Association's second annual pilgrimage, spawned a tradition that endured for more than sixty years. Early programs included a mass meeting, a well-attended concert, the presentation of a prize to a local high school student for an essay on John Brown, and a wreath-laying ceremony at Brown's grave. Each program featured a principal speaker, and some eminent black and white names graced the roster over the years:

- Oswald Garrison Villard, editor of the *Nation* and grandson of Boston abolitionist William Lloyd Garrison (1925)[13]
- Clarence Darrow, renowned lawyer and leading member of the American Civil Liberties Union, best known for his defense of

teenage killers Leopold and Loeb and his role in the Scopes "Monkey Trial" (1927)[14]

- Philip Randolph, organizer and president of the first predominantly black union, the Brotherhood of Sleeping Car Porters (1930)[15]
- Dr. Malaku Bayen, personal physician to Emperor Haile Selassie of Ethiopia (1937)[16]

The advance program for 1928 announced the usual caravan to Lake Placid from Philadelphia in order to encourage participation among those hesitant to undertake a solo journey into unfamiliar "white" territory. Automobiles "decorated with John Brown Memorial Pennants" and carrying "copiously filled lunch baskets" were to stop, it was announced, "to lunch together far up in New York State. Pictures are snapped, jokes are swapped and the whole atmosphere is permeated with jolly comraderie [*sic*]." "Car seats" were available at minimal expense to pilgrims without vehicles. The Philadelphia motorcade started at three in the morning on the day before the gathering, mustered with caravans from elsewhere at Saratoga that night, and traveled with them to Lake Placid the following day. Organizational advances that year included a "publicity committee" and the assignment of $500 to a fund to be devoted to "propaganda."[17]

The *Lake Placid News* felt it necessary during the pilgrimage's early years to reassure local residents that the visiting blacks were "cultured negroes," enumerating "four physicians, two dentists, two clergymen and other prominent colored men" among the 1924 attendees.[18] The delegation was headquartered through 1925 at the National Hotel, a commercial establishment directly across from the railroad station purchased by the Lake Placid Club later that year for use as staff apartments. In 1926 it was headquartered at Pinehurst Cottage (Mrs. Rosa Vassar, proprietor), and in 1929 and 1930 at Mapledale Cottage, a small Main Street inn across the street from the North Elba Town Hall from which guests were "distributed" to homes around town.[19]

Subsidiary associations organized to lend their support to Barber's national organization and to assist in raising funds for the projected

21. Gathering at John Brown Homestead, July 1959. Courtesy of Mary MacKenzie Collection, Lake Placid Public Library.

John Brown statue. At one time or another there were ancillary chapters in Manhattan; Brooklyn; Springfield, Massachusetts ("organized in the Colored church where [former resident] John Brown used to preach to Colored people"); Kansas City, Missouri; Norristown, Pennsylvania; and Harpers Ferry, West Virginia, a chapter initiated by students at traditionally black Storer College. (A Storer student described the 1929 Lake Placid pilgrimage as punctuated by "about a dozen snow squalls" during which "heavy wraps and overshoes felt good."[20]) Lake Placid enthusiasts formed their own chapter in 1934, raising funds through strawberry socials, music recitals, and fashion shows. Manhattan's Frederick Douglass chapter was particularly active, offering youth programs, "Pilgrimage Meetings" open to the public, and excursions to Harpers Ferry.[21]

Attendance at the annual John Brown memorial event reflected the national economy and the country's international commitments.

It dropped precipitously during most of the Depression years: "hard times," as Barber pointed out, "which affect the negro as much or more than the white man." It fell again during World War II due to travel restrictions and "the pressure of war activities." Only Barber and a small, unheralded group of Philadelphians made the trip in 1942, "their avowed aim to keep the idea alive and to call attention to John Brown as a symbol of the goals of the Allied nations."[22] The largest pilgrimage in the association's history took place in 1935, during the midst of the Depression, when the longstanding dream of dedicating a monument to honor Brown was realized. Some 1,500 people gathered at the gravesite for the unveiling that May of an eight-foot-tall statue by New York City sculptor Joseph P. Pollia (best known for his Cuban war memorial on San Juan Hill) of Brown in conversation with a young black boy.[23] It had been the original intent of the association to mount the statue atop the huge boulder inside the grave enclosure so that the figures "would be silhouetted against the sky," but the state rejected the proposal as an intrusion on the historic site, and the statue went up outside the graveyard on a granite base.[24]

While blacks took the lead in honoring Brown on his birthday, the Lake Placid community gave valuable assistance to ensure that the annual pilgrimage ran smoothly. The president or other senior officer of the Chamber of Commerce was always on hand to greet pilgrims, and other organizations and individuals contributed generously to the endeavor, particularly the pastors and parishioners of the local Methodist Church and the Community Church that succeeded it in 1927. Ironically, despite a well-known prohibition against minority memberships, the Lake Placid Club made its premises available to early event attendees, granting visitors "special permission as a body" to tour the facility and hosting concerts at which the club organist sometimes played.[25] The club took on the responsibility, too, of providing cash prizes to winners of the high school's annual John Brown essay contest (thirty dollars in gold in 1929). Harry Wade Hicks, once general secretary of the Christian Education Movement and longtime secretary of the Lake Placid Club, was one of the association's staunchest supporters and introduced Dr. Barber to the assembled audience at the 1924 pilgrimage.[26]

Brown's gravesite saw a trickle of black visitors at times other than the annual association visits. Julius Fremont Bulles, for example, a white resident of New Russia, Essex County, arranged an outing to the site in the summer of 1926 for some forty black laborers working on road construction in the Boquet Valley. He and his neighbors furnished the cars that transported the group to Lake Placid, where two of the workers spoke briefly at the gravesite.[27]

Alice L. Walker purchased a Lake Placid property in 1919 and became the first of three black proprietresses of local boardinghouses catering to black lodgers to play active roles in the association.[28] The women's original connections to Lake Placid are uncertain, but all three may have arrived in the community as domestic staff members with vacationing white families and recognized an unmet need and a business opportunity.

Alice Walker's home at 41 McKinley Street was located about two blocks from the railroad station, south of the Central School in "downtown" Lake Placid. Dr. Barber, the organizer of the 1922 pilgrimage to Brown's gravesite, spoke of Walker as "a colored woman who runs a sanitorium for tubercular people" when acknowledging her role in making his exploratory visit to the John Brown homestead a success.[29] If this had been Walker's original intent, she immediately expanded her market. Her Uretta Cottage was advertised as a tourist accommodation in the African American newspaper *Chicago Defender* as early as 1920 and was popular with railroad porters. Open from mid-June through mid-September, it boasted "large, light, airy rooms with a wonderful view."[30] Walker's social life was tied to that of the black community in Saranac Lake, and her name appeared regularly in social columns submitted by that group to New York City's African American newspapers. Bridge-teas and a masquerade party sponsored by Our Ladies Social Club were among the events held at her home.[31]

Eva Watson Franklin, later Durant, was a part-time resident of Lake Placid by the mid-1920s. In 1931, when she was in her late forties, her name began to appear in African American newspapers as the proprietress of seasonal Camp Parkside at 41 Woodland Terrace. This address placed her in an "uptown" neighborhood of private residences and boardinghouses catering to a white clientele that was considered by class-conscious local residents to be superior to the "downtown" neighborhood where Alice Walker's lodging house was situated.[32] "A quiet restful and friendly place to spend your vacation," according to an advertisement in *New York Age*, Camp Parkside took its name from its location on a back lot near a small park and was housed in an old, barnlike structure with a garage for multiple automobiles on the ground floor. On the second story were a series of perhaps twenty small bedrooms, a large dining room furnished with long, family-style dining tables, and a private apartment with a tiny balcony for the proprietress.[33] Franklin went largely unnoticed by her adult white neighbors, but not by their children. As one later recalled:

> My grandmother had warned me not to go near the "colored" lady. Other parents and guardians in the vicinity had probably done the same; and when we gathered there to play, there was much discussion involving reasons why we were not allowed to visit with Mrs. Franklin. We would look up at her smiling down on us from her perch at the top of the stairs. One day, we decided to disregard orders to keep our distance and smiled back. She then called down to us and asked if we would like to come up for cookies and cocoa. We looked at each other and also all around us to see if anyone was watching. Nodding assent, we headed up the stairs. Mrs. Franklin was a warm, friendly person and a great baker of cookies. From then on, we were frequent visitors; and to my knowledge, my grandmother never found out. (My grandfather knew, however; but he secretly liked her too and never squealed.)[34]

Franklin married James M. Durant, a onetime treasurer of Brooklyn's black Democratic organization, in the mid-1930s. When Durant died in 1949, he left his Brooklyn home to his widow—information disseminated through the *Lake Placid News* and provided, no doubt, by the legatee herself in the hope of achieving some status in

22. Eva Franklin Durant, Lake Placid boardinghouse keeper and JBMA officer. *Thirty-fourth Annual Pilgrimage*, advance program, 1954. Courtesy of John Brown Farm, Lake Placid; New York State Office of Parks, Recreation and Historic Preservation.

the community that ignored her. Mrs. Durant "of Lake Placid and Brooklyn" continued to run Camp Parkside.[35]

Parkside catered to black staff members of white families vacationing in Lake Placid, and to a wide range of tourists whose names Durant often supplied to African American newspapers. Her guests, she noted, enjoyed "picnics, bathing, fishing, horse back riding, hikes, and other

23. Inez Carter, Lake Placid boardinghouse keeper and JBMA officer. *Thirty-fourth Annual Pilgrimage*, advance program, 1954. Courtesy of John Brown Farm, Lake Placid; New York State Office of Parks, Recreation and Historic Preservation.

sports which are customary in the mountain resorts."[36] Among those who returned regularly to Camp Parkside in the 1950s was the family of Kenneth and Mamie Clark, whose research and expert testimony contributed in the landmark 1954 US Supreme Court case, *Brown v. Board of Education*, to the ruling that racial segregation in public education was unconstitutional.

Alice Walker last advertised the amenities of Uretta Cottage in the summer of 1935 before quietly disappearing from the Adirondack scene. By 1938 her McKinley Street cottage had been rented to Inez Carter, identified in the 1940 census as a forty-four-year-old African American widow born in Alabama and recently of Chicago. Her occupation was given as cook in a private home. Mrs. Carter continued the boardinghouse tradition of her predecessor, welcoming black guests to her renamed Dreamland Cottage and publishing her guest list in the *Chicago Defender*. (One item was entitled "Mrs. Inez Carter Entertains Friends.") Occasionally she provided a home to an elderly white boarder. In 1948 Carter bought the house in which she had been living for more than ten years.[37]

Like Alice Walker before them, Durant and Carter were committed to the John Brown Memorial Association. Durant, as Eva Franklin, was the first president of the local chapter. Carter was local chapter president by 1942 and was listed as such on a plaque installed by the association at the Brown farm honoring the women of his family in 1946.[38] Durant was president of the national organization from 1951 through at least 1959, while Carter served with her as its first vice president. The two women cochaired the entertainment committee for an association reception at the Brown farm in August 1957 honoring Mrs. William Herberger, a great-granddaughter of John Brown.[39] Inez Carter sold her Lake Placid home in 1961.[40] Eva Durant died two years later at the age of seventy-nine in a nursing home in Richmond, Virginia. She had, according to a brief local obituary, been a resident of Lake Placid for forty-two years.[41]

Durant and Carter both kept an eye on the aging Lyman Epps Jr., who had sung at John Brown's 1859 funeral and was the last survivor in Lake Placid of Gerrit Smith's black colony. Epps spent his adult life as a farmhand and then a laborer, generally for the town of North Elba. He basked in his family's connection with John Brown, attended all memorial association pilgrimages, and unveiled the John Brown statue at the 1935 association gathering.[42] Epps confided to a neighbor in 1936 that his "most earnest wish" was "to be permitted to live in the old Brown homestead; to wear a cap with an emblem on it in the shape of a golden eagle; and to be allowed to tell the summer tourists what he knew about John Brown and his family." The neighbor put the question to a number of state bureaus on his behalf, from the governor's office on down, but the request was denied.[43]

In a 1936–37 interview, Epps called attention to the loneliness he felt as a black man in a predominantly white community. As he explained, he had never married because there were "no real colored people" in the area, "just some of them city-folks." At the same time, he downplayed racial differences in positioning himself as a respected member of the community: "People don't treat me as though I was colored; they act as though I was just like them, and that's how I want to be."[44] Epps died in November 1942 at the age of ninety-six. His funeral service was largely attended, but his burial in the Epps family plot in North Elba was not, according to the town clerk, who reported that he, "the undertaker and two colored women wrapped in large woolen shawls against the bitter cold, were all that followed the body to its grave."[45] George Tyre, formerly of Saranac Lake, presided over a local ceremony the following September at which a marker sponsored by the John Brown Memorial Association's Lake Placid chapter was unveiled on his grave.[46] The association's Frederick Douglass chapter in New York City held a memorial service for Epps in Harlem and presented a scholarship in his name to historically black Knoxville College in Tennessee.[47]

Epps shares his family burial plot with his parents, a brother, and a brother-in-law, William Appo. The stone provided by the John Brown Memorial Association honored both Lyman Jr. and his youngest sister, Kate Epps Robinson, who died in 1920. Robinson is not, however, buried in North Elba. According to her death certificate and cemetery records, she lies alone in an unmarked plot in Cypress Hills Cemetery, a huge, privately owned burial ground straddling Brooklyn and Queens that opened in 1851 shortly before passage of a law prohibiting further burials in Manhattan. Born in 1857, Kate married Richard Robinson, a black music teacher in New York City whom she may have met through her musician brother-in-law William Appo. The couple lived in Manhattan and had no children. Richard Robinson was, by 1910, an assistant supervisor of music for New York City's Board of Education. Kate's occupation was recorded in the 1900 census as dressmaker and in 1905 as housework. What became of her husband after her death is unknown.

A recently arrived black resident of Lake Placid took on an official role in the John Brown Memorial Association in 1948, when Charles Curtis Walker Jr. became the group's treasurer.[48] Walker, born in 1921, was raised in West Chester, Pennsylvania. After serving in the Marine Corps from 1941 to 1946, where he rose to the rank of corporal, he located in Lake Placid as houseman for a local family. It was not long before his "loving heart and bright sprit" touched everyone in town. Walker became an enthusiastic participant in the sport of ice skating, so central to the culture of Lake Placid. He was a member of the Lake Placid Skating Club, performed in its shows, and was eventually elected president of the club. In 1963 he was appointed by the United States Figure Skating organization as one of its first black judges. Despite his achievements in skating, Walker was best known locally for his deep baritone singing voice. He sang for years in the choir of the Adirondack Community Church, belonged to a barbershop group, and performed at private and public events (including John Brown Memorial Association pilgrimages). He also took part in local theater, was a member of the Kiwanis Club and the first board of the Lake Placid Center for the Arts, and volunteered countless hours of community service in many capacities. Walker was inducted into the Lake Placid Hall of Fame in September 2012 in tribute to "his outstanding accomplishments and great personality." He died not many months after attending the Lake Placid ceremony at his home in Middletown, New York, where he lived with his wife after a late marriage.[49]

John Brown's grave was singled out in the 1964 American Oil Company's *American Traveler's Guide to Negro History* as one of four significant New York "places that have special relevance to the proud part that Negroes have played in our nation's history."[50] The John Brown Memorial Association continued to organize trips to Lake Placid through at least 1985, although these were no longer as ambitious or reverential as they had been in earlier years. New features were added: a 1947 Inter-Racial Card Tournament in the home economics classroom at Lake Placid's high school, and tourist excursions to Santa's Workshop in nearby Wilmington. Association pilgrimages continued, however, to incorporate the placement of a wreath on the North Elba grave of John Brown, and originated a new tradition in placing one on the grave of Harry Wade Hicks (died 1960), the supportive secretary of the Lake Placid Club after whom the Lake Placid chapter had been named.[51]

During the more than six decades in which the annual John Brown Memorial Association celebrated John Brown for his role in emancipating the black race, it provided a broadly based social outlet in which resident African Americans were encouraged to, and did, take on leadership roles. It was the only organization in the Adirondack Park to do so.

14

Public and Publicly Supported Institutions

LIKE ALL AMERICANS, Adirondack residents interfaced occasionally or often with government at the local, state, and federal levels. This chapter presents brief overviews of public institutions with which at least some regionally based African Americans had contact. Sketches are offered, too, of three public or publicly supported entities that brought disparate outsiders into the region. The largest and most tenacious of these, Clinton Prison in Dannemora, Clinton County, became one of the largest facilities in New York State's penal system. In admittedly odd juxtaposition were two organizations financed by private individuals and organizations to transport underprivileged children from New York City to the Adirondacks for short summer getaways.

Education

It was in the 1790s that New York State first promoted public education by offering matching grants to towns providing schools for children in their constituencies. An 1812 law established a statewide system of school districts, each serving a defined locality and governed by trustees elected by local voters. The education offered in rural areas was generally in one- or two-room schoolhouses serving all comers between the ages of five and fifteen; expenses were met by town and county taxes and state aid based on the number of students served. This system lasted into the twentieth century with only a few changes, among them a requirement that the school year be increased from three months in the 1830s to more than seven months by the 1890s. A law making attendance compulsory went into effect in 1874 but was, for many years, little enforced.[1] Census records indicate that many young people living in the Adirondacks through the first decades of the twentieth century had limited schooling. As a black New Yorker explained, the eighth grade was an important marker for his race, as New York State passed a law in 1921 allowing anyone over the age of twenty-one with an eighth grade education to vote in state and local elections. For many, this meant that formal schooling ended at age fourteen.[2]

New York State declared public schools open to "all" children in 1841. Six years later the state superintendent of schools clarified the law, stating that "colored children are entitled equally with all others to the privileges and advantages of the district schools." The state permitted the creation of separate black schools within districts as of that year. Such schools were sometimes initiated by white residents and sometimes by black. (Dr. James McCune Smith, black advisor to Gerrit Smith, called for special schools for African American children after discovering in 1846 that only one of the first seventeen blacks from Westchester County to receive Smith land grants was able to sign his name.)[3] Adirondack towns, with their small black populations, never considered segregated education. But black students could be subject to harassment and humiliation in the region's schools. As an 1858 historian wrote of early school life in Ticonderoga: "Among the urchins who swung their feet from the front benches, was a black girl from Samuel Deall's family, but it is related that the children of 1800 would not sit on the same seat with her, and so she was taken home."[4]

New York did a decent job of providing basic education to African Americans. Some 15.14 percent of resident blacks over the age of twenty were unable to read or write in 1850, compared to 2.99 percent of whites. By 1910, the state's illiteracy rate for black children over the age of ten was the lowest of any state in the country at 5 percent. (Louisiana's was the highest, at 48.7 percent.)[5] Fifty-nine blacks were enrolled in New York State colleges in the 1870s—a number that decreased to fifty-five before 1880 and did not rise significantly until

1910, when there were 245 in attendance.[6] The first African American student known to have attended a school of higher education in the Adirondack region was James Augustus Wilson, who graduated in 1902 from Plattsburgh State Normal and Training School (now SUNY Plattsburgh), an institution opened in 1890 with a mandate to train high school graduates as teachers. It is unclear how Wilson, born in Alabama and a schoolteacher for three years before entering Plattsburgh, came to be at the school, but he was a strong student and was involved in extracurricular activities: organizing and directing the YMCA choir and chosen as a commencement speaker. He went on to earn a bachelor's degree in divinity from Wesleyan University in 1906 before returning to Alabama, where he worked at Tuskeegee Institute with its founder, Booker T. Washington, in the school's teacher-training program.[7] Within the park, Paul Smith's College in Franklin Country (founded 1948), enrolled two black men in September 1950 as members of the class of 1952; the New York State Ranger School in Wanakena (founded 1912) in St. Lawrence County graduated one black student in 1963.[8]

Government

Three early black residents of the Adirondacks were elected to minor public offices: James Henderson and Lyman Epps as North Elba's Inspectors of Elections in 1851, and William Satchel as Elizabethtown's Sealer of Weights and Measures in 1886. But only the lowest paid public service jobs were given to blacks through the first half of the twentieth century, the most prevalent of them being heavy labor on town and county road projects.

Public Assistance

Material aid provided by communities to destitute citizens in their homes, or "outdoor relief," was the foundation of early welfare policy in the United States. Tax-supported residential poorhouses or almshouses, introduced at the beginning of the nineteenth century, were considered the cutting edge of poor-relief policy in their day. Their establishment was a response to theories that the "unworthy poor" would be less inclined to ask for government aid if such assistance entailed their leaving their homes, and that relief provided in group settings came at less cost to taxpayers. The often cheerless and degrading poorhouse survived as an institution well into the twentieth century, gradually taking on a new identity as an old-age home.[9]

The poorhouse served a variety of clients. It was a refuge of last resort for the sick poor and the indigent elderly as well as a temporary refuge for individuals and families left without resources because of harsh growing seasons, periods of unemployment, and family emergencies. Aging men became inmates more often than elderly women—generally because they had no children, had deserted their children earlier in life, or were dissolute in their habits. Younger women entered poorhouses to give birth or because there were no men in their lives to help support their children.[10] New York State legislation made poorhouses obligatory in counties throughout the state in 1824, although exemptions were granted. (An Adirondack exception was Hamilton County, which provided for its poor in the institutions of other counties or in family homes.)[11] The poorhouses of Essex and Warren counties, both tied to working farms, were physically within the boundaries of the eventual Adirondack Park.

Blacks in the North were, as in the South, often shut out of white institutions, but Adirondack poorhouses exercised little or no racial bias when it came to accommodating African American applicants. They appeared in poorhouse populations in proportion to their small demographic presence, and landed there for the same reasons.

Homer Jackson was a seventy-year-old boatman when he arrived in the Warren County Poor House in 1880. According to poorhouse records, he had been self-supporting until entering the facility. His residence was due to "Old Age and was hurt in going over Cohoes Dam Mohawk River." Born in Arkansas, where his father had been a slave who "bought his own and his wife's freedom," Jackson was in and out of the poorhouse before he died there in 1882.[12]

Living in the Essex County Poor House, later the Essex County Home, in 1877 were Thomas Johnson, a seventy-eight-year-old uneducated farmer, "temperate," with no living children, and seventy-six-year-old George Washington Bell, a common laborer with no children who was partially blind and had received outdoor relief for about five years before entering the facility. In 1910 the Essex County Home housed one black resident in a population of fifty (thirty-two men and eighteen women); the Warren County Almshouse accommodated two in a population of sixty-seven (fifty-eight men and nine women).[13]

In a few cases dependency could last for years. An 1879 report detailed the history of a family of three living in the Essex County Poor House: "a black woman, widowed, aged forty-nine years, and her daughter, single, aged twenty-four years, and her grandson, a mulatto, four years old, illegitimate, and born in the house. Both women are intemperate and thoroughly depraved, and quite certain to remain public burdens, each having already been nineteen years in the house." A child's spending such an extended period in a poorhouse was rare after passage of New York State's Children's Act in 1875, which called for the removal of minors between the ages of two and sixteen from such institutions. But poorhouses continued to provide a refuge for children. As the administrator of Fulton County's poorhouse noted of a two-year-old, biracial child accepted in 1889, her parents were a "bad couple" and the home had taken her in "for Humanity sake."[14]

The 1932 death of William "Billy" Brown in the Essex County Home "after a life of disappointments and setbacks, principally due to his race and color," led to an outpouring of affectionate reminiscence in the *Ticonderoga Sentinel* from those who knew his story. Born in Virginia around 1850, the son of a slave and her master, Brown had traveled north after the Civil War and landed in Ticonderoga, where he became a domestic employee, painter, and handyman. He "spent most of his evenings studying," it was said, and in due course enrolled in Syracuse University, working for board and books, before taking up teaching. "There arose dissension regarding having a Mulatto as a teacher, so, eventually he was discharged and drifted back to Ticonderoga." Brown's "moral character was unblemished," it was recalled, and it was only in the last years of his "long, admirable, self-sacrificing life" that he was compelled to ask for charity. A letter to the newspaper's editor mentioned the time Brown approached its writer to hand him a five-dollar bill toward a planned new town hospital, "stating that he would like to do his bit toward a cause that meant so much to the community." The author suggested that it would be "entirely fitting" if a room in the new building were dedicated in his memory (which it was not).[15]

The outmoded poorhouses in both Essex and Warren counties did not close until the final decades of the twentieth century. It had taken government a long while to evolve toward coping humanely with the needs of the chronic poor and elderly.

New Deal policies formulated in response to the Great Depression brought about a vast expansion of government activity in the field of social welfare. While most programs officially prohibited discrimination, they were limited in their success. The Works Progress Administration (WPA), however, has been singled out as one of the most important New Deal agencies in terms of creatively benefiting black Americans: relieving their poverty during the national emergency in greater proportion than their numbers in the population, and enabling them to participate in relief projects commensurate with their skills and education.[16] Organized in 1935, the agency provided paid jobs on public works projects for out-of-work men and women until the economy recovered. Its reach extended into almost every American town, and, at its 1938 peak, it employed 3.3 million workers—most of them unskilled men.[17] It wound up operations in 1943 as the economy gained momentum in response to World War II needs.

Many of the jobs offered by the WPA were on traditional public works schemes: roads, bridges, dams, civic buildings. A high percentage of projects in the Adirondack Park related to recreational facilities, among them ski slopes, bathing beaches, an improved boat channel for Cranberry Lake, the bobsled run at Mt. Hoevenberg, and three new or enlarged golf courses.[18] Charles Johnson of Saranac Lake worked as a teamster on a (never completed) Saranac Lake golf course expansion. His children visited the job site on weekends with their father when he went to tend to the horses used on the project. Road schemes employed a number of regional black men. Fifty-four-year-old Lucy

Cutting, daughter of Port Henry's George and Lucy Jackson, worked in a WPA "sewing room" in 1940.

Clinton Prison, Dannemora

New York State's prison system has historically been one of its more egalitarian racial settings. This is not to say that there was never a predisposition to segregate miscreants by color. Bias was evident in 1817 suggestions to Governor DeWitt Clinton that the state's black convicts might be pardoned if they accepted transfer to one of the southwestern states or territories as agricultural laborers—proposals the governor rejected for, among other reasons, fear of retaliation by southern states.[19]

Blacks were included in the state's prison population from the system's beginning, when Newgate Prison opened in New York City's Greenwich Village in 1797. In October 1848 there were eight blacks among the 133 inmates of Clinton Prison, a facility opened three years earlier in the Adirondack wilderness just south of the Canadian border.[20] Iron had been discovered in this section of Clinton County in the 1830s, and iron mining was the prison's first labor venture in the days when financial recompense drove New York's penitentiary management. The village that grew up around the prison was optimistically named Dannemora after the well-known Swedish mining center, and the prison itself has long been nicknamed Dannemora. It became something of a North Country tourist attraction in the late nineteenth century, serving to enhance the region's romantic reputation as a remote and untamed landscape. A pamphlet detailing "little trips" from Hotel Champlain, south of Plattsburgh, referred to the bright lights of the institution, some twenty miles away, which "can be plainly seen, glittering like diamonds, in the distance to the west on clear nights, from the hotel."[21] Depression in the iron industry and overestimation of the amount of ore in the prison tract led to early failure of the mining enterprise. Later industries at Clinton, restricted to those that did not compete in the free market, included the manufacture of cloth, clothing, nails, brooms, and tinware for use in state-owned facilities.

As the prison expanded, so did its black population. Thirty-five, or 7 percent, of Dannemora's 484 inmates were black in 1860; by 1910 the percentage had risen to 11 percent (156 among 1,467 internees).[22] Prison management was rebuked in 1856 for making "especial pets" of two or three black inmates who were allowed to run errands outside prison walls for the institution's officers and to act as their "waiters, servants and menials"—even accompanying them in these roles on fishing and pleasure trips into the wilderness.[23]

Photographs showing inmates on work crews and in group settings during Clinton's first decades suggest full integration of blacks into prison life. A Plattsburgh doctor visiting the penitentiary on business in 1891 commented on the "white and black and young and old men" in the prison's band, then comprising twenty-eight inmates. (An Ulster County newspaper reported in 1903 that an African American from Ellenville recently committed for the fifth time to Dannemora for burglary was one of the band's "leading members.")[24] Not only did music account for a portion of band members' "daily work," as they were required to practice every day under the eye of a prison guard, but it also provided a recreational respite—one prisoner writing to ask a reporter for the *New York Amsterdam News* in 1932 if he would inquire of entertainers he knew "if any of them has an old tenor banjo lying around taking up room." He would, he added, "appreciate having it for company during the next twenty years."[25]

Prisoners of both races worked closely together in the shops, and friendships across color lines occurred, although other inmates sometimes resented such associations.[26] Racial separation increased within the prison as the number and percentage of black prisoners grew. By the end of fiscal year 1936, nearly 21 percent of the Clinton Prison population was black (380 of 1,787 inmates), a percentage that remained constant in a larger population of 2,121 prisoners six years later.[27] The self-segregation by ethnic background and color that marked prison life was thought to reflect the culture found in the larger metropolitan areas from which prisoners were drawn and was not considered to be hostile. As one white prisoner wrote in reference to Dannemora's culture in the 1930s, it was impossible to ignore the "old caste system." The cliquish alliances that "owned" the 350-odd, patio-like recreational "courts" informally laid out on the facility's terraced hillside were largely but not entirely exclusive: "Wops [Italians] fraternized with Donkeys [Irish], Kikes [Jews] with Goyim [non-Jews], even the occasional 'right' nigger might be invited to have coffee or spaghetti on a white man's court. But no one would obey an order to share his court with convicts he regarded as unfit for his company."[28]

African American newspapers reported in the 1930s on criticisms leveled against Clinton Prison management by paroled and released black prisoners. Complainants charged that Dannemora guards and officials (all of whom were white and most of whom came from the predominantly rural surrounding area) encouraged racial hatred among white prisoners. When interracial altercations took place, they noted, blacks were likely to be charged while white participants were not. Despite their qualifications, they were said to be routinely denied "soft" job assignments as clerks, nurses, kitchen mechanics, tailor and butcher shop helpers, prison truck drivers, boiler room assistants, and workers in the barn, mess hall, and bakery. On the other hand, the "ebony boys" could purportedly be found in large numbers wherever "a pick and shovel gang" was needed and in the most backbreaking jobs in the cotton and weave shops that dominated prison employment at the time. A few "lucky" blacks might be allowed to serve as porters or to clean up the cell halls. Despite such accusations, determined the *New York Amsterdam News* in 1938, "being called Nigger and everything else to heap insult upon their heads, the Negro prisoner at Clinton fares very well."[29]

It was ascertained in 1936 that two-thirds of Clinton Prison inmates had never advanced beyond grammar school; a 1939 survey determined that the average level of educational attainment among the prison's black prisoners was grade 5.8, and grade 7.0 for white inmates.[30] Although designated a prison for "incorrigibles" and repeat offenders, Dannemora was a leader in modern rehabilitation methods, and all prisoners had access to academic education as well as to commercial and vocational training. Some 1,400 inmates were enrolled in the prison school in 1936, where they were taught by civilian and inmate teachers.[31]

The African American press reported in the 1930s that blacks were no longer permitted to play in the Clinton Prison band, that athletic teams were segregated, and that baseball teams comprised of black inmates were not allowed to play against white teams, "even when the latter request it."[32] A different version of recreational separatism occurred in 1934, when the Clinton Prison School of Dramatic Art (directed by the prison's popular Catholic chaplain) mounted a show called "Big Time Radio Revue Vaudeville and Hot from Harlem." This undertaking was comprised of two independent, side-by-side shows produced for a single program. The "Big Time" revue was shaped by white inmates and featured white performers; its "associate" show, "Hot from Harlem," was a wholly black production. Some two thousand residents drove in subzero weather from surrounding towns to Dannemora to attend the opening-night performance in the prison auditorium. A "colorful presentation of a darky scene on the levee" closed the second, black portion of the entertainment, and was praised by a local reporter as an "absolutely . . . snappy and peppy show" with "exceptionally good" dancing and "fine" singing—some of it performed by obvious professionals. An overflow crowd was on hand the following evening for a second performance, giving the entertainment "a tremendous burst of applause as the curtain rang down on the final act." Not long afterward, the two branches of the production merged extracts from the show in an hour-long radio concert produced by a station in nearby St. Albans, Vermont.[33]

The community outside the prison walls was largely white, but the racial mix within the facility and among inmates' visitors led to an unusual degree of tolerance in the village of Dannemora. As Allen Walton, a black man who became a Port Henry miner in the 1930s, wrote of his early residence in the Adirondack region, "During all my traveling, Dannemora was the least discriminating place I ran into. In Dannemora I could go into any place and sit down and eat. Or any person who had a boardinghouse, I could stay if I had the money. These people up there, most of them had come out of Vermont or

24. Clinton Prison, "colored winning baseball team of 1945." Clinton Photograph Collection, Department of Correctional Services, New York State Archives B0095-77.

New Hampshire or French Canada, and they was good and kind. Occasionally we would run into married people up there, a colored and a white. Never down South. Never. That would never happen."[34]

Lita Kelly, the daughter of a prison guard, mentioned race in recalling her 1950s Dannemora childhood: "It wasn't at all unusual to be playing outdoors and glance up to see a group of convicts coming toward me, walking down the middle of the street, on their way to a job detail. . . . Many of the prisoners weren't white, which I noticed but never thought to question. . . . The only black people I saw at the time were related to the convicts. When buses pulled in from out of town and people began to file out and go inside the prison, we noticed. There were so many, and they were so sad."[35]

The Fresh Air Fund

The Fresh Air Fund of New York City, founded by the *New York Tribune* in 1877, was a philanthropic response to inner-city conditions based on middle-class assumptions about poverty and the benefits of nonurban life. Placing city youngsters with volunteer families in the countryside and in small towns for two-week summer vacations, it served some 1.8 million poor New York City children between the ages of five and twelve by 2014.

Adirondack residents were active in the program from its earliest days, with the *Tribune* reporting in August 1883 on the homecoming of one hundred Fresh Air–sponsored children by way of Troy and the night boat from the Lake Champlain region surrounding Plattsburgh. The returnees, it noted, carried with them country mementoes in "inverse ratio of the size of the bearers," among them cages of live chickens and "every manner of vegetable thing from string beans to bright red apples."[36] It was only in the first decade of the twentieth century that black children were included in the program. Alice Walker, African American boardinghouse proprietor in Lake Placid, hosted Fresh Air Fund children in 1932 and 1933.[37] The local press explored cultural differences between regional participants and their African American guests in the 1940s, noting well-intentioned efforts to bridge the racial gap, among them the report of a five-year-old girl's host "seen surreptitiously sneaking a water melon home to make her heaven perfect."[38] The press also detailed the racial distribution among the region's young guests:

- Keeseville, Clinton and Essex counties, 1951: Twenty-five children, including "three little wide-eyed negro girls and two little Spanish boys."[39]
- North Creek, Warren County, 1953: Ten children, including one black girl. "Although their need is just as great," explained the *North Creek News* to its readers, "Negro and Puerto Rican youngsters are sent . . . only to hosts who request them."[40]

Police Athletic League of New York City

Established in 1914, the Police Athletic League (PAL) aspired to positively channel the energies of inner-city children through recreational and athletic programs. In 1938 it was gifted with Foxlair, the one-time lavish estate on 1,200 acres in Johnsburg, Warren County, that

25. Boys at New York City's Grand Central Station en route to Police Athletic League's Fox Lair Camp, 1939. Acme Photo. Author's collection.

had belonged to Richard Hudnut, a wealthy New York City cosmetics manufacturer. Retaining a variant of the estate's name, PAL developed Fox Lair as a boys' camp, where from 300 to 600 underprivileged boys were welcomed each summer for short vacations during which they played baseball, swam, fished, and hiked mountain trails. Plagued with financial problems from the beginning, Fox Lair was sold by PAL to New York State in 1964, after which the buildings were destroyed and the land added to the Adirondack Park.[41]

Pete Hamill, a renowned New York City journalist who began writing for the *New York Post* in 1960, spent three weeks as an eleven-year-old camper at Fox Lair in the summer of 1946. Of Irish descent and raised in a Brooklyn tenement, Hamill described the camp as "up close, much more complicated than any paradise." For the first time, he met "poor boys from the great city beyond the borders of the Neighborhood: Italians from Red Hook and Bensonhurst; blacks from distant Harlem and mysterious Bedford-Stuyvesant; Jews out of Brownsville and the Lower East Side." As Hamill acknowledged, despite his upbringing in what he considered a "pretty tough" neighborhood, "these kids made me feel like some sheltered boy." At Fox Lair he learned about sex, how to talk rough, and how to drink wine in the woods under the influence of Arnold, a black campmate. Returning home a "changed boy," Hamill concluded years later that his Fox Lair experience had been his "first true opening to consciousness." As a longtime New York City denizen, he added, "he hadn't seen a brook since Fox Lair Camp, had never fished in any serious way, associated woods with the place where Arnold hid his bottle of wine."[42]

15

Miners of Moriah

AFRICAN AMERICANS began before the Revolutionary War to mine iron in Essex County when Philip Skene, a British soldier who settled Skenesborough (now Whitehall, Washington County), sent slaves to extract ore from a rich bed at Cheever, just north of Port Henry, on land granted to him by the British Crown. Skene's miners transported the ore up Lake Champlain to Skenesborough, stopping overnight when necessary at shelters built for the purpose on a point of land six miles south of Ticonderoga that became known as Nigger's Marsh. When the State of New York stripped Skene of his lands after the war, his petition to the British government for financial restitution listed among his lost property "six healthy Negro men and six healthy women" valued at 600 pounds, "six young Negroes" at 80 pounds, and a "house for workers and Negroes" at 150 pounds.[1]

Witherbee, Sherman and Company, with the nominally independent but associated Port Henry Iron Ore Company, started mining in 1862 on some 38,000 acres of mostly contiguous Essex County land it owned in Moriah—a township encompassing the village of Port Henry and two outlying hamlets, Mineville and Witherbee. The majority of the company's employees were unskilled immigrants, most of them recruited by agents in their home countries or at New York City dockside when they landed in the United States. They came in national waves, reacting to political and economic crises at home and triggering frequent changes in Moriah's ethnic mix. The Irish arrived first, followed by Austrians, Russians, Slavs, and Italians. French Canadians came down from the north, and the occasional Mexican or Brazilian drifted up from the far south. In 1912, 44 percent of Witherbee, Sherman's workforce was classified as "Poles," 18 percent as "Hungarians," and 14.2 percent as "Americans."[2] The company encouraged ethnic clustering in housing and work assignments, as this deterred communal action against the company and stimulated competitive rivalry on the job.[3] Turnover at the mines was high, with defectors citing "no like," "small pay," "too wet," and "going away" among reasons for their departure.[4] Many employees left more than once.

African Americans were drawn to the Adirondack iron industry as early as the first decade of the twentieth century. Five black workers from the South were employed in 1910 in a blast furnace in Standish, a hamlet in the Clinton County town of Saranac. With families, they totaled sixteen residents. Standish was not itself a mining center, but its blast furnace processed the product mined in Lyon Mountain, an adjoining hamlet in the town of Dannemora. The black employees worked either in the furnace's machine shop or in "carrying iron"—probably from the Lyon Mountain mines to the furnace. Some of them would have been involved in the Adirondack region's only recorded race riot. This 1913 free-for-all was instigated by an Italian furnace employee whose efforts to interfere with a black coworker's job performance led the victim to threaten reporting him to his foreman. As an ethnic group, Italians had been known during the Adirondack and St. Lawrence Railroad construction project to dislike working with African Americans, an antipathy they expressed again here. As the black man "was passing one of the Italians," it was recounted, "the foreigner applied a vile name to him and in return was promptly knocked down. Every Italian in the room then turned on him, throwing iron, sticks and anything they could get their hands on at him. He finally escaped through a window," and a battle between blacks and Italians involving guns and knives ensued. Two Italians landed in hospital as a result of the fracas.[5]

Standish's black community expanded to a high of thirty in 1915, held steady through 1920, and then dwindled as the hamlet's iron industry faltered: to twenty-three residents in 1925 and eleven in 1930. It disappeared altogether by 1940—a year after lack of demand led to the dismantling of the Standish blast furnace.[6] No African Americans were employed during these census years at the nearby Lyon Mountain iron mines, but several men who worked at the Standish furnace would go on to have long careers as Moriah miners.

Standish's short-lived black settlement absorbed no more than a single drop of the steady trickle of southern blacks to the North that began with the dismantling of Reconstruction in the late nineteenth century. It preceded by several years the accelerated black relocation phenomenon that commenced with the 1914 outbreak in Europe of World War I. The "fever" of the "Great Migration," as it was later called, "rose without warning or notice or much in the way of understanding by those outside its reach."[7] Over 400,000 African American migrants left their southern homes between 1916 and 1918 in reaction to demeaning Jim Crow laws and increased mob violence. The immediate stimulus, however, was job availability: the result of military conscription and restricted immigration from abroad, which plunged from 1.2 million in 1914 to 110,000 in 1918.

Some 4.6 million workers across the country, driven by a sense of empowerment as they watched industry expand to meet wartime production needs, took part in labor disputes in the several years before 1920. The War Labor Board conceded workers' rights to organize and bargain collectively in March 1918, and the labor movement experienced a powerful surge.[8] Witherbee, Sherman, which had undergone a discomfiting but noncrippling strike in January 1913, considered itself threatened by the War Labor Board's edict and had no intention of facing another strike. The company had taken on one African American miner in 1917. In the summer of 1918, it quietly but deliberately added eighty-one more to its employment roster in the course of a scant six-week period.[9] This June 19–July 27 hiring spree was a cynical, proactive attempt by the company to stir up racial hostility within its work force. It did so in order to advance what was considered sound anti-organizing policy in the steel industry during a period of explosive relations between industrial management and employees.

The collective unwillingness of African Americans to support organized labor was one of their most appealing characteristics as far as industry was concerned. They had been employed as strikebreakers since the 1850s, when they first suffered exclusion from union organizations and eagerly took up jobs relinquished by striking white union members. (Less than 1 percent of the roughly 5 million black workers in the United States would be unionized as of 1925.)[10] The Delaware and Hudson Railroad took the regional lead in threatening to hire compliant blacks to replace white employees when faced with a possible job action in the years before the war. It announced in 1916 that it was bringing in one hundred African Americans from New Orleans to supplant track workers who had not yet settled with the company on job pay, including those employed on the railroad's Adirondack branch from Glens Falls to Lake George. The threat, which went so far as the construction of a camp to house the anticipated strikebreakers below Saratoga Springs, was apparently sufficient to settle the protest, for the scheme was not carried through.[11]

The black miners engaged by Witherbee, Sherman as prospective strikebreakers in June and July 1918 joined a workforce that would total 1,347 employees that year.[12] Most of them arrived in clusters: fifteen on June 19, for example, and thirteen on July 24. Seventy-three listed their previous address as Baltimore, a receiving station for southern blacks who followed the well-traveled eastern rail corridor north, and a recruiting base for northern job agents. Three recorded Boston as their last place of residence.[13] All were assigned to the lowest-paid job in the mining hierarchy, that of "trammer," whose duties entailed assisting miners by loading broken ore onto conveyors and filling and hauling mine cars.[14] Few of the hastily recruited African Americans stayed with Witherbee, Sherman for long; none of their names appeared in the town's 1920 federal census. But the company would henceforth be a consistent employer of black miners, most of them enlisted from among the migrants who continued to flow north until the Great Migration statistically ended in 1970.[15] It took on forty-nine African Americans during the 1920s and thirty-three in the 1930s before ceasing to keep records with the transfer of the company's operations to another proprietor, Republic Steel, in 1937.[16]

Witherbee, Sherman survived the war and early postwar period of labor unrest without strike actions. But the company did not always prosper, and a cyclical pattern of years of industrial activity followed by months or years of inactivity became the Witherbee, Sherman norm. Erratic iron ore production and sales during the early 1920s led to several years of unprofitable operation; mining was suspended in 1924 and 1925. Production increased between 1928 and 1930, after which the company succumbed to the nationwide Depression, again closing its mines in 1932 and 1933. Some 700 Moriah families were dependent on home and work relief during the era's darkest days, and job uncertainty led to a high rate of population displacement.[17]

Blacks never achieved in Moriah the 1 percent of population they represented in Saranac Lake in 1910, but they made up the largest black community in the park in the 1940s. From one African American (a female servant) in a population of 6,754 in 1910, it increased to 17 (in eight black and mixed-race households) in a diminished Moriah population of 6,626 in 1920. In 1930 there were 28 blacks (9 black households) among 6,191 residents and, in 1940, 36 (12 black and mixed-race households) in a population of 5,952.[18] Housing was not segregated, but black families tended to cluster in a mixed neighborhood on and near quarter-mile-long Elizabeth Street at the edge of Port Henry's downtown. As of 1940, one mixed-race family was living in Mineville and one in Witherbee.

Moriah's black miners were not all from the South, but a high percentage of them were. South Carolina predominated as the birthplace of transplants enumerated in the 1930 and 1940 censuses—the majority of them coming from the city of Greenville and the farms and small towns of nearby Anderson County. Like many newcomers, they arrived through a pattern of chain migration known as laddering up, whereby those who had already made the move north induced relatives and onetime neighbors to join them. Such recruitment from home, attended by promises of help in finding jobs and settling in, was a way for migrants to surround themselves with people whose lifestyle and folkways were familiar to them.[19] Not all new hires had relevant experience, although some had worked in the mining industry before, both in the Standish blast furnace and in related jobs elsewhere in the country. A few came from hotel, industrial, and transportation backgrounds in New York and nearby Vermont. Occasional recruits showed up by chance, as did three members of an Ohio-based, fifteen-rail-car Gentry Brothers' traveling circus that played Port Henry on July 31, 1929, who signed on together.[20]

Moriah was a company town. Witherbee, Sherman's management oversaw all aspects of town life, providing school buildings for the three communities of Port Henry, Witherbee, and Mineville as well as a recreation and community center, a hospital, and land for church buildings. Single miners resided in company-owned boardinghouses, and married miners lived with their families in company-owned tenements and multifamily houses. By the 1930s the town was known as a rough place to live. Housing was run-down (and would not have indoor plumbing until the late 1940s). Living accommodations were often overcrowded, as many mining families took in boarders. Drinking, integral to the mining culture, meant that taverns were plentiful and popular and alcohol abuse was widespread. So was prostitution.[21] Allen Walton, the black Tennesseean who settled in Port Henry in the 1930s, remembered boozy "rent parties" at which folks sold food and spirits to friends and strangers from their homes and charged admission to help make that month's rent. At such gatherings, according to Walton, "one was inclined to dance too close to some one else's mate. This always caused a real house brawl."[22]

Black miners, who worked in intimate contact with whites below ground, often struck up friendships across racial barriers—at least during shift hours. But life in Moriah could be lonely for their wives. Although families looked largely within their community for social life, neighborhood proximity led to occasional, often durable, cross-race friendships. An African American church, a pillar of southern life, was launched in Port Henry in the 1950s. Services were held at least once a month in a simple wooden building on Elizabeth Street, and black choirs from Albany paid occasional visits. Despite its importance to parishioners, it was able to survive for only a few years.[23] Thus,

26. Moriah miners, unknown date. Courtesy of Town of Moriah Historical Society.

black residents of Port Henry and the hamlets worshiped primarily in local Baptist, Methodist, and Presbyterian churches.

Witherbee, Sherman's mines produced as much iron in 1936 and 1937 as they had in 1930. In 1938 the company leased its operations to the Republic Steel Corporation, which had been running them since late 1937 and would later purchase them.[24] Republic Steel's timing was fortuitous, as wartime demand for iron increased dramatically between 1939 and 1944.

There were few blacks in defense industries before World War II, but a June 1941 presidential executive order creating the Committee of Fair Employment Practices banned discrimination in defense employment. The federal government invested heavily in Republic's Moriah operation, although it practiced segregationist policy in industry as it did in the military. Responding to a government war contract with the company that anticipated 1,400 supplementary workers, the Federal Public Housing Administration oversaw the construction of several hundred new housing units as well as five dormitories to accommodate 310 unattached men—one of which was designated specifically for African Americans.[25]

Republic Steel's war contracts brought the United Services Organizations (USO) to Mineville for the better part of 1943. A nonprofit association providing programs, services, and live entertainment to American troops and "industrial transients" in the defense industry, it opened a local office under the direction of a YMCA staffer and provided a drop-in center with a phonograph, a library of books, and equipment for tabletop games such as ping pong and table hockey.[26] The USO was committed to racial and religious inclusiveness, and the local director reported on interactions with African Americans in his monthly reports, describing race relations as "good." Tessie Stewart, a black machine operator from South Carolina who had followed his twin brother, Jesse, to the Moriah mines in 1935, was the judge of a jitterbug contest at a USO dance; his wife was elected to membership on the community-based USO Council. (Stewart would die in a mine accident in 1946 at the age of forty-five.)[27]

Despite the preparations made for their arrival, the expected influx of war employees to Moriah never materialized, and few recruits stayed long. (Five of seven blacks from Alabama hired by Republic in late 1943 moved on within two weeks.)[28] Departing workers cited dissatisfaction with wages as a reason for leaving, as well as the community's isolation from ordinary recreational outlets: restaurants, stores, movie theaters, and sports facilities. Only fifty-six of 430 housing units at the Grover Hills family housing project were occupied as of December 1943, and four of the five new dormitories were subsequently shut down, leaving a single dormitory to be shared by fifteen men, "both white and colored." The USO closed its Mineville operation that month due to the absence of clientele.[29]

Unionization came to Moriah at about the same time as Republic Steel. By early 1939 the mineworkers had organized an integrated local of the Iron Ore Miners' Union under the umbrella of the American Federation of Labor. Promotions for African Americans became more forthcoming (the 1940 census reported one black foreman at the blast furnace), although racial progress made little headway at the white-collar level. A longtime company employee later recalled a "difficult problem" that arose in 1943 when Republic considered taking on a highly qualified black engineer. Many would-be coworkers in the Port Henry office threatened to quit if he were engaged, so the Mineville field survey staff was queried as to how it felt about such a hiring. The leader of the group, despite his Maryland background, reported no objection to a black engineer, and he went to work in its office. "He did excellent map work, was congenial and I don't think anyone ever gave much thought to the color of his skin," it was recalled. The new hire was the star of a talent show held in the high school not long after his arrival with his musical rendition of "Deep in the Heart of Texas."[30]

Race-based hate crimes were infrequent in Moriah, but they did occur. Port Henry was the scene of a 1947 incident that took place after the black chef at a local restaurant, filling in for an absent bartender, forcibly ejected a client from the bar for using racially abusive language. Piqued, the expelled man recruited two cronies and sought revenge. The trio abducted the chef after he left work, drove him into the woods, and beat him so badly that he was unable to work again. Convicted of the crime, the three men served brief jail sentences. The primary offender was additionally fined one thousand dollars.[31]

Life was, predictably, not easy for black children in Moriah's largely white schools. Frostiness, tactless curiosity about physical differences, and taunting were commonplace. School friendships seldom extended beyond the schoolyard, and did so to an even lesser degree as children reached adolescence.[32] Nevertheless, the school system did quite well by its black students, sending many of them on to higher education. As Allen Walton, who raised five children in Port Henry, phrased it in 1996, "Every kid that want to go to college went off to college. Some become doctors, lawyers, politicians."[33] Racial boundaries could be breached by athletic ability. Pallbearers at the 1929 Port Henry funeral of John Gilbo (twenty-eight-year-old son of a well-known local family) were all white except for one: African American Albert Parnell, "who represented baseballdom in which the deceased attained much fame in this section."[34]

The fortunes of the Moriah mining industry continued to fluctuate after the close of World War II. A lengthy strike in 1946 led to a wage increase for miners, but layoffs became more frequent and drawn-out. "A period of consolidation" reduced employment numbers in the 1950s, and the Moriah communities continued to decrease in size. One black family that stayed on during these years of diminishing economic activity was that of miner William Payden, whose wife and children arrived late in the 1940s from Greenville, South Carolina, and spent twenty-two years in the hamlet of Witherbee. Alice Paden Green, only six years old when her family settled in Moriah, writes honestly and eloquently about her experience growing up as an African American in the Adirondacks in her autobiographical afterword to this book.

Republic closed down operations altogether in 1971.[35] By then most of the town's miners, black and white, had moved on to other job opportunities, usually outside of the region. Allen Walton was one of the few blacks who remained, becoming a local activist, particularly on behalf of Moriah's poor and senior citizens, and receiving an award from the Essex County Bar Association in 1991 as an "Outstanding Citizen" of the county.[36] Walton neatly summarized the local black population as it existed in 1994, not long before his death, as "one Black lady, 2 growned children, myself."[37] Another isolated black community in the Adirondacks had largely disappeared.

16

Pullman Porters

Railroad Stories

THERE WERE MORE African American workers employed in connection with rail lines serving the Adirondacks than those who furnished brute labor to build the Adirondack and St. Lawrence Railroad. Porters, waiters, bartenders, and members of the kitchen workforce on trains traversing the region were routinely black from the late 1860s, when what became the Delaware and Hudson Railway first penetrated the region's southern reaches. By the close of 1875 the D and H was serving towns along the eastern Adirondack border between New York City and Montreal.[1] The New York Central did the same in the central and western Adirondacks after 1892. Both lines ran spurs to popular resort areas.

The Chicago-based Pullman Company, organized in 1867, owned and staffed dining, observation, lounge, and overnight sleeping cars (or sleepers), leasing them to individual railroads. George M. Pullman, the company's founder, determined early on that hiring black workers from the South to tend to the needs of his middle- and upper-class clientele made business sense. As glorified servants, they could be looked upon by travelers as "part of the furniture" of train travel because of their racial and social distance from themselves.[2]

Thanks to inter-rail cooperation, Pullman sleeping cars, each staffed with a black porter, could be switched between lines so that travelers were able to cover long distances without changing berths. Most porters stayed with the same cars for the duration of their runs.

Those with seniority were assigned to the same routes year after year. Although they were overworked and underpaid, their professionalism, courtesy, and deference became hallmarks of Pullman service. Highly respected within the black community, Pullman porters helped lay the foundation of the African American middle class. While they welcomed the financial stability and group fraternity they enjoyed, as well as the public's generally friendly attitude toward them, the groveling stereotype they projected as dependent on passengers' tips for a good portion of their income was difficult to counteract. Their jobs, moreover, offered no prospects of advancement. Porters were answerable to conductors in charge of their cars—who were always white and who held positions to which blacks could never aspire. Many well-known African Americans served stints as Pullman porters, among them Supreme Court Justice Thurgood Marshall, photojournalist Gordon Parks, and social activist Malcolm X.

Sleeping cars outnumbered passenger coaches during the heyday of train travel, and engines hauling a long string of Pullman sleepers were a common sight in the Adirondacks through the 1930s. A resort employee clearly exaggerated when he reported seeing thirty or forty Pullman cars cut off from a single summer train at the station that served the large and luxurious Saranac Inn on Upper Saranac Lake around 1907, but his estimate signifies the local perception of the huge Pullman presence.[3] Porters who served in the Adirondacks generally called New York City, Albany, or Buffalo home; Montreal was the customary base for three- to four-day stopovers between trips.[4] Some Pullman porters were regularly or occasionally laid over at regional terminals in Lake Placid or Lake George. Others might be employed on special trains that had long downtimes between arrival and departure at Adirondack locations. While the Pullman Company provided dormitories for porters' use between runs in large centers,[5] it did not do so in the Adirondacks, and off-duty porters were on their own when it came to finding accommodations. The Lake Placid boardinghouse for African Americans run by Alice Walker and later by Inez Carter was a popular overnight venue.

27. Pullman porter with President and Mrs. Calvin Coolidge, Gabriels, hamlet of Brighton, Franklin County, 1926. Photograph by William F. Kollecker. Courtesy of Adirondack Collection, Saranac Lake Free Library.

Interactions between porters and regional travelers could enrich the experience of one or both parties. Alabama-born Frederick Douglas Funderburg, a Pullman porter during summer breaks from his medical school education in the late 1910s and early 1920s, attracted the attention of a Manhattan-based passenger on a New York-to-Adirondacks run who subsequently provided him with a small subsidy for school expenses. (Funderburg went on to become a doctor in Monticello, Georgia.)[6] Porter W. J. Grandy was remembered after his 1922 death for the "unusual patience, tact and sympathy" he displayed on the route between New York City and Saranac Lake to which he was assigned for most of the twenty years he worked for the Pullman Company.[7] Tuberculosis patients who rode what was nicknamed the Lungers' Special were likely to be so ill that they were delivered to the train on stretchers,[8] and an acquaintance recalled seeing Grandy "handle an invalid with such ease and solicitude that a professional nurse could not have done better. Many times passengers who knew him would delay their trip if he were not on the job; not that they would not get service, but they felt they were in care of a friend when he was in attendance."[9]

There was some discussion in the early twentieth century about the health danger faced by the numerous Pullman porters who tended to actively ill tuberculosis patients, as they came "into closer contact with passengers than other railroad employee[s]," and "in making up berths . . . [were] constantly exposed to dust." It was determined, however, that the danger of infection, "while present in limited degree, [was] not great." For riders' protection, porters were required to fumigate cars that carried sick passengers to or from Loon Lake, Saranac Lake, and Lake Placid, and to take their berths "off sale" until they reached the end of their runs.[10] Porters overseeing tuberculosis patients had to contend with other special situations as well. According to the wife of William Hunton, the WMCA's international secretary, her husband was well cared for by two young students from southern schools employed as porters during the summer of 1914 when Hunton journeyed to Saranac Lake for tuberculosis treatment. They were not working in his sleeping car, she noted, but saw him carried onto a Pullman sleeper in New York City and "came quickly to speak to him and to offer themselves for any service. We did want some milk," Mrs. Hunton recalled, "and they promised to get it for us. From somewhere along the road during the night they secured a fresh new pail of very good milk," and they assisted in taking Hunton off the train upon its early morning arrival in Saranac Lake.[11] In another tuberculosis-related incident, a Buffalo-based Pullman porter discovered the 1934 suicide of a forty-one-year-old patient returning after a Christmas leave to Sunmount, the veterans hospital in Tupper Lake.[12]

Porters were subject to accusations of all kinds, many of them originating in the racist sensibilities of train passengers. A 1906 legal case grew out of an incident on the Delaware and Hudson's New York–to–Montreal route involving the claim of a white passenger that a porter had stolen his pocketbook. The porter involved, a former schoolteacher, was briefly imprisoned as a result of the unfounded allegation. He sued his accuser for "malicious intent" as well as for the "public disgrace" and "trouble and expense" he suffered because of the episode. The passenger, president of the Brady Brass Company of New Jersey, was quoted as unabashedly stating during the trial that he "knew how thoroughly untrustworthy and unreliable" Pullman porters were, that he thought none of his respectable-looking fellow passengers could have committed the theft, and that "when it came to a matter of accusing or of deciding whether a white man or a colored man would steal a purse, he would decide in favor of the colored man stealing it always." A jury awarded the porter the sizable sum of $2,500 in damages, an amount reduced on appeal to $300, for, as the trial judge determined, "a black person's humiliation was not the equivalent of a white's and, thus, blacks should be awarded lower damages." The ruling, labeled "distinctly shocking" by the liberal *New York Times*, was upheld by an appellate division of the New York State Supreme Court.[13]

Another Pullman car incident, leading to a trial with broad ramifications, occurred on the Adirondack Division of the New York Central en route to Lake Placid in 1931, when a conductor reportedly dragged twenty-nine-year-old porter James E. Smith from the berth of a protesting white woman passenger. This gave rise, according to the conductor, to a melee that necessitated his subduing the physically aggressive perpetrator with the assistance of two other railroad employees and four passengers. (One railroad employee spent several months in hospital as a result of the encounter.) Smith was handed over to the police at Thendara, a hamlet west of Old Forge in the Herkimer County town of Webb, and charged with first- and second-degree assault. The $5,000 necessary to secure the release on bail of its union member was provided by the International Brotherhood of Sleeping Car Porters and Maids, the union for black train personnel founded by A. Philip Randolph in 1925 that was then struggling for adherents and recognition after a diminution in membership fueled by a failed 1929 strike attempt.[14]

Both male and female passengers routinely propositioned porters, and Smith contended that he had entered the woman's berth at her invitation. He claimed self-defense in having struck out at the conductor and subsequent assailants.[15] There were no witnesses to the triggering episode, and the woman involved, who made no charge against the porter, quietly slipped away. But crossing the color line when it came to sexual relations between black men and white women raised red flags among whites (although there were few legal or social repercussions for white men who forced themselves upon black women). Smith's supporters decided that he needed a strong defense lawyer to counteract the influence of racial hostility injected into the case by regional newspapers, and New York Democratic Congressman Fiorello LaGuardia volunteered his services without charge to represent the porter. LaGuardia paid his own travel expenses to and from Rome, Oswego County, where the trial was held. He was able to maneuver his client's acquittal thanks to the prosecutor's inability to locate the woman passenger in the case and the contradictory testimony of thirteen prosecution witnesses. The decision was hailed as benefitting not only railroad porters but all black Americans, "who suffer many grave injustices based upon fictitious charges and allegations of their attempting to force their attentions."[16] Smith lost his job but worked for several years as a field agent for the Brotherhood of Sleeping Car Porters in New York City before resigning in 1938.[17]

Prohibition, introduced with the passage in 1919 of the Eighteenth Amendment to the US Constitution that proscribed the manufacture, transportation, and sale of alcohol and alcoholic beverages, proved to be a resounding failure as government policy. Many people believed the amendment to be a "bum law," and Prohibition served as an economic driver in the Adirondacks during the years between 1920 and 1933, when the law was repealed. Small-time liquor smugglers were attracted to the possibilities offered by the railroads that daily passed through the region on their way to and from Canada, and Pullman passengers, counting on lax federal enforcement, concealed liquor in their luggage as well as in train ventilators, light fixtures, seat springs, upper berths, mattresses, and behind the wall panels of staterooms and bathrooms.[18] It was among the official job responsibilities of Pullman porters to assist customs officers in rooting out alcohol in their cars,[19] but rail crew members were sometimes as guilty as passengers of illegally importing liquor from Canada—both for their own use and for resale, often to train passengers. Sometimes they were caught. Among unlucky porters was Buffalo-based Grover Meadows, taken into custody at Malone in 1928 by custom agents who confiscated thirty-eight bottles of whiskey from a Pullman stateroom on a southbound New York Central train from Montreal.[20] Meadows, who had been with the company for barely two years before his arrest, was no doubt let go as a result of his exploit.

Another porter on the same run, Frank G. Whitted, was arrested for transporting several suitcases of "choice liquors" in his Pullman car in 1925. His case was tried in Malone, where Whitted explained that a Red Cap railroad station porter in New York City had handed him the suitcases and told him to deliver them to Tupper Lake, where he was to leave them on the train platform to be called for by their owner. Whitted did as he was instructed, but when he saw that the baggage was not claimed returned it to the train and carried it on to Malone. The suspect was cleared after several witnesses, including a conductor on Whitted's train, corroborated his story as he had told it to them during the course of the journey north. It was assumed that the owner of the liquor stash had seen a trooper or other officer at Tupper Lake and been afraid to claim his belongings.[21]

The only result of the incident for Whitted, who had been a Pullman employee for eleven years and the subject of a number of commendatory letters from passengers, was that he was "restricted from further operation into International territory" to keep him out of temptation's way. He remained with the Pullman Company until at least 1936 and survived "cautions," "instructions," and "warnings" for unexplained absences (during one of which he claimed to be helping out on his father's farm), drinking on duty, and run-of-the-mill blunders such as leaving a laundry bag containing "sheets and slips not tied tight, linen exposed." In 1929 the company granted Whitted a loan of one hundred dollars.[22]

It has been estimated that only a fraction—perhaps 5 to 20 percent—of contraband liquor was ever seized during Prohibition.[23] Thus the smuggling of liquor between Montreal and other cities was no doubt a modestly rewarding sideline over a nearly fourteen-year period for a number of Pullman porters and other personnel working Adirondack railroad routes. A new opportunity for smuggling arose with World War II and the imposition of food rationing. Four New York City–based porters on the Delaware and Hudson's Montreal–to–New York run were arrested in 1945 in Rouse's Point, Clinton County, for attempting to bring in some four hundred pounds of Canadian ham and bacon at a time when meat, particularly pork, was scarce and commanding high prices.[24]

A few tales passed down by and about Pullman porters traversing the region relate to curious incidents that befell them in the course of their employment. One sleeping-car porter was written up for forgetting to awaken his charges in time to prepare for the early-morning detraining of passengers on a New York Central run that stopped at Childwold, St. Lawrence County. This led a member of the party ("an influential man in Western Union") to insist that the train be held until everyone was dressed—not only causing a delay in the train schedule but also marring the job record of the porter involved.[25]

The Adirondack misadventure of another sleeping-car porter was unfortunate for the Pullman employee but made for an amusing story. Its protagonist had gathered a dozen or so pairs of shoes laid out for polishing on his New York–to–Chicago night run, and had taken them to a baggage car where he hoped to find some company to pass the time while buffing. Excursions beyond one's own car were against Pullman rules but not uncommon, and the porter fell into conversation with another shoeshiner to whom he commented on the unusual bumpiness of the ride. That, explained his knowledgeable companion, was because some of the train's cars, including the one they were on, had been switched to a Montreal-bound train at Troy. "Laws," his dismayed companion was said to have lamented, "an all them feets on their way to Chicago." The Pullman Company purchased new shoes for the inconvenienced passengers in Chicago; what happened to the porter involved is unknown.[26]

Twenty thousand African Americans were employed across the country as sleeping-car porters and other Pullman personnel during the mid-1920s. The company's busiest year was 1925, when it carried more than thirty-five million passengers nationwide, but railroad custom foundered during the Great Depression and never revived. A Pullman porter reported in July 1931 that his cars were running full out of New York en route for Lake George, but that most of his loads were camp girls, who "as a rule are not the most desirable patrons in the world, from the porter's angle."[27] New York Central reportedly broke its Adirondack travel records during the 1932 Winter Olympics, when more than ten trains pulling Pullman sleepers arrived in Lake Placid on a Friday morning. Most of their four thousand passengers returned home the same way Sunday night when eight trains, of which seven were "specials" put on for the event, hauled a total of sixty-one sleeping cars and a few coaches back to their originating cities.[28] Sixty-one sleeping cars meant, of course, sixty-one porters in the village for the weekend, none of whom were likely to have been Olympic spectators.

The summer season of 1940 marked a new low in passenger traffic to and through the Adirondacks during a period that also saw the beginnings of inroads by Mexicans and Filipinos into Pullman jobs held until then almost exclusively by African Americans.[29] Railroad business increased briefly during the Second World War, when the company was responsible for 66 percent of US troop movements, but overnight rail travel continued its decline, a trend hastened by the rise in popularity of automobiles, faster and more comfortable day trains, and the slow growth of commercial airlines.[30] The Pullman Company ceased operation of its sleeper cars and terminated all leases in 1968, bringing to an end a long era of specialized, generally black, employment.

The Delaware and Hudson abandoned its money-losing Lake Placid train route in 1946 and cut the Lake George branch back to

Glens Falls in 1958.[31] Amtrak, its eventual successor, continues to run infrequent passenger trains to Montreal. The New York Central steadily shrank service to the Adirondacks, and passenger trains disappeared altogether on the line's Adirondack Division line in 1964 (except for a brief revival of service during the 1980 Winter Olympics).

Overall, work opportunities for African Americans in railroading advanced little over the years. A 1957 survey conducted jointly by New York and New Jersey state commissions against discrimination found that African Americans held 93 percent of service jobs—waiters, chefs, and cooks—on the nineteen railroads then operating in the two states, but that only 8 percent of their supervisors were black. At the same time, blacks accounted for less than 1 percent of "operating transportation" jobs: engineer, motorman, agent, ticket collector, switch tender, etc. Fifty-five percent of common laborers on railroads, but only 6 percent of gang foremen, were black.[32]

Railroad service workers were perhaps the Adirondacks' largest and most mobile, if least visible, part-time black population during the one hundred years between 1850 and 1950. The occasional porter may have commented upon the "beautiful country" he passed through during his runs through the region,[33] but no rail personnel have yet been discovered who documented their Adirondack experiences in any way. If only they had. As a onetime Pullman porter recalled, to be in his position "was like getting a ten-second flash of every movie ever filmed."[34]

17

The Twentieth-Century Military

REGIONAL DEMOGRAPHICS suggest that the number of blacks who enlisted or were drafted into the armed forces from the Adirondacks during the twentieth century would have been small. Nevertheless, there were a few black soldiers with Adirondack roots. Other African Americans settled in the region after military service; at least one arrived only after death. Most of the men cited in this chapter repose in local cemeteries, some buried beneath headstones recalling their service units or celebrated with markers furnished by the US Department of Veterans Affairs.

There was little debate in the military about race during the second half of the nineteenth century. The army as reorganized during Reconstruction included four black infantry regiments, consolidated into two in 1869 (the Twenty-Fourth and Twenty-Fifth infantries), and two cavalry regiments. This arrangement remained virtually unchanged for nearly forty years. The regiments moved outside of mainstream American culture: usually assigned to fight Indians and Mexicans on the western frontier, where they "won the reputation of being tough, brave, efficient, though often brawling troopers," and in 1898 taking part in the Spanish-American War in Cuba. In 1899 they were posted to the Philippines during the Philippine-American War, where they ironically supported keeping other people of color "in their place" as they assisted in putting down the local "insurrection" against colonial rule after the United States took over the island.[1]

It was rumored in 1908 that some units of the Twenty-Fourth would be posted to Plattsburgh Barracks, the military base just outside of the Adirondack Park that intermittently accommodated soldiers during and after the War of 1812. "Regardless of protests from New York congressmen and residents in the vicinity of Plattsburg and Madison barracks," announced the *Elizabethtown Post* in an article headlined "Negroes for Plattsburg," the regiment, then en route from the Philippines, was to be assigned to Plattsburgh and to Madison Barracks in Sackets Harbor, west of Watertown in Jefferson County.[2] The decision was eventually made not to station units at Plattsburgh, but headquarters, the band, and two battalions were based between March 1908 and November 1911 at Madison Barracks and one battalion at Fort Ontario in Oswego County in the regiment's first assignment east of the Mississippi River.[3] (It was later reported of the Madison Barracks assignees "that there had never been a regiment so soldierly, so self-respecting, and which gave so little trouble").[4] Eighteen officers and 357 enlisted men of the Twenty-Fourth, including the band, took part in a July 1909 Plattsburgh parade commemorating Lake Champlain's tercentenary.[5]

Claud Reid, husband of Saranac Lake boardinghouse proprietor Mattie Ramsey Reid, was a member of the Twenty-Fourth Infantry Regiment. Born in 1885, he enlisted from Lincoln County, Georgia, in the peacetime army in 1913 and was assigned to Company L of the regiment's Third Battalion. His years as an army regular coincided with a troubled period for the unit that was instrumental in determining the role of blacks in the armed forces during the two major wars of the first half of the twentieth century.[6]

Soldiers of the Twenty-Fourth, used to living in tight-knit communities and legendary for their discipline, were able to sidestep many of the worst manifestations of Jim Crow. The regiment's several postings to the Philippines in 1899–1902, 1906–8, and 1912–15 imbued unit members with an elitist spirit that was rudely contested when its Third Battalion was posted to Houston, Texas, in July 1917. The unit settled in barely three months after the United States declared war on Germany and was assigned to guard the construction site of a new military installation, Camp Logan. Triggered directly by a white policeman's unwarranted mistreatment of a black woman, and indirectly by increasing resentment of Houston's blatant racism, soldiers from the battalion broke on August 23, rampaging through the city during a two-hour nighttime spree. The "mutiny" resulted in the killing of fifteen civilians and four soldiers and brought immediate retribution. The battalion was returned posthaste to its earlier New Mexico camp. A series of courts-martial brought in 110 convictions against participating soldiers, including twenty-nine death sentences—of which nine were later commuted to life imprisonment. The Third Battalion was disbanded in late 1922 and later reformed from soldiers at the Infantry School at Fort Benning, Georgia.[7]

Claud Reid is likely to have been present in Houston during the Third Battalion incident, but as a seasoned soldier he appears not to have been directly involved. He was promoted from private to corporal to sergeant before being discharged from the army in New Mexico in 1919 with "severe disabilities": high blood pressure and heart disease. He spent, as noted in chapter 10, much of his later life in veterans hospitals, but joined his wife during summers at her Saranac Lake boardinghouse. He died in 1959 and is buried by Mattie Reid's side in the Ramsey family plot in Brookside Cemetery, Bloomingdale, Essex County.[8]

The Houston riot unsettled the War Department, which henceforth reduced the number of black combat units.[9] Some African Americans, angered by the government's failure to penalize whites involved in the Houston melee and the harsh punishments meted out to black rioters, proposed that black Americans sit out the First World War, arguing that sending black soldiers "to defend 'the American Way' would be a mockery."[10] But the majority of them believed, as they had in the Civil War, that "the black man has nothing to lose and everything to gain" from wartime loyalty, and that their participation and war records would encourage "a grateful nation" to bestow on them "the rights and privileges of true and loyal citizens of these United States."[11] Some 367,700 blacks served in the army during World War I, 200,000 of them in support units overseas.[12]

The concept of black commissioned officers was anathema to the military hierarchy, and officers overseeing black regiments continued to be, as they had been since the Civil War, almost universally white. Black candidates were not invited to apply to the fourteen camps established across the country to train army officers on the eve of the United States' entry into the First World War. Pressure brought to bear by black universities and the NAACP, however, led to promises in early 1917 that one "parallel" military "Camp for Colored Men" would be established in conjunction with a white training camp at Plattsburgh Barracks if two hundred black men of college grade could be obtained.[13] Fifteen hundred names were presented to the War Department within ten days.[14] Some blacks approved the scheme, but others criticized the idea of a segregated training camp as "un-American," protesting that "to go to a Jimcrow Plattsburg to learn how to lead Jimcrow regiments is too much."[15] The scheme was abandoned in any event, but an officer-training camp for black high school graduates and noncommissioned officers was organized at Fort Des Moines, Iowa, in June 1917, from which 639 men graduated four months later. No further specific opportunities were offered for black soldiers to attain commissioned-officer rank, although some seven hundred trained in various other facilities.[16]

As *Crisis*, journal of the NAACP, phrased it in 1918, Saranac Lake was "not as appreciative of her colored soldiers as some other cities." On August 3, it noted, two "colored men, through draft were sent to camp. The morning of their departure, they were sent away with two or three boxes of cigarettes and matches. . . . Two days later one man of the opposite race left for the same cause, and was sent away with a trunkful of all sorts of things and also full military honors consisting of a company of home guards and the firing-off of a couple of rounds of ammunition."[17] One of the unidentified black draftees may have been Herbert Minnifield, born in 1889 into the large family of stonemason Wallace Minnifield in the Franklin hamlet of Vermontville. Minnifield was drafted on August 2 of that year and served until July 14, 1919.

The Department of Veterans Affairs gave no details of Minnifield's war service in recording his 1976 death, but there is a good chance that he was one of the 70 percent of black army men assigned to labor units.[18] These corps, the military equivalent of chain gangs, made up an estimated one-third of all labor troops during the war and did the dirty work necessary to support modern warfare: loading and unloading materiel at railheads and docks; digging ditches; repairing roads; "policing" (cleaning) camps; hauling wood, coal, and stone; disposing of garbage; and caring for animals. Even those trained for more technical duties—such as drivers or mechanics—were likely to end up digging, hauling, or performing general fatigue duties.[19] Colonel E. D. Anderson, chairman of the Operations Branch of the Army General Staff, contemptuously outlined army policy in May 1918 with regard to the majority of black draftees. The "backwoods" and "ignorant illiterate day laborer class," he wrote, or what remained after the "cream of the colored draft" had been "skimmed off" for possible combat service, would, "instead of laying around camps accomplishing nothing of value," be "kept out of trouble by being kept busy at useful work" in labor battalions in white "cantonments" or camps. Their noncommissioned officers, he added, should be "forceful whites," the kind of men who as civilians "had been overseers of black work gangs" and could "get work out of the colored men."[20]

Herman Payton (born 1897) and Ambrose Gambrell (1896), Moriah miners who arrived in the Adirondacks in the 1920s, came from the rural "backwoods" background delineated by Colonel Anderson. Payton was a hired man on a "mulatto"-owned South Carolina farm in 1920; Gambrell was a tenant farmer. Both men could read and write, Payton having completed the sixth grade and Gambrell the eighth grade in the separate and unequal school system of the South. Payton was drafted in August 1918 and served as a private until February 1919 with the Headquarters 432nd Residence Labor Battalion at Camp Jackson, a Columbia, South Carolina, training camp established as the United States entered the war.[21] His assignment to a South Carolina camp was in keeping with army policy not to antagonize white citizens by placing southern blacks, who made up a high percentage of black draftees, in regions unaccustomed to their presence. As rationalized by Colonel Anderson, "Each southern state has negroes in blue overalls working throughout the state with a pick and shovel. When these colored men are drafted they are put to work in blue overalls (fatigue clothes) and continue to do work with pick and shovel in the same state where they were previously working."[22] Payton died in 1968. His gravestone in Port Henry's Union Cemetery records his service with the 432nd.

Ambrose Gambrell, drafted in July 1918, was assigned for one month to a labor unit, the 156th Depot Brigade, at the same Camp Jackson before being transferred to Company B of the all-black 534th Engineers Service Battalion. This was one of forty-six labor battalions delegated to support the overseas work of the American Expeditionary Forces under the direction of the US Army Corps of Engineers. Gambrell was shipped with his unit to France in late August, where the 534th toiled close to the front lines: supporting a September offensive in and near the town of St. Mihiel (south of Verdun) by laying railroad tracks forward toward the enemy line from railheads and maintaining roads and bridges.[23] Honorably discharged in March 1919, Gambrell died in 1948 at the age of forty-eight in a mine collapse in Moriah.[24]

No African Americans with Adirondack connections have yet come to light who counted themselves among the thirty thousand combat soldiers serving with the army's black Ninety-Second and Ninety-Third combat divisions in Europe during World War I: a war in which blacks could not serve in the marine corps and only in limited, menial positions in the navy and army air force. Negative white opinion in the United States regarding African Americans' performance in combat (despite the successful integration of the Ninety-Third Division for most of the war into the French army), and fear, particularly in the South, that black soldiers were "spoiled" by their war experience, meant that returning African American troops were not warmly embraced at the war's close.[25] Elevated racial tensions led to anti-black riots in twenty-six cities across the United States in the summer and fall of 1919. Lynchings of black men increased, from fifty-eight in 1918 to seventy-seven in 1919. At least ten victims were war veterans, some still in uniform.[26]

Disillusion and a newfound self-respect intensified the level of black political activism after World War I, spurred on by race leaders, the

NAACP, and the African American press. Despite the discriminatory treatment they had experienced during the war, many blacks believed that participation in the military, particularly as officers, provided a means of socioeconomic advancement. Opportunities were limited, but by mid-1919 junior or senior Reserve Officers' Training Corps (ROTC) units had been placed at twelve historically black colleges and universities; a very few blacks were admitted to ROTC programs at predominantly white universities. The Citizens' Military Training Camps (CMTC), a program established under the Army Reorganization Act of 1920 to train reserve officers and noncommissioned personnel for use if needed, was, however, effectively closed to African American applicants. A black candidate accepted in 1922 to a CMTC training camp at Plattsburgh Barracks was given orders to report and had his fare paid north by the government, only to be told on arrival that a mistake had been made and he was summarily shipped home.[27]

The American public had to be sold on World War II.[28] Blacks, nevertheless, were still willing to do their part. As army enlistee and heavyweight boxing champion Joe Louis is said to have phrased it, "There may be a whole lot wrong with America, but there's nothing that Hitler can fix."[29] Regardless of the heightened level of pressure applied, integration was not a military priority and, according to Army Chief of Staff George C. Marshall, "the settlement of vexing social problems can not be permitted to complicate the tremendous task of the War Department and thereby jeopardize discipline and morale."[30] Segregation continued to be the military's organizational norm, although there was a marked increase in the number of blacks in the armed services over the course of the war, from a level of 5,000 in the prewar peacetime army to over 900,000 by 1945. Seventy-five percent of black soldiers were assigned to service and supply units.[31]

The impact of the Second World War on black Americans as represented through the stories of Adirondack participants is as idiosyncratic as that of the First World War, and no doubt as incomplete. Edward Plummer, a college graduate who grew up in Saranac Lake, became a sergeant with the 293rd Company of the 504th Port Battalion Transportation Corps, a unit that served in the Pacific theater and was responsible for managing ports of embarkation and debarkation and moving soldiers from training bases to the front.[32]

Pilots were the romantic heroes of popular culture in the late 1930s and early 1940s. When the US Army Air Corps, predecessor to the Department of the Air Force and in its time considered the most prestigious branch of the armed services, embarked in 1939 on an expansion program, black leaders mounted a vigorous crusade to ensure that training on the new planes would be open to African Americans. The military resisted these efforts, using the old argument that the army was "not a social laboratory," but concerns about the black vote in Roosevelt's 1940 reelection campaign led the White House to announce two months before the election that the Air Corps would soon begin training black pilots and air support units.[33] The program was, of course, to be entirely segregated in keeping with army policy. Tuskegee Air Base in Tuskegee, Alabama, home of Tuskegee Institute, was built from scratch to house a black training facility at a cost of several million dollars, despite the fact that one of the service's largest and best-equipped facilities, Maxwell Field, was only forty miles away.[34] Those involved in what career military men disparagingly referred to as the Tuskegee Experiment were referred to as Tuskegee Airmen.

Roland M. Brown, whose father would in 1947 purchase a golf course in Indian Lake, Hamilton County, became a Tuskegee Airman. Born in 1923 in the largely white enclave of Morristown, New Jersey, Brown interrupted his education at Drew University to join the army in April 1943. Assigned to a segregated unit at Missouri's Jefferson Barracks, he saw a sign on the base reading "You, too, can learn to fly" that propelled him to apply and be accepted into the Tuskegee flight school.[35]

Tuskegee's first class, which commenced training in July 1941, learned to pilot single-seater planes designed as escort fighters and fighter bombers (thus avoiding what Army Air Corps General Henry H. Arnold called the "impossible social problem" of having black officers—that is, pilots—commanding whites in flight crews). Brown joined the program after it expanded to include segregated training for service on multiengine, multicrew bombers. He was assigned as a bombardier-navigator trainee to the 477th Medium Bombardment Group, activated in January 1944. Pilots continued to be instructed at the Tuskegee Army Flying School, but the base had no facilities for preparing other trainees, and they mastered their specialties in small groups at bases throughout the country—bases that were not always equipped to handle them.[36] As Brown later recalled, he was one of some eighty-four trainees sent to Tyndall Field in Florida for gunnery instruction, where the group was kept waiting on a hot bus because the facility "didn't have accommodations for blacks. They wouldn't integrate us with the white cadets on the base," but eventually solved the problem by kicking black enlisted men out of their quarters.[37] Because of the chaotic nature of specialty training, the unit never developed an esprit de corps; some members of the 477th moved more than thirty times in the twenty months between its inception and the close of the war, in which it never saw action.[38]

Brown returned to college after the war, graduating in 1949 from Pennsylvania's Lafayette College, which he served as a trustee from 1975 to 1990. Most of his professional life was spent as an engineer with the US Army Electronic Command in Fort Monmouth, New Jersey, but during summers he and his family spent as much time as possible at his father's Cedar River Golf Club. After his death in 2004, Brown was buried near his father in the Cedar River Cemetery in Indian Lake, "a community," recalled his son, Roland Brown Jr., "we all loved." In 2011 Brown Jr. presented his father's Congressional Gold Medal to the Adirondack Museum, a medal given in 2007 by President George W. Bush to all Tuskegee Airmen as "a gesture to help atone for all the unreturned salutes and unforgivable indignities" they had encountered during World War II.[39]

Allen W. Gambrell was the only known black war casualty from the Adirondacks of World War II. Born in South Carolina in 1924 but living in Port Henry by the age of three, he was a son of World War I veteran Ambrose Gambrell and completed one year of college at Tuskegee Institute before being drafted into the army in late 1942. A member of the black Ninety-Second Infantry Division, he was assigned in 1944 to its 370th Regiment: a heterogeneous, hand-picked fighting team drawn from all units of the division in response to black demands for the use of African American soldiers as combatants. The regiment, hastily readied at remote Fort Huachuca, Arizona, for deployment to the Mediterranean Theater of Operations, arrived in Italy in the late summer and early fall of 1944. Gambrell was killed on the first day of an October 1944 attack in what came to be known as the Italian Campaign on Mount Cauala, one of a series of heights guarding the way to the heavily guarded German stronghold of Massa.[40] He is buried in the American Cemetery in Florence.

The Lake Placid Club had a long history of racial discrimination. (Members' "colored" chauffeurs were fed in 1912 in a dining room with "a special outside entrance door" so that white chauffeurs eating in another dining room would not have to encounter them.)[41] The club was thus a surprising choice for what became an integrated "redistribution center" for army servicemen in 1944. The center was designed both to provide one- or two-week rest-and-rehabilitation breaks to soldiers recently returned from abroad, and to give the military an opportunity to assess their mental states prior to reassigning them—to renewed overseas combat, if possible. In keeping with the standard military policy of racial separation, the club was initially intended as one of five facilities for white soldiers; blacks were to be housed in two hotels in New York City and Chicago. Pressure from the black community led to a decision to integrate the centers in Lake Placid and Santa Barbara, California, thought to be areas of minimal racial strife. As the *Baltimore Afro-American* headlined its article announcing the revised policy: "Army Drops Plan to Jim Crow Vets."[42]

Opening in October 1944, the Lake Placid facility quickly reached its capacity of 1,200 servicemen (plus wives of some one-fifth of them, for whom their husbands paid a daily boarding fee). Six thousand enlisted men passed through the center within its first three months of operation, among them a few African Americans. Soldiers assigned to the club were offered—in addition to their physical and psychological examinations and the therapeutic group "sound off" or "gripe" sessions intended to deliver "organized emotional catharsis"—a program

28. Recreation at Lake Placid Redistribution Center, 1945. Acme Photo. Author's collection.

of outdoor sports and other entertainments, including a nightclub.[43] One sardonic black journalist suggested that, while the anti-segregation battle might have been won in forcing the issue of integrated army redistribution centers, black soldiers might have been "much more able to relax and have that 'helluva good time'" promised them by the army in the urban hotels originally selected for their use. "How many," he queried, "would enjoy the below-zero temperatures and skiing at Lake Placid?"[44] The center was a feature of Lake Placid life for fourteen months before closing in November 1945.[45] Some 50 percent of the soldiers who passed through were deemed fit to return to duty abroad.[46] The brief flirtation at the Lake Placid Club with integration had no lasting consequences. A 1963 guest noted a sign posted in the window of its office reading, "The Lake Placid Club does not accept membership applications from Jews, Negroes, Orientals, or tuberculars."[47]

Plattsburgh Barracks came in once again for race-based attention late in the war when several black airmen were admitted in January 1945 as patients to its Air Corps Convalescent Hospital specializing in occupational and physical therapy. It was announced in June that the practice of admitting African Americans would be discontinued. Justification for the policy change was said to be based on interviews with four black patients during which "it was found that the colored personnel assigned there were very unhappy . . . due largely to severe winter climate and . . . the fact that there is a negligible colored population in that vicinity . . . one family." The "fallacious reasoning" behind the exclusion of black airmen from the barracks' hospital was condemned in a letter to the Secretary of War by Thurgood Marshall, special counsel to the NAACP and later a Supreme Court justice. "It is unbelievable," he declared, "that the Air Command . . . should suddenly assume that colored men are 'unhappy' because of the winter climate at Plattsburg. There is no doubt that many white patients from homes in Dixie might also be unhappy in Plattsburg."[48]

An enterprise untinged by racism took over Plattsburgh Barracks briefly in 1946, when the facility was declared surplus military property. New York State was planning for the expected return of some 500,000 discharged soldiers during the first six months of that year, most of whom, it was assumed, would choose to take advantage of the educational and training opportunities promised by the 1944 Servicemen's Readjustment Act, otherwise known as the GI Bill of Rights. An estimated 60,000 former soldiers were expected to seek higher education, a potential problem alleviated by a unique response: the creation of the Associated Colleges of Upper New York (ACUNY) and a pledge to open three "emergency" junior colleges under their guidance in former military installations in time for the fall semester.[49] Champlain College, based at Plattsburgh Barracks, opened on September 23, 1946, with 1,047 freshmen students. Sampson College, fifteen miles south of the city of Geneva, and Mohawk College in Utica opened the following month.[50] Students who satisfactorily completed the emergency college program were eligible to transfer to other colleges and universities within the state.

Fewer black veterans enrolled in college-level programs than whites (an estimated 12 percent black compared to 28 percent white).[51] But as the project's historian noted in 1950, the ACUNY agenda, "allowed to develop from student need and impetus," had "several trends that reflected the youth of the three campuses." There were "no organizations with racial discrimination," and "Negro, white, and yellow shared dormitory rooms." Black faculty members taught at all three campuses.[52] Enrollment counts by race were not publicized, but photographic evidence indicates that there were black students at Champlain. Mohawk College closed in June 1948 and Sampson in June 1949 when it was determined that emergency colleges were no longer necessary. Champlain was approved in January 1950 by the state as a four-year liberal arts college within the recently organized New York State University system. In 1953, however, the federal government reclaimed Plattsburgh Barracks for use as an air force bomber base, and Champlain closed in June of that year. A proposal to relocate the college to Bolton Landing with the purchase of the Sagamore Hotel and related property was "deemed not feasible" by the state university's board of trustees.[53]

The hopes of black soldiers that their military service would guarantee their futures as equal participants in American society remained unfulfilled. They returned from World War II to a segregated country in which they were still regarded as second-class citizens. Their service did, however, have positive results in breaking down military barriers to racial integration. President Harry S. Truman, facing 1948 opposition in Congress to civil rights legislation, issued an executive order calling for full integration of the armed services—well ahead of civilian acceptance of the idea. American forces went into the Korean War in 1950 in rigidly segregated units, but under Truman's successor, President Dwight D. Eisenhower (who once publicly supported segregation), the armed forces integrated, more or less, from top to bottom. It had taken a long time to do so.

18

Tourism

THE WEALTHY BLACK ELITE, representing perhaps 10 percent of the African American population of the United States in the late nineteenth century, patronized some of the country's most celebrated resorts. Vacation centers close to New York and other northeastern cities included Saratoga Springs; Newport, Rhode Island; and Atlantic City, Cape May, and Sea Isle, New Jersey.[1] The Adirondacks were not a popular destination, but the Cleveland, Cincinnati, Chicago and St. Louis Railway, also known as the Big Four Railroad, operating in affiliation with the New York Central, advertised the region among its tourist destinations in the African American newspaper *Indianapolis Freeman* in 1894.[2]

Vacation options diminished as custom turned against blacks after the Supreme Court's 1896 *Plessy v. Ferguson* decision institutionalized segregation in public accommodations. "The white New Yorker," noted a 1912 column in the NAACP journal *Crisis*, "may choose from a thousand different places the one to which he will go with his family. . . . But you, if you are colored, will knock in vain at the farmhouse door for board and lodging. The beautiful, inexpensive, out-of-the way places are out of your way indeed."[3] Word-of-mouth recommendations and the classified columns of African American newspapers were the most assured means of locating vacation venues. Not many advertisements touted Adirondack facilities to black tourists. Those that did so were not splashy. A 1911 listing in *New York Age* read simply, "Lake George Cottage, Mrs. W. Lewis, Prop., Canada Street, Rates Reasonable."[4]

Anxiety was the constant companion of middle-class black travelers who took to the open road after the dramatic post–World War I expansion of automobile tourism. It was not only a matter of finding accommodations. It was hard, too, to locate accessible restrooms at gas stations or discover friendly eating places in towns where the racial etiquette was unknown. As William Nunn, managing editor of the influential African American newspaper *Pittsburgh Courier*, wrote of his 1935 visit to boxer Max Bauer's training camp in the village of Speculator, Hamilton County: "Friendly people . . . who look at us askance until they find out why we're here! Swell sandwiches . . . we can't eat in the resort hotel . . . you know why!"[5]

The Adirondacks may have been more hospitable than some northern regions to black tourists. A journalist with the *New York Amsterdam News* recommended the region in a 1928 article summarizing weekend trips from New York City, suggesting visits to the John Brown homestead and Ausable Chasm (Keeseville) as well as Montreal and Quebec as part of the itinerary. "I have never found myself," he reported, "unwelcome at any tourist camp nor have I been refused at any house where rooms are advertised for tourists. If a little judgment is exercised in the selection, and a little intelligence used in the manner of approach, rarely will one meet the least affront."[6]

The town of Lake Placid, home to the inhospitable Lake Placid Club, was the focus of a well-publicized race-based incident in 1937. Two black nurses from New York City hospitals were among the one thousand delegates at a New York State Nurses Association convention; both had confirmed reservations at the Lake Placid Inn. Told upon arrival that "a mistake had been made," the nurses were asked to relocate but refused to do so. They were rebuffed again the following morning in being informed that no seats were available for breakfast in the hotel's dining room. After waiting outside the room for twenty minutes, they went elsewhere to eat and then moved to a tourist cottage. This was the first confrontation of its sort in the association's twenty-year history of conventions, and there was talk of taking legal action against the hotel, but nothing concrete was done beyond lodging formal protests with the association.[7] In fact, few blacks denied hotel or restaurant service contested such actions. As black journalist George S. Schuyler wrote in 1929, "The average Negro just turns away when refused. . . . After several such experiences he becomes conditioned and stays away from places where he knows he isn't wanted. . . . It takes time and trouble to fight a case of discrimination and then one is liable to lose, so why bother?"[8]

Hotel policies of racial exclusion in and near the Adirondacks extended even to the celebrated. When Jack Benny's gravel-voiced radio and television sidekick, comedian Eddie "Rochester" Anderson, wished to spend a week in 1941 at the Saratoga races with his wife, there was "no room for them at the inn all the way up to Huletts Landing" on the eastern shore of Lake George, nearly sixty miles to the north. Summer resident Delphine Knight, a child at the time, remembered the owner of Hulett's Hotel, Arthur Wyatt, phoning her mother to ask if it would be all right if he rented the cottage adjoining theirs to the Andersons. "We were so thrilled" to have such "famous people" living nearby, reported Knight, and "they had a good time with it. They came out and posed for pictures . . . and they just looked so happy because they had this tremendous meeting with these very enthusiastic children."[9] Anderson bought four racehorses in Saratoga that week.[10] One of them, Burnt Cork, ran two years later in the Kentucky Derby, becoming the first horse owned by an African American to participate in the sixty-eight-year-old annual event and placing tenth in a field of ten.

A tourist guidebook specifically catering to black travelers was issued in response to a perceived need in 1930. *Hackley and Harrison's Hotel and Apartment Guide for Colored Travelers: Board, Rooms, Garage Accommodations, etc. in 300 Cities in the United States and Canada* was compiled by the New London, Connecticut, office of the Negro Welfare Council.[11] Victor H. Green, a Harlem postal carrier, launched the most successful and long-lived of a number of similar ventures in 1936. His *Negro Motorist Green-Book* (later the *Negro Traveler's Green Book* and popularly known as the *Green Book*), was modeled on Jewish prototypes and undertook to provide the black automobilist with information to "keep him from running into

29. Eddie "Rochester" Anderson and wife at Huletts Landing, 1941. Courtesy of Judy Firth Haggett and the Friends of Huletts Landing.

difficulties, embarrassments, and to make his trip more enjoyable."[12] The first edition of the no-frills manual covered only New York City. In 1937 the guide expanded to include New Jersey and Westchester County, and in 1938 it began national coverage with the intention of listing hospitable "hotels, road houses, taverns, night clubs, tourist homes, trailer parks and camps, restaurants, garages, service stations, summer resorts, barber shops, beauty parlors, dance halls, [and] theatres."[13] The guide provided a promotional vehicle for enterprises that actively sought a black clientele, and advertisers paid to be listed by city or town within states. Two Adirondack lodgings, both in Essex County, were entered in the "summer resorts" category offered in the late 1930s: one in Saranac Lake, the other in Schroon Lake.[14]

"Mrs. V. Ramsey," as the Saranac Lake establishment was identified in 1938 and 1939, referred to the boardinghouse at 24 Lake Flower Avenue that Viola Ramsey had operated since the 1920s, in part as a cure cottage for blacks suffering from tuberculosis. She had by now left the town's dwindling private sanatorium business (as had her sister-in-law Mattie Reid, recorded in the 1940 census as housekeeper for a private family and the only resident of her former Saranac Lake boarding cottage at 155 Pine Street). Ramseys became the go-to accommodation for black visitors to Saranac Lake, and was later referred to casually by a former manager of the town's prominent Hotel Saranac in recalling the segregationist attitude of local hoteliers in the early 1940s. "Those years we, as a nation, were still practicing race discrimination," she wrote. "At the hotel (and I am sure at other public places) it was the practice, as guests were registering, to tactfully suggest that the Black maid or chauffeur might be more comfortable at the tourist home on Lake Flower Avenue that was operated by Black people. This was acceptable to all and was routine."[15]

"Claver Villa," a tourist home in Schroon Lake, first appeared in the *Green Book*'s list of resort accommodations in 1939. Its owner, Mrs. Anna Brown, widow of Civil War veteran Lloyd Brown, had lived in Schroon Lake for nearly sixty years and celebrated her eighty-third birthday that year. Identified as a laundress in the 1892 Schroon Lake census, she had bought a house at 30 Main Street in her own name in 1904 that she marketed as a boardinghouse catering to the black chauffeurs of guests at seasonal Schroon Lake hotels before advertising it as a vacation destination for middle-class blacks.[16]

Brown well understood the power of promotion. She was a longtime contributor of social news to local newspapers, garnering free publicity for Claver Villa by deftly introducing its name and those of its guests into the social reportage of Essex County and Troy journals. She used the same technique with New York City's African American newspaper *New York Age*. One 1931 issue of the publication included a social column tagged "Schroon Lake" in which only Mrs. Brown and her boardinghouse guests' names were listed.[17] This was not surprising, as she was then the only black resident of Schroon Lake. Brown spent winters with a daughter in Queens, New York. She died in 1940 and is buried with her husband in the Schroon Lake Protestant Cemetery.

Black journalist George Schuyler tested the racial policies of northeastern summer holiday destinations in early July 1942, querying the management of 105 hotels then advertising accommodations about the possibility of putting up "a colored family of three planning a two-week vacation between now and Labor Day." Among the thirty-one responses he received (of which only one was favorable), two came from the Adirondacks. Like other replies, they included enigmatic phrasing that meant "nothing available." The first, from the Hotel Windsor in Elizabethtown, refused Schuyler obliquely in stating that "seventy-five per cent of our guests come before July fifth and remain until September."[18]

"In view of the assertion of resort managers elsewhere that they were filled until Labor Day," noted Schuyler dryly of the second response, "we were caught off balance by the reply from the *Hotel Monoquaya* that 'due to conditions of the country and business, we have been obliged to reduce our service and staff to a minimum, and can only provide accommodations for the guests we now have for the season.' Hard times must have hit the Adirondacks," concluded Schuyler. The author confessed himself charmed by the candid reply received from a hotel manager on the Vermont side of Lake Champlain who "hesitated to suggest that we come as it would be quite a grave experiment for you and for us."[19]

New York State expanded its liberal antidiscrimination tradition in 1945, passing the nation's first law to explicitly bar places of public accommodation, resort, and amusement from refusing patronage to anyone on the basis of race, color, creed, or national origin.[20] Despite the public ban, hoteliers who chose not to interact with black patrons, among them a number in the Adirondacks, could be creative in inventing devices to effect exclusion. Phrasing in letters to potential clients suggesting that a hotel's patrons were "carefully selected and no objectional [*sic*] person is tolerated" was generally a sufficient deterrent.[21] Newspapers published in the state, however, had to be careful about implied hate speech in advertising they accepted. The proprietor of Camp-of-the-Pines, a family resort in Willsboro, Essex County, lost a 1945 lawsuit against the *New York Times* over what he considered the newspaper's illegal substitution of the phrase "congenial following" for his own wording, "selected clientele," in a published ad for the resort.[22]

"Summer Resorts" disappeared as a listing category with the 1940 edition of the *Green Book*, and it was not until the 1950s that Adirondack accommodations again showed up in the guide. The spring 1956 edition of the *Green Book* included four Adirondack hotel options: two in Lake Placid, one in Lake George, and one in Horicon, Warren County. The two Lake Placid hostelries, black-owned Dreamland Cottage and Camp Parkside, were discussed in chapter 13. The Lake George listing, Woodbine Cottage, was owned by Samuel "Pink" McFerson, an African American who moved north from Alabama in the early 1930s to take a job as a bellman/porter available through an uncle working at the Hotel Rockwell in Glens Falls. McFerson married a Glens Falls woman and stayed on. By the mid-1930s he rented, and later owned, the small, seasonal Woodside hotel accommodating around thirty guests at 75 Dieskau Street in Caldwell (now Lake George).[23] He advertised widely, not only in the *Green Book* and in classified advertisements in New York City's black newspapers, but also in the *Washington Afro-American*, the *Negro Business Directory of the State of Wisconsin* (which listed hotels across the country "owned and operated for or by Negro people"), and an odd, twelve-page, mimeographed guide published in 1939 and for at least two years thereafter by the US Department of the Interior's Travel Bureau entitled *Directory of Negro Hotels and Guest Houses in the United States.*[24] McFerson's brother Elmore opened McFerson's Hotel in 1945, a year-round, eight-bedroom roadhouse with a bar and dining room some five miles south of Lake George in Glens Falls. The two McFerson establishments, with their quality southern-style food and good jazz music, provided a local "hub of Negro social and economic life." McFerson's Hotel burned down in 1965. Pink McFerson's Woodbine became a magnet for black musicians who performed during the summer at local hotels. Diahann Carroll stayed there as a young girl in the 1940s with her aunt, a well-known organist and choir director.[25]

The Crystal Lake Lodge in Horicon, the fourth Adirondack listing in the 1956 *Green Book*, was an unconventional advertiser. Known as an "adult summer camp" catering to "a mostly Jewish middle-class clientele of socialist schoolteachers,"[26] it was owned by members of the politically left-wing Slutsky family: Jewish hoteliers in the "Borscht Belt" of the Catskill Mountains. (The lodge was referred to as a "hotbed of Communist influence" in 1956 by a New York State legislative committee.)[27] Crystal Lake modeled itself after nearby Scaroon Manor, an elegant Jewish resort in Schroon Lake famous for its roster of celebrity entertainers. It maintained its own repertory theater company, and "dine with live actors" was a phrase incorporated into advertising brochures; even the band was expected to disperse and join guests at mealtimes.[28] As Crystal Lake's 1959 theater director recalled of an interracial couple employed that summer as set and costume designers, they "fitted into the social scene of the lodge more than the somewhat primitive backstage environs."[29] Paul Robeson, Ossie Davis, and Ruby Dee were among well-known black entertainers who relaxed at the resort.[30] A fire of suspicious origin consumed the lodge in the 1960s. Rebuilt, it closed for good in the 1970s.

The Hotel Saranac, which once so routinely rerouted Saranac Lake's African American guests to Viola Ramsey's boardinghouse, reversed its race policy in the late 1940s. It was one of the earliest and most consistent advertisers in another guide for black automobilists: *Travelguide*, first published in 1946 with the motto "Vacation and Recreation without Humiliation." Eleven other Adirondack hostelries advertised at different times in the guide as well.[31]

The need for specialized guides diminished with the proliferation of interstate highways after 1956. These high-speed arteries provided a level of protection to traveling African Americans in bypassing unfamiliar towns and offering impersonal, standardized facilities dispensing gas, food, and overnight lodgings. The *Travelguide* ceased publication in 1957; the *Green Book* dropped *Negro* from its title and hobbled along until 1964.[32]

The *New York Amsterdam News*, which had published its first piece touting the Adirondacks as a vacation destination in 1928, continued to offer similar articles. In 1952 and 1958 it felt no need to give advice to would-be holidaymakers about securing hospitable lodgings. Both pieces hyped the region's "medium-priced accommodations" as well as the kind of spectator entertainments that attracted mainstream tourists: water carnivals, town anniversary celebrations, ice skating exhibitions, and sailboat races. Also recommended were several historical and commercial venues: the Adirondack Museum, Fort Ticonderoga, Frontier Town, Old McDonald's Farm, and Enchanted Forest. Another suggested leisure activity in 1958 was canoeing, a "popular vacation attraction, particularly with Boy Scouts and husky canoe paddlers."[33]

Canoeing has long been a recreational pursuit associated with wilderness tourism, or "roughing it" in the great outdoors. With the 1869 publication of William H. Murray's popular *Adventures in the Wilderness: Or, Camp Life in the Adirondacks*, an increasing number of visitors were attracted to the Adirondacks to enjoy the backwoods pleasures of camping out, hiking, fishing, hunting, and boating. Perhaps the earliest African American to give an account of an Adirondack canoe trip was William L. Brown, a longtime staff member at Virginia's Hampton Institute, who wrote up an excursion he made with a companion through the Bog River country of Hamilton County after a fundraising visit to the region in 1897. Describing periods "of busy activity and hearty effort" interspersed with days dedicated to "the fishing gear, the camera and the lunch," Brown extolled the region's beauty and wildness, which "will ever conjure up in our memories visions of the sublime."[34]

With the rise of automobile travel and an increase in paid vacations for wage earners after 1910 (of whom about 50 percent received the benefit by 1940), working-class families embraced the idea of auto camping, with its relatively low entry costs. The expanding national park system strove to meet user needs, adding picnic areas and auto campgrounds as it experienced dramatic increases in visitation: from 31,000 in 1906 to 7,358,000 in 1940.[35] Race was an issue in the national parks from the beginning. Yellowstone, established in 1872 as the first park in the national system, launched a conscious but unpublicized policy to discourage black visitors, and at a 1922 conference of park superintendents it was agreed that, while "we cannot openly discriminate against them, they should be told that the parks have no facilities for taking care of them." Some national parks in southern states developed segregated facilities, a step vigorously protested by the NAACP in 1937.[36] "Inclusion" did not become a watchword in national park policy until the second half of the twentieth century, when the park service discovered that African Americans were among those who made little use of park facilities. Numerous studies since then have attempted to understand differences between ethnicities in patterns of outdoor recreation. Answers have been varied, complex, and inconclusive, but have highlighted the necessity for the park service to redefine its role if national parks are to remain relevant to the evolving American population.[37]

No agency involved with New York State's Adirondack Park management since its 1892 creation claims to have tracked historical racial and ethnic patterns of park use, but proportions are thought to have been historically similar to those at the national park level. A few black outdoor recreationists other than canoeist William Brown, however, appear to have been early Adirondack Park users.

Hunting wild animals for food has always been popular with park residents, despite the passage of proscriptive game laws in the late nineteenth century. (Lyman Epps Jr. of Lake Placid recounted in 1940 "that when he was a boy hunting was a chore not a sport," and he claimed "to have killed every type of animal native to this section including wolves"—one of which he shot in Lake Placid's business district.)[38] Visitors from outside have long hunted in the park as a recreational activity, and African American newspapers have reported, generally in social columns, on the occasional foray of middle-class black hunters into the Adirondacks:

- *Chicago Defender*, November 9, 1918: Samuel Johnson of Utica "is preparing for a big deer hunt in the Adirondacks."
- *New York Age*, October 18, 1919: A trio "spent ten days in the Adirondacks, camping and hunting big game. They returned Tuesday and brought home a deer."
- *New York Amsterdam News*, November 23, 1932: The assistant manager of a Manhattan branch of the Unity Life Insurance

Company returned from his Adirondack hunting trip "with a deer and a bear."

- *Pittsburgh Courier*, December 9, 1939: Robert Goode, developer of Lucy Depp, a summer resort community for African Americans outside of Columbus, Ohio,[39] and his wife were en route home "from their annual hunting trip to the Adirondacks."

On the other side of the hunting equation, Adirondack resident William Jackson, "a young negro of splendid courage," lost his life in 1897 as deputy to a game constable in Schroon Lake, Essex County, when he attempted to serve a warrant against one Frank LaGoy, "known as a desperate character" and wanted for killing a deer out of season. This was likely a game-related rather than a race-based crime, as LaGoy was reported to have known that a warrant was out for his arrest and "threatened to shoot any person who attempted to serve it." He assaulted and murdered Jackson with an ax, for which he served a twenty-year sentence in Clinton Prison.[40]

A 1977 survey of black and white respondents from roughly similar social and economic backgrounds by the US Department of the Interior determined that, while 21 percent of whites in the survey hunted, only 9 percent of blacks did so.[41] Fishing, on the other hand, was highlighted as a pastime in which black and white participation rates were nearly equal, with 49 percent of black and 56 percent of white respondents taking part. (Other activities with similar participation rates were nature walks, horseback riding, and driving vehicles and motorcycles in off-road areas.)[42] Pink McFerson, owner of Woodbine Cottage in Caldwell/Lake George, catered to both hunters and fishing enthusiasts, advertising in the *Washington Afro-American* in 1953 that "Woodbine Cottage is opened early in the year for the fishing season and does not close until November, the end of the hunting season."[43]

Frank "Jake" Tompkins of Canton, St. Lawrence County, was famous for his prowess as an Adirondack recreational fisherman. His father, Walker Tompkins, had been the son of former slaves and was believed to have traveled north to Morley, a hamlet of Canton, with

30. Fisherman Jake Tompkins and friend, unknown date. Town and Village of Canton New York Historian, Linda Casserly, Collection. Donated by Marilyn Infantine Mintener.

a Civil War officer as a boy.[44] Frank, born in 1885, stayed on in the region and became a barber. A "veteran trouter," he could be counted on from the 1920s through the 1940s to be one of the two hundred fishermen gathered at midnight along the shores, inlets, and outlets of Cranberry Lake in the western Adirondacks to cast their lines at the April 1 kick-off of the trout season, often in the midst of swirling snow and in temperatures close to zero. Tompkins usually caught the most or the largest fish of the day, and it was said that he could "charm a trout with his smile until he comes and eats out of his hand."[45]

The 1977 Interior Department survey determined that only 1 percent of black respondents skied in comparison with 11 percent of whites. African Americans' lack of interest in skiing, a sport that began attracting winter tourists to the Adirondacks in the early twentieth century, has been attributed to the sport's northern orientation, its distance from urban centers, and the high cost of participation.[46] One assumes that the journalist detailing a 1939 square dance held by the Gore Mountain Ski Club at the Garnet Lodge in North Creek (a Warren county hamlet of Johnsburg said to be the birthplace of the alpine skiing industry in New York) was not writing with tongue in cheek when he reported of his skill as a dancer that "Al Sterling, the obliging and jovial Negro major domo of the Lodge, showed he was as talented a jigger as he is a skier."[47]

A longtime guide from the Cranberry Lake area provided a local white perspective on the Adirondack experience of African American sportsmen in recalling two black hunters peripherally involved in an early 1960s shooting accident. The pair had been camping near the lake, he reported, keeping "pretty much to themselves," when they were talked into joining an "organized drive" for bear by three local hunters who, like them, had not had much luck in finding game. They staked out their assigned position beside a hunter from the other group who, seeing movement, shot at what he thought was a bear and killed one of his partners. The black men were asked to remain with the dead man's body while one of the others reported the incident, and apprehensively greeted the arrival of local authorities. As the guide told his story, he allowed that he could "see why those Colored boys were so nervous. They were definitely in [a] minority." The men, he noted, returned to the same camping spot for several years and "were the most polite people you would ever want to meet, never causing anyone the slightest trouble." Continuing to reflect his Adirondack perspective, he admitted that, "to save my life, I could never tell one from the other."[48]

The kind of racial unease noted by the guide in his reportage of this hunting accident, as well as the longtime absence of black faces in tourist advertising for the region, explains to some degree the level of historical disinterest shown by blacks in the Adirondack Park as a recreational playground. Yet, as is the case with the national parks, attracting black and other members of minority groups to the region as tourists—"wilderness" or otherwise—becomes a crucial issue when it comes to maintaining state political support and public funding for the Adirondack Park in a changing demographic society.

19

1940 to 1950 and Beyond

DEMOGRAPHIC SHIFTS during the decade between 1940 and 1950 altered the dynamics of race relations in upstate New York. The catalyst for change was, as it had been during the years before 1920, war. In mid-1941 the African American journal *New York Age* addressed what it anticipated as "another migration of Negroes from the South to the large industrial centers of the country" to meet demands for increased production. Advising prospective migrants to the state to "decide against stopping in Harlem where their presence can only aggravate a situation now acute due to overcrowding and little work," it suggested instead that they focus on upstate cities. Utica, Albany, Troy, and Schenectady (home to General Electric) were listed among options.[1]

Many southern migrants followed this advice. It was estimated in 1943 that Utica was "now adding Negroes at a rate of about one a day," and was home to 800 or 900 more African Americans than it had been a year earlier—perhaps 1,500 more than two years earlier.[2] The Albany-Schenectady-Troy metropolitan area experienced an 83 percent growth in nonwhite population—including Asian and Indigenous people—during the decade between 1940 and 1950.[3] As African Americans from the South crowded into older upstate cities, they met with cordial receptions from neither white nor black residents. The deteriorating housing in which they were forced to live, as well as high rates of disease and crime, created black ghettos in these areas for the first time. Settled African Americans saw seemingly unbridgeable cultural differences between themselves and the newcomers and were said to view "the old days" with nostalgia.[4]

Changing demographics to the south had little impact on the Adirondacks, which offered few assembly-line jobs. But the influx of migrants reinvigorated racial stereotyping at the regional level and increased prejudice (or, at the very least, unpredictability) in contacts across racial lines in even the smallest upstate communities. In the mid-1940s, businesses in the town of Bolton on Lake George, which had once sustained so many seasonal African American employees at its Saratoga Hotel, allegedly barred black students attending an interracial summer school of dance from their stores.[5]

The two New York counties wholly within the park provide the only easy comparisons in terms of race-based population change between 1940 and 1950. Essex County, with 78 African Americans in an overall population of 34,178 in 1940, grew this number to 139 among 35,086 residents (an increase from 0.23 percent to 0.40 percent of the county's population, but a number increase of only 16 above its black population of 1860). Hamilton County, which had no African Americans in its 1940 population of 4,188, had none in its 1950 population of 4,105.

Other Adirondack communities experienced similarly modest demographic shifts: Saranac Lake decreased its African American population from 40 in a 1940 population of 7,138 to 39 among 6,913 in 1950. Moriah, home to 36 blacks in a 1940 population of 5,952, added 5 to its 1950 total of 4,189. The bustling village of Lake Placid counted only 2 black residents in its year-round 1950 population of 2,999. Parts of the region, moreover, like the towns of Saranac Lake and Moriah as indicated above, were losing overall population by 1950 as citizens fled rural areas in search of job opportunities.

The late 1930s and 1940s saw a slight increase in African American achievement in the Adirondacks, with a very few individuals experiencing modest career success in capacities other than that of boardinghouse keeper. Ulysses Grant Bethel, known as Grant, was the first black to become a different kind of entrepreneur. Born in 1891 in Reidsville, North Carolina, he spent a number of years in Connecticut and a brief period in Tupper Lake, Franklin County, before arriving with his family on the Saratoga/Warren County border in 1927 and shortly thereafter settling in Lake Luzerne, Warren County. He acquired a Socony gas station on good terms near the site of the nearly completed Conklingville Dam built to harness the Sacandaga River. He got off to a shaky start, however, operating, as well as the gas station, an unpretentious roadhouse/restaurant in a building on his premises that attracted occasional police attention as a place of drinking and "wagering" during Prohibition.[6] Abandoning the gas station in 1933, Bethel turned his attention to horticulture, eventually owning a garden center/nursery in Lake Luzerne and overseeing a staff of white employees and a number of sizeable landscaping projects: among them Million Dollar Beach, the largest and best known beach on Lake George.

Dewey Brown fulfilled a dream in 1947 in becoming the owner of the seasonal Cedar River House and its nine-hole golf course in Indian Lake, Hamilton County. Born in 1899, Brown had learned to golf as an eight-year-old caddie after his family relocated from North Carolina to New Jersey. He became a professional golfer, making his way in what was throughout much of the twentieth century a notoriously segregated sport—primarily as a teacher and maker of clubs (including a set for President Warren G. Harding). In 1928 he became the first black member of the Professional Golfers' Association. The light-skinned Brown's PGA membership was revoked without explanation in 1934 shortly before a "Caucasian only" clause was written into the organization's constitution and bylaws. This clause was not rescinded until 1961; Brown was formally re-elected to membership in the association the following year.[7]

Brown and his wife operated a New Jersey catering service and restaurant during the winter months. Hiring a Scottish couple to assist his family in the summer management of what was renamed the Cedar River Golf Club, Brown focused his energy on administration, food service, and teaching, while improving the facility physically with the addition of a driving range, a swimming pool, and two cottages for groups wishing to lodge together. He introduced his section of the

Adirondack Park to some of the best black professionals in the sport, who, thanks to his close relationship with the pro at the eighteen-hole Tupper Lake Golf Club, were welcomed at its annual tournaments in the 1950s and 1960s.[8] Among those who triumphed at Tupper Lake were Lee Elder, who set a 135, seven under par, course record in 1965 and in 1975 became the first black to play the Masters Tournament;[9] Charlie Sifford, six-time winner of the National Negro Open and in 2004 inducted as the first black golfer into the World Golf Hall of Fame; and Teddy "Rags" Rhodes (nicknamed for his natty sartorial style), an older player who took home the $200 winner's check in 1963. J. Peter Martin, an Adirondack youth who went on to become the golf professional at Lake Placid's Whiteface Club and Resort, said later that he would never forget his first sight of black golfers emerging in groups of four or five from their "big old cars" at the tournament, immaculately dressed in the latest golfing fashions and smoking cigars. "Those guys could play," he said, "certainly better than the local entrants, and they were colorful. Crowds of fans followed them around the course."[10] Dewey Brown, described by sportswriters as the "'Knight of the Fairways' because he was one of God's great gentlemen and sincerity was his trademark,"[11] was elected in 1958 to the Golf Club Superintendents Association of America.[12] He was buried after his 1972 death across the road from his beloved golf club in the Cedar River Cemetery.

Grace Briggs Bethel, wife of garden-center owner Grant Bethel, succeeded professionally in another sphere. Born in Boston in 1898, she married Bethel in 1920. The mother of six children, she became the author of a popular newspaper column, "From My Window," in the *Glens Falls Post-Star*. Laced with gentle wit, Bethel's column appeared irregularly from 1947 through 1956 and touched on the natural world, family and community life, mild politics, and the classical music and literature she loved.[13] She rarely mentioned race. Indeed, when in 1949 she touched on the "discrimination, disenfranchisement and lack of educational opportunities" faced by black soldiers returned from World War II, the *Post-Star* felt compelled to observe in a supportive editorial that few of the column's admirers "were likely to have been aware that its writer . . . is a Negro."[14]

The middle-class achievements of the Bethels and Dewey Brown hardly constituted a trend, but they represented an accomplishment in upstate New York, where, according to a 1950 study by the New York State Commission against Discrimination, most African Americans were confined to laboring, service, domestic, and routine assembly-line jobs at the bottom of the employment hierarchy.[15] Another measure of racial success was the appearance of several African Americans as renters and owners of second homes in the region. These newcomers exhibited self-assurance in choosing the quiet of the Adirondacks over better-known residential resort areas catering to blacks in the Northeast. Among the new arrivals was Dr. Samuel Sweeney, for eighteen years (1940–58) minister of Harlem's St. Mark's Church: home to the largest Methodist church congregation in the Northeast during his pastorate. Sweeney and his wife purchased a "small tumbledown cabin" in 1946 from black property owner Queenie Simmons as a summer home in Lake Clear, Franklin County, a place they "loved more than anywhere else in the world."[16] Sweeney participated in John Brown Memorial Association events and in the Methodist Church community of Tupper Lake, where he occasionally preached. The couple died in an automobile crash in traveling between the Adirondacks and New York City in 1965.[17]

Saranac Lake's history as a health resort resonated with a mixed-race couple, Canadians who bought property in 1950 in a new village development called Breezy Acres so that a daughter with a history of tuberculosis might spend time in the famously reinvigorating Saranac Lake air. George Turner, a black Montreal machinist from British Honduras, joined his white English-born wife, Ruth, and the couple's children on summer weekends at the family's Breezy Acres cottage.[18]

Walter Maxfield began his Adirondack sojourn as a summer resident but became a beloved year-rounder in the Saratoga County town of Hadley on the Warren County border. He discovered the region through his in-laws, the James E. Browns, who maintained a second home in Hadley in the late 1940s.[19] Like his father-in-law, Maxfield was employed in the Brooklyn Post Office, where both men had begun their careers as letter carriers and worked their way into clerical positions: placements with civil service perquisites that gave them job stability and situated them firmly in the black middle class.[20] Maxfield's wife, Alice, was a registered nurse and onetime instructor in obstetrics and supervisor of the maternity ward at Lincoln Hospital in the Bronx.[21]

The Maxfields bought a home on 150 Hadley acres in 1952 to which the couple moved permanently after Maxfield's 1966 retirement. He became one of the village's most active citizens as member and president of the school board; deacon, elder, trustee, and choir member of the local Presbyterian church and moderator of the Albany Presbytery; member and president of the Lions Club; founder and chairman of the Hadley-Luzerne Economic Development Corporation; and a volunteer in the middle school instructional program.[22] The road leading past the Maxfield home was renamed in his honor after his 1984 death.

The issue of race was at the forefront of a turbulent period in the United States during the 1950s and 1960s. The nascent civil rights movement, in which the NAACP took a leading role with its focus on law and the courts, brought attention to the country's color divide, and federal legislation and Supreme Court decisions changed the way in which blacks were treated in national society. The 1954 landmark Supreme Court decision *Brown v. Board of Education* toppled the "separate but equal" policy enshrined in public education and applied elsewhere after the *Plessy v. Ferguson* decision of 1896, while the Civil Rights Act of 1964 ended segregation in public places and banned discrimination in employment on the basis of race, color, religion, sex, or national origin. The Voting Rights Act of 1965 prohibited racial discrimination in voting. While these laws and court decisions were aimed primarily at abuses in the South, wider awareness bolstered the growing sense of racial unity and self-confidence of black New Yorkers in confronting bias.

Civil rights activism was not an issue addressed aggressively by blacks resident in the Adirondacks. There were, however, occasional race-based lawsuits filed in the region from the 1930s on. All brought by outsiders, they targeted local businesses. Among the known cases were

- *William Warfield*, head of the transfer squad of officers at New York City's Riker's Island prison and secretary of the Prison Keepers' Benevolent Association, who filed a complaint in 1936 against a Plattsburgh tavern for refusing him service when he and a white officer stopped in after transferring a prisoner to Clinton Prison. The tavern faced the loss of its license and a five hundred dollar fine.[23]
- *Hattie Durant*, a registered nurse, who sued a Saranac Lake cocktail lounge in 1945 for refusing to serve her while she was in the company of white friends.[24]
- Orchestra leader *William Lowery*, who filed suit against a Lake George barber in 1955 for refusing to cut his hair. The barber, who stated that he was not "trained to cut colored people's hair" and didn't care to learn, was fined one hundred dollars.[25]

The Adirondack region first grappled with blatant discrimination on a community-wide scale when the Plattsburgh Air Force Base opened on the grounds of the former Plattsburgh Barracks in 1954. While many black air force families lived on base, others chose to settle elsewhere in the city. As a local newspaper columnist wrote in 1957, Plattsburgh, previously home to few black residents, had "never been faced with a Negro integration problem" before. How was it coping? According to the white columnist, "Quite well." There had been, he noted, "isolated incidents of difficulty, but nothing glaring." He outlined his own take on the race situation in Plattsburgh public schools, noting that "little tots show no racial feeling whatsoever. . . . In high school, the Negro is accepted, but he is not a leader of students, nor is he asked to join groups and cliques too frequently. He is sort of a lone wolf."[26] Blacks who found themselves "having a hard time adjusting" to Plattsburgh were advised in another article to join a church.[27]

Plattsburgh's recent black immigrants were not as sanguine about race issues as white journalists. As one African American serviceman wrote in a 1960 letter to the editor of the *Plattsburgh Press-Republican*, the city was "the most prejudiced place we have ever lived."[28] Problems were reported to be particularly pronounced in housing, where blacks faced the same kind of bias found elsewhere in the North: houses, apartments, and trailer park units available until the owners/agents met the applicants in person; offers rescinded after complaints from potential neighbors; exorbitant rents demanded for substandard units. One black woman, a "qualified stenographer," admitted to having had difficulty in landing a job, but noted that there were "two sides to the story of racial discrimination or the absence of it" in Plattsburgh. She had, she related, received "good care and attention" at the local hospital when she needed it. She had also found that the city's white residents were not always attuned to the difficulties faced by their black fellow citizens. "When people become aware of this problem," she noted, "many are anxious to help those who have met with discrimination." The NAACP established a Plattsburgh branch in late 1961. As its African American head (a six-year Plattsburgh resident) phrased it that year, "When more Negroes came to Plattsburgh as a result of the Air Force Base expansion, I expected a certain amount of discrimination. But the high percent of discrimination against Negroes which has been evident in the past few years was not expected."[29]

The racial tensions awakened in Plattsburgh were rarely experienced elsewhere in the region. As long as numbers remained insignificant, which they did in terms of both residents and tourists, African Americans were left undisturbed. Burton Bernstein, who wrote about contemporary Essex County in the early 1970s, reported on a 1968 luncheon meeting of the Essex County Board of Supervisors, at which "law and order was the most commonly discussed issue." It soon became synonymous, he discovered, with "the Negro problem." As one supervisor announced, "there's never been any trouble with the few colored we've got, and that includes colored tourists and the colored servicemen from Plattsburgh Air Force Base." Bernstein also recorded the comments of a number of community leaders who expressed comfort with Essex County's ongoing lack of heterogeneity. A businessman, he wrote, offered "with harsh bluntness" one reason for the area's discouraging lack of new industry in saying, "The truth of the matter is that some of the folks around here don't want industry of any kind moving in, because they're afraid that with it will come more wops and Polacks or even—heaven forbid!—niggers and spiks. . . . They don't want to upset the ethnic balance of things. They like it the way it is, depression and all."[30]

The demographics of the Adirondack Park have not changed dramatically in the decades leading up to publication of this book. Blacks still represent a tiny minority of the regional population, although local colleges enroll an increasing number of black students, and a few communities have added full-time black residents. Homogeneity continues to be lauded by some as a regional attribute. As recently as 2014 a writer responded to a call for welcoming a wider range of people to the Adirondacks as residents and visitors in writing, "People go to the Adirondacks, or any remote place for that matter, to get AWAY from urban and suburban problems, one of which is diversity."[31] There were, moreover, disturbing racial confrontations in the region in the summer of 2016, when black clients were harassed in a Ticonderoga bar, and a store representative at a nearby Walmart asked the black victims of racial insults, rather than their harasser, to leave the store to calm a tense situation. At about the same time, Aaron Mair, the first black president of the Sierra Club, was subjected to racial slurs while taking a lazy canoe ride on Essex County's Schroon River. As Mair said of the offensive incident, places that lack racial diversity can "be perceived by whites to be their territory."[32] The Adirondack Park is hardly a black Eden.

Concerned residents, black and white, are taking steps to change the future. But, in returning to the past, one wonders how pioneer African Americans felt about themselves and their regional interactions as visitors, part-time, or full-time residents in the Adirondacks during the previous more than 150 years. Were they comfortable in the roles they played in the predominant white community? Were the tradeoffs they made in foregoing the warmth of a broad-based common identity worthwhile? Were they aware of them? Were their experiences similar to, or different from, those of other African Americans who spent time in comparable settings? Did their presence affect change? Until more is known, we can only guess. But meaning can be found in celebrating the lives of previously unrecorded or little-recorded African Americans who chose, for whatever reasons, to spend at least some of their lives in the remote Adirondacks and, in doing so, enriched the regional story.

Afterword

Autobiographical Reflections

ALICE PADEN GREEN

VERY FEW RESEARCHERS or writers have explored the history of black people in the Adirondacks. Sally Svenson's book is the first definitive examination of the history and presence of black people in this mountainous region of New York. Through impeccable research, the author introduces us to how the few members of this minority community ventured into a land that has often seemed reserved for whites.

Although their numbers have always been small in the Adirondacks, society there is to this day shaped by the way blacks were treated over the past two centuries. This is of particular concern today as the region's residents confront the lack of diversity and the continued practice of discrimination. To move forward on this front, we need to clearly understand the nature of that treatment and come to terms with the past. *Blacks in the Adirondacks* points to the intertwining of slavery and prejudice with life in the Adirondacks and how whites have benefitted from these forces of oppression.

This history raises related questions that cry out for exploration and explanation of black people's involvement in the political life of the region and the impact of the civil rights movement on their lives. Among the key questions is why some business and social enterprises in the region came to reject blacks whom they seemed to have welcomed before World War II. That discrimination may have profoundly influenced African Americans' decisions about whether to visit or settle in the region and the quality of life of those determined to make the Adirondacks their home.

Most important, this book speaks personally to those of us who migrated to and grew up in the Adirondacks during and right after World War II. We knew nothing of our black history, which left us feeling disconnected, like strangers, without a way to develop a positive self-image and identity. I cannot help believing that if we had known the history presented here, it would have provided a lifeline to us. It can still be helpful in filling some of the gaps in our life stories that can connect us to our past.

Much of this book is also of special interest to me because it includes people and events I personally knew and witnessed. My account of my family's life in the Adirondacks can provide a window on what it was like for us and others trying to survive in a land perceived to be white and often hostile. This autobiographical afterword can also give voice to some of the blacks present in the region before 1950, providing the reader with a fuller understanding of the Adirondack community and their relationship to it.

The Great Migration—Greenville to Witherbee

The thin almond-colored woman felt anxious but also excited when the D&H Railroad conductor announced the next stop would be Port Henry. It would mark the end of Annie Payden's long and difficult trip from Greenville, South Carolina, to the small iron-ore-mining hamlet of Witherbee, New York. Eager to get a glimpse of this new land, she peered out the window into the frosty August night but found only deep darkness that forced her to wonder anew whether she had made the right decision to leave the South and follow her husband, Bill, to this distant land in 1948.

Although this was new territory for Annie, it was not for her husband. Some twenty years earlier, at the urging of his older brother, Herman Payton, who spelled the family name differently, Bill left Greenville to join him in the iron-ore industry in upstate New York near the town of Plattsburgh, not far from the Canadian border. Herman, who had served in the army during World War I, had been recruited to leave the South and work for Witherbee Sherman and Company, which was later sold to the Republic Steel Corporation. At this time, he worked in the mining hamlets of Standish and Lyon Mountain. Both brothers worked there together for a couple of years, mostly carrying iron to the blast furnace in Standish.

Due to a bleak social life that included no young women of color and the uneven demand for iron ore, Bill decided to leave his brother and return to Greenville to live with his mother, Alice Moore.

Back home, Bill soon met and courted Annie. They were wed in 1940 and had six children by 1948, when Bill became exasperated and spoke out against what he called the "slave wages" paid by the Dunean Cotton Mill that could not support his family. He, Annie, and his mother grew increasingly fearful of the Ku Klux Klan and the constant surveillance of Bill by the police, who made life difficult for black males in the Jim Crow South. For his own safety, he decided to go back to the Adirondacks. Annie hated the thought of leaving the South and her family and friends. But after days of heated discussions, she relented. They agreed that Bill should return to the Adirondacks and the iron-ore industry. Once employed, he would secure a home and send for her and the children to join him. His best guess was that this ambitious plan would take six months to complete, allowing his family to arrive in August.

As the train inched closer to the next stop, Annie cast aside her doubts, realizing she had to hurry and awaken her six small children huddled together in two seats across the aisle. Time forced her to quickly prepare them for what was about to happen. They would step from the train into the darkness and into a new world where their father was ardently awaiting a reunion with the family he had left behind to go north to a promised land.

Wearily wiping the sleep from their tiny eyes, the three girls, Geraldine, Alice, and Joan, and their younger brothers, William, Ralph, and baby Clyde, awoke to busy confusion and the strange hissing and clanging of the slowing train engine. Five of them begrudgingly followed their mother's instruction to grab each other's hands while she gathered her infant son in one arm and slung her bulging brown handbag over the other. At that moment, the conductor roared, "Port Henry, Port Henry, this way out!" The car's lone passengers inched their way to the open door of the stopped train and the extended hand of the conductor. As they descended the huge steps, their ears picked up the familiar sound of their Daddy's voice. In unison, they squealed with excitement and ran through the chilly dark night to be smothered in his outstretched arms. Through a small space Bill soon caught a glimpse of Annie holding tight to their baby boy.

From a distance, two other black men watched the joyful reunion. Bill's brother, Herman, and their friend Homer Matthews had arrived in two cars to drive the family to their new home. Annie demanded that special care and attention be given to the big black trunk that held all their worldly possessions, including the family Bible containing birth records and other important information. They would travel from Port Henry on Lake Champlain to their new home located six miles north in Witherbee, a small hamlet surrounded by natural mountains and several gray ones made from iron ore pilings.

Life in Witherbee—The Payden Family

After more than sixty-five years, my recollection of our arrival is still vivid. During that car ride to Witherbee, I recall hearing Uncle Herman and my dad in the front seat discussing something that would remain etched in my memory. They spoke of a funeral earlier that day. As a young child of six, I already knew about death, having attended the funerals of two family members. The most recent had been in June when my great-grandmother, Cicely Cauthan, died at the age of eighty-nine on my birthday. She was born enslaved in 1859.

Listening carefully, I was able to discern that a black man named Ambrose Gambrell had been killed a week earlier while drilling in the Old Bed Mine of the Republic Steel Corporation. Uncle Herman, his working partner and close friend, was present at the accident site and escaped injury. That event alerted me to how dangerous their work was. Miners were threatened not only by industrial accidents, but also by silicosis, a dreadful lung disease brought on by prolonged inhalation of silica dust deep inside the mines.

When we stepped off the train on August 13, 1948, we joined the other blacks living in three mining communities. Port Henry, the largest settlement in the town of Moriah, was the site of the greatest concentration of black people in Essex County and possibly the Adirondacks. Some fifteen black families lived on one block of the two-block-long Elizabeth Street. Four miles north, three families resided in the hamlet of Grover Hills. My father found a two-bedroom house for us in nearby Witherbee where one other black family of three had been living for four years since their arrival from Alabama. All the men in these families had come north for the same reason: to work in the mines and escape the brutality of the Jim Crow South. They were refugees of a racist regime that replaced the system of slavery.

Slowly, we took stock of the Adirondack area around us. Much of it was forestland interrupted by steep hills, small ponds, bubbling brooks, wild apple trees, and wild berry bushes. And, of course, high mountain peaks in the distant background. The wild blackberry bushes abundant in the wooded areas near our home later provided me a source of solace and comfort throughout my childhood. During the summer when there were no friends to play with or I felt lonely, sad, or depressed, I retreated to the woods to pick buckets of blackberries for hours on end. The activity allowed me to be both productive and alone to contemplate a situation or figure out how to solve a problem. Soon I became known as the champion blackberry picker. My mother welcomed the blackberries as a source of free food, using them to make pies, muffins, and jelly to help feed her hungry children. The irony of it all was that I hated blackberries. I never ate any of the hundreds of buckets of blackberries that I picked during my childhood.

Our family sought other sources of free food in the Adirondacks. My mother found multiple uses for wild apples and insisted that we go together as a family to collect as many apples as possible from trees we found on vacant land. Again, she used every piece of an apple to make pies and applesauce and the peeling, core, and seeds to boil for jelly.

Unfortunately, wild apples were small, sour, wormy, and not tasty to eat from the tree.

The forest near our home provided another source of free food. My father hunted rabbits and possum as his family had done in the South. But, it was my mother who supplied the bulk of our food. Her garden allowed her to grow some of the southern vegetables that were not available in Adirondack stores. For example, the stable of any soul food diet, collard greens, was not even heard of in the local stores. Nor was chow chow made from green tomatoes. Each summer, she spent days harvesting and canning the foods she had grown to ensure that we would have enough to eat during the winter. My father and brothers often added fish and sometimes frogs from the pond near our home. All of this, coupled with federal government surplus food, kept us fed and healthy.

As our lives took hold in our new home in New York, we saw no evidence that blacks had ever before inhabited Essex County or other parts of the Adirondack Mountains. If they had, their presence seemed to have been erased from everything we came in contact with—the people, schools, churches, businesses, resort industry, and even the mines. We felt stuck inside a world that seemed to view us as alien and inferior. Our family's struggle became one of how to survive and to shape a healthy identity. It was a daunting challenge that included a search for other blacks in the Adirondacks. Early on, we saw a few in Westport who arrived during the summer as servants to wealthy white people on vacation in the Adirondacks. Several worked in resorts in Paradox Lake, Westport, and Schroon Lake. As time passed, they disappeared. Their presence was replaced to some extent by small groups of black migrant workers brought north in the 1950s to pick apples. Our family befriended some who resided in migrant camps and housing in nearby Crown Point and Elizabethtown. Our parents seemed especially happy to visit with the workers because they brought news and information about the South. They invited some of them for Sunday dinner and used these visits as opportunities to share in cultural activities of singing, dancing, and eating soul food such as fried chicken, potato salad, and Mom's homegrown collard and turnip greens. The meals were usually topped off with the special southern cultural tradition of making and sharing homemade ice cream together.

Although we lived only six miles from Port Henry, the lack of transportation made it difficult for my family to maintain regular contact with black residents there, but we were visited on occasion by several of the men who had cars. They enjoyed getting together with my father to reminisce about the hard life they left back in Greenville. Although our parents tried to shield us from such talk, we positioned our ears to the upstairs floor to listen in awe as they talked and sometimes laughed into the night.

It seemed to take a while for our white neighbors to achieve a modicum of comfort in our presence. Many had not seen a black person before and remained suspicious of us and curious about our bodies. I endured endless questions about my hair and skin color. And if someone accidentally or intentionally touched me, their spontaneous reaction would be to wipe their hands, seemingly fearful that they had touched something dirty or that some of my color had rubbed off on them. Such prejudicial behavior served to strengthen our family internally. A strong bond developed between us, causing us to feel safest when we were together even as we developed positive relationships with white neighbors and classmates. Being alone together took the pressure off; we could let down our guard and feel free to be who we were.

We adapted quickly to school life, although it could not offer us the knowledge we craved about our black history and the presence of African Americans in the Adirondacks. Most of our teachers knew nothing of such things. Our textbooks, newspapers, and the academic and social experiences and values we shared reflected the life of whites, most of whom were European immigrants lured to upstate New York by agents of the iron-ore industry desperate for workers, and their first-generation American relatives. We were forced to learn their history and culture, but not our own.

Sometimes, we found the way race and ethnicity were approached in the classroom downright embarrassing and humiliating. My siblings and I always dreaded the first day of school, when teachers invariably asked each student to tell the class where his or her ancestors came from. One by one, the white students would proudly call out their country of origin: "Poland, Spain, Italy." Each time this happened I sunk deeper into my seat dreading my turn to be called upon. I could hear my heart pounding and feel sweat dripping down my face as my mouth and throat dried up. I knew that when I weakly and self-consciously uttered, "Africa" the students would laugh, as they always did. Africa must have seemed to them like a deep, dark, uncivilized land, filled with black, dumb natives who were ruled by Tarzan. My brothers and sisters experienced the same humiliation. We had no proud black history or heroes to buffer us from this onslaught. Our history books carved out one or two sentences about African Americans, mentioning only that they had been slaves, and to their credit, they had Lena Horne and Jackie Robinson among them. That was the sum total of our black history lesson.

As in most small American towns, school sports took on added importance in Witherbee and Port Henry. Black males gained ready acceptance throughout the region for their prowess on the court and on the field. Away from these venues, the athletes were subjected to all the racial venom that the rest of us endured. Yet most of them competed in sports; some were able to gain limited social acceptance through their achievements and went on to make a name for themselves throughout the region and sometimes beyond. Murray "Pop" Bullock, Norman Gates, Kenneth Hagood, my brothers, William "Duke" and Ralph Paden, and close Witherbee friend Calvin Twilley were among those who gained legendary stature in the 1950s and early 1960s.

Sports, recreation and school activities gave us an opportunity to occasionally visit other parts of the Adirondacks, but we never felt a connection to any of the sites. We passed through Lake Placid with its outdoor skating rink, surrounding ski slopes, fancy resort hotels, and well-manicured beaches, but they had no significance for us. We rode past waterfalls, beautiful vegetable gardens, and horse farms, but they belonged to people we could not know or were places we dared not go.

On the academic front, some of us were determined to destroy the deeply held and often openly expressed stereotype that blacks were intellectually inferior. Kenneth Hagood of Port Henry was equally driven to excel in sports and academics. He went on to Cornell Law School and became a successful attorney in New York City. I was class salutatorian, and my goal was to fulfill my mother's wish that I become a schoolteacher. I did that and later earned graduate degrees in education, social work, and criminology, including a doctorate in criminal justice.

Most of the sons and daughters of black miners quickly left the Adirondacks after graduating from high school, eagerly seeking to join urban communities and connect with other African Americans. Upon relocating, most of them succeeded in a variety of professions including education and medicine.

Their departure was hastened by the lack of jobs, especially in the failing mining industry that had summoned their parents north. Most of us had already felt the sting of racial discrimination when we sought summer employment in the resort industry during the 1950s, 1960s, and well into the 1970s. The hotels that had earlier welcomed black waiters, cooks, and cleaning staff no longer wanted to hire blacks. When they did, they relegated them to humiliating conditions in segregated, barely habitable living quarters. They were paid less than the other workers and barred from hotel lobbies and front yards. My brothers, William and Ralph, and I experienced such treatment first hand. Our black peers saw no other alternative but to leave the Adirondacks.

The landscape near our home provided some sense of security to me. It closeted me from an uncertain and more frightening world that I envisioned beyond the Adirondacks. I had hoped to remain in Witherbee and teach at the Moriah Central School in order to help care for my failing parents. I was denied that opportunity even though there was a suitable opening, forcing me to take a job in Rochester, New York, where I taught in an urban ghetto school far from my parents.

Religion played a major role in life in the Adirondacks. Catholicism loomed large, but our mother was a devout southern Methodist.

Her grandmother, Cicely Cauthan, who raised her, was known as a founding member of Trinity CME church in Toccoa, Georgia. Since there was no Methodist church in the Witherbee/Mineville area and Catholicism was so foreign to her, Mom decided that we would become Presbyterians and members of the Mineville Presbyterian Church, the only Protestant church nearby. The black Methodist church that was formed in Port Henry was out of reach since we had no reliable transportation. A couple of the other black families in the Witherbee/Mineville area converted to Catholicism, which was seen as a path to acceptance and assimilation. They feared the label of "heathen," which some Catholics branded Protestants.

The Presbyterian Church community was extremely supportive of our family. Aside from Sunday school and religious services, they offered picnics, choirs, youth groups, holiday parties and dinners, clubs, and occasional educational trips to other area towns. When they learned that I had cancelled my plans for college because I had absolutely no money to attend the University at Albany where I was accepted, several families in the church came together to provide financial assistance to me during my first year in college. The church minister also found housing for me with an Albany area family. I did childcare and light housekeeping duties in exchange for room and board.

Perhaps the most difficult challenge for us came during adolescence, when we faced the problem of how to survive socially and have a healthy and normal life like our white peers. My sisters and I had the same interests in boys as white girls. We longed for their attention, wanted to date, and needed to feel valued and desired as young women. But there was only one black boy in our high school, and public interracial interactions of all kinds between boys and girls were strictly forbidden. I recall the time when I was walking to school and a friendly new boy in town caught up to me a block from school. We walked together while he asked me questions about the school. As we approached the school, we caught the attention of students in the schoolyard. Male students started making fun and bitterly teasing and humiliating him for being with me. He did not realize that our association, no matter how innocent, was taboo. It never happened again.

A couple of white male classmates, who were our close neighbors and dear friends of our brothers, freely associated with me and my sisters in our neighborhood at night. We talked, laughed, and danced together. We even played teen kissing games like spin the bottle. During those times, I felt adored and almost normal. However, during the day, in public and at school, the very same boys would totally ignore and shun us.

This treatment reinforced our feelings of separateness, mistrust, and isolation because of something we had no control over: the color of our skin. We felt hopelessly locked out of the white world and confined to our own, which lacked a critical mass of black peers to sustain our need for honest and meaningful social interactions.

Surprisingly, the Plattsburgh Air Force Base offered us the greatest opportunity for "normal" dating, even though the airmen were a little older. The black airmen stationed there were experiencing some of the same problems we were: no eligible blacks to date and social taboos against interracial dating. On Friday afternoons, many of them would speed to Montreal, where interracial dating was less restricted and more women of color could be seen. After a chance meeting with several airmen in Plattsburgh, they became interested in visiting us at our home in Witherbee. Their visits became more frequent, and my sisters and I ended up with dates for the junior prom and other social events.

Some townspeople expressed fear that other airmen might come to Witherbee to seek dates with local white girls, but that didn't happen. Instead, healthy relationships developed between the airmen and several of the black girls in Witherbee and Port Henry, resulting in marriages that have endured until today. My sister Joan married Airman Jesse Lee; their marriage produced three children and lasted forty-three years until his death.

Black males did not fare as well socially. When my brothers became teenagers, tensions mounted as local residents became intent on preventing them from becoming romantically involved with the white girls their age that they had counted as friends. My brother William's white peers told him straight out that when he went with them to "look for girls," he was not to touch any of them. It sounded a lot like the South to me.

Pressure on them was not limited to verbal warnings. On a number of occasions, my teenage brothers, William and Ralph, were forced to defend themselves and fight their way out of area night spots after they were verbally assaulted and physically attacked by gangs of white men. My sister Geraldine and I were present during one of those vicious attacks on William in Witherbee. Shocked by the suddenness of the blistering assault, we did all we could to stop it and get our brother out of the building and to safety, which we somehow managed to do. The scene called to mind some of the stories we had overheard when our father and some of his black friends from Port Henry got together to reminisce about their life in the South.

My family was largely isolated from the civil rights movement, which began in earnest in 1954 with a landmark Supreme Court decision. The politically conservative Adirondack region seemed to barely notice *Brown v. Board of Education*. We heard nothing about this important ruling that outlawed segregation in public schools. Nothing about the case was openly discussed in our classrooms, the church, or public spaces. In Witherbee, radio and television reception was spotty and weak, so we saw or heard little. Our family was occasionally gifted with a copy of *Ebony* or *Jet* from a Port Henry friend who frequently traveled outside of the area. These black magazines introduced us to two epic civil rights events that were discussed only within the confines of our home. One was the Little Rock High School desegregation battle in 1957; we were terrified by the vicious treatment of black children who simply wanted to attend school. The other event, two years earlier, that made an indelible mark on our psyche was the killing of Emmett Till. The photo of his battered face so deeply frightened, angered, and disturbed me that I refused to travel to the South for almost twenty-five years. My deep anger resurfaced recently upon learning that the woman who claimed young Emmett disrespected her in 1955 admitted that she lied. These two events and another remain constant reminders of the destructive power of racism.

We not only faced overt employment discrimination, but were called "niggers" and were the targets of hate speech. Sometimes, the attacks were not intentionally directed at us, but were used in ordinary exchanges with whites. As a high school senior, I was engaged in a friendly conversation with the cafeteria manager at Mineville High School when a fellow student approached us and asked the manager's help with a task. She responded sharply to the interruption, saying something to the effect of "Whose nigger waiter do you think I am?" She quickly apologized to me, but I walked away, deeply wounded, never to speak to her again. On other occasions, I learned that "nigger" was part of many white friends' vocabulary and it would slip out to their embarrassment.

Our parents had migrated from the South to escape racism and poverty, but these forces remained our constant companions in the Adirondacks. Employment discrimination and some bad luck in the 1950s sent our family deeply into poverty. The misfortune struck a scant few weeks after our arrival in Witherbee when our father was seriously injured in a mining accident. A loaded trolley car crushed his legs. Fortunately, the Republic Steel physician, the venerable Doc Cummings, was able to wire his broken bones back together. However, his recovery required months of hospitalization, forcing our mother to be a single parent for her six young children once again.

After regaining the ability to walk, our father was no longer employable as a miner. He was given the lowest level job at Republic Steel—locker room janitor. The miners' union periodically went on strike for safer working conditions and better pay. Those work stoppages were extremely costly for the poorest families such as ours, and worse still for black families, for none of them could get temporary jobs to help out. Occasionally, my mother secured a housecleaning assignment that helped with expenses. Small welfare grants and government surplus cheese, canned meats, and dried milk saved us from starvation.

While poverty and racism placed many obstacles in our way, there were some kind, loving, compassionate, and supportive people who understood our plight and were willing to lend us a helping hand. Aside from members of the Mineville Presbyterian Church, we developed close friendships with a few schoolmates and particularly a family who lived two doors away. From the time of our arrival, we bonded with four of the children—twin sisters, Millie and Mollie, and two of their brothers, Alvin and Roger. We were all close in age. Their two older brothers were ten or more years older and had joined the US Air Force. As youngsters we played together and shared many life experiences, but our relationship had its limitations. Whenever their oldest brother came home on leave, he forbade his siblings and parents to associate with any member of my family. Their obedience seemed largely based on their fear of losing his financial support. They also saw him as an authority figure, for this miner's son from Witherbee was now an air force officer. So, we were totally shunned by our closest friends while their brother was in town. Immediately upon his departure, they resumed their contact and friendship with us. We found this hurtful but accepted this limitation on our otherwise good relationship. As we grew older, we expressed our disappointment and hurt, but their behavior never changed even into adulthood.

Several of our elementary and high school teachers took special interest in me and my two brothers, William and Ralph. Early on, they recognized my academic potential and their athletic abilities and provided us with extra attention and encouragement. One of our high school teachers, James Sotis, who came to our school from Brooklyn, took an interest in our entire family. He encouraged me to seek a college education, regularly played basketball with my brothers, and took us on special trips to introduce us to blacks who visited the area—gospel singers in Ticonderoga, semiprofessional basketball players in Port Henry, and Jackie Robinson in Burlington. We learned that Robinson's appearance was cancelled while we were en route to Burlington in a bad snowstorm. As an added incentive to excel, Mr. Sotis promised to attend my college graduation in Albany. Yet, I was still surprised and shocked when he appeared as promised. Long after he left Witherbee, he returned to participate in the Paden Family Reunion when we celebrated our fiftieth year in the Adirondacks. He inspired us all and maintained a close relationship with our family until his death about ten years ago.

Annie and Bill Payden did all within their power to give their children an opportunity to achieve a life better than they had known in the South. They far exceeded that mission as they struggled to overcome sickness, poor healthcare, and poverty compounded by racial discrimination, isolation, and culture shock in the Adirondacks. Although they never really recovered from the death of their youngest child in a car accident at the age of thirteen, they lived to see their five remaining children go out into the world to establish their own lives and start their own families. Their sacrifice of moving to the Adirondacks in hopes of providing their children with a better life and opportunities to achieve all that they could paid off. We believe that they would be extremely proud of all of us and our accomplishments. At times they felt that the barriers and obstacles their children faced would destroy their will, but they believed that our sense of family, their love, and their spiritual guidance would provide the support we needed. But we felt that it was their sacrificial efforts to ensure that we received a good education that impressed and encouraged us the most. Mom kept in constant touch with our teachers, attended every parents' night, carefully reviewed our report cards, and scratched every penny from her meager budget to make sure we had needed school supplies. She strongly believed that a good education was the way to success and happiness. Her grandmother, who was born enslaved, instilled that lesson in her and she passed it on. I got it and graduated with a perfect attendance record throughout my school years and beyond.

Although our father was supportive of education, he left the children's schooling to Mom. He must have also felt incapable, because, like a number of the southern iron-ore miners, he was illiterate, unable to read or write.

Life after Witherbee

Our parents worried most about their oldest child, Geraldine, who freely and openly expressed her deep hatred for the Adirondacks and the racism and hypocrisy she saw in some white people. Her deep anger forced her to leave Witherbee before graduating from high school. She went to Albany then to New York City, where she was able to finish school and become a registered nurse committed to working in the emergency room at Harlem Hospital. Upon her retirement, she was honored for serving the Harlem community for more than thirty-five years. Geraldine now lives in Troy and has four grandsons. One of her two sons has passed away; her older son, Leon, has for twenty years lived in the Payden homestead, where he raised two of his sons. One is a graphic artist and the other is a senior at Moriah Central School. A third son lives in Albany where he is one of several black firefighters in the city.

Joan was one of the girls who married an airman stationed at the Plattsburgh Air Force Base. She and her husband Jesse Lee raised a son and two daughters in Maryland near Washington, DC. Now widowed and retired, she worked for years as a developmental specialist in Rochester, New York. Her son is a retired US airman and health care worker. Both of her daughters work for the federal government in Washington.

William, our parents' oldest son, distinguished himself as a high school football player. Duke, as he is called, remains bitter over the social and employment discrimination he experienced in the Adirondacks during his teen years. He left Witherbee and joined the US Navy. After leaving the armed services, he trained as an electrician and then worked for years for the IBM Corporation, where he was recognized and cited for the quality of his work and service. Duke continued his education and received a degree in criminal justice from Dutchess Community College. His greatest achievement has been as a father of three sons and a daughter. The oldest son, Mark, lives in Virginia with his wife. His second son, William III, works for the National Basketball Association, which allows him to travel around the world with professional ball teams. His youngest son works as a youth counselor with developmentally handicapped children, and his daughter just received her BA in education. They all live in the Poughkeepsie and Hyde Park area but visit the Adirondacks during the summer.

Ralph lives in Largo, Maryland. He, like Duke, distinguished himself in sports, particularly football and basketball. Ralph also earned a reputation in Witherbee as a track star and went on to become a miler at the University of Maryland Eastern Shore, where he excelled in the classroom and on the track. He recalls that, in Witherbee, he was always in the loop except when social moments came up. He often laments that "I was President of the student council, captain of the sports teams, King of the Prom, but I never had a date, I used sports to keep from being depressed." Ralph was head football coach at Fairmont Heights High School in Maryland for twenty-eight years. No one coached there as long or won as many games. His record of two hundred wins still stands and includes a number of county, regional, and state championships. On five different occasions, various organizations named him Coach of the Year. He also has been honored by the Washington Redskins, WHUR Radio Station, and Prince Georges County Board of Education. In 2003, Ralph was selected by the Maryland State High School Football Coaches Association as a member of its Hall of Fame, making him only the second African American chosen for this honor. Retired and still living in Maryland with his wife of forty years, Ralph has three sons and two grandchildren.

Perhaps the most socially and politically conscious of the five living children, I have always felt the profound impact of enslavement, Jim Crow, and mass incarceration on our lives in the South, the Adirondacks, and urban communities across the country. I have never forgotten that my great-grandmother was born enslaved, that my Dad was a chain gang prisoner and fled the South to escape the overarching threat of the convict leasing system during Jim Crow segregation, and the devastating reach of the criminal justice system into the lives of my family members and all black people in the country. I have spent most of my adult life working to reform the system, defeat the War on Drugs, and abolish prisons and the disproportionate incarceration of blacks. To that end, I founded the Albany-based Center for Law and Justice more than thirty years ago and have openly, abrasively, and somewhat successfully challenged government officials through political protests and civil disobedience.

In 1985, Governor Mario Cuomo appointed me to the position of Deputy Commissioner of the New York State Division of Probation and Correctional Alternatives. I resigned three years later in protest over the governor's increased building of prisons to house a rapidly growing population that was disproportionately black. I was particularly pained when in 1989 the state opened the Moriah Shock Prison, converted out of existing iron-ore-mining buildings and grounds to house a maximum of 250 young men as part of the Department's growing Shock Incarceration program. Adding insult to injury, the prison was built practically in the backyard of the Payden homestead in Witherbee. I watched in horror as the prison population in the Adirondacks grew rapidly. Ironically, this growth meant increased jobs and services in the now economically depressed Adirondack region, even as it removed young urban black men from their families and communities.

While the free black population in the Adirondacks steadily decreased during this period, the black imprisoned population increased as the prison industrial complex took hold and gave rise to antiprison protests across the state, led in large part by my Center for Law and Justice.

Mom and Dad died within eleven weeks of each other in 1970 and lie buried with their beloved son, Clyde, and grandson, Jeffrey, in Port Henry, not far from the train station where the family was reunited on that night in the summer of 1948.

After our parents died, my siblings and I closed our family home of twenty-two years and left the Adirondacks behind us. We settled in Rochester, Albany, Poughkeepsie, New York City, and Washington, DC, and focused on our new lives and families.

After our parents died we felt even more disconnected from our past that we knew little about. They were our strongest connection to it. Soon, I yearned to return to Greenville to rediscover the place that we left as children in 1948. In 1978, I found the courage to go to Greenville, believing that it would now be safe due to the positive changes made by the civil rights movement. So, my sister Joan and I decided to return to our homeland together.

We traveled by train. As we approached the Greenville train station, my heart seemed to be pounding out of control. We arrived before sunrise on a cool November morning. Here was where our journey to the Adirondacks began thirty years earlier. Our eyes searched the building that held faint memories of our earlier departure. We were a little fearful as we climbed into a taxi driven by a white driver, but we soon relaxed as he started a friendly conversation about the comfort of our train ride.

Our weeklong visit to Greenville was filled with visiting several distant family members and a couple of our peers who remembered Grandmother Alice. One claimed to have remembered me. We visited the home where we had been born and searched for anything familiar. The house seemed so much smaller but caused us to stand in silence and reflect on our brief life there. Vague memories connected us to a few other buildings and landscapes as we toured our section of the city.

We left Greenville feeling more complete and satisfied that we had returned to our homeland, but we felt no strong bond to it. We were from the Adirondacks.

Return to the Adirondacks

A couple of years after our return trip to Greenville something beckoned me and my siblings back to the Adirondacks, where we discovered the beauty of the region that we were unable to appreciate while growing up there. It was as if Lake Champlain, the golden ponds, rushing streams, high peaks, colorful forests and wildlife were all new. We now felt free to explore the entire Adirondack region. To our surprise it was more expansive than we had ever imagined. It covers much of the northeastern part of upstate New York. We learned that most of it falls within the Adirondack Park which has eighteen major mountain peaks, fifteen lakes, twelve rivers, huge wilderness areas, and interesting communities including Saranac Lake, Lake Placid, Tupper Lake, and Keeseville. While visiting in the summer, we took family trips to many of these communities and sites. With our children in tow, we visited theme parks, chasms, and caves, took them fishing and camping along Lincoln Pond and Lake Champlain, and explored waterfalls and swimming holes near Elizabethtown.

I suspect that our new sense of freedom in the Adirondacks came from the many changes that had occurred in our lives after leaving the area. We were all becoming more comfortable in our skin. Living in urban settings allowed us to learn more about our blackness and our history, which we, at last, took great pride in. The civil rights movement had taught us to be more assertive about our rights and claims to America. I finally got the nerve to go south and discover it for myself and came to believe that this land, all of it, was mine, too. Although we realized that people in the area might still stare at us because they are not accustomed to seeing blacks, we no longer feared blatant acts of racism following passage of the Civil Rights Act of 1964. Although we were not wealthy, we were no longer poverty-stricken. We possessed the means to enjoy and purchase some of what we saw in the area for our children. But, most important, we started to realize that we had a bona fide claim and connection to the Adirondacks that we could not forget, ignore, or deny. After all, our home, with all its memories—good and bad—was still there. We were a part of the Adirondacks' history, and we wanted our children to know that and take some comfort in it. To this day, when people ask me where I am from, I unabashedly tell them that I am from the Adirondacks, rarely mentioning my birthplace.

My husband also inspired us to return to the Adirondacks and experience it anew. In 1973, I married Charles Touhey of Albany, who had spent all of his summers in the town of Essex, where his family owned property overlooking Lake Champlain. It included a large home that dated to the Revolutionary War era and was reputed to have been a station on the Underground Railroad that smuggled runaway slaves to Canada and freedom. Charles, who is white, encouraged my siblings and me to restore the Payden homestead and use it as a family summer home. We all enjoyed pitching in to fix up our deteriorating home and completed the job in 1982. Each summer, for nearly twenty-five years, our growing family and circle of friends gathered for a Payden family reunion and large picnic on July Fourth. (Charles and

I have two children, John and Brenda, and now three grandchildren, Olivia, Ava, and Kaiya. John, a trained teacher, works as legislative representative for the New York State United Teachers, and Brenda works for the Internal Revenue Service in Washington.)

Our friends included some of the former black residents of Port Henry and their children. The Witherbee home became sort of a home base for their return to the area to see and chat with old friends. Sitting around a big campfire on July Fourth became a well-known annual ritual. We reminisced about our early lives in the Adirondacks; we looked back, laughed, and shared stories of that time while our children tried hard to imagine what it must have been like to live in a land that had so few black people. Year after year, we found ourselves eagerly retelling, and often embellishing, the tales to grab the attention of our young people.

In 1998, eighty of us gathered to celebrate our fiftieth year in the Adirondacks. The highlight was a visit to the gravesite of our parents and brother. We were joined by several of the old miners' children and well-wishers from nearby towns. Special visitors included my high school teacher, Mr. Sotis, onetime basketball stars "Pop" Bullock and Norm Gates, and Calvin Twilley, who had been a celebrated football and track star. He was a member of the only other black family in Witherbee in the 1950s and, anxious to leave Witherbee, moved to Detroit the day after his high school graduation in 1959.

At the gravesite we were all mindful of the fact that all of the southern-born black miners had died. Allen Walton, the last member of that group, died of cancer in October 1994, the day before our scheduled meeting to discuss more of the history of blacks in the Adirondacks. A few years before his death, he had become a renowned local historian, holding court and talking to any who would listen to tales of his travels throughout the North Country and life among the black miners who lived and worked in Lyon Mountain, Standish, and other towns. He recalled being with my father and Uncle Herman as they arrived from the South to work for Witherbee Sherman and Company. We always listened with delight, eager to learn as much as we could about our uncle and especially our father, who never shared with his children his own stories about his early life in the Adirondacks. Allen Walton helped me and my siblings make an important connection between our southern roots and our life in the Adirondacks. Fortunately, Adirondack historian Amy Godine got to know Walton through her many interviews with him. She has written extensively about his life and recollections.

Changing of the Guard

By the year 2000 only a few children of the black miners from the 1940s and 1950s still lived in Essex County. We found several in Ticonderoga, Port Henry, and Witherbee. Others we had known were now spread across New York and the nation.

According to the US census, some Adirondack counties showed both modest increases and declines in population. However the prison population in these areas steadily increased. In the period between 1974 and 2002, the New York state prison population rose by almost 500 percent from 14,400 to 70,700.[1]

It is staggering to the imagination that so many people were placed in its archipelago of prisons built to accommodate the influx known as mass incarceration. Much of the growth had to do with the 1973 Rockefeller Drug Laws that handed out stiff mandatory prison sentences for possession of a small amount of narcotics. Blacks and Latinos were disproportionately prosecuted and sentenced under these laws and many of them confined to prisons in upstate New York. More than 94 percent of those sentenced under those drug laws were black and Latino.[2]

In both the 2000 and 2010 US censuses, these imprisoned people—most of whom come from the New York City area—were counted as residents of the counties in which they were confined instead of their home communities. Some in the region welcomed the count because it increased the official local population used to determine legislative seats. Furthermore, prisoners, who are legally disenfranchised, provide the Adirondack region with prison jobs and increased per capita federal assistance based on census data that reports them as residents. In a partial fix, in 2010 New York State enacted legislation to ensure that incarcerated persons are counted as residents of their home communities when state and local legislative districts were redrawn.[3]

On the other hand, counting persons imprisoned in this manner makes it difficult to get an exact count of the black resident population in the Adirondack region. According to the 2000 census, 233,885 people lived in northern New York. Whites comprised 96 percent of that population while blacks made up 3 percent, or 7,000 residents. The New York State Department of Corrections' 2010 count of people imprisoned tells us that close to 5,000 men were incarcerated in the region.[4] This would mean that approximately 71 percent of persons of color in upstate New York are imprisoned. The disparity is even worse in the Adirondack Park. It is estimated that blacks make up 2.5 percent of the park's total population of 137,938 people or 3,390. But, 2,686—or roughly 80 percent of the black population—are imprisoned.[5] This suggests an even worse parallel to Michelle Alexander's claim that there are more blacks under the control of the criminal justice system in America today than there were enslaved in 1850.[6]

Whatever their number, the current free black population can be thought of as sparsely sprinkled in a number of communities, with no sizable or recognized community presence anywhere other than Plattsburgh, which the 2010 census showed as having a black population of 594 blacks, or 3 percent of the city's population. During the summer and fall, blacks have a greater presence in the Adirondacks. Black seasonal workers, especially Jamaican apple pickers, are visible in some of the twenty-one orchards in the region. A number of them work in the Jay and Keeseville area. Over the past several years, I have seen black workers in some of the area's hotels and resorts. I have met several who remain in the area during the winter in places like Lake Placid and Hague.

Adirondack Residents React to Prisons and Human Rights

Starting in the 1980s, relatives and friends of prisoners reported to the Center for Law and Justice in Albany claims of mistreatment while traveling to prisons in the Adirondack region. They related that they were denied lodging at local motels and the use of public toilets, that they were stared at, and that racial epithets were hurled at them. Many reported that they were aware that the buses from New York City carrying them to the Adirondack prisons were referred to as "The African Queen."

Disturbed by the mass incarceration and the disproportionate incarceration of blacks and Latinos in state prisons, by reported violations of civil rights and acts of racial discrimination, and by the lack of racial diversity in the area, a number of black and white residents have been working to reverse these patterns of mistreatment. Individuals and organizations are educating young people and adults about African American history in the Adirondacks and the importance of promoting civil and human rights.

A number of blacks stand out as prominent community leaders. Among them are the Rev. Fred Shaw in Elizabethtown, Robin Caudell, a longtime reporter for the *Plattsburgh Press-Republican*, J. W. Wiley, Chief Diversity Officer and Director of the Center for Diversity at SUNY Plattsburgh, and Vivian Papson, a guiding force in the establishment of the North Country Underground Railroad Historical Association and the North Star Underground Railroad Museum, which explores the history and modern-day importance of the fight against slavery and racism. The museum, located in Chesterfield, opened in 2011. Each year it draws thousands of visitors from the Adirondacks and around the world.

One of the hardest-working and most effective groups has been John Brown Lives, a human rights and freedom education project led by activist Martha Swan, a resident of Westport. The group developed a traveling and now permanent Timbuktu exhibit located at the John Brown Museum in North Elba depicting one of the first attempts to encourage and welcome blacks to the Adirondacks: wealthy abolitionist Gerrit Smith's 1846 gift of 120,000 acres of land to attract free black families to the Adirondacks to escape poverty. John Brown Lives has sponsored and organized many important community discussions about racism, slavery, and mass incarceration. The organization also sponsors an annual May gathering at the John Brown Farm and Museum to celebrate the birth and legacy of John Brown.

Paul Smith's College, the only private four-year college in the Adirondack Park, offered a "Nature and Culture" course that examined diversity in the Adirondacks. Other environmentalists have taken up the cause of promoting racial and economic diversity in the Adirondacks. In 2014, I attended the first ever Adirondack Diversity Symposium at the Adirondack Interpretive Center in Newcomb along with other civil rights leaders, community activists, and social scientists. A highlight of the symposium was a focus on Brother Yusuf's Youth Ed-Venture & Nature Network, which brings urban young people to the Adirondacks to learn about and enjoy nature. Shortly thereafter Brother Yusuf, educator and environmentalist extraordinaire, died, but his widow, Cherry, and others are actively committed to continuing his work to help make the Adirondacks more inclusive and welcoming to people of color.

My husband and I founded the Paden Institute and Retreat for Writers of Color in 1997, named in my parents' honor by using their final change in the spelling of our surname. Ten years ago we began collaboration with SUNY Plattsburgh, Brenda Greene of Medgar Evers College in Brooklyn, and the Paden Institute that allowed students and skilled writers to work together in the summer at Valcour, south of Plattsburgh. The Paden Institute continues to host writers during the summer at a cottage located on Touhey family property in Essex. Writers have a chance to quietly work on their writing projects, meet residents of the town, and read their works at sites such as the Belden Noble Public Library in Essex and other venues in Elizabethtown and Plattsburgh.

Several Adirondack libraries, schools, and museums, including the Adirondack Museum in Blue Mountain Lake, have recently added materials and curricula to educate the public about African American history and specifically the presence of blacks in the Adirondacks. John Brown Lives has been cited for its curricula on racism for high school students. The Adirondack Museum is adding to its exhibit on iron-ore mining and showing renewed interest in black miners and their families. What a grand tribute to all those who came to the region looking for opportunity and acceptance during a most difficult time in the history of this country.

To add to this wonderful recognition of these black trailblazers, other organizations are working to honor those blacks who dared to settle in the Adirondacks. Renee Moore of Saratoga helped rescue the abolitionist Solomon Northup from virtual anonymity. Northup, born free in Minerva, Essex County, in 1808, was kidnapped and sold into slavery in 1841. He and his family were respected residents of Saratoga when he was kidnapped while in Washington, DC. Moore founded a Solomon Northup Day and in the 1990s arranged annual celebrations of his life with music, food, and lectures on Northup and his legacy. Moore also helped to secure him a plaque in Saratoga to memorialize him. In 2013, Solomon's memoir was made into a film entitled *12 Years a Slave*. The film received critical acclaim around the world, winning several prizes from a number of media outlets, and it was named best picture at the Academy Awards.

Any one of these individuals or organizations and their examination of black history would have made an enormous difference in my life as a young person. They would have helped me understand who I was and what I might achieve as a black woman. My hope is that young blacks and all people take note of black achievements in the Adirondacks and elsewhere and learn of our great past and potential for the future.

Even though blatant attacks on blacks in the Adirondacks seem to have lessened after the civil rights movement, the press has recently reported on open racial taunts and threats.[7] Today's racism is more subtle than the blatant form that my family and I experienced when I was growing up. For example, in the 1980s my husband Charles and I purchased from his aunt a cottage on his family's property in Essex. Although we had visited and stayed with his grandmother next door for years during the summer, I had long been forbidden to step onto the aunt's property. But when she became ill, she decided to sell the property and we purchased it. For close to five decades, Charles's family had belonged to the nearby private Crater Club, which provided services to its members and also rented cottages. We had heard about the club's long-held policy of discrimination against Jews and blacks. To challenge the ban, we applied for membership soon after my husband's grandmother's death in 1987. She had been a member for nearly fifty years. But we were rejected without explanation. In turn, we filed a formal complaint against the club with the New York State Human Rights Commission, which ultimately upheld the private club's right to discriminate. It determined that the club was not engaging in public accommodation since they were renting to members.

While much is being done to fight racial discrimination and improve the relationship between blacks and whites in the Adirondacks, it seems that not everyone promoting racial diversity has fully grasped its true importance and meaning. For some, diversity is achieved simply through numbers and often for the personal, political, and economic benefit of whites. I find this problematic for achieving systemic change and the true inclusion of all people in the Adirondacks, our state, and nation.

At the Adirondack Diversity Symposium held in Newcomb in August 2014, I expressed my concern that diversity without total inclusion and acceptance of new and different people as equals in all aspects of life in a community can be hollow and harmful to those left out. From my own experience in Witherbee, I recall that while I was ostensibly accepted by my peers in the school setting, I was not invited to participate in most of their social events. Although I had been elected president of the school drama club, my classmates appeared to think it absurd that I should actually want to be included in the cast of any of the selected plays. Their limited experience and understanding, and that of faculty advisers, as well, was that in both theater and film, blacks were only cast in the familiar roles of servants or slaves. The fact was that I was made to feel excluded; they did not seem to know how much I wanted to act in a school play and feel equal to them.

Inclusion is undoubtedly a complex and uncomfortable process. It calls upon white people to learn about and embrace the true history and culture of others and to examine their own implicit biases and unearned privileges. In addition, it demands that whites accept change that can disturb their comfort level, such as having a person of color move next door to them, and to think about and treat them as equals.

Change is undoubtedly hard, and even well-meaning people will have to struggle to implement it. But it must start somewhere. Learning and understanding other's cultures and true histories may be the key to unlocking the door to implementing real diversity and inclusion. History helps us understand change. It offers a wealth of information about how people and societies have connected, how we all came to be who we are, and what is happening in the world, today. Ultimately, it is history that connects us to the future.

Sally Svenson's book begins that understanding of our history in the Adirondacks and beyond. I founded the Paden Institute and Retreat for Writers of Color to inspire others to become involved in telling our history. Perhaps this work will serve as a springboard to further research and truth-telling of our history. I truly hope so.

Notes

Bibliography

Index

Notes

Federal and state census data, a significant resource in the preparation of this book, is increasingly available online in a variety of formats and is not referenced in the notes. Census dates are provided in the text in connection with all census material; census designations for occupations are enclosed within quotation marks. Similarly, enlistment and other information relating to the Civil War and overseas wars (available only through World War I draft records as of 2017) can generally be found online and are not referenced in notes.

Online links to books now out of copyright as well as older journal articles available online are not included here. I would suggest searching all book titles online that are likely to be out of copyright, an approach that often works with journal articles as well.

Preface

1. Coonrod, "Roads to Yesterday," unpaged.
2. *Christian Inquirer*, June 16, 1860.
3. McElrath, "Richard Harding Davis's 'The Boys in the Adariondacks [*sic*],'" 205.
4. *North Creek News-Enterprise*, Jan. 2, 1975.
5. *New York Tribune*, Aug. 2, 1869. Thanks to Larry Miller for this item.
6. Hurston, *Dust Tracks on a Road*, 292.
7. Wilkerson, *Warmth of Other Suns*, 55n13.

Introduction

1. Banks, introduction to "John Brown's Body," 250.
2. Hough, "New York State Census," 206–7.
3. Hochschild and Powell, "Racial Reorganization," 63, 66.
4. United States Bureau of the Census, *Negro Population in the United States: 1790–1915*, 210.
5. Hochschild and Powell, "Racial Reorganization," 70–71.
6. Dollarhide, *New York State Censuses*, passim.

7. Kenneth Prewitt, "A Nation Imagined, a Nation Measured: The Jeffersonian Legacy," in *Across the Continent: Jefferson, Lewis and Clark, and the Making of America*, ed. Douglas Seefeldt, Jeffrey L. Hantman, and Peter S. Onuf, quoted in Hochschild and Powell, "Racial Reorganization," 63.

8. Baker, *Following the Color Line*, 110.

9. Litwack, *North of Slavery*, 182; Itabari Njeri, "Sushi and Grits," 17.

10. Hough, "New York State Census," 209.

11. William James, "The Will to Believe: An Address to the Philosophical Clubs of Yale and Brown Universities," first published in *New World*, June 1896, and frequently republished, quoted in Early, editor's introduction to *Lure and Loathing*, xx.

12. Loury, "Free at Last? A Personal Perspective," 2.

13. Lewis and Ardizzone, *Love on Trial*, 37.

14. Smith-Pryor, *Property Rites*, 3; Lewis and Ardizzone, *Love on Trial*, 37.

15. "Rhinelander Tells of Baring Letters," *New York Times*, Nov. 17, 1925; "Rhinelander's Wife Cries Under Ordeal," *New York Times*, Nov. 24, 1925.

16. Wilkerson, *Warmth of Other Suns*, 386.

1. Slavery: Backdrop to the Adirondack Story

1. Desjardins and Pharoux, *Castorland Journal*, 246–47.

2. Calarco, *Underground Railroad in the Adirondack Region*, 18n.

3. Wanda Burch, "'He Was Bought at Public Sale': Slavery at Johnson Hall," *Gloversville Leader-Herald*, Feb. 27, 2000; Williams-Myers, "Contested Ground," 102; *History of Montgomery and Fulton Counties, NY*, 188.

4. McManus, *History of Negro Slavery in New York*, 172.

5. McManus, *History of Negro Slavery in New York*, 154–59; Foner, *Gateway to Freedom*, 33.

6. In 1841, New York State Governor William H. Seward signed the repeal of an 1817 law that allowed slaves to be brought to the state "in transit" for up to nine months. Slaves entering the state were henceforth declared automatically free. Foner, *Gateway to Freedom*, 78.

7. Philip L. White, *Beekmantown, New York*, 90.

8. Kellogg, *Doctor at All Hours*, 19.

9. Mayfield, *Town Minutes*, 155.

10. Ibid., 154.

11. Stewart, *Mysterious Black Migration*, 88–89.

12. Mayfield, *Town Minutes*, 152; Stewart, *Mysterious Black Migration*, 89.

13. Peckham, *History of Cornelis Maessen Van Buren*, 84. "Boy," "girl," and "wench" were degrading designations for slaves of any age.

14. From the act, passed in the General Assembly of New York, June and September 1706, quoted in Williams-Myers, *Long Hammering*, 44.

15. Mayfield, *Town Minutes*, 41.

16. Unidentified newspaper clipping, June 2, 1892, on file in Mayfield Historian's Office; Mayfield, *Town Minutes*, 47; [Birney], *American Churches*, 6–7.

17. Aber and King, *History of Hamilton County*, 623–25, 627.

18. Northup, *Twelve Years A Slave*, 6, 8–10, 12–13, 17–18, 22.

19. Philip L. White, *Beekmantown, New York*, 106.

20. Calarco, *Search for the Underground Railroad*, 79–80; "Plattsburgh's Anti-Slavery Interpretive Panel Unveiling," New York History Blog: Historical News and Views from the Empire State, Feb. 9, 2010, http://newyorkhistoryblog.org/2010/02/09/plattsburghs-anti-slavery-interpretive-panel-unveiling/.

21. Calarco, *Underground Railroad in the Adirondack Region*, 157. Keeseville is in the towns of Au Sable and Chesterfield in Clinton and Essex counties.

22. Foner, *Gateway to Freedom*, 19.

23. Calarco, *Underground Railroad in the Adirondack Region*, 6, 188.

24. Dorothy Williams, *Road to Now*, 28.

25. Calarco, *Underground Railroad in the Adirondack Region*, 100.

26. Seaver, *Historical Sketches of Franklin County*, 310.

27. Laird and Bowman, *Black Heritage in Fulton County*, 4.

28. Howell and Tenney, *Bi-Centennial History of Albany*, 2:725–26.

29. Corbett, *Making of American Resorts*, 146–49.

30. Armstead, "*Lord, Please Don't Take Me in August*," 29, 71; Hotaling, *They're Off! Horse Racing at Saratoga*, 66–67.

31. Armstead, "*Lord, Please Don't Take Me in August*," 39, 84.

32. DeAmicis, "Search for Community," 9–10, 20.

33. "The Negro Settlement on Post Street Soon Will Be Only a Memory; Most of Its Carefree Denizens Have Migrated to the Second Ward," *Utica Sunday Tribune*, Dec. 1, 1912.

34. *Johnstown Daily Republican*, July 13, 1892; *Gloversville Daily Leader*, Aug. 18, 1893; *Johnstown Daily Republican*, June 24, 1896. Thanks to Paul Larner for pointing out these items.

35. Robert L. Jeffers, "History of Gloversville," *Gloversville Daily Leader*, Oct. 28, 1899.

36. Whitfield, "African Americans in Burlington," 103.

37. Whitfield, "African Americans in Burlington," 114–15; Armstead, "*Lord, Please Don't Take Me in August*," 81.

2. Gerrit Smith: Essex and Franklin County Colonists

1. Smith also made land grants in the old Totten and Crossfield Patent lands in Hamilton County, but no recipients are known to have taken them up. Grover, *Make a Way Somehow*, 220.

2. Davis, "Three Dark Centuries Around Albany," 11.

3. Steward, *Twenty-Two Years a Slave*, 166–67.

4. M. A. Shadd, letter to the editor, *North Star*, Mar. 23, 1849, quoted in Grover, *Make a Way Somehow*, 110.

5. Gerrit Smith, "Account of My Distribution of Land Among Colored Men," 88:26, 92.

6. Watson, *Military and Civil History of the County of Essex*, 218; MacKenzie, *Plains of Abraham*, 130.

7. Benjaminsen and Berge, "Myths of Timbukto," 32. The contemporary use of the word *Timbucto(o)* in reference to Smith's North Elba colony has been exaggerated. In 2010, W. Caleb McDaniel, an assistant professor at Rice University, researched references in period sources. He identified six occurrences of the word in pre-1850 letters of abolitionist John Brown, and one instance of its use by a colonist, also pre-1850. "In Search of John Brown's Timbucto, Part I," Aug. 11, 2010, http://wcm1.web.rice.edu/john-brown-timbuctoo-part1.html.

8. James Henderson to Henry Garnet, Jan. 29, 1849, quoted in Sernett, *North Star Country*, 197.

9. MacKenzie, *Plains of Abraham*, 144–45.

10. "Personalities," *The Independent, Devoted to the Consideration of Politics, Social and Economic Tendencies, History, Literature, and the Arts*, Dec. 11, 1890; MacKenzie, *Plains of Abraham*, 131–35.

11. *New York Evening Post*, Dec. 20, 1859.

12. Sanborn, *Life and Letters of John Brown*, 97.

13. James Henderson to Henry Garnet, Jan. 29, 1849, quoted in Sernett, *North Star Country*, 197.

14. Watson, *Military and Civil History of the County of Essex*, 222.

15. Harlow, *Gerrit Smith*, 246.

16. Two of Thompson's brothers fought and died with Brown at Harpers Ferry. Calarco, *Underground Railroad in the Adirondack Region*, 267.

17. Quoted without specific source of Brown attribution in Stauffer, *Black Hearts of Men*, 173.

18. *Chicago Defender*, July 2, 1938. Epps leased John Brown's farm for a number of years after Brown's death and his family's departure from North Elba. An 1885 letter from two Brown sons laid out the rental terms to Epps if he "would like to keep the place for another year . . . $10 (Ten dollars) a year and the taxes, and such attention to fences and other matters about the place as shall save it from running down from lack of care." John Jr. and Owen Brown (Put-in-Bay Island, OH) to Lyman Epps, Nov. 1, 1885, John Brown/Boyd B. Stutler Collection Database, West Virginia Memory Project, http://www.wvculture.org/history/wvmemory/jbdetail.aspx?Type=Text&Id=659.

19. Gatewood, *Aristocrats of Color*, 97.

20. *Historical, Statistical and Industrial Review of the State of Connecticut*, Part I, s.v. "St. John Appo," 227; Southern, *Biographical Dictionary of Afro-American and African Musicians*, 16–17; Davies, "Saint-Dominguan Refugees," 119.

21. Gatewood, *Aristocrats of Color*, 97.

22. *Utica Daily Gazette*, Jan. 30, 1846.

23. New York City Common Council, *Manual of the Corporation*, 261. 262.

24. MacKenzie, *Plains of Abraham*, 136–38.

25. Foner, *Gateway to Freedom*, 119–20, 134.

26. Sernett, *North Star Country*, 200–201; Harlow, *Gerrit Smith*, 243–34; Frothingham, *Gerrit Smith*, 105, 112.

27. Watson, *General View and Agricultural Survey of the County of Essex*, 725–26; O'Brien, "Timbuctoo," 16.

28. Watson, *Military and Civil History of the County of Essex*, 218.

29. O'Brien, "Timbuctoo," 20.

30. *Proceedings of the National Convention of Colored People and Their Friends*, 28, 29.

31. Quoted without attribution in Edward J. Blankman, "Under the North Star," 36.

32. John Brown to William Hodges, Springfield, MA, Oct. 28, 1848, Jan. 22, 1849, and May 7, 1849, reproduced in *New York Evening Post*, Dec. 20, 1859.

33. Blankman, "Under the North Star," 36.

34. *Malone Palladium*, May 10, 1894.

35. John Thomas to Gerrit Smith, Aug. 26, 1872, Gerrit Smith Papers.

36. Seaver, *Historical Sketches of Franklin County*, 644–45.

37. John Thomas to Gerrit Smith, Aug. 26, 1872, Gerrit Smith Papers.

38. Stewart, *Mysterious Black Migration*, 250n241.

39. Gerrit Smith, "Account of My Distribution of Land Among Colored Men," 88:106.

40. Deed of sale from Ira Marks to Margaret Ann Hazzard, Charles Henry Hazzard, Alexander Hazzard. Lavinia Eppes, Leonard Hazzard, George Hazzard, Jane Ann Hazzard, Lucinda A. Hazzard, and Anna Mary Hazzard, heirs of Avery Hazzard, Dec. 23, 1864 (recorded Apr. 7, 1865), Essex County, *Book of Deeds* 56, 392–93, County Clerk's Office, Elizabethtown, NY.

41. Guyette, *Discovering Black Vermont*, 86.

42. *Cleveland Gazette*, Sept. 12, 1936.

43. *Saranac Lake Methodist Church Records Book 1*, Marriages, Johnson to Smith, Oct. 1, 1877. Copy on file in Adirondack Room, Saranac Lake Free Library.

3. Soldiers of the Civil War

1. James Henry Estes to his mother, Oct. [15], 1862, Estes Family Correspondence, 1856–1916, Special Collections, Feinberg Library, SUNY Plattsburgh. Estes was in camp near Relay House, Maryland, when this letter was written.

2. Seraile, *New York's Black Regiments*, 18–20.

3. Emilio, *Brave Black Regiment*, 11–12.

4. Ibid., 166, 301.

5. *Herkimer County Journal*, Apr. 16, 1863, reprinted from *Albany Statesman*. Thanks to David Krutz for this item.

6. "Remembering Amos King," *Gloversville Leader-Herald*, Aug. 5, 1996.

7. Amos King, his wife, and two young sons were living in East Fishkill, Dutchess County, in 1850. One son apparently did not survive to maturity.

8. Deed of sale from Morgan Burton to Philip Leonard, Apr. 19, 1851, Fulton County, *Book of Deeds* 17, 481–82, County Recorder's Office, Johnstown, NY.

9. McMartin, *Caroga*, 31.

10. Seraile, *New York's Black Regiments*, 22.

11. Jessie Carney Smith, *Notable Black American Women, Book II*, s.v. "Helen Appo Cook," 137–40; Taylor, *Original Black Elite*, 127–28; Hobbs, *Chosen Exile*, 62–63; *Brooklyn Daily Eagle*, Jan. 10, 1928; *New York Evening Post*, Nov. 9, 1905.

12. Louisa Brady died in 1894 and is buried with members of the Thomas family in the Union Cemetery, Franklin, Franklin County.

13. *Elizabethtown Post*, Jan. 7, 1915.

14. New York State, *Annual Report of the Adjutant-General of the State of New York for the Year 1901*, Serial 29, Vol. 4, 521.

15. Wiley, *Life of Billy Yank*, 124–25.

16. United States National Archives, Civil War Widows Pension Files, "Lafayette Mason," Certificate #374223.

17. Thomas Pike, "Salisbury Prison Was Final Stop for Many," *Rochester (MN) Post Bulletin*, Oct. 16, 2012.

18. *Au Sable Forks Adirondack Record*, July 25, 1919.

19. United States National Archives, Civil War Widows Pension Files, "Lafayette Mason," Certificate #374223.

20. Louis Brown, *Salisbury Prison*, 13.

21. Drummond, *Religious Pray, the Profane Swear*, 64–65.

22. Louis Brown, *Salisbury Prison*, 165.

23. United States National Archives, Civil War Widows Pension Files, "Lafayette Mason," Certificate #374223.

24. Berlin, Reidy, and Rowland, eds., *Freedom*, Series 2, *Black Military Experience*, 18n29.

25. Union League Club, *Report of the Committee on Volunteering*, 5.

26. There were two state exceptions to the USCT designation: Massachusetts, where Governor Andrew refused to allow what he considered a discriminatory label to be applied to the three state units made up of black soldiers; and Connecticut, where black regiments were formed before the creation of the USCT designation and did not transfer to federal authority.

27. Seraile, *New York's Black Regiments*, 26.

28. Cunningham, *Three Years with the Adirondack Regiment*, 220.

29. Union League Club, *Report of the Committee on Volunteering*, including quotation from the *New York Independent*, Mar. 10, 1864, 40–42.

30. Berlin, Reidy, and Rowland, *Freedom*, 501.

31. New York State Division of Military and Naval Affairs, Military Museum and Veterans Research Center, "Civil War Colored Troops Units with New York Soldiers or Officers," s.v. "20th Infantry, US Colored Troops," accessed June 7, 2017, https://dmna.ny.gov/historic/reghist/civil/other/coloredTroops/coloredTroopsMain.htm#20thInf.

32. Matthews, *Freedom Knows No Color*, 2:309.

33. Ibid., 313.

34. Ibid., 316.

35. Ibid.

36. Ibid., 321.

37. Ibid. 324.

38. Ibid., 321.

39. MacKenzie, *Plains of Abraham*, 157.

40. Royce, *Bessboro*, 537–38.

41. United States National Archives, Civil War Widows Pension Files, "Silas Frazier," Certificate #185533.

42. "Augusta Dinsmore," Naval History and Heritage Command, June 9, 2015, https://www.history.navy.mil/research/histories/ship-histories/danfs/a/augusta-dinsmore.html.

43. Reidy, "Black Men in Navy Blue," 156–62.

44. United States National Archives, Civil War Widows Pension Files, "Silas Frazier," Certificate #185533.

45. Ron Bruno Sr. (Willsboro Town Historian), email message to author, June 6, 2015.

46. United States National Archives, Civil War Widows Pension Files, "Lafayette Mason," Certificate #374223.

47. Ibid.

48. *Minneapolis Appeal*, Sept. 8, 1900.

49. Deed of sale from A. B. Mowry to Amos King, Oct. 28, 1865, Fulton County, *Book of Deeds* 32, 147–48, County Recorder's Office, Johnstown, NY.

50. *Gloversville Leader-Herald*, Aug. 5, 1996.

51. MacKenzie, *Plains of Abraham*, 151, 160. The Hasbrooks returned occasionally to the Adirondacks to visit the family of Jane Hasbrook's late brother, Charles Henry Hazzard. A 1906 social item in *New York Age* reported that R. C. Barber, a Manhattan barber visiting Saranac lake, had met the Hasbrooks, "who lived in the family of John Brown for many years." *New York Age*, Aug. 16, 1906.

52. *Johnstown Daily Republican*, Dec. 10, 1892; *Amsterdam (NY) Evening Recorder*, July 28, 1927.

53. Svenson, "'Devoted to Patriotic Reminiscence,'" 43.

54. Gannon, *Won Cause*, 5–7, 21, 37, 164–65.

4. Wartime and Early Postwar Migration

1. "Dr. Langdon Ithiel Marvin," http://www.northhamptonnyhistory.com/dr-langdon-i-marvin.html.

2. Wiley, *Life of Billy Yank*, 110.

3. Clarkson, *An Adirondack Archive*, 40.

4. *Gloversville Morning Herald*, Apr. 14, 1924.

5. *Gloversville Morning Herald*, Apr. 17, 1915; May 7, 1918; Sept. 18, 1925.

6. Quoted text is from the Confiscation Act as approved on August 6, 1861.

7. Rael, *Eighty-Eight Years*, 259–60.

8. Royce, *Bessboro*, 555.

9. Don Papson, "The John Thomas Story: From Slavery in Maryland to American Citizenship in the Adirondacks," *Lake Champlain Weekly*, Nov. 29, 2006; Kirstein, "Vermontville's Black Community," 24–27.

10. Notice of sale in foreclosure by Francis Skiff against Walter and Caroline Scott, Nov. 6, 1916, Franklin County, *Book of Deeds* 157, 244–47, County Clerk's Office, Malone, NY.

11. Kirstein, "Vermontville's Back Community," 26.

12. "J. Herring, 89, Civil War Vet, Taken by Death," *Gloversville Morning Herald*, Apr. 7, 1933.

13. An exception was John H. Jackson of Glens Falls, Warren County, who enlisted as a "colored cook" in the 175th New York Infantry in Plattsburgh in August 1864. A "boatman" before the war, Jackson returned to Glens Falls at its close and continued his maritime-oriented career: as a "caulker," "boat builder," and "engineer." He died in 1895. New York State, *Annual Report of the Adjutant-General of the State of New York for the Year 1905*, Serial 41, Vol. 3, 773.

14. United States National Archives, Civil War Widows Pension Files, "William Satchel," Certificate #859959.

15. Bristol, "From Outposts to Enclaves," 594.

16. United States National Archives, Civil War Widows Pension Files, "William Satchel," Certificate #859959; *Adirondack Record-Elizabethtown Post*, Dec. 15, 1927.

17. *Elizabethtown Post and Gazette*, Nov. 7, 1889.

18. *Elizabethtown Post and Gazette*, Mar. 4, 1886.

19. United States National Archives, Civil War Widows Pension Files, "William Satchel," Certificate #859959.

20. Foner, *Forever Free*, 121–22.

21. *Au Sable Forks Adirondack Record-Elizabethtown Post*, Aug. 2, 1934; Kollatz, *True Richmond Stories*, 59–61; *Plattsburgh Sentinel*, Apr. 28, 1871.

22. *Au Sable Forks Adirondack Record-Elizabethtown Post*, Aug. 2, 1934.

23. *Lake Placid News*, Oct. 27, 1993.

24. This photo was taken at the Vernon Portrait Gallery in Richmond, a studio that operated from 1886 to circa 1891.

25. Karen Campbell, "Warner W. Curtis," *Harveysburg on Caesar's Creek*, Jan. 25, 2007, http://harveysburg.blogspot.com.

26. *Ticonderoga Sentinel*, Apr. 27, 1899.

27. Ticonderoga Historical Society, *Ticonderoga*, 283, 277.

28. *Ogdensburg Daily Journal*, Nov. 14, 1908; *Au Sable Forks Adirondack Record-Elizabethtown Post*, Feb. 22, 1923.

29. Information on Edward Jackson from Crown Point historian, Aug. 1913.

30. United States National Archives, Civil War Widows Pension Files, "Lloyd Brown," Certificate #804490.

31. *Ticonderoga Sentinel*, Feb. 14, 1935.

32. Obituary of William Pickhardt, *New York Times*, June 28, 1895.

33. *Lake Placid News*, June 19, 1936; *Au Sable Forks Record-Post*, June 10, 1937.

34. Marjorie Ochs Powers, conversation with author, Jan. 2013.

35. Ward, *Dark Midnight When I Rise*, 376.

36. Logan, *The Negro in American Life and Thought*, 208–9.

37. Loewen, *Teaching What Really Happened*, 189; Pollard, "Last Great Battle of the West," 42–43.

38. Wilkerson, *Warmth of Other Suns*, 161.

5. Making a Living

1. Johnson, *Patterns of Negro Segregation*, 6, 83–84.

2. Williams-Myers, *Long Hammering*, 142.

3. Frazier, *Black Bourgeoisie*, 19.

4. Lindsay, "Economic Condition of the Negroes of New York," 198.

5. Madison and Jefferson, *Tour to the Northern Lakes*, 20.

6. *African American National Biography*, vol. 11, s.v. "Taylor, Prince (1755–1828)"; Ticonderoga Historical Society, *Ticonderoga*, 39; Cook, *Home Sketches of Essex County*, 58.

7. Glenn Harris, "Hidden History of Agriculture," 182; McMurry, "Evolution of a Landscape," 133.

8. McMurry, "Evolution of a Landscape," 129–32.

9. Glenn Harris, "Hidden History of Agriculture," 174.

10. Hyde, *Adirondack Forests*, 121.

11. Watson, *Military and Civil History of the County of Essex*, 481.

12. According to Hyde, one sugar maple produces ten to fourteen gallons of sap per season, and thirty to fifty gallons of sap are required to make eight pounds of sugar. Hyde, *Adirondack Forests*, 86, 91.

13. Gosselink, *Benjamin Van Buren's Bay*, 11–13.

14. Glenn Harris, "Hidden History of Agriculture," 196.

15. Gosselink, *Benjamin Van Buren's Bay*, 11–13.

16. McMurry, "Evolution of a Landscape," 133.

17. *Ticonderoga Sentinel*, June 21, 1917.

18. Hopper and Cantor, *Migrant Farm Workers in New York State*, 1, 4.

19. New York State Department of Labor, Division of Placement and Unemployment Service, *Farm and Food Processing Labor: Annual Report* (1956), 7.

20. New York State Department of Labor, Division of Placement and Unemployment Service, *Farm and Food Processing Labor: Annual Report* (1959), 10; (1958), 19.

21. Hyde, *Adirondack Forests*, 146–47.

22. H. P. Smith, *History of Essex County*, 721.

23. Tuttle, *Three Centuries in Champlain Valley*, 115.

24. *Plattsburgh Republican*, Apr. 3, 1875; Jan. 28, 1893.

25. McLaughlin, "A History of the Redford Crown Glass Works," 369–70; Deed of sale from Matthew Lane to George Tankard, Apr. 10, 1838, Clinton County, *Book of Deeds* 7, 67–68, County Clerk's Office, Plattsburgh, NY.

26. Facsimile in Vanderhorst-Rodriguez, *Tan Americans of Clinton County, New York*, unpaged.

27. *Plattsburgh Press*, Apr. 7, 1896; *Plattsburgh Republican*, Apr. 11, 1896.

28. Pelatiah Richards, will dated Apr. 14, 1869. Copy on file at Richards Library, Warrensburg, NY.

29. "Diary of Grace Noyes," *Glens Falls Post-Star*, Feb. 27, 1994; Grace Noyes, "Diary," as transcribed in *Warrensburgh Historical Society Quarterly* (Summer 2000–Winter 2000/2001), passim.

30. Grace Noyes, will dated Jan. 4, 1881. Copy on file at Richards Library, Warrensburg, NY.

31. Chappell and Curtis, *Grasse River Outing Club*, 26–27.

32. Trowbridge, *Durand Camp*, 6, 101, 107, 122.

33. *New York Age*, Sept. 2, 1907.

34. Starling, *Starling of the White House*, 39; *Pittsburgh Press*, Sept. 26, 1926; *St. Petersburg (FL) Independent*, Sept. 8, 1926.

35. *Youngstown (OH) Vindicator*, July 12, 1926; *Buffalo Courier-Express*, Sept. 11, 1926.

36. *New York Amsterdam News*, Aug. 19, 1931.

37. *New York Age*, Mar. 20, 1937.

38. "Something for James," *Time* magazine, May 29, 1950, 59; Stephen Elliott, email message to author, Jan. 5, 2017.

39. Elliott, "Trip to Willsboro," 28.

40. Elliott, email message to author, Jan. 5, 2017.

41. *Ogdensburg Journal*, Aug. 7, 1945; Michael Brick, "A Storm-Tossed Hero, Now Dry; New Roof Repays Family's Debt to Savior of 170 in 1945 Fire," *New York Times*, Nov. 2, 2003.

42. Farley, "Working in a Camp on Upper St. Regis Lake," 9.

43. *Essex County Republican*, Aug. 22, 1930.

6. Railroad Building

1. *Fort Covington Franklin Gazette*, June 19, 1891.

2. Charles H. Burnett, *Conquering the Wilderness*, 28, 32–33.

3. "Back to the South," *Syracuse Weekly Express*, Mar. 31, 1892.

4. "The Gun and Club," *Utica Saturday Globe*, Apr. 2, 1892; *Herkimer Democrat*, Apr. 6, 1892.

5. The New York State Census of 1892 recorded national background but not state of origin.

6. The now-defunct town of Wilmurt, Herkimer County, from which the town of Webb was detached in 1896, also housed railroad workers in 1892. The manner in which the population was enumerated makes it difficult to determine if there were one or more camps in the town, or the number of individuals who were connected with the railroad project. A 1911 fire in the New York State Library destroyed many 1892 census records, including those for Franklin County, where other railroad camps would have been located.

7. "Brutal Contractors," *Cleveland Gazette*, June 18 1892; "Brutal Treatment," *Shenandoah (PA) Evening Herald*, Mar. 26, 1892; "Contractor Redmond in Trouble," *Utica Weekly Herald*, Apr. 5, 1892; *Walhalla (SC) Keowee Courier*, Apr. 14, 1892.

8. "Shot by an Angry Boss," *New York Times*, Oct. 7, 1891.

9. "Italians Deserting the Railroad Construction Camps in the Adirondacks," *Ogdensburg Daily Journal*, Dec. 2, 1891; "On Dr. Webb's Road," *St. Regis Falls Adirondack News*, Dec. 19, 1891.

10. Charles H. Burnett, *Conquering the Wilderness*, 29; *Herkimer Democrat*, Apr. 6, 1892.

11. *Keowee (SC) Courier Walhalla*, Apr. 14, 1892.

12. "A Negro's Pitiful Story," *Shenandoah (PA) Evening Herald*, Mar. 16, 1892; "Hardships Endured by Adirondack Railroad Laborers," Mar. 26, 1892.

13. Marleau, *Big Moose Station*, 46.

14. Thomas, *Tales from the Adirondack Foothills*, 115.

15. "A Story of Abuse," *Oswego Daily Palladium*, Mar. 23, 1892.

16. Ibid.

17. "The Other Side Told," *Rome Semi-Weekly Citizen*, Apr. 6, 1892; Thomas, *Tales from the Adirondack Foothills*, 116.

18. "The Tennessee Laborers," *Cleveland Gazette*, Apr. 9, 1892.

19. "On Their Way South," *Batavia Daily News*, Mar. 30, 1892.

20. *Utica Morning Herald*, Mar. 31, 1892.

21. *Herkimer Democrat*, Apr. 6, 1892.

22. "In the Adirondacks," *Lowville Journal and Republican*, Apr. 7, 1892.

23. *Sacramento (CA) Record-Union*, Apr. 1, 1892; "In the Adirondacks," *Lowville Journal and Republican*, Apr. 7, 1892.

24. Harter, *Fairy Tale Railroad*, quoting undated article from *Utica Observer*, 42.

25. "A Story of Abuse," *Oswego Daily Palladium*, Mar. 23, 1892.

26. "The Other Side Told," *Rome Semi-Weekly Citizen*, Apr. 6, 1892; *Utica Sunday Tribune*, Apr. 3, 1892; "Adirondack Slave Drivers," *New York Times*, Mar. 30, 1892.

27. *Herkimer Democrat*, Apr. 6, 1892.

28. Harter, *Fairy Tale Railroad*, 43.

29. "Florence F. Donovan in Trouble," *New York Times*, Jan. 27, 1893.

30. "Trying to Get Home," *Cleveland Gazette*, June 4, 1892; "Back to the South," *Syracuse Weekly Express*, Mar. 31, 1892.

31. Charles H. Burnett, *Conquering the Wilderness*, v; *Locomotive Firemen's Magazine* 16, no. 6 (June 1892): 493.

7. The Summer Resort Industry

1. "Labors of the Summer Time," *New York Globe*, July 7, 1883.

2. Shelton, "Queen of Spas," 387.

3. Guest capacity of hotels referenced comes from Tolles, *Resort Hotels of the Adirondacks*, 223–24.

4. *National Anti-Slavery Standard*, quoting *Newark (NJ) Advertiser*, Aug. 19, 1865.

5. "Going to the Watering Places," *Christian Recorder*, June 16, 1866.

6. Shelton, "Queen of Spas," 388.

7. Bullock, *History of Negro Education*, 123.

8. From speech of white philanthropist William H. Baldwin Jr. at the second Capon Springs Conference for Education in the South, 1899, quoted in Bullock, *History of Negro Education*, 102.

9. Bullock, *History of Negro Education*, 77, 79.

10. Ibid., 79, 209–10.

11. *New York Globe*, July 7, 1883.

12. *Washington Bee*, Aug. 27, 1887.

13. *Washington Bee*, July 7, 1888; July 28, 1888.

14. *Washington Bee*, Aug. 27, 1887; Sept. 3, 1887.

15. Tolles, *Resort Hotels of the Adirondacks*, 64.

16. *Essex County Republican*, July 8 1897.

17. Hogan, *Shades of Glory*, 21–22; Maccannon, *Commanders of the Dining Room*, 20–23.

18. *Plattsburgh Press*, Aug. 13, 1896; Aug. 14, 1896.

19. *Indianapolis Freeman*, May 7, 1904; Dec. 30, 1905; June 2, 1906.

20. *Lake George Mirror*, June 30, 1894; Aug. 25, 1894.

21. Maccannon, *Commanders of the Dining Room*, 165–66.

22. *Indianapolis Freeman*, Sept. 17, 1904.

23. Hollis, "'The Black Man Almost Has Disappeared from Our Country,'" 18.

24. *Lake George Mirror*, July 5, 1913.

25. *New York Sun*, June 7, 1914.

26. *Baltimore Afro-American*, Aug. 2, 1947; Nancy Graff, "In This State: Son of a Slave Became an Orchardist, a Legislator, and More," VTDigger, Oct. 26, 2014, https://vtdigger.org/2014/10/26/state-son-slave-became-orchardist-legislator/.

27. Sam Roberts, "Recalling First Black Appointed to New York Police Dept.," *New York Times*, June 27, 2011; Browne, *One Righteous Man*, 14, 25, 37, 46.

28. Clark-Lewis and Sprow, "Duty and 'Fast Living'," 61–63. The Fort William Henry referred to in Sprow's diary was a replacement for the first Fort William Henry Hotel, which burned to the ground in 1909 and was rebuilt the following year as a facility to house 150–200 guests.

29. Harold Hochschild, *Township 34*, 214; *Philadelphia Times*, Jan. 19, 1890; Elijah Hodges, "Old Timer Remembers: When Girls Wore Clothes," *Philadelphia Tribune*, Nov. 29, 1941.

30. *Warrensburgh News*, June 28, 1906.

31. *Pittsburgh Courier*, Aug. 17, 1929; *Norfolk (VA) New Journal and Guide*, Aug. 2, 1930.

32. *Lake George Mirror*, Aug. 24, 1907.

33. Maccannon, *Commanders of the Dining Room*, 17, 22.

34. *Washington Bee*, Sept. 11, 1915.

35. *Ticonderoga Sentinel*, July 1, 1920.

36. *Norfolk (VA) New Journal and Guide*, June 29, 1946.

37. Wilson, *Rogers Rock*, 26–28, 56–57, 175.

38. Ibid., 61–62.

39. Hampton Institute, Obituary of Bishop Brown, *Southern Workman* 47 (1918), 511.

40. *Lake George Mirror*, July 13, 1907; "Bell Boys at Rogers Rock," *Lake George Mirror*, July 27, 1907.

41. Wilson, *Rogers Rock*, 57, 59, 150–51.

42. *Ticonderoga Sentinel*, Aug. 16, 1923.

43. Wilson, *Rogers Rock*, 151, 154.

44. Bloch, "Discrimination Against the Negro in Employment in New York," 365–66.

45. On rare occasions the names, but no other details, of seasonal black employees who arrived in Lake George towns by the early June date when census data was gathered did show up in census documents.

46. Champion was not listed as a Caldwell resident in the 1915 state census, but her twenty-two-year-old "waitress" daughter, Susie Howard, appeared that year as the head of a household comprising a younger "chambermaid" cousin and a niece. Champion headed essentially the same household in the 1925 census; it is likely that she had not yet returned from her winter job at the time the 1915 census was taken.

47. *Baltimore Afro-American*, Feb. 11, 1928.

48. *Saratogian*, July 8, 1949.

8. Resort Entertainment: Employees and Students

1. *Washington Bee*, Sept. 3, 1887.

2. *St. Paul (MN) Western Appeal*, copying item that originally appeared in the *Louisville Courier Journal*, Sept. 10, 1887.

3. *Baptist Standard: A Record of Christian Progress*, Feb. 1, 1902, 11; "Dr. Charles S. Morris, Minister, Orator, Dies," *Chicago Defender*, Aug. 1, 1931.

4. *Indianapolis Freeman*, Aug. 29, 1903.

5. Taylor and Austen, *Darkest America*, 77.

6. Toll, *Blacking Up*, 234, 237.

7. Taylor and Austen, *Darkest America*, 27, 31, 54; Trav, *No Applause—Just Throw Money*, 107–8.

8. Taylor and Austen, *Darkest America*, 39–40.

9. *Indianapolis Freeman*, Aug. 29, 1903; Abbot and Seroff, *Ragged but Right*, 28.

10. *Lake George Mirror*, July 15, 1905.

11. *Lake George Mirror*, Aug. 13, 1898; Aug. 20, 1898.

12. *Lake George Mirror*, Aug. 13, 1898; Aug. 26, 1899.

13. Jayna Brown, *Babylon Girls*, 130–34.

14. *Lake George Mirror*, July 14, 1900; July 21, 1900; *Warrensburgh News*, Aug. 2, 1901.

15. Peabody served on the boards of Hampton Institute from 1884 to 1930; Tuskegee Institute from 1900 to 1911; Penn Normal Industrial and Agricultural School, St. Helena Island, South Carolina, from 1901 to 1927; and the Fort Valley High and Industrial School, Fort Valley, Georgia. (He joined the latter board after learning that its singers "pleased the summer cottagers with their spirituals" during its 1901 appearance in Lake George.) Ware, *George Foster Peabody*, 115–16.

16. Ibid., 214. Another George Peabody (1795–1869), a distant cousin of Bolton's George Peabody, established the Peabody Education Fund in 1867 that was active in setting up common schools for blacks in the South.

17. Vernon Lee Smith, "Hampton Institute Choir," 30–33, 52–58.

18. Hampton Normal and Agricultural Institute, *Treasurer's Statement for the Year Ending June 30, 1902*, 17, 22, 23, 24, 35, 47.

19. Marable, "South African Nationalism in Brooklyn," 24–25.

20. *Essex County Republican*, Oct. 29, 1874.

21. Hurston, *Dust Tracks on a Road*, 279–80.

22. Shaw University, *Lake George Mirror*, July 25, 1902; Tuskegee Institute, *Lake Placid News*, Aug. 11, 1916, and Aug. 5, 1927; Wilberforce University, *Lake Placid News*, July 15, 1927.

23. *Rome Daily Sentinel*, July 16, 1901.

24. "More Race Prejudice," *Sumter (SC) Watchman and Southron*, Sept. 18, 1901.

25. Enck, "Black Self-Help in the Progressive Era," 74, 78.

26. Moton, "Hampton's Summer Campaign in the North," 505; Enck, "Black Self-Help in the Progressive Era," 86.

27. *Chicago Broad Ax*, May 16, 1914; Hampton Institute, "Hampton's Summer Campaign," *Southern Workman* 49 (1920), 444–46.

28. *St. Regis Falls Adirondack News*, Aug. 22, 1925.

29. Bailey, "Cotton Blossom Singers," 135–37.

30. *Gloversville and Johnstown Morning Herald*, May 31, 1933; publicity card for "Cotton Blossom Singers" at Star Lake, n.d., Edward Comstock Jr. Collection, Saranac Lake, NY; *Utica Daily Press*, Aug. 18, 1932.

9. Baseball, and a Little Basketball

1. Keetz, *Mohawk Colored Giants of Schenectady*, 5.

2. McNary, *Black Baseball*, 13.

3. Morris, *Catcher*, 98.

4. Sol White, *Sol White's History of Colored Baseball*, lvii–lx. White was a member of the Hotel Champlain staff and baseball team during the summer of 1892; *Pittsburgh Courier*, Mar. 12, 1927.

5. Lomax, *Black Baseball Entrepreneurs*, 94.

6. *Plattsburgh Sentinel*, Aug. 22, 1890.

7. *Plattsburgh Sentinel*, June 26, 1891.

8. *Plattsburgh Daily Press*, Aug. 16, 1898; *Plattsburgh Sentinel*, Aug. 22, 1890.

9. *Plattsburgh Daily Press*, Aug. 16, 1898.

10. Frost, *Hotel Champlain to Clinton Community College*, 42, quoting an undated 1898 article from the *Plattsburgh Sentinel*.

11. *Plattsburgh Daily Press*, June 4, 1904.

12. Lomax, *Black Baseball Entrepreneurs*, 76.

13. *Plattsburgh Daily Press*, Aug. 10, 1897.

14. Lindholm, "Rumors and Fads," 45.

15. Needham, "College Athlete," 128; Lindholm, "Black Matty," passim. Matthews's tenure with the Harvard team was problematic. The popular shortstop was forced to sit out games against southern schools (Georgetown, Annapolis, Virginia); the team gave up its annual southern trip in Matthews's senior year in a show of support. Lindholm, "Black Matty," 62. In a 1908 analysis of the hardening color line at Harvard, where black students had long enjoyed exceptional opportunities, journalist and historian Ray Stannard Baker noted that recently "a Negro baseball player was the cause of so much discussion and embarrassment to the athletic association that there will probably never be another coloured boy on the university teams." Baker, *Following the Color Line*, 123.

16. *Lake George Mirror*, Aug. 1, 1896; July 31, 1897.

17. *Lake George Mirror*, July 27, 1895.

18. *Warrensburgh News*, Aug. [7?], 1912; *Lake George Mirror*, July 5, 1913.

19. Keetz, *Mohawk Colored Giants of Schenectady*, 33, 37.

20. *Ticonderoga Sentinel*, July 26, 1923.

21. Keetz, *Mohawk Colored Giants of Schenectady*, 7, 21 32.

22. Ibid., 160.

23. *Ticonderoga Sentinel*, June 26, 1924; July 24, 1924.

24. *Ticonderoga Sentinel*, July 2, 1925; Aug. 6, 1925.

25. Craig, *Chappie and Me*, 3–4.

26. *Ticonderoga Sentinel*, July 24, 1924.

27. *Lake Placid News*, June 28, 1929; *Ogdensburg Republican-Journal*, July 27, 1925.

28. *Ticonderoga Sentinel*, June 11, 1936.

29. Craig, *Chappie and Me*, 48.

30. Keetz, *Mohawk Colored Giants of Schenectady*, 32, 64.

31. *Ticonderoga Sentinel*, Mar. 6, 1941.

32. Keetz, *Mohawk Colored Giants of Schenectady*, 11, 37–38; *Ticonderoga Sentinel*, Mar. 4, 1926.

33. *Warrensburgh News*, July 29, 1926; Aug. 5, 1926; Aug. 12, 1926.

34. Keetz, *Mohawk Colored Giants of Schenectady*, 49.

35. *Philadelphia Tribune*, Sept. 29, 1927.

36. Keetz, *Mohawk Colored Giants of Schenectady*, 46.

37. *Ticonderoga Sentinel*, June 2, 1927; June 9, 1927; June 16, 1927.

38. *Lake Placid News*, Aug. 2, 1929.

39. *Chicago Defender*, June 17, 1933.

40. *Ogdensburg Journal*, Apr. 8, 1935.

41. Pietrusza, *Baseball's Canadian-American League*, 137.

42. *Ogdensburg Journal*, Aug. 16, 1935.

43. *Baltimore Afro-American*, Aug. 27, 1949.

44. *Ticonderoga Sentinel*, July 8, 1937.

45. Peterson, *Cages to Jumpshots*, 15–18, 11.

46. Ibid., 97–101.

47. Ibid., 12.

48. *Saratogian*, Feb. 18, 1927.

49. *North Creek News*, Mar. 10, 1948; *Plattsburgh Daily Press*, Jan. 8, 1931.

50. Peterson, *Cages to Jumpshots*, 107.

51. League teams that season represented Schenectady, Mechanicville, Saratoga, Fort Edward, Hudson Falls, South Glens Falls, Argyle, Corinth, and Port Henry. *Essex County Republican*, Nov. 27, 1953.

52. *Ticonderoga Sentinel*, Mar. 19, 1954.

10. Saranac Lake and Tuberculosis

1. Gallos, *Cure Cottages of Saranac Lake*, 2–3.

2. Tanner, "Story of an Artist's Life,"11664.

3. Collins, *Brighton Story*, 7, 20–21.

4. Tanner, "Story of an Artist's Life": 11664; Mosby, *Across Continents and Cultures*, 15, 19.

5. Gallos, *Cure Cottages of Saranac Lake*, viii, 6, 16.

6. Seaver, *Historical Sketches of Franklin County*, 383.

7. Ames, "Tuberculosis Survey," foldout map insert.

8. Spencer, *Medical Symphony*, 29, 53.

9. *Rochester Democrat and Chronicle*, Jan. 7 and 8, 1939.

10. Payne, "Leading Causes of Death Among Negroes: Tuberculosis," 225.

11. *Saranac Lake Adirondack Enterprise*, Feb. 18, 1946.

12. Spencer, *Medical Symphony*, 64.

13. New York City Department of Health, *First Report of the Clinic for the Treatment of Communicable Pulmonary Diseases*, 30.

14. Johnson, *Patterns of Negro Segregation*, 76.

15. Gallos, *Cure Cottages of Saranac Lake*, 16–17.

16. Ames, "Tuberculosis Survey," 234.

17. Saranac Lake Department of Health, *Disinfection Register*, vol. 1 (Jan. 1911–Oct. 1913): 124. Disinfection registers recorded the names and cottage addresses of vacating tuberculosis patients, whose rooms had to be disinfected before reuse. On file in the Adirondack Room, Saranac Lake Free Library.

18. Ibid., 119.

19. *Baltimore Afro-American*, July 24, 1915.

20. *Indianapolis Freeman*, Dec. 12, 1914; *Chicago Defender*, Jan. 19, 1918.

21. Deed of sale from Francis Barry Cantwell and Genevieve G. Cantwell to John Ramsey, Aug. 10, 1921, Essex County, *Book of Deeds* 168, 293, County Clerk's Office, Elizabethtown, NY.

22. *Saranac Lake Adirondack Enterprise*, May 15, 1958.

23. *Saranac Lake Adirondack Enterprise*, Aug. 9, 1965.

24. Saranac Lake Department of Health, Tuberculosis Patient Registration Records, "A Report of a Case of Tuberculosis" registration card for Eugene Aiken; *New York Age*, Aug. 27, 1927.

25. *New York Amsterdam News*, July 8, 1939.

26. *Norfolk (VA) Journal and Guide*, Mar. 28, 1931.

27. *New York Amsterdam News,* Oct. 24, 1928. It is likely that the Peter Green referred to in census records as born in Ohio was the same Peter Green who, according to his 1958 Saranac Lake obituary, came from Georgia and was employed for house and janitorial work by several local homeowners and churches. Among his employers was the family of Dr. Lawrason Brown, for whom Green worked for thirty years. They arranged to have him buried in their family plot in the village's Pine Ridge Cemetery under a stone inscribed "Loyal friend, Faithful servant." The staff of the Saranac Lake Free Library eulogized Green after his death as "a 'gentleman of the old school' who served our institution so faithfully over the years, always beyond the call of duty." *Saranac Lake Adirondack Enterprise*, Mar. 28, 1958.

28. *New York Amsterdam News*, Sept. 9, 1931.

29. Gallos, *Cure Cottages of Saranac Lake*, 78–79.

30. Hunton, *William Alphaeus Hunton*, 2–4, 144; *Encyclopedia of African American History*, s.v. "William Alphaeus Hunton"; *Indianapolis Freeman*, Nov. 7, 1914.

31. Gallos, *Cure Cottages of Saranac Lake*, 22.

32. Hunton, *William Alphaeus Hunton*, 152. Hunton Jr. became a leading intellectual and civil rights activist in the 1940s.

33. Caldwell, *Last Crusade*, 132.

34. Hunton, *William Alphaeus Hunton*, 154–55.

35. Ibid., 155.

36. *New York Age*, Aug. 3, 1923; *Utica Observer-Dispatch*, Dec. 10, 1923; *Lowville Journal and Republican*, Mar. 13, 1924.

37. *Watertown Daily Times*, July 6, 1916; *Amsterdam (NY) Evening Recorder*, July 12, 1922; *Gloversville Morning Herald*, June 28, 1923.

38. *Lowville Journal and Republican*, Mar. 13, 1924; *Pittsburgh Courier*, May 10, 1924; *Gloversville Morning Herald*, Mar. 8, 1924.

39. *Pittsburgh Courier*, May 10, 1924; *Lowville Journal and Republican*, Mar. 13, 1924.

40. *Watertown Daily Times*, Oct. 18, 1939; *Saranac Lake Adirondack Enterprise*, Jan. 26, 1953; *Saranac Lake Adirondack Enterprise*, Mar. 26, 1957.

41. New York State Hospital for the Treatment of Incipient Pulmonary Tuberculosis, *Sixth Annual Report* (1907), 6.

42. Slade, "Selection of Patients for a Tuberculosis Sanatorium," 190.

43. New York State Hospital for the Treatment of Incipient Pulmonary Tuberculosis, *Sixth Annual Report* (1907), 6; *Eleventh Annual Report* (1912), 3–4.

44. Gallos, *Cure Cottages of Saranac Lake*, 19.

45. *Milwaukee Sentinel*, Oct. 25, 1959.

46. *Pittsburgh Courier*, Dec. 15, 1934.

47. *Negro Actors Guild of America Newsletter*, June 1, 1952; Nov. 1, 1952; *New York Amsterdam News*, Jan. 7, 1961. Bailey's moonwalk was filmed for the 1943 movie *Cabin in the Sky.*

48. *Los Angeles Tribune*, June 13, 1958.

49. Chalmers, "The Mascot of 'Troop 1,'" 315–29.

50. Edgar T. Rouzeau, "This Thing Called Love," *Norfolk (VA) New Journal and Guide*, Sept. 16, 1939.

51. United States Bureau of the Census, *Negro Population in the United States: 1790–1915*, 100–101.

11. Community Life in Saranac Lake

1. Caldwell, *Last Crusade*, 128–31.

2. Chalmers, "Watching the Hour-Glass," 294.

3. Packard, "A Fortune Awaits You in Saranac Lake," 40.

4. A "teamster" drove a team of draft animals; "general trucking" meant the trucking or transporting of goods.

5. Saranac Lake Methodist Church, *Methodist Marriages, 1898–1916*, 626. Copy on file in the Adirondack Room, Saranac Lake Free Library. Charles Hazzard, born in Pennsylvania, was a son of William and Lucinda Hazzard.

6. *Lake Placid News*, Oct. 22, 1948.

7. *Saranac Lake Adirondack Enterprise*, Sept. 29, 1948.

8. Kim Smith Dedam, "Generations of Freedom: Legacy of John Thomas Lives on Through Family," *Plattsburgh Press-Republican*, Feb. 18, 2007.

9. *Saranac Lake Adirondack Enterprise*, Oct. 28, 1955.

10. In 1920, 70 percent of all laundresses in the United States were black women who worked at home. Grover, *Make a Way Somehow*, 128.

11. Cited in John Blassingame, ed., *The Frederick Douglass Papers*, vol. 3, *Series One: Speeches, Debates, and Interviews* (New Haven, CT: Yale Univ. Press, 1989), 71, and quoted in Grover, *Make a Way Somehow*, 107.

12. *Saranac Lake Adirondack Enterprise*, Aug. 3, 1923.

13. Baer and Singer, *African American Religion*, 101, 102, 109; Frazier, *Black Bourgeoisie*, 128.

14. Haley, "Klan in Their Midst," 42; Bernstein, *Sticks*, 154.

15. Haley, "Klan in Their Midst," 42.

16. *Saranac Lake Adirondack Enterprise*, Jan. 8, 1927.

17. Gordon and Gordon, *On Wandering Wheels*, 58–63, 65, 67–69.

18. Glenn, "Negro Prestige Criteria, 647–48.

19. Johnson, *Patterns of Negro Segregation*, 233.

20. Frazier, *Black Bourgeoisie*, 179, 195, 199, 234.

21. Tyler, "*In Them Thar Hills*," 45; Minnifield family history, Minorities folder, Adirondack Room, Saranac Lake Free Library.

22. Deed of sale from Anna E. Otis to Q. M. Davis, Oct. 8, 1906, Franklin County, *Book of Deeds* 128, 329; Deed of sale from Henry Lewis to Queen Minifield Davis, May 1, 1907, Franklin County, *Book of Deeds* 130, 284; Deed of sale from Joseph and Josephine Otis to Q. M. Davis, May 29, 1907, Franklin County, *Book of Deeds* 130, 428–29; Deed of sale from Anna E. Otis to Queenie E. M. Davis, Apr. 18, 1910, Franklin County, *Book of Deeds* 138, 516, County Clerk's Office, Malone, NY.

23. "Queenie Minnifield Davis Simmons," Minorities folder, Adirondack Room, Saranac Lake Free Library.

24. *Saranac Lake Adirondack Enterprise*, Jan. 13, 1970.

25. *Saranac Lake Adirondack Enterprise*, Mar. 10, 1972; Oct. 5, 1964; Mar. 30, 1965.

26. Alice Wareham, conversation with author, Aug. 2013. A Saranac Lake social column with the Tyre byline appeared in the *Baltimore Afro-American* on May 23, 1936.

27. *Ticonderoga Sentinel*, June 13, 1918.

28. *Mount Vernon Daily Argus*, Nov. 12, 1920.

29. Alice Wareham, conversation with author, Aug. 2013.

30. Ibid.

31. Ibid.

32. *Saranac Lake Adirondack Enterprise*, Apr. 4, 1960.

33. Alice Wareham, conversation with author, Aug. 2013.

34. Ibid.

35. Packard, "A Fortune Awaits You in Saranac Lake," 40.

36. Village of Saranac Lake to William C. and Sadie H. Hall, May 10, 1946, Franklin County, *Book of Deeds* 261, 427, County Clerk's Office, Malone, NY.

37. *Saranac Lake Adirondack Enterprise*, July 26, 1965; Mar. 31, 1966.

38. Payne, "Leading Causes of Death Among Negroes: Tuberculosis," 225.

12. Popular Culture: Professional Performers

1. Jeffery, *Jeffery's Guide*, 222–52.

2. Southern, *Music of Black Americans*, 229; *Plattsburgh Sentinel*, Dec. 13, 1866.

3. Taylor and Austen, *Darkest America*, 51.

4. Southern, *Music of Black Americans*, 229; *Malone Palladium*, Oct. 21, 1875; *Gloversville Intelligencer*, Feb. 23, 1878; Toll, *Blacking Up*, 203.

5. Riis, *Just Before Jazz*, 32.

6. *Schuylerville Standard*, Aug. 20, 1903; *Gloversville Daily Leader*, July 29, 1902; *Amsterdam (NY) Evening Recorder*, July 15, 1905.

7. *Ogdensburg Daily Journal*, Aug. 23, 1898.

8. *Variety*, May 19 1916, 3; *Lake George Mirror*, June 6, 1902; July 4, 1902; Aug. 2, 1902.

9. *Syracuse Journal*, Feb. 11, 1907; *Oswego Daily Times*, June 8, 1905.

10. *Ogdensburg Daily Journal*, May 3, 1906.

11. *Elizabethtown Post*, May 10, 1906.

12. *Malone Farmer*, May 16, 1906. *Chateaugay Record and Franklin County Democrat*, May 18, 1906.

13. Southern, *Music of Black Americans*, 289.

14. *Ticonderoga Sentinel*, Dec. 6, 1906; Nov. 22, 1906.

15. Price, *Encyclopedia of African American Music*, 697.

16. *New York Age*, Aug. 18, 1910.

17. *Ticonderoga Sentinel*, Nov. 20, 1913; *Au Sable Forks Adirondack Record*, Nov. 22, 1917.

18. *Ticonderoga Sentinel*, June 26, 1913; July 3, 1913; *Tupper Lake Herald*, June 17, 1913.

19. *Elizabethtown Post*, July 9, 1914; *St. Regis Falls Adirondack News*, July 1, 1916.

20. *New York Clipper*, Apr. 22, 1919.

21. *Billboard*, Dec. 21, 1959.

22. *Ticonderoga Sentinel*, Nov. 15, 1923; Abbott and Seroff, *Out of Sight*, 198.

23. *Chicago Defender*, May 7, 1921; Nov. 24, 1923.

24. *Billboard*, Nov. 3, 1923.

25. *Ticonderoga Sentinel*, Nov. 15, 1894; Jan. 16, 1902; Jan. 1, 1903.

26. Southern, *Music of Black Americans*, 228; *Ticonderoga Sentinel*, Nov. 15, 1894; Jan. 16, 1902.

27. Abbott and Seroff, *Out of Sight*, 176–77.

28. *Chateaugay Journal*, May 14, 1896; *Chateaugay Record and Franklin County Democrat*, Feb. 3, 1905; *Ticonderoga Sentinel*, Nov. 5, 1903; Jan. 30, 1908; Jan. 13, 1910; Feb. 17, 1910.

29. *Ticonderoga Sentinel*, Apr. 13, 1933; *Essex County Republican*, Apr. 2, 1937; Dec. 16, 1938; *Hamilton County Record*, Oct. 13, 1938; May 18, 1939.

30. *North Creek News*, Dec. 14, 1938.

31. arwulf arfulf, "Utica Institute Jubilee Singers," AllMusic, accessed June 2, 2017, http://www.allmusic.com/artist/utica-institute-jubilee-singers-mn000025293 5/biography.

32. Erenberg, *Steppin' Out*, 150–52.

33. *Lake George Mirror*, July 31, 1915; "Philadelphia Orchestra Musicians Roster: A Listing of All the Musicians of the Philadelphia Orchestra," The Stokowski Legacy, accessed May 20, 2017, www.stokowski.org/Philadelphia_Orchestra_Musi cians_List.htm; *New York Evening Post*, June 1, 1923.

34. *Lake George Mirror*, July 31, 1915.

35. *Lake George Mirror*, Aug. 28, 1915; Erenberg, *Steppin' Out*, 153.

36. *Lake George Mirror*, July 3, 1915; Southern, *Music of Black Americans*, 287–88; Curtis-Burlin, "Black Singers and Players," 502–4.

37. *Ticonderoga Sentinel*, Oct. 13, 1949; Nov. 7, 1929.

38. Shipton, *Hi-De-Ho*, 30–31; *Ticonderoga Sentinel*, May 6, 1937.

39. *Essex County Republican*, July 29, 1921; *Lake Placid News*, Aug. 10, 1934; "Out of Town," *New Yorker*, July 1, 1928, 43.

40. *Lake Placid News*, Jan. 20, 1928; July 29, 1932.

41. *Saranac Lake Adirondack Enterprise*, May 9, 1974.

42. *Saranac Lake Adirondack Enterprise*, Jan. 16, 1953.

43. *Warrensburgh News*, July 30, 1931; *Glens Falls Post-Star*, July 3, 1929.

44. *Warrensburgh News*, July 17, 1930; July 30, 1931; Aug. 21, 1930; *Schenectady Gazette*, Jan. 7, 1931; *Troy Times*, Aug. 23, 1930; *Greene County (NY) Examiner-Record*, Dec. 9, 1948; *Kingston Daily Freeman*, Dec. 4, 1957.

13. Lake Placid and the John Brown Memorial Association

1. Gee, "Stone on John Brown's Grave," passim.

2. Scharnhorst, *Kate Field*, 74.

3. "Monument to John Brown," *New York Times*, July 22, 1896.

4. *Plattsburgh Daily Press*, Aug. 31, 1899.

5. D. J. Max Barber (1878–1949), the South Carolina–born son of former slaves, was educated at Virginia Union University and became the editor-in-chief of *Voice of the Negro*, a short-lived, Atlanta-based, literary magazine with a robust circulation and a militant insistence on full Constitutional rights for blacks. Accommodationist Booker T. Washington disliked Barber's radicalism, and his interventions caused Barber to lose jobs in publishing and teaching and led him to retrain for the nonpolitical profession of dentistry. Harlan, "Booker T. Washington," 46, 60–62. Dr. T. Spotuas Burwell (1876–1938), born in North Carolina, was educated at Lincoln University and Jefferson Medical College. An internist who rose to the position of Chief of the Chest Department at Philadelphia's Douglass Hospital serving the local black community, he was at one time president of the National Medical Association, a professional organization of black doctors created in 1895 in response to the American Medical Association's refusal to accept African Americans as members. Like Barber, he served as a president of the Philadelphia chapter of the NAACP. "In Memoriam: T. Spotuas Burwell," *Journal of the National Medical Association* (Aug. 1938): 134.

6. Harlan, "Booker T. Washington," quoting from a speech given by Barber at North Elba, 62.

7. Two seasonal residents of the Adirondacks, John Milholland of Lewis, Essex County (his birthplace), and Edwin Seligman of Lake Placid, were members of the Preliminary Committee on Permanent Organization that founded the NAACP. Milholland was the organization's first treasurer. Sullivan, *Lift Every Voice*, 14–15.

8. Barber, "Pilgrimage to John Brown's Grave," 167–69.

9. *Lake Placid News*, May 12, 1922.

10. *Philadelphia Tribune*, May 24, 1924.

11. *Pittsburgh Courier*, May 24, 1924.

12. *Lake Placid News*, May 14, 1924; John Brown Memorial Association, *Program*, 1928. The final cost of the memorial was $5,000 for the statue and $1,000 for the granite base. *Baltimore Afro-American*, May 4, 1935.

13. *Lake Placid News*, May 15, 1925.

14. *Ticonderoga Sentinel*, May 19, 1927. Darrow's sister, Viola ("Jennie") Darrow Moore, was a member of and spent summers at the Lake Placid Club.

15. *Ticonderoga Sentinel*, May 22, 1930.

16. *Lake Placid News*, May 14, 1937.

17. John Brown Memorial Association, *Program*, 1928; *Pittsburgh Courier*, June 2, 1928.

18. *Lake Placid News*, May 8, 1924; May 14, 1924.

19. *Lake Placid News*, Apr. 30, 1926; *Philadelphia Tribune*, Apr. 10, 1926; Apr. 25, 1929; May 1, 1930.

20. *Chicago Defender*, Apr. 23, 1927; *Harpers Ferry (WV) Storer Record*, June 1, 1929.

21. *Essex County Republican*, Sept. 7, 1934; *Saranac Lake Adirondack Enterprise*, Sept. 8, 1955; Quarles, *Allies for Freedom*, 188.

22. *Lake Placid News*, Apr. 22, 1932; May 4, 1942; Quarles, *Allies for Freedom*, 191.

23. A pamphlet, *John Brown in Bronze*, containing the dedication program and texts of speeches delivered at the event was published in late 1935 by the John Brown Memorial Association. Copy on file at the Schomburg Center for Research in Black Culture, New York Public Library, New York City.

24. *Essex County Republican*, Sept. 7, 1934.

25. *Philadelphia Tribune*, May 24, 1924; June 4, 1936.

26. *New York Age*, May 25, 1929; *Lake Placid News*, May 16, 1924.

27. *New York Herald Tribune*, July 3, 1926.

28. *Troy Times*, Sept. 17, 1919.

29. Barber, "Pilgrimage to John Brown's Grave," 168–69.

30. *Chicago Defender*, July 3, 1920; *New York Amsterdam News*, Sept. 12, 1928.

31. *New York Amsterdam News*, Aug. 12, 1931; Sept. 23, 1931.

32. *Baltimore Afro-American*, Aug. 1, 1931; *New York Amsterdam News*, Aug. 12, 1931; Barbara Tyrell Kelly, *Growing Up in Lake Placid*, 41.

33. *New York Age*, July 16, 1949; Barbara Tyrell Kelly, *Growing Up in Lake Placid*, 120; Alice Wareham, conversation with author, Aug. 2013.

34. Barbara Tyrell Kelly, *Growing Up in Lake Placid*, 120.

35. *New York Age*, June 15, 1935; *Lake Placid News*, June 10, 1949; May 15, 1959.

36. *Afro-American*, Sept. 9, 1939.

37. *Chicago Defender*, Sept. 27, 1941; Deed of sale from Lamb Lumber Co., Inc., to Inez Carter, June 14, 1948, Essex County, *Book of Deeds* 260, 226–27, County Clerk's Office, Elizabethtown, NY.

38. *Lake Placid News*, Oct. 2, 1942.

39. *Baltimore Afro-American*, Aug. 6, 1957; *Saranac Lake Adirondack Enterprise*, Aug. 5, 1957.

40. Deed of sale from Inez Carter to Lamb Lumber Co., Inc., Sept. 20, 1961, Essex County, *Book of Deeds* 392, 588, County Clerk's Office, Elizabethtown, NY.

41. *Saranac Lake Adirondack Enterprise*, May 31, 1963.

42. MacKenzie, *Plains of Abraham*, 135; *Baltimore Afro-American*, May 18, 1935.

43. Heald, "A Man to Remember," 41–42.

44. Walker, "Collecting Folk Histories," 72–73.

45. Heald, "A Man to Remember," 42.

46. *Lake Placid News*, Sept. 10, 1943.

47. *Lake Placid News*, June 11, 1943.

48. *Lake Placid News*, Sept. 3, 1948.

49. Obituary of Charles Curtis Walker Jr., *Lake Placid News*, Apr. 12, 1913.

50. American Oil Company, *American Traveler's Guide*, 29.

51. John Brown Memorial Association, *Program*, 1947.

14. Public and Publicly Supported Institutions

1. Mabee, *Black Education in New York State*, 70, 82.

2. Driggins, *History of the Negro Community in Corning*, 13.

3. Mabee, *Black Education in New York State*, 73–74.

4. Cook, *Home Sketches of Essex County*, 36. Samuel Deall was a Ticonderoga merchant and son of a town founder, another Samuel Deall.

5. Hough, "New York State Census, 1855," 216; Duncan, *Changing Race Relationship*, 18.

6. Williams-Myers, *Long Hammering*, 156.

7. Skopp, *Bright with Promise*, 45.

8. Neil Surprenant (Director of Library Services, Paul Smith's College), email message to author, June 2015; Michel R. Bridgen (Director, Wanakena Ranger School), email message to author, Aug. 2013.

9. Katz, *In the Shadow of the Poorhouse*, 3–4, 18, 86.

10. Ibid., 87–88, 91.

11. New York State Board of Charities, *Directory*, 273.

12. New York State Board of Charities, *Census of Inmates in Almshouses and Poorhouses.*

13. Ibid.

14. New York State Board of Charities, *Census of Inmates in Almshouses and Poorhouses*; Katz, *In the Shadow of the Poorhouse*, 109.

15. "South Ticonderoga," *Ticonderoga Sentinel*, Mar. 23, 1932; "Billy Brown, Once Negro Slave in South, Dies Friendless in the Essex County Home," *Ticonderoga Sentinel*, Mar. 24, 1932; *Ticonderoga Sentinel*, Mar. 31, 1932.

16. Wolters, "New Deal and the Negro," 188; Frazier, *Black Bourgeoisie*, 45.

17. United States Works Progress Administration, *WPA in the Adirondacks* [Albany: NY, 1938]. Pamphlet, unpaged. Copy in the Adirondack Museum Library, Blue Mountain Lake, NY.

18. Ibid.

19. Lewis, *From Newgate to Dannemora*, 61.

20. Prison Association of New York, *Fourth Annual Report*, 208. (Crimes relating to blacks for which white New Yorkers were imprisoned that year included "negro stealing," "harboring a slave," "selling free man of color," "giving forged pass to slave," and "seducing slaves," 545, 566.)

21. Hotel Champlain, *Little Trips* (Bluff Point, Clinton County, undated). Pamphlet, unpaged. Copy in the Adirondack Museum Library, Blue Mountain Lake, NY.

22. "Ethnic Composition of Dannemora Village," in New York State Department of Correction, Clinton Prison, Division of Administration, Prison and Reformatory Records. On file at New York State Archives.

23. *Plattsburgh Republican*, Oct. 11, 1856.

24. Kellogg, *Doctor at All Hours*, 85; *Kingston Daily Freeman*, Aug. 3, 1903.

25. "Clinton Prison at Dannemora," *New York Times*, Nov. 24, 1895; Lewis Theophilus, "Harlem Notebook: Gentlemen Behind Bars," *New York Amsterdam News*, May 4, 1932.

26. Cormier, *Watcher and the Watched*, 229, 236, 249.

27. New York State Department of Correction, Clinton Prison, *Annual Report*, 1936, unnumbered page; New York State Department of Correction, Clinton Prison, Correspondence and Subject Files of the Warden, 1932–1951, Box 1, Folder 1, letter from Walter B. Martin (prison warden) to sixth-grade pupils of the Rugar Street School, Plattsburgh, Mar. 3, 1942. On file at New York State Archives, Albany, NY.

28. Resko, *Reprieve*, 167.

29. "Lehman Asked to Probe Bias at Dannemora," *New York Amsterdam News*, June 15, 1935; "Prison Life at Clinton for Negro Bared by Number 17455," *New York Amsterdam News*, Aug. 6, 1938.

30. Locke, "Various Factors in a Penal Population," 318.

31. "New York State Department of Correction, Clinton Prison, Correspondence and Subject Files of the Warden, 1932–1951, Box 1, Folder 1, "Clinton Prison," May 21, 1936.

32. *New York Amsterdam News*, June 15, 1935; Aug. 6, 1938.

33. *Plattsburgh Daily Press*, Jan. 18, 1934; Jan. 19, 1934; Jan. 24, 1934.

34. Godine, "Oral History: Allen Walton," 20.

35. Lita Kelly, "In the Shadow of the Walls," 50.

36. *New York Tribune*, Aug. 9, 1883.

37. *Lake Placid News*, July 22, 1932; July 21, 1933.

38. *Essex County Republican*, July 15, 1949.

39. *Essex County Republican*, Aug. 3, 1951.

40. *North Creek News*, June 24, 1953.

41. Wessels, *Adirondack Profiles*, 211.

42. Hamill, *Drinking Life*, 75–82, 182.

15. Miners of Moriah

1. Morton, *Philip Skene of Skenesborough*, 26, 64.

2. Farrell, *Through the Light Hole*, 105.

3. Denton, "Social and Economic Decline of a Mining Community," 31–32.

4. Witherbee, Sherman and Company, Employee Records.

5. *Ticonderoga Sentinel*, July 10, 1913.

6. *Ticonderoga Sentinel*, Nov. 23, 1939.

7. Wilkerson, *Warmth of Other Suns*, 8.

8. Cliff Brown, "Racial Conflict and Split Labor Markets," 321, 328.

9. Witherbee, Sherman and Company, Employee Records. Blacks were identified as "American Negro" in the space allotted to "nationality" on record cards.

10. Litwack, *North of Slavery*, 160; Cliff Brown, "Racial Conflict and Split Labor Markets," 327.

11. *Ballston Spa Daily Journal*, July 1, 1916.

12. Farrell, *Through the Light Hole*, 103.

13. Witherbee, Sherman and Company, Employee Records.

14. Farrell, *Through the Light Hole*, 124.

15. Wilkerson, *Warmth of Other Suns*, 398.

16. Witherbee, Sherman and Company, Employee Records.

17. Farrell, *Through the Light Hole*, 124, 133; *Essex County Republican*, Apr. 12, 1935.

18. Single persons and family groups living as boarders in nonrelated households are counted here as separate families.

19. Wilkerson, *Warmth of Other Suns*, 536.

20. Witherbee, Sherman and Company, Employee Records; "Gentry Bros. and Trained Wild Animal Circus, 1921," Circus Historical Society, Aug. 2012, http://www.circushistory.org/Routes/GentryBros.htm.

21. Rosenquist, *Iron Ore Eaters*, 132–33; Denton, "Social and Economic Decline of a Mining Community," 18–19.

22. Rosenquist, *Iron Ore Eaters*, 92.

23. Green, "An African in the Adirondacks," 134–35.

24. Farrell, *Through the Light Hole*, 134, 137.

25. Rosenquist, *Iron Ore Eaters*, 131; Kautz Family YMCA Archives, "Progress Report," May 20, 1942.

26. Kautz Family YMCA Archives, "Narrative Report," July 1943.

27. Kautz Family YMCA Archives, "Episodes," "Historical Records, Section 2:7—Race Relations," "Historical Records, Section 3:2—Minutes of the USO Council," June 24, 1943; *Essex County Republican*, Sept. 10, 1943; Jan. 25, 1946.

28. Kautz Family YMCA Archives, "Narrative Report," Nov. 1943.

29. Kautz Family YMCA Archives, "Narrative Report," Aug. 1943; "Narrative Report," July 1943; "Narrative Report," Dec. 1943; *Essex County Republican*, Jan. 25, 1946.

30. Farrell, *Through the Light Hole*, 160.

31. *Lake Placid News*, Nov. 28, 1947; Feb. 6, 1948; "Attempt to Lynch New Yorker," *New York Amsterdam News*, Mar. 29, 1947; *Philadelphia Tribune*, Nov. 18, 1947.

32. Green, "An African in the Adirondacks, 141.

33. Godine, "Oral History: Allen Walton," 26.

34. *Plattsburgh Daily Republican*, Nov. 8, 1929.

35. Farrell, *Through the Light Hole*, 176, 189, 208.

36. *Plattsburgh Press Republican*, Oct. 27, 1994.

37. Godine, "Voice of Tradition: Allen Walton of Essex County," 91n1.

16. Pullman Porters: Railroad Stories

1. Shaughnessy, *Delaware and Hudson*, 69, 151.

2. Tye, *Rising from the Rails*, 2–3.

3. J. Fred Maloney, interview by William Langlois, Sept. 4, 1970, in Constable, NY, "Oral and Digital History of Reynoldston and Franklin County New York," http://www.reynoldstonnewyork.org.

4. Dorothy Williams, *Road to Now*, 42.

5. Holbrook, *Story of American Railroads*, 336.

6. Funderburg, *Pig Candy*, 148–51.

7. *New York Age*, Oct. 7, 1922.

8. Chalmers, "Watching the Hour-Glass," 292.

9. *New York Age*, Oct. 7, 1922.

10. A. D. Foster, "Interstate Migration of Tuberculous Persons," 755; J. S. Merrill (Superintendent, Pullman Company, Northeastern Division), confidential memorandum to District Superintendents, New York and Montreal, and Agent, Saranac Lake, Sept. 2, 1903, St. Regis Yacht Club records, MS 75-013, Adirondack Museum Library, Blue Mountain Lake, NY.

11. Hunton, *William Alphaeus Hunton*, 142.

12. *Tupper Lake Free Press*, Jan. 4, 1934.

13. *Griffin v. Brady*, 132 App. Div. 928 (N.Y. App. Div. 1909), Case on Appeal, Brief of the Appellant, 1909: 6; McBride, "Fourteenth Amendment Idealism," 225–26.

14. *New York Age*, May 16, 1931; Oct. 8, 1932.

15. *New York Age*, May 16, 1931.

16. *Los Angeles California Eagle*, Oct. 7, 1932; *New York Age*, Oct. 8, 1932.

17. *Baltimore Afro-American*, June 4, 1938.

18. Everest, *Rum Across the Border*, 82, 33.

19. Tye, *Rising from the Rails*, 40.

20. *Watertown Daily Times*, Sept. 4, 1928.

21. "Pullman Porter Has Large Load," *Au Sable Forks Adirondack Record-Elizabethtown Post*, May 7, 1925; "Pullman Porter is Freed in Rum Case," *Au Sable Forks Adirondack Record-Elizabethtown Post*, May 14, 1925.

22. Pullman Company, Personnel Administration Department, Employee Service Records, ca. 1890–1969, Special Collections, Newberry Library, Chicago, "Frank F. Whitted," Box 295.

23. Everest, *Rum Across the Border*, 82.

24. *Chateaugay Record and Franklin Democrat*, Oct. 18, 1945.

25. Myers and Hancock, *History of the Grasse River Club*, 27.

26. *Schenectady Gazette*, May 30, 1932.

27. *New York Age*, July 25, 1931.

28. *Saranac Lake Adirondack Enterprise*, Feb. 15, 1932.

29. Johnson, "Negroes in the Railway Industry," 202.

30. *Baltimore Afro-American*, Sept. 7, 1940; Tye, *Rising from the Rails*, 194.

31. Shaughnessy, *Delaware and Hudson*, 355, 360.

32. New York State Commission against Discrimination, *Railroad Employment in New York and New Jersey*, 5–6.

33. Turner, *Memories of a Retired Pullman Porter*, 113.

34. Holbrook, *Story of American Railroads*, 330.

17. The Twentieth-Century Military

1. Barbeau and Henri, *Unknown Soldiers*, 15–16.

2. *Elizabethtown Post*, Feb. 27, 1908. The spelling of Plattsburgh as "Plattsburg" reflected a postal address directive of 1894 that sometimes was, and sometimes was not, reflected in newspaper coverage. The city's name remained "Plattsburgh."

3. Squire, "24th Infantry Regiment," 71–72.

4. *Watertown Daily Times*, July 29, 1916.

5. New York Lake Champlain Tercentenary Commission, *The Champlain Tercentenary: First Report*, 75, 80, 81.

6. Nalty, introduction to Barbeau and Henri, *Unknown Soldiers*, xiii.

7. Lentz-Smith, *Freedom Struggles*, 58; Squire, "24th Infantry Regiment," 79–82.

8. Also buried in the Ramsey family plot in Brookside is another brother, Doy Ramsey. He is not thought to have been a Saranac Lake resident, but was gathered into the family upon his death. A "washer" in a Manhattan mirror company before being drafted in August 1918, Ramsey served during the final months of World War I with three stateside labor units.

9. Nalty, introduction to Barbeau and Henri, *Unknown Soldiers*, xiii; Barbeau and Henri, *Unknown Soldiers*, 33, 39.

10. Bill Harris, *Hellfighters of Harlem*, 13.

11. Atlanta minister Reverend James Bond, quoted in Lentz-Smith, *Freedom Struggles*, 38; Barbeau and Henri, *Unknown Soldiers*, 7.

12. Bill Harris, *Hellfighters of Harlem*, 22, 32. Numbers given in reference to World War I black soldiers vary. Daniel K. Gibran refers to 404,000 officers and enlisted men, or nearly 11 percent of the army, as black. Gibran, *92nd Infantry Division and the Italian Campaign in World War II*, 1.

13. Sullivan, *Lift Every Voice*, 14–15.

14. "How We Got Army Officers in the World War of 1917," *Baltimore Afro-American*, Oct. 7, 1939.

15. *Baltimore Afro-American*, Mar. 10, 1917; Oct. 7, 1939.

16. Barbeau and Henri, *Unknown Soldiers*, 61–62; Bryan, "Fighting for Respect."

17. "A Contrast," *Crisis*, 280.

18. Barbeau and Henri, *Unknown Soldiers*, 91. Minnifield located away from the Adirondacks to Philadelphia after his war service. His name is listed on Saranac Lake's monument honoring soldiers of the First World War.

19. Barbeau and Henri, *Unknown Soldiers*, 89, 90, 93–94, 191.

20. Ibid., 95, 191–93.

21. South Carolina Adjutant-General's Office, *Official Roster*, 1578.

22. Barbeau and Henri, *Unknown Soldiers*, 90, 94.

23. South Carolina Adjutant-General's Office, *Official Roster*, 1350; Hendricks, *Combat and Construction*, 192–94.

24. *Ticonderoga Sentinel*, Aug. 12, 1948.

25. Gibran, *92nd Infantry Division*, 3; Barbeau and Henri, *Unknown Soldiers*, 33, 121, 129, 131, 136.

26. Bryan, "Fighting for Respect."

27. Patton, *War and Race*, 134, 138, 141.

28. Buckley, *American Patriots*, 280.

29. An often-quoted phrase attributed to Louis by a public speaker and repeated in Gero, *Black Soldiers of New York State*, 75.

30. George C. Marshall to Henry L. Stimson, Dec. 1, 1941, quoted in Potter, *Liberators*, 66–67.

31. Buckley, *American Patriots*, 280, 279.

32. Plummer is buried in Arlington National Cemetery.

33. Moye, *Freedom Flyers*, 14, 25–26, 28.

34. Potter, *Liberators*, 90; Moye, *Freedom Flyers*, 75.

35. "Flying for Freedom: Roland Brown '49 and David Showell '51 Served with the Tuskegee Airmen."

36. Moye, *Freedom Flyers*, 14, 125.

37. "Flying for Freedom."

38. Moye, *Freedom Flyers*, 125.

39. "Flying for Freedom"; Obituary of Roland Brown Sr., Higgins Home for Funerals, 2004, http://higginsfuneralhome.com/tribute/details/754/Roland-Brown-Sr/obituary.html; "Bush, Congress Honor Tuskegee Airmen," *USA Today*, Mar. 29, 2007; Robin Caudell, "Adirondack Museum Honors Tuskegee Airman," *Plattsburgh Press Republican*, June 25, 2011.

40. Gibran, *92nd Infantry Division*, 4, 5, 55; *Ticonderoga Sentinel*, Mar. 22, 1945.

41. Campbell, *Inside the Club*, 72–73, quoting from club publication.

42. *Baltimore Afro-American*, Oct. 14, 1944.

43. Ross, "What They Dreamed of at the Front," 8–9.

44. *Cleveland Call and Post*, Sept. 23, 1944.

45. Manchester, *Lake Placid Club*, 25.

46. Ross, "What They Dreamed of at the Front," 8.

47. Moses, "Lake Placid No Melting Pot," 32.

48. "Air Heroes Barred from Hospital," *Baltimore Afro-American*, June 2, 1945.

49. Gilbert, *ACUNY*, 64–65. The project was overseen by a board of trustees composed of the presidents of ten upstate colleges and universities: Clarkson College of Technology, Colgate University, Colleges of the Seneca, Cornell University, Hamilton College, Rensselaer Polytechnic Institute, University of Rochester, St. Lawrence University, Syracuse University, and Union University.

50. Hartzell, *Empire State at War*, 283–87.

51. Turner and Bound, "Closing the Gap or Widening the Divide," 149n7.

52. Gilbert, *ACUNY*, 326.

53. Gilbert, *ACUNY*, 161, 247; *Plattsburgh Press-Republican*, May 19, 1953.

18. Tourism

1. Gatewood, *Aristocrats of Color*, 201.

2. "We Travel 251.7 Miles North of New York to See Baer's Camp in Vaunted Adirondacks," *Indianapolis Freeman*, June 9, 1894.

3. "Vacation Days," 186.

4. *New York Age*, Aug. 3, 1911.

5. *Pittsburgh Courier*, Sept. 14, 1935.

6. Adolph Hodge, "Week-End Trips," *New York Amsterdam News*, May 30, 1928.

7. *New York Amsterdam News*, Oct. 16, 1937.

8. Schuyler, "Keeping the Negro in His Place," 476.

9. Delphine Knight, interview by Marian Knight, July 13, 2011, Hulett's Landing, NY, transcript, Friends of Historic Hulett's Landing, http://www.historichuletts.org/collections/oral-histories/.

10. "'Rochester' Starts Stable of Race Horses, Buying Four Yearlings Here," *Saratogian*, Aug. 7, 1941.

11. Clay Williams, "*Guide for Colored Travelers*," 71.

12. Rugh, *Are We There Yet?* 77; Mark Foster, "In the Face of 'Jim Crow,'" quoting from the first (1936) edition of the *Negro Motorist Green Book*, 142.

13. *Green Book*, 1938, front cover.

14. *Green Book*, 1938, 21; *Green Book*, 1939, 48.

15. Munn, "Early Days of the Hotel Saranac," 3–4.

16. Metcalfe, *Leland House*, 44.

17. *New York Age*, Sept. 5, 1931.

18. Schuyler, "Vacation Daze," 41–44.

19. Ibid. Location of Hotel Monoquaya unknown.

20. McBride, "Fourteenth Amendment Idealism," 233.

21. Advertising piece for Ara-Ho, Inlet, from "hotels" folder, vertical file, Adirondack Museum Library, Blue Mountain Lake, NY.

22. "Paper's Refusal of Biased Ad Backed by N.Y. Court," *Baltimore Afro-American*, Mar. 17, 1945.

23. McFerson, "Coming Home a Stranger," 309–11.

24. *Washington Afro-American*, Aug. 4, 1953; *Negro Business Directory of the State of Wisconsin*, 107; United States Travel Bureau, *Directory of Negro Hotels and Guest Houses in the United States*, 5.

25. *New York Age*, Sept. 17, 1949; McFerson, "Coming Home a Stranger," 314.

26. Whitcover, *My Road Less Traveled*, 243.

27. *Yonkers Herald Statesman*, May 28, 1956.

28. Hebald, *Heart Too Long Suppressed*, 120.

29. Whitcover, *My Road Less Traveled*, 246.

30. Godine, "Red Woods," 52, 92.

31. *Travelguide* listings for accommodations within the Adirondack Park between 1947 and 1957 included: *Bolton Landing* (Warren County): Port Jerry—Vacation Camping, 1952. *Lake George* (Warren County): Woodbine Cottage, 1953–57. *Lake Placid* (Essex County): Dreamland Cottage, 1952 summer supplement, 1953–55; Hotel Marcy, 1949–57; Mirror Lake Inn, 1950; Parkside, 1947, 1949–51; St. Moritz Hotel, 1955–57. *Loon Lake* (Warren County): Carlisle Cabin Village, 1953–54. *Saranac Lake* (Essex County): Keough's Motel, 1955; Hotel Saranac, 1949–55. *Tupper Lake* (Franklin County): Altamont Hotel, 1949–56; Prince Albert Hotel—Cabins (Moody), 1955–56. (Issues for 1946 and 1948 not consulted.)

32. Seiler, "'So That We as a Race Might Have Something Authentic to Travel By,'" 1109–10.

33. "Adirondacks Offer Great Variety in Vacation Fare," *New York Amsterdam News*, June 28, 1952; George Jackson, "Trip Tips," *New York Amsterdam News*, July 19, 1958.

34. William L. Brown, "Following the Indian Trail," 199.

35. Young, "'A Contradiction in Democratic Government,'" 653–54.

36. Ibid., 651–52, 656.

37. Weber and Sultana, "Why Do So Few Minority People Visit National Parks?" 459–60.

38. *Watertown Times*, Dec. 26, 1940.

39. *Columbus (OH) Dispatch*, Jan. 12, 2012.

40. *Ticonderoga Sentinel*, Sept. 23, 1897; *Warrensburgh News*, Sept. 23, 1897; *Plattsburgh Daily Press*, Sept. 29, 1897; *Au Sable Forks Adirondack Record-Elizabethtown Post*, Jan. 6, 1922. Jackson, born in Essex County in 1873, was the son of another William Jackson, who claimed Franklin County as his circa-1840 birthplace, and a white mother from Canada. The family moved around in the eastern Adirondacks while Jackson was growing up, his father sometimes working as a laborer in the woods around North Hudson.

41. Washburne and Wall, *Black-White Ethnic Differences*, 1, 4.

42. Ibid., 1, 3–4.

43. *Washington Afro-American*, Aug. 4, 1953.

44. Walter Brown Leonard, "Tells the Story of Walker Tompkins," *Canton Commercial Advertiser*, Aug. 24, 1937.

45. *Canton Commercial Advertiser*, Apr. 4, 1939; *St. Lawrence Plaindealer*, Apr. 4, 1933; G. Atwood Manley, "Frank Tompkins, Canton's Only Negro Barber Dies Following Brief Illness," *St. Lawrence Plaindealer*, Nov. 17, 1955.

46. Washburne and Wall, *Black-White Ethnic Differences*, 4.

47. *Warrensburg News*, Mar. 2, 1939.

48. Jim Burnett, *Adirondack Snow Flurries*, 35–37.

19. 1940 to 1950 and Beyond

1. "The Empire State as a Refuge for Migrants," *New York Age*, July 12, 1941.

2. "Negroes," *Upstate Ministry*, 1942–43, quoted in Judith Owens-Manley, *Final Evaluation.*

3. New York State Commission against Discrimination, Division of Research, *Negroes in Five New York Cities*, 20.

4. DeAmicis, "Search for Community," 30; New York State Commission against Discrimination, Division of Research, *Negroes in Five New York Cities*, 8, 19; Haley, "Afro-Americans in Upstate New York; 1890–1980," 55.

5. "New York and the Boas School of Dance," Dance Collection Danse, http://www.dcd.ca/exhibitions/sullivan/newyork.html. The school was run between 1944 and 1948 by Franziska Boas, daughter of well-known anthropologist Franz Boas.

6. *Ballston Daily Journal*, Nov. 8, 1927.

7. Sinnette, *Forbidden Fairways*, 31–32; Kennedy, *Course of Their Own*, 20–21.

8. Martin, "Open to All," 82.

9. *Tupper Lake Free Press*, Aug. 5, 1992.

10. J. Peter Martin, telephone conversation with author, Oct. 2014.

11. Martin, *Adirondack Golf Courses*, 102.

12. "Dewey Brown: Superintendent, Professional, Gentleman," 31, 34.

13. Bethel, *From My Window*, passim.

14. *Glens Falls Post-Star*, Mar. 25, 1949; Mar. 26 1949.

15. New York State Commission against Discrimination, Division of Research, *Negroes in Five New York Cities*, 8, 19.

16. Wilkins, *They Raised Me Up*, 123–25.

17. *Saranac Lake Adirondack Enterprise*, May 25, 1960; *Tupper Lake Free Press and Herald*, Aug. 13, 1964; *Pittsfield (MA) Berkshire Eagle*, Feb. 12, 1960; Wilkins, *They Raised Me Up*, 125.

18. Dawn Richardson (granddaughter of George and Ruth Turner), email message to author, July 1913.

19. *New York Amsterdam News*, Aug. 25, 1951.

20. "Post office clerk" topped a 1939 survey list of twenty-two jobs realistically aspired to by black teenage boys in New York City; "mail carrier" placed sixth. McDougald, "Negro Youth Plans Its Future," 224–25.

21. *New York Amsterdam News*, Aug. 5, 1931.

22. *Warrensburg-Lake George News*, May 6, 1981; Apr. 4, 1984.

23. "Italian May Lose License for Jim Crow," *Baltimore Afro-American*, Mar. 28, 1936.

24. "Civil Rights Suit," *(Canada) People's Voice*, July 14, 1945.

25. "Refuses to Cut Negro's Hair; Pays," *Baltimore Afro-American*, Dec. 10, 1955.

26. Bill Babel, "Off the Beaten Track," *Plattsburgh Press-Republican*, Dec. 10, 1957.

27. *Plattsburgh Press-Republican*, Jan. 6, 1960.

28. Ibid.

29. *Plattsburgh Press-Republican*, Dec. 16, 1961. The Plattsburgh NAACP branch no longer exists. The organization has never been represented in the park itself; Glens Falls, Warren County, established a (still extant) branch in 1967.

30. Bernstein, *Sticks*, 127–28, 150.

31. Comment by "Outlier" reacting to Pete Nelson's blog entry "Voices from the Diversity Forum," *Adirondack Almanack*, Oct. 4, 2014, http://www.adirondackalmanack.com/2014/10/toward-a-more-diverse-adirondacks-voices-from-the-symposium.html.

32. Odato, "Aaron Mair," 29.

Afterword: Autobiographical Reflections

1. Felker, "Failure of the Rockefeller Drug Laws."

2. Ibid.

3. "An End to Prison Gerrymandering," *New York Times*, Aug. 23, 2010.

4. New York State Department of Correctional Services, *Security Level and Facility by Ethnic Status Under Custody*, Dec. 31, 2010.

5. Vink, "Adirondack Park Population by Race."

6. Alexander, *The New Jim Crow*.

7. Chris Churchill, "Adirondack Beauty Marred by Ugly Bigotry," *Albany Times Union*, Nov. 8, 2010, B.

Bibliography

Abbott, Lynn, and Doug Seroff. *Out of Sight: The Rise of African American Popular Music, 1889–1895*. Jackson: Univ. Press of Mississippi, 2002.

———. *Ragged but Right: Black Travelling Shows, "Coon Songs," and the Dark Pathway to Blues and Jazz*. Jackson: Univ. Press of Mississippi, 2007.

Aber, Ted, and Stella King. *History of Hamilton County*. Lake Pleasant, NY: Great Wilderness Books, 1965.

African American National Biography. Edited by Henry Louis Gates Jr. and Evelyn Brooks Higginbotham. 2nd ed. New York: Oxford Univ. Press, 2013.

Alexander, Michelle. *The New Jim Crow: Mass Incarceration in the Age of Colorblindness*. New York: The New Press, 2010.

American Oil Company. *American Traveler's Guide to Negro History*. 2nd ed. Chicago: American Oil Company, [1964].

Ames, Forrest B. "Tuberculosis Survey of the Residents of Saranac Lake, New York." *American Review of Tuberculosis* 2, no. 4 (May 1918): 207–36 and foldout map.

Armstead, Myra B. Young. *"Lord, Please Don't Take Me in August": African Americans in Newport and Saratoga Springs, 1870–1930*. Urbana: Univ. of Illinois Press, 1999.

Baer, Hans A., and Merrill Singer. *African American Religion: Varieties of Protest and Accommodation*. 2nd ed. Knoxville: Univ. of Tennessee Press, 2002.

Bailey, Ben E. "The Cotton Blossom Singers: Mississippi's Black Troubadours." *Black Perspective in Music* 15, no. 2 (Autumn 1987): 133–52.

Baker, Ray Stannard. *Following the Color Line: An Account of Negro Citizenship in the American Democracy*. New York: Doubleday, Page, 1908.

Banks, Russell. Introduction to "John Brown's Body: James Baldwin and Frank Shatz in Conversation." *Transition* 9, nos. 1 and 2 (2000): 250–66.

Barbeau, Arthur E., and Florette Henri. *The Unknown Soldiers: African-American Troops in World War I.* 1974. Reprint, Boston: Da Capo Press, 1996.

Barber, J. Max. "A Pilgrimage to John Brown's Grave." *Crisis* 24, no. 4 (Aug. 1922): 167–69.

Benjaminsen, Tor A., and Gunnvor Berge. "Myths of Timbukto: From African El Dorado to Desertification." *International Journal of Political Economy* 34, no. 1 (Spring 2004): 31–59.

Berlin, Ira, Joseph P. Reidy, and Leslie S. Rowland, eds. *Freedom: A Documentary History of Emancipation, 1861–1867.* Series 2, *The Black Military Experience.* Cambridge: Cambridge Univ. Press, 1982.

Bernstein, Burton. *The Sticks: A Profile of Essex County, New York.* New York: Dodd, Mead, 1971, 1972.

Bethel, Grace. *From My Window.* Compiled by Jeane Bethel Mayo. S.l.: Jeane Bethel Mayo, 1987. Copy at Crandall Public Library, Glens Falls.

[Birney, James G.]. *American Churches, the Bulwark of American Slavery*, 2nd Am. ed. Newburyport, MA: Charles Ripple, 1842. Pamphlet originally published in England in 1840.

Blankman, Edward J. "Under the North Star." *Adirondack Life*, Mar./Apr., 1983, 33–38.

Bloch, Herman D. "Discrimination against the Negro in Employment in New York, 1920–1963." *American Journal of Economics and Sociology* 24, no. 4 (Oct. 1965): 361–82.

Bristol, Douglas, Jr. "From Outposts to Enclaves: A Social History of Black Barbers from 1750 to 1915." *Enterprise and Society* 5, no. 4 (Dec. 2004): 594–606.

Brown, Cliff. "Racial Conflict and Split Labor Markets: The AFL Campaign to Organize Steel Workers, 1918–1919." *Social Science History* 22, no. 3 (Autumn 1998): 319–47.

Brown, Jayna. *Babylon Girls: Black Women Performers and the Shaping of the Modern.* Durham, NC: Duke Univ. Press, 2008.

Brown, Louis. *The Salisbury Prison: A Case Study of Confederate Military Prisons, 1861–1865.* Wendell, NC: Avera Press/Broadfoot's Bookmark, 1980.

Brown, William L. "Following the Indian Trail: Some Vacation Days of a Canoeist." *Southern Workman* 26, no. 10 (Oct. 1, 1897): 199.

Browne, Arthur. *One Righteous Man: Samuel Battle and the Shattering of the Color Line in New York*. Boston: Beacon Press, 2015.

Bryan, Jami. "Fighting for Respect: African-American Soldiers in WWI." Military History Online, 2003. http://www.militaryhistoryonline.com/wwi/articles/fightingforrespect.aspx.

Buckley, Gail. *American Patriots: The Story of Blacks in the Military from the Revolution to Desert Storm*. New York: Random House, 2001.

Bullock, Henry Allen. *A History of Negro Education in the South: From 1619 to the Present Period*. Cambridge, MA: Harvard Univ. Press, 1967.

Burdick, Neal and Natalia Rachel Singer, eds. *Living North Country: Essays of Life and Landscapes in Northern New York*. Utica, NY: North Country Books, 2001.

Burnett, Charles H. *Conquering the Wilderness: The Building of the Adirondack and St. Lawrence Railroad by William Seward Webb, 1891–92*. [Norwood, MA]: Privately printed, 1931.

Burnett, Jim. *Adirondack Snow Flurries*. Cranberry Lake, NY: Halstead, 1987.

Calarco, Tom. *The Search for the Underground Railroad in Upstate New York*. Charleston, SC: History Press, 2014.

———. *The Underground Railroad in the Adirondack Region*. Jefferson, NC: McFarland, 2004.

Caldwell, Mark. *The Last Crusade: The War on Consumption 1862–1954*. New York: Atheneum, 1988.

Campbell, Barbara A. *Inside the Club: Stories of the Employees of the Former Lake Placid Club*. Troy, NY: Troy Book Makers, 2008.

Chalmers, Stephen. "The Mascot of 'Troop 1.'" In *The Boy Scout Book of Stories*, edited by Franklin K. Mathiews, 315–29. New York: D. Appleton, 1920.

———. "Watching the Hour-Glass." *Pearson's Magazine*, Mar. 1909, 289–97.

Chappell, Charles A., and Frank W. Curtis. *The Grasse River Outing Club*. Syracuse, NY: Chappell, 1972.

Clark-Lewis, Elizabeth, and Mary Johnson Sprow. "Duty and 'Fast Living': The Diary of Mary Johnson Sprow, Domestic Worker." Edited and with an introduction by Elizabeth Clark-Lewis. *Washington History* 5, no. 1 (Spring/Summer 1993): 46–65.

Clarkson, Elisabeth Hudnut. *An Adirondack Archive: The Trail to Windover.* Utica, NY: North Country Books, 1993.

Collins, Geraldine. *The Brighton Story: Being the History of Paul Smiths, Gabriels and Rainbow Lake.* Lakemont, NY: North Country Books, 1977.

"Contrast, A." *Crisis* 16, no. 6 (Oct. 1918): 280.

Cook, Flavius J. *Home Sketches of Essex County.* Keeseville, NY: Lansing, 1858.

Coonrod, Harry. "Roads to Yesterday." Unpublished manuscript, 1937. Original at Lewis, Essex County, Town Hall, as is a copy typed in 2009 by Jean W. Dickerson, Lewis Town Historian.

Corbett, Theodore. *The Making of American Resorts: Saratoga Springs, Ballston Spa, Lake George.* New Brunswick, NJ: Rutgers Univ. Press, 2001.

Cormier, Bruno M. *The Watcher and the Watched.* Plattsburgh, NY: Tundra Books, 1975.

Craig, John. *Chappie and Me.* New York: Dodd, Mead, 1979.

Cunningham, John L. *Three Years with the Adirondack Regiment, 118th New York Volunteers Infantry.* N.p.: Privately printed, 1920.

Curtis-Burlin, Natalie. "Black Singers and Players." *Musical Quarterly* 5, no. 4 (1919): 499–504.

Davies, John. "Saint-Dominguan Refugees of African Descent and the Forging of Ethnic Identity in Early National Philadelphia." *Pennsylvania Magazine of History and Biography* 1314, no. 2 (Apr. 2010): 109–26.

Davis, Thomas J. "Three Dark Centuries Around Albany: A Survey of Black Life in New York's Capital City Area before World War I." *Afro-Americans in New York Life and History* 7 (1983): 7–23.

DeAmicis, Jan. "The Search for Community: Utica's African-Americans." In *Ethnic Utica*, edited by James S. Pula, 7–35. Utica, NY: Ethnic Heritage Studies Center, Utica College, 2002.

Denton, Barbara. "The Social and Economic Decline of a Mining Community." Undergraduate independent study project, Plattsburgh State Teachers College, Nov. 1981. Copy at the Essex County Historical Society, Elizabethtown, NY.

Desjardins, Simon, and Pierre Pharoux. *Castorland Journal: An Account of the Exploration and Settlement of Northern New York State by French Émigrés in the Years 1793 to 1797.* Ithaca, NY: Cornell Univ. Press, 2010.

"Dewey Brown: Superintendent, Professional, Gentleman." *Golf Superintendent,* July 1974, 31–34.

Dollarhide, William. *New York State Censuses and Substitutes.* Baltimore, MD: Genealogical Publishing, 2006.

Driggins, John L. *A History of the Negro Community in Corning, New York.* Corning, NY: Painted Post Historical Society, 1995.

Drummond, Robert Loudon. *The Religious Pray, the Profane Swear: A Civil War Memoir: Personal Reminiscences of Prison Life during the War of the Rebellion.* Aurora, CO: Davies Group, 2002.

Duncan, Hannibal Gerald. *The Changing Race Relationship in the Border and Northern States.* Philadelphia: Univ. of Pennsylvania, 1922.

Early, George, ed. *Lure and Loathing: Essays on Race, Identity, and the Ambivalence of Assimilation.* New York: Allen Lane, Penguin Press, 1993.

Elliott, Stephen. "Trip to Willsboro." In *Bark Book: Recollections of Pok-O-MacCready Camps' History, 1905–2009,* edited by Judy Murphy, 28. Willsboro, NY: Privately printed, 2010.

Emilio, Luis F. *Brave Black Regiment: History of the Fifty-Fourth Regiment of Massachusetts Volunteer Infantry, 1863–1865.* 1894 edition. Reprinted with introductions by James M. McPherson and Edwin Gittleman. Salem, NH: Ayer, 1990.

Enck, Henry S. "Black Self-Help in the Progressive Era: The 'Northern Campaigns' of Smaller Southern Black Industrial Schools, 1900–1915." *Journal of Negro History* 61, no. 1 (Jan. 1976): 73–87.

Encyclopedia of African American History: 1896 to the Present. Edited by Paul Finkelman. New York: Oxford Univ. Press, 2009.

Erenberg, Lewis A. *Steppin' Out: New York Nightlife and the Transformation of American Culture, 1890–1930.* Chicago: Chicago Univ. Press, 1981.

Everest, Allan S. *Rum Across the Border: The Prohibition Era in Northern New York.* Syracuse, NY: Syracuse Univ. Press, 1978.

Farley, Evelyn. "Working in a Camp on Upper St. Regis Lake." *Franklin Historical Review* 20 (1983): 8–10.

Farrell, Patrick. *Through the Light Hole: A Saga of Adirondack Mines and Men.* Utica, NY: North Country Books, 1996.

Felker, Alex. "Failure of the Rockefeller Drug Laws." CRJ 481 Thesis Paper. State Univ. of New York at Albany, Dec. 13, 2015. http://www.albany.edu/honorscollege/files/Felker_Honors_Thesis.pdf.

"Flying for Freedom: Roland Brown '49 and David Showell '51 Served with the Tuskegee Airmen." *Lafayette Alumni News*, Sept. 1998. https://news.lafayette.edu/2006/12/07/flying-for-freedom-2/.

Foner, Eric. *Forever Free: The Story of Emancipation and Reconstruction*. New York: Knopf, 2005.

———. *Gateway to Freedom: The Hidden History of the Underground Railroad*. New York: Norton, 2015.

Foster, A. D. "Interstate Migration of Tuberculous Persons: Its Bearing on the Public Health, with Special Reference to the States of North Carolina and South Carolina." *Public Health Reports* 30, no. 11 (Mar. 12, 1915): 745–74.

Foster, Mark S. "In the Face of 'Jim Crow': Prosperous Blacks and Vacations, Travel and Outdoor Leisure, 1890–1945." *Journal of Negro History* 84, no. 2 (Spring 1999): 130–49.

Frazier, E. Franklin. *Black Bourgeoisie*. 1957. Reprint, New York: Free Press Paperbacks, 1997.

Frost, Richard B. *Hotel Champlain to Clinton Community College: A Chronicle of Bluff Point*. [Bluff Point, NY]: Clinton Community College Foundation, 2011.

Frothingham, Octavius Brooks. *Gerrit Smith: A Biography*. New York: G. P. Putnam's, 1878.

Funderburg, Lise. *Pig Candy: Taking My Father South, Taking My Father Home—A Memoir*. New York: Free Press, 2008.

Gallos, Philip L. *Cure Cottages of Saranac Lake: Architecture and History of a Pioneer Health Resort*. Saranac Lake, NY: Historic Saranac Lake, 1985.

Gannon, Barbara A. *The Won Cause: Black and White Comradeship in the Grand Army of the Republic*. Chapel Hill: Univ. of North Carolina Press, 2011.

Gatewood, Willard B. *Aristocrats of Color: The Black Elite, 1880–1920*. Bloomington: Indiana Univ. Press, 1990.

Gee, Clarence S. "The Stone on John Brown's Grave." *New York History* 42, no. 2 (Apr. 1961): 157–68.

Gero, Anthony F. *Black Soldiers of New York State: A Proud Legacy*. Albany: State Univ. of New York Press, 2009.

Gerrit Smith Papers. Special Collections Research Center, Syracuse University Libraries.

Gibran, Daniel K., *The 92nd Infantry Division and the Italian Campaign in World War II*. Jefferson, NC: McFarland, 2001.

Gilbert, Amy M. *ACUNY, the Associated Colleges of Upper New York; a Unique Response to an Emergency in Higher Education in the State of New York*. Ithaca, NY: Cornell Univ. Press, 1950.

Glenn, Norval D. "Negro Prestige Criteria: A Case Study in the Bases of Prestige." *American Journal of Sociology* 68, no. 6 (May 1963): 645–57.

Godine, Amy. "Oral History: Allen Walton," *Adirondack Life*, Jan./Feb. 1996.

———. "The Red Woods." *Adirondack Life*, July/Aug. 2003.

———. "Voice of Tradition: Allen Walton of Essex County, Adirondack Knight of the Road." *New York Folklore* 20, nos. 1 and 2 (1994): 67–93.

Gordon, Jan, and Cora Gordon. *On Wandering Wheels*. New York: Dodd, Mead, 1928.

Gosselink, Charles G. *Benjamin Van Buren's Bay*. Silver Bay, NY: Boathouse Books, 2002. Copy at Hague Historical Society.

Green, Alice Paden. "An African in the Adirondacks: Growing Up in the Fifties." In *Living North Country: Essays of Life and Landscapes in Northern New York*, edited by Burdick and Singer, 130–49. Utica, NY: North Country Books, 2001.

Green Book. See *Negro Motorist Green Book*.

Grover, Kathryn. *Make a Way Somehow: African-American Life in a Northern Community, 1790–1965*. Syracuse, NY: Syracuse Univ. Press, 1994.

Guyette, Elise A. *Discovering Black Vermont: African American Farmers in Hinesburgh, 1790–1890*. Burlington: Univ. of Vermont Press, 2010.

Haley, Charles T. "Afro-Americans in Upstate New York; 1890–1980: Critical Reflections of a Study in Progress." *Afro-Americans in New York Life and History* 9, no. 1 (Jan. 1985): 51–57.

———. "The Klan in Their Midst: The Ku Klux Klan in Upstate New York Communities." *Afro-Americans in New York Life and History* 7, no. 1 (Jan. 1983): 41–53.

Hamill, Pete. *A Drinking Life: A Memoir*. Boston: Little, Brown, 1994.

Hampton Institute. "Hampton's Southern Campaign." *Southern Workman* 49, no. 10 (Oct. 1920): 444–46.

———. Obituary of Bishop Brown. *Southern Workman* 47, no. 10 (Oct. 1918): 510–11.

Hampton Normal and Agricultural Institute. *Treasurer's Statement for the Year Ending June 30, 1902*. Hampton, VA: Hampton Institute, 1902.

Harlan, Louis R. "Booker T. Washington and the *Voice of the Negro*, 1904–1907." *Journal of Southern History* 45, no. 1, (Feb. 1979): 45–62.

Harlow, Ralph Volney. *Gerrit Smith: Philanthropist and Reformer*. New York: Henry Holt, 1939.

Harris, Bill. *The Hellfighters of Harlem: African-American Soldiers Who Fought for the Right to Fight for Their Country*. New York: Carroll and Graf, 2002.

Harris, Glenn. "The Hidden History of Agriculture in the Adirondack Park, 1825–1875." *New York History* 83, no. 2 (Spring 2002): 165–202.

Harter, Henry A. *Fairy Tale Railroad: The Mohawk and Malone: From the Mohawk, through the Adirondacks to the St. Lawrence*. Sylvan Beach, NY: North Country Books, 1979.

Hartzell, Karl Drew. *The Empire State at War; World War II*. Albany, NY: State of New York, 1949.

Heald, Anne A. "A Man to Remember: The Shadow of John Brown." *Negro Digest* 11, no. 9 (July 1962): 40–45.

Hebald, Carol. *Heart Too Long Suppressed: A Chronicle of Mental Illness*. Boston: Northeastern Univ. Press, 2001.

Hendricks, Charles. *Combat and Construction: U. S. Army Engineers in World War I*. Hyattsville, MD: US Army Corps of Engineers, Office of History, 1993.

Historical, Statistical and Industrial Review of the State of Connecticut. Part I. New York: W. S. Webb, 1883.

History of Montgomery and Fulton Counties, NY: With Illustrations and Portraits of Old Pioneers and Prominent Residents. New York: F. W. Beers, 1878.

Hobbs, Allyson. *A Chosen Exile: A History of Racial Passing in American Life*. Cambridge, MA: Harvard Univ. Press, 2014.

Hochschild, Harold K. *Township 34, a History, with Digressions, of an Adirondack Township in Hamilton County in the State of New York*. N.p.: published by author, 1952.

Hochschild, Jennifer L., and Brenna Marea Powell. "Racial Reorganization and the United States Census 1850–1930: Mulattoes, Half-Breeds, Mixed Parentage, Hindoos, and the Mexican Race." *Studies in American Political Development* 22 (2008): 59–96.

Hodges, Willis Augustus. *Free Man of Color: The Autobiography of Willis Augustus Hodges.* Edited and with an introduction by Willard B. Gatewood Jr. Knoxville: Univ. of Tennessee Press, 1982.

Hogan, Lawrence D. *Shades of Glory: The Negro Leagues and the Story of African-American Baseball.* Washington, DC: National Geographic Society, 2006.

Holbrook, Stewart H. *Story of American Railroads.* New York: Crown, 1947.

Hollis, Sylvea. "'The Black Man Almost Has Disappeared from Our Country': African American Workers in Cooperstown, New York, 1860–1900." *New York History* 88, no. 1 (Winter 2007): 13–31.

Hopper, Mabel Lewis, and Marjorie Cantor. *Migrant Farm Workers in New York State.* New York: Consumers League of New York, 1953.

Hotaling, Edward. *They're Off! Horse Racing at Saratoga.* Syracuse, NY: Syracuse Univ. Press, 1995.

Hough, Franklin B. "New York State Census, 1855." *Journal of the American Geographical and Statistical Society* 1, no. 7 (July 1859): 205–17.

Howell, George Rogers, and Jonathan Tenney. *Bi-Centennial History of Albany: History of the County of Albany, N.Y. from 1609 to 1886.* 2 vols. Albany, NY: W. W. Munsell, 1886.

Hunton, Addie Waite. *William Alphaeus Hunton: A Pioneer Prophet of Young Men.* New York: Association Press, 1938.

Hurston, Zora Neale. *Dust Tracks on a Road.* 1942. Reprinted with restored text, New York: HarperPerennial, 1996.

Hyde, Floy S. *Adirondack Forests, Fields, and Mines.* Mountain View, NY: published by author, 1974.

Jeffery, Jno. B. *Jno. B. Jeffery's Guide to the Opera Houses, Theatres, Public Halls, Bill Posters, Etc. of the Cities and Towns of America.* 11th ed. Chicago: published by author, 1889.

John Brown Memorial Association, Inc. Miscellaneous programs of the annual JBMA North Elba pilgrimage. On file at John Brown Farm State Historic Site, North Elba, New York.

Johnson, Charles S. "Negroes in the Railway Industry: Part II." *Phylon* 3, no. 2 (Second Quarter, 1942): 196–205.

———. *Patterns of Negro Segregation*. New York: Harper and Brothers, 1943.

Katz, Michael B. *In the Shadow of the Poorhouse: A Social History of Welfare in America*. New York: Basic Books, 1986.

Kautz Family YMCA Archives. National Board of the Young Men's Christian Associations. Armed Services Dept. USO-related Records. Industrial Clubs: Mineville, NY, 1943. University of Minnesota Libraries, Archives and Special Collections. Y.USA.4-2, Box 15.

Keetz, Frank M. *The Mohawk Colored Giants of Schenectady*. Schenectady, NY: N.p., 1999.

Kellogg, David S. *A Doctor at All Hours: The Private Journal of a Small-Town Doctor's Varied Life, 1886–1909*. Edited by Allan S. Everest. Brattleboro, VT: Stephen Greene Press, 1970.

Kelly, Barbara Tyrell. *Growing Up in Lake Placid*. Jay, NY: Graphics North, 2012.

Kelly, Lita. "In the Shadow of the Walls." In *Adirondack Reflections: On Life and Living in the Mountains and the Valleys*, edited by Neal Burdick and Maurice Kenny, 47–54. Charleston, SC: History Press, 2013.

Kennedy, John H. *A Course of Their Own: A History of African American Golfers*. Kansas City, MO: Andrews, McMeel, 2000.

Kirstein, Thelma Buck. "Vermontville's Black Community." In *They Told Me So. . . . A Booklet of Recollections and History Written by the Residents of Vermontville, Town of Franklin*. Vol. 5, 1993: 24–27. Copy at Adirondack Room, Saranac Lake Free Library.

Kollatz, Harry, Jr. *True Richmond Stories: Historic Tales from Virginia's Capital*. Charleston, SC: History Press, 2007.

Laird, Audrey, and Audrey Bowman. *Black Heritage in Fulton County*. Gloversville, NY: City of Gloversville Bi-Centennial of the U.S. Constitution Committee, 1990.

Lentz-Smith, Adriane. *Freedom Struggles: African Americans and World War I*. Cambridge, MA: Harvard Univ. Press, 2009.

Lewis, David W. *From Newgate to Dannemora: The Rise of the Penitentiary in New York, 1796–1848*. Ithaca, NY: Cornell Univ. Press, 1965.

Lewis, Earl, and Heidi Ardizzone. *Love on Trial: An American Scandal in Black and White*. New York: W. W. Norton, 2001.

Lindholm, Karl. "The Black Matty: William Clarence Matthews, 'Harvard's Famous Colored Shortstop,' and the Color Line." *Black Ball* 7 (2014): 54–78.

———. "Rumors and Fads: William Clarence Matthews' 1905 Challenge to Major League Baseball's Color Barrier." *NINE: A Journal of Baseball History and Culture* 17, no. 1 (Fall 2008): 37–53.

Lindsay, Arnett. "The Economic Condition of the Negroes of New York Prior to 1861." *Journal of Negro History* 6, no. 2 (Apr. 1921): 190–99.

Litwack, Leon F. *North of Slavery: The Negro in the Free States, 1790–1860.* Chicago: Univ. of Chicago Press, 1961.

Locke, Bernard. "Various Factors in a Penal Population." *Journal of Criminal Law and Criminology* 33, no. 4 (Nov./Dec. 1942): 316–20.

Loewen, James W. *Teaching What Really Happened: How to Avoid the Tyranny of Textbooks and Get Students Excited About Doing History.* New York: Teachers College Press, 2010.

Logan, Rayford Whittingham. *The Negro in American Life and Thought: The Nadir, 1877–1901.* New York: Dial Press, 1954.

Lomax, Michael E. *Black Baseball Entrepreneurs, 1860–1901: Operating by Any Means Necessary.* Syracuse, NY: Syracuse Univ. Press, 2003.

Loury, Glenn C. "Free at Last? A Personal Perspective on Race and Identity in America." In *Lure and Loathing: Essays on Race, Identity, and the Ambivalence of Assimilation*, edited by George Early, 1–12. New York: Allen Lane, Penguin Press, 1993.

Mabee, Carleton. *Black Education in New York State: From Colonial to Modern Times.* Syracuse, NY: Syracuse Univ. Press, 1979.

Maccannon, E. A. *Commanders of the Dining Room: Biographic Sketches and Portraits of Successful Head Waiters.* New York: Gwendolyn, [1904].

MacKenzie, Mary. *The Plains of Abraham: A History of North Elba and Lake Placid.* Edited by Lee Manchester. Utica, NY: Nicholas K. Burns, 2007.

Madison, James, and Thomas Jefferson. *The Tour to the Northern Lakes of James Madison and Thomas Jefferson, May–June 1791: A Facsimile Edition of Their Travel Journals*, edited by Robert Maquire. Ticonderoga, NY: Fort Ticonderoga, 1995.

Manchester, Lee. *The Lake Placid Club, 1890 to 2002.* Saranac Lake, NY: Adirondack Publishing Co., 2003.

Marable, Manning. "South African Nationalism in Brooklyn: John L. Dube's Activities in New York State, 1887–1899." *Afro-Americans in New York Life and History* 3, no. 1 (Jan. 1979): 23–38.

Marleau, William R. *Big Moose Station.* Eagle Bay, NY: Marleau Family Press, 1986.

Martin, J. Peter. *Adirondack Golf Courses: Past and Present.* Lake Placid, NY: Adirondack Golf, 1987.

———. "Open to All." *New York Golf,* Oct. 2002, 82–90.

Matthews, Harry Bradshaw. *Freedom Knows No Color: African American Freedom Journey in New York and Related Sites 1823–1870: Roll Call, Men of the 20th USCT and 26th USCT: Historical and Genealogical Connections.* Vol. 2. Oneonta, NY: USCT Institute, Hartwick College, [2006].

Mayfield, Fulton County, Town of. *Town Minutes (1794–1825).* Mayfield Historian's Office.

McBride, David. "Fourteenth Amendment Idealism: The New York State Civil Rights Law, 1873–1918." *New York History* 71, no. 2 (Apr. 1990): 207–33.

McDougald, Elizabeth. "Negro Youth Plans Its Future." *Journal of Negro Education* 10, no. 2 (Apr. 1941): 223–29.

McElrath, Joseph R. Jr. "Richard Harding Davis's 'The Boys in the Adariondacks [*sic*].'" *American Literary Realism, 1870–1910* 14, no. 2 (Autumn 1981): 195–215.

McFerson, Shirley. "Coming Home a Stranger." In *Living North Country: Essays of Life and Landscapes in Northern New York,* edited by Burdick and Singer, 309–15. Utica, NY: North Country Books, 2001.

McLaughlin, Warner. "A History of the Redford Crown Glass Works at Redford, Clinton County, N.Y." *New York History* 26, no. 3 (July 1945): 368–77.

McManus, Edgar J. *A History of Negro Slavery in New York.* Syracuse, NY: Syracuse Univ. Press, 1966.

McMartin, Barbara. *Caroga: An Adirondack Town Recalls Its Past.* 2nd ed. Caroga, NY: Town of Caroga, 1998.

McMurry, Sally. "Evolution of a Landscape: From Farm to Forest in the Adirondack Region, 1857–1894." *New York History* 80, no. 2 (Apr. 1999): 117–52.

McNary, Kyle. *Black Baseball: A History of African-Americans and the National Game.* New York: Sterling, 2003.

Metcalfe, Ann Breen. *Leland House: An Adirondack Innovator.* Elizabethtown, NY: Essex County Historical Society, 1994.

Morris, Peter. *Catcher: How the Man Behind the Plate Became an American Folk Hero*. Chicago: Ivan R. Dee, 2009.

Morton, Doris Begor. *Philip Skene of Skenesborough*. Granville, NY: Grastorf Press, 1959.

Mosby, Dewey. *Across Continents and Cultures: The Life and Art of Henry Ossawa Tanner*. Kansas City, MO: Nelson-Atkins Museum of Art, 1995.

Moses, Stefan B. "Lake Placid No Melting Pot." *American Libraries*, Dec. 1998, 32.

Moton, Robert R. "Hampton's Summer Campaign in the North." *Southern Workman* 38, no. 9 (Sept. 1909): 505–7.

Moye, J. Todd. *Freedom Flyers: The Tuskegee Airmen of World War II*. New York: Oxford Univ. Press, 2010.

Munn, Eleanor H. "The Early Days of the Hotel Saranac." Nov. 30, 1989. Unpublished manuscript. On file in Adirondack Room, Saranac Lake Free Library.

Myers, William A., and John V. Hancock. *A History of the Grasse River Club*. N.p., 2008. Copy at Adirondack Museum Library.

Nalty, Bernard C. Introduction to *The Unknown Soldiers: African-American Troops in World War I*, by Arthur E. Barbeau and Henri Florette. 1974. Reprint, Boston: Da Capo Press, 1996.

Needham, Henry Beach. "The College Athlete: How Commercialism is Making Him a Professional. Part I: Recruiting and Subsidizing." *McClure's Magazine*, June 1905, 11–28.

Negro Business Directory of the State of Wisconsin. Milwaukee, WI: M.E. Shadd, 1950.

Negro Motorist Green Book. New York: Victor H. Green, 1937–41, 1948–57, 1962. Title varies.

New York City Department of Health. *First Report of the Clinic for the Treatment of Communicable Pulmonary Diseases*. New York: City of New York, [1906].

New York City Common Council. *Manual of the Corporation of the City of New York*. New York: 1870.

New York Lake Champlain Tercentenary Commission. *The Champlain Tercentenary: First Report of the New York Lake Champlain Tercentenary Commission*. Albany: J. B. Lyon Company, State Printers, 1913.

New York State. *Annual Report of the Adjutant-General of the State of New York for the Year. . . . Register[s of New York Regiments in the War of the Rebellion].* Albany: James B. Lyon, State Printers, 1894–1906. Imprint varies.

New York State Board of Charities. *Census of Inmates in Almshouses and Poorhouses, 1826–1921.* Records for individual counties are available from New York State Archives, Albany, NY.

———. *Directory of the Charitable, Eleemosynary, Correctional and Reformatory Institutions of the State of New York.* Albany: James B. Lyon, 1892.

New York State Commission against Discrimination. *Railroad Employment in New York and New Jersey: A Joint Study by the New York State Commission against Discrimination and the New Jersey Division against Discrimination.* New York, [1958].

———. Division of Research. *Negroes in Five New York Cities: A Study of Problems, Achievements and Trends.* [New York, 1959].

New York State Department of Correction. *Annual Reports.* On file at New York State Archives, Albany, NY.

New York State Department of Labor, Division of Placement and Unemployment Service. *Farm and Food Processing Labor: Annual Report[s].* Rochester, NY: New York State Employment Service, 1955–1959. Reports provide data for preceding year as well as comparative data.

New York State Hospital for the Treatment of Incipient Pulmonary Tuberculosis, Ray Brook, New York. *Annual Reports*, 1906–1928. Albany: State Printers. On file at New York State Library.

Njeri, Itabari. "Sushi and Grits: Ethnic Identity and Conflict in a Newly Multicultural America." In *Lure and Loathing: Essays on Race, Identity, and the Ambivalence of Assimilation*, edited by George Early, 13–40. New York: Allen Lane, Penguin Press, 1993.

Northup, Solomon. *Twelve Years A Slave.* 1853. Reprinted with introduction by Ira Berlin; general editor Henry Louis Gates Jr. New York: Penguin Books, 2012.

Noyes, Grace. "Diary." 1878. Transcribed by Sarah Farrar in *Warrensburgh Historical Society Quarterly* (Summer 2000): 1, 6–8; (Fall 2000): 7–8; (Winter 2000–2001): 5–6; (Spring 2001): 4–5; (Spring 2002): 4; (Summer 2002): 5–6; (Winter/Spring 2003): 5–6. Original 1878 diary preserved at the Richards Library, Warrensburg, NY.

O'Brien, Maurice H. "Timbuctoo, An Attempt at Negro Settlement in the Adirondacks." Unpublished report for New York State Division for Historic Preservation, 1977. Copy at Adirondack Museum Library, Blue Mountain Lake, NY.

Odato, James M. "Aaron Mair: The Sierra Club President on Race in the Adirondacks and His Vision for a Trail to Honor Fallen Soldiers." *Adirondack Life*, Nov./Dec. 2016.

Owens-Manley, Judith. *Final Evaluation, the Municipal Housing Authority of the City of Utica, New York HOPE VI Grant Number NY06URD006 1102, Washington Courts Development, 2003–2008*, 22–23. Accessed June 6, 2017. http://www.hamilton.edu/documents/hope_vi_final_evaluation-july09-1.pdf.

Packard, John M. "A Fortune Awaits You in Saranac Lake: The Ties That Bind in the City of the Sick." *Adirondack Life*, Mar./Apr. 2010.

Patton, Gerald W. *War and Race: The Black Officer in the American Military, 1915–1941*. Westport, CT: Greenwood Press, 1981.

Payne, Howard M. "Leading Causes of Death Among Negroes: Tuberculosis." *Journal of Negro Education* 18, no. 3 (Summer 1949): 225–34.

Peckham, Harriett C. Waite Van Buren. *History of Cornelis Maessen Van Buren, Who Came from Holland to the New Netherlands in 1631, and His Descendants, Including the Genealogy of the Family of Bloomingdale Who Are Descended from Maas, a Son of Cornelis Maessen*. New York: Tobias A. Wright, 1913.

Peterson, Robert W. *Cages to Jumpshots: Pro Basketball's Early Years*. New York: Oxford Univ. Press, 1990.

Pietrusza, David. *Baseball's Canadian-American League: A History of Its Inception, Franchises, Participants, Locales, Statistics, Demise and Legacy 1936–1951*. Jefferson, NC: McFarland, 2005.

Pollard, Alton B., III. "The Last Great Battle of the West: W. E. B. Du Bois and the Struggle for African America's Soul." In *Lure and Loathing: Essays on Race, Identity, and the Ambivalence of Assimilation*, edited by George Early, 41–54. New York: Allen Lane, Penguin Press, 1993.

Potter, Lou. *Liberators: Fighting on Two Fronts in World War II*. New York: Harcourt Brace Jovanovich, 1992.

Price, Emmett G., III, *Encyclopedia of African American Music*. Santa Barbara, CA: Greenwood, 2011.

Prison Association of New York. *Fourth Annual Report.* 2nd ed. Albany, NY: Weed, Parsons, 1849.

Proceedings of the National Convention of Colored People, and Their Friends, Held in Troy, N.Y., on the 6th 7th, 8th and 9th October, 1847. Troy, NY: J. C. Kneeland, 1847.

Quarles, Benjamin. *Allies for Freedom: Blacks and John Brown.* New York: Oxford Univ. Press, 1974.

Rael, Patrick. *Eighty-Eight Years: The Long Death of Slavery in the United States, 1777–1865.* Athens: Univ. of Georgia Press, 2015.

Reidy, Joseph P. "Black Men in Navy Blue During the Civil War." *Prologue: Quarterly of the National Archives and Records Administration* 33, no. 3 (Fall 2001): 156–67.

Resko, John. *Reprieve: The Testament of John Resko.* 1956. Reprint. Westport, CT: Greenwood Press, 1975.

Riis, Thomas Laurence. *Just Before Jazz: Black Musical Theater in New York, 1890–1915.* Washington, DC: Smithsonian Institute Press, 1989.

Rosenquist, Valerie. *The Iron Ore Eaters: A Portrait of the Mining Community of Moriah, New York.* New York: Garland, 1990.

Ross, Donald D. "What They Dreamed of at the Front: Lake Placid Station Helps Vets Relax After Overseas Duty." *PM*, Jan. 22, 1945, 8–9.

Royce, Caroline Halstead. *Bessboro: A History of Westport, Essex Co., N.Y.* N.p.: published by author, 1902.

Rugh, Susan Sessions. *Are We There Yet? The Golden Age of American Family Vacations.* Lawrence: Univ. Press of Kansas, 2008.

Sanborn, Franklin Benjamin. *Life and Letters of John Brown: Liberator of Kansas, and Martyr of Virginia.* Boston: Roberts Bros., 1891.

Saranac Lake Department of Health. Tuberculosis Patient Registration Records. On file in Adirondack Room, Saranac Lake Free Library.

Saranac Lake Methodist Church. *Methodist Marriages, 1898–1916.* On file in Adirondack Room, Saranac Lake Free Library.

Scharnhorst, Gary. *Kate Field: The Many Lives of a Nineteenth-Century Journalist.* Syracuse, NY: Syracuse Univ. Press, 2008.

Schuyler, George S. "Keeping the Negro in His Place." *American Mercury* 17 (Aug. 1929): 469–76.

———. "Vacation Daze." *Common Ground* 3, no. 3 (Mar. 1943): 41–44.

Seaver, Frederick J. *Historical Sketches of Franklin County.* Albany, NY: Lyon, 1918.

Seiler, Cotton. "'So That We as a Race Might Have Something Authentic to Travel By': African American Automobility and Cold-War Liberalism." *American Quarterly* 58, no. 4 (Dec. 2006): 1091–1117.

Seraile, William. *New York's Black Regiments during the Civil War.* New York: Routledge, 2001.

Sernett, Milton C. *North Star Country: Upstate New York and the Crusade for African American Freedom.* Syracuse, NY: Syracuse Univ. Press, 2002.

Shaughnessy, Jim. *Delaware and Hudson.* 1982. Reprint, Syracuse, NY: Syracuse Univ. Press, 1997.

Shelton, John G. "The Queen of Spas." *Colored American*, Sept. 1901, 379–93.

Shipton, Alyn. *Hi-De-Ho: The Life of Cab Calloway.* New York: Oxford Univ. Press, 2010.

Sinette, Calvin H. *Forbidden Fairways: African Americans and the Game of Golf.* Chelsea, MI: Sleeping Bear Press, 1998.

Skopp, Douglas R. *Bright with Promise: From the Normal and Training School to SUNY Plattsburgh, 1889–1989: A Pictorial History.* Norfolk, VA: Donning, 1989.

Slade, Charles B. "Selection of Patients for a Tuberculosis Sanatorium." *American Medicine*, New Series 6, no. 4 (Apr. 1911): 189–99.

Smith, Gerrit. "Account of My Distribution of Land Among Colored Men." Gerrit Smith Papers. Special Collections Research Center, Syracuse University Libraries. Vol. 88.

Smith, H. P. *History of Essex County, with Illustrations and Biographical Sketches of Some of Its Prominent Men and Pioneers.* Syracuse, NY: Mason, 1885.

Smith, Jessie Carney, ed. *Notable Black American Women, Book II.* Detroit, MI: Gale Research, 1996.

Smith, Vernon Lee. "The Hampton Institute Choir 1873–1973." PhD diss., Florida State University, 1985. Copy at Schomberg Center, New York Public Library, New York.

Smith-Pryor, Elizabeth M. *Property Rites: The Rhinelander Trial, Passing, and the Protection of Whiteness.* Chapel Hill: Univ. of North Carolina Press, 2009.

South Carolina Adjutant-General's Office. *Official Roster of South Carolina Soldiers, Sailors and Marines in the World War, 1917–18.* Vol. 2, *Colored.*

Columbia, SC: Joint Committee on Printing, General Assembly of South Carolina, 1929.

Southern, Eileen. *Biographical Dictionary of Afro-American and African Musicians.* Westport, CT: Greenwood Press, 1982.

———. *Music of Black Americans: A History.* 2nd ed. New York: W. W. Norton, 1983.

Spencer, Gerald A. *Medical Symphony: A Study of the Contributions of the Negro to Medical Progress in New York.* New York: Spencer, 1947.

Squire, Willard S., III. "The 24th Infantry Regiment and the Racial Debate in the U.S. Army." Master's Thesis. United States Army Command and General Staff College, 1997.

Starling, Edmund W. *Starling of the White House.* New York: Simon & Schuster, 1946.

Stauffer, John. *The Black Hearts of Men: Radical Abolitionists and the Transformation of Race.* Cambridge, MA: Harvard Univ. Press, 2001.

Steward, Austin. *Twenty-Two Years a Slave, and Forty Years a Freeman; Embracing a Correspondence of Several Years, While President of Wilberforce Colony, London, Canada West.* Rochester, NY: William Alling, 1857.

Stewart, L. Lloyd. *The Mysterious Black Migration 1800–1820: The Van Frankens and Other Families of African Descent in Washington County, New York.* N.p.: Xlibris, 2013.

Sullivan, Patricia. *Lift Every Voice: The NAACP and the Making of the Civil Rights Movement.* New York: New Press, 2009.

Svenson, Sally E. "'Devoted to Patriotic Reminiscence': The New Hampshire Veterans' Association Campground at the Weirs." *Historical New Hampshire* 54, nos. 1 and 2 (Spring/Summer 1999): 41–56.

Tanner, H. O. "The Story of an Artist's Life." Part I. *World's Work* 18, no. 2 (June 1909): 11661–66.

Taylor, Elizabeth Dowling. *The Original Black Elite: Daniel Murray and the Story of a Forgotten Era.* New York: Amistad/HarperCollins, 2017.

Taylor, Yuval, and Jake Austen. *Darkest America: Black Minstrelsy from Slavery to Hip-Hop.* New York: W. W. Norton, 2012.

Thomas, Howard. *Tales from the Adirondack Foothills.* Prospect, NY: Prospect Books, 1957.

Ticonderoga Historical Society. *Ticonderoga: Patches and Patterns from Its Past.* Ticonderoga, NY: Ticonderoga Historical Society, 1969.

Toll, Robert C. *Blacking Up: The Minstrel Show in Nineteenth-Century America.* New York: Oxford Univ. Press, 1974.

Tolles, Bryant E., Jr. *Resort Hotels of the Adirondacks: The Architecture of a Summer Paradise, 1850–1950.* Hanover, NH: Univ. Press of New England, 2003.

Trav, S. D. *No Applause—Just Throw Money, or, The Book That Made Vaudeville Famous: A High-class, Refined Entertainment.* New York: Faber and Faber, 2005.

Travelguide, Inc. *Travelguide.* New York: 1947–57, 1962–63.

Trowbridge, Catherine C., editor and compiler. *Durand Camp: History and Reminiscences of Durand Camp on Long Lake from 1906.* Tucson, AZ: published by editor, 1975.

Turner, Robert E. *Memories of a Retired Pullman Porter.* New York: Exposition Press, 1954.

Turner, Sarah, and John Bound. "Closing the Gap or Widening the Divide: The Effects of the G.I. Bill and World War II on the Educational Outcomes of Black Americans." *Journal of Economic History* 63, no. 1 (Mar. 2003): 145–77.

Tuttle, Maria Jeannette Brookings. *Three Centuries in Champlain Valley: A Collection of Historical Facts and Incidents.* Plattsburgh, NY: Saranac Chapter D.A.R., 1909.

Tye, Larry. *Rising from the Rails: Pullman Porters and the Making of the Black Middle Class.* New York: Henry Holt, 2004.

Tyler, Helen Escha. *"In Them Thar Hills": Folk Tales of the Adirondacks.* Saranac Lake, NY: Currier Press, 1968.

Union League Club. *Report of the Committee on Volunteering.* New York: Union League Club, 1864.

United States Bureau of the Census. *Negro Population in the United States: 1790–1915.* Washington, DC: Government Printing Office, 1918.

United States National Archives. Civil War Widows and Other Dependents Pension Files, 1861–1934. Record Group 15. Records of the Veterans Association, Washington, DC.

United States Travel Bureau. *Directory of Negro Hotels and Guest Houses in the United States.* Washington, DC: Government Printing Office, 1939.

"Vacation Days." *Crisis* 4, no. 4 (Aug. 1912): 186–88.

Vanderhorst-Rodriguez, Guadalupe. *Tan Americans of Clinton County, New York.* N.p: published by author, 2009.

Vink, Jan. "Adirondack Park Population by Race." Program for Applied Demographics, Cornell Univ., 2010.

Walker, William S. "Collecting Folk Histories: Harold W. Thompson and Student Field Research in the 1930s." *Public Historian* 37, no. 3 (Aug. 2015): 45–75.

Ward, Andrew. *Dark Midnight When I Rise: The Story of the Jubilee Singers, Who Introduced the World to the Music of Black America*. New York: Farrar, Straus and Giroux, 2000.

Ware, Louise. *George Foster Peabody: Banker, Philanthropist, Publicist*. Athens: Univ. of Georgia Press, 1951.

Washburne, Randel, and Paul Wall. *Black-White Ethnic Differences in Outdoor Recreation* (Research Paper INT-249). Ogden, UT: USDA Forest Service, Intermountain Forest and Range Experiment Station, 1980.

Watson, Winslow C. *A General View and Agricultural Survey of the County of Essex. Taken under the Appointment of the New-York State Agricultural Society*. [Albany, NY: N.p., 1852].

———. *The Military and Civil History of the County of Essex, New York*. Albany, NY: Munsell, 1869.

Weber, Joe, and Selima Sultana. "Why Do So Few Minority People Visit National Parks? Visitation and the Accessibility of 'America's Best Idea.'" *Annals of the Association of American Geographers* 103, no. 3 (May 2013): 437–64.

Wessels, William L. *Adirondack Profiles*. Lake George, NY: Adirondack Resorts Press, 1961.

Whitcover, Walt. *My Road Less Traveled: Becoming an Actor, a Director, a Teacher*. N.p.: Xlibris, 2011.

White, Philip L. *Beekmantown, New York: Forest Frontier to Farm Community*. Austin: Univ. of Texas Press, 1979.

White, Sol. *Sol White's History of Colored Baseball, with Other Documents on the Early Black Game, 1886–1936*. Compiled and introduced by Jerry Malloy. Lincoln: Univ. of Nebraska Press, 1995.

Whitfield, Harvey Amani. "African Americans in Burlington, Vermont, 1880–1900." *Vermont History* 75, no. 2 (Summer/Fall 2007): 101–23.

Wiley, Bell Irvin. *The Life of Billy Yank: The Common Soldier of the Union*. Baton Rouge: Louisiana State Univ. Press, 1952.

Wilkerson, Isabel. *The Warmth of Other Suns: The Epic Story of America's Great Migration*. New York: Random House, 2010.

Wilkins, Carolyn Marie. *They Raised Me Up: A Black Single Mother and the Women Who Inspired Her*. Columbia: Univ. of Missouri Press, 2013.

Williams, Clay. "*The Guide for Colored Travelers*: A Reflection of the Urban League." *Journal of American and Comparative Cultures* 24, nos. 3 and 4 (Fall/Winter 2001), 71–79.

Williams, Dorothy. *The Road to Now: A History of Blacks in Montreal*. Montreal: Véhicule Press, 1997.

Williams-Myers, A. J. "Contested Ground: Hinterland Slavery in Colonial New York." *Afro-Americans in New York Life and History* 33, no. 1 (Jan. 2009): 91–137.

———. *Long Hammering: Essays on the Forging of an African American Presence in the Hudson River Valley to the Early Twentieth Century*. Trenton, NJ: Africa World Press, 1994.

Wilson, Geoffrey. *Rogers Rock (Ticonderoga, New York): The Hotel, the Club, the Cottage Colony: A History and Personal Memoir*. Bloomington, IN: AuthorHouse, 2005.

Witherbee, Sherman and Company. Employee Records, 1910–1937. Essex County Historical Society, Elizabethtown, NY.

Wolters, Raymond. "The New Deal and the Negro." In *The New Deal: The National Level*, edited by John Braeman, Robert H. Bremner, and Robert Brody, 188–93. Columbus: Ohio State Univ. Press, 1975.

Young, Terence. "'A Contradiction in Democratic Government': W. L. Trent, Jr., and the Struggle to Desegregate National Parks." *Environmental History* 14, no. 4 (Oct. 2009): 651–82.

African American Newspapers

Baltimore Afro-American (1892–present). At its circulation peak, the paper published weekly editions in other cities including Washington, DC.

Broad Ax: Salt Lake City (1895–99); Chicago (1899–1931)

Chicago Daily Defender (1956–2003)

Chicago Defender (1905–56)

Christian Recorder, journal of the African Methodist Church (1854–1902)

Cleveland Call and Post (1927–present)

Cleveland Gazette (1863–1945)

Indianapolis Freeman (1884–1927)

Los Angeles California Eagle (1879–1964)

New York Age (1887–1953)

New York Amsterdam News (1909–present)
New York Globe (circa 1880–84)
Norfolk (VA) New Journal and Guide (1900–present)
Philadelphia Tribune (1884–present)
Pittsburgh Courier (1907–66)
St. Paul (MN) Western Appeal (1885–1923)
Washington Bee (1882–1922)

Index

Italic page numbers denote illustrations.

Sally E. Svenson has been writing about the Adirondack region of upstate New York for more than fifteen years. Her first book, *Adirondack Churches: A History of Design and Building*, was reviewed as a "highly recommended" academic title in *Choice* magazine and praised as a "model for future studies of regional church architecture." Her second, *Lily, Duchess of Marlborough (1854–1909): A Portrait with Husbands*, was a biography of an obscure American duchess with an Adirondack connection. She writes occasionally on diverse topics for *Adirondack Life* magazine.

A graduate of Cornell University, Svenson holds master's degrees from Columbia University and Teachers College, Columbia. She and her husband are winter residents of New York City and summer residents of the Adirondacks, where she serves on the executive committee of the Adirondack Museum.